The Politics of Opposition in Contemporary Africa

Edited by

Adebayo O. Olukoshi

Nordiska Afrikainstitutet, Uppsala 1998

Indexing terms
Democratisation
Political opposition
Political participation
Political power
State
Africa

Cover: Anna Bengtsson
Language checking: Elaine Almén

ISBN 91-7106-419-2

Printed in Sweden by Elanders Gotab, Stockholm, 1998

Contents

Preface and Acknowledgements 5

Chapter 1
Economic Crisis, Multipartyism, and Opposition Politics
in Contemporary Africa. 8
Adebayo O. Olukoshi

Chapter 2
Contestation over Political Space: The State and the Demobilisation
of Opposition Politics in Kenya 39
Karuti Kanyinga

Chapter 3
Opposition Politics in Zimbabwe: The Struggle within the Struggle 91
Tandeka C. Nkiwane

Chapter 4
The Senegalese Opposition and its Quest for Power 113
Aminata Diaw and Mamadou Diouf

Chapter 5
The Rise to Power of an Opposition Party: The MNSD in Niger Republic . . . 144
Jibrin Ibrahim and Abdoulaye Niandou Souley

Chapter 6
The Dilemmas of Directed Democracy:
Neutralising Ugandan Opposition Politics under the NRM 171
John Ssenkumba

Chapter 7
From Peoples' Politics to State Politics:
Aspects of National Liberation in South Africa 195
Michael Neocosmos

Chapter 8
Political Opposition and Democratic Transitions in Nigeria, 1985–1996 242
Osita Agbu

Notes on Contributors 265

Appendix 1: Directory of Parties and Elections i Contemporary Africa. 267

Appendix 2: Select Bibliography on Political Liberalisation and
Multipartyism in Contemporary Africa. 306

Index 319

Preface and Acknowledgements

In December 1995, the Nordic Africa Institute in Uppsala, Sweden, organised a conference in Accra, Ghana, devoted to a discussion, in the main, of the experiences of the opposition political parties that have emerged as part of the movement towards the re-introduction of multiparty politics in many African countries. Opposition groups have always existed in Africa, even under the regime of single party and military rule that was to envelop much of the continent shortly after independence in the 1960s. The problem, though, was that many of these opposition groups were mostly compelled to operate clandestinely or in exile or, where they were barely tolerated, under severe restrictions that hampered their effectiveness as vehicles for the mobilisation of political opinion. What was, therefore, interesting about the reform movement that gathered speed across the continent from the late 1980s onwards was that, after some two decades of *de facto* and *de jure* political monopoly in most countries, the political playing field was once again, by and large, re-opened for opposition political parties to function legally. Yet, as the debate on Africa's experience with the transition from political monopoly to multipartyism developed, very little attention was paid to the fortunes of the opposition political parties whose presence and capacity are crucial to the enhancement of the environment for the development of democratic politics. It was against this background that the Accra meeting was conceived and convened.

In convening the Accra conference, the primary intention was to focus attention mainly on opposition political parties as central players in the emergence and consolidation of the democratic process in Africa. If in the late 1980s and early 1990s, the euphoria that greeted the upsurge of popular pressures for democratisation and the defeat of a number of authoritarian governments resulted in the neglect of opposition political parties in scholarly analysis and discourse, by the mid-1990s when the Accra meeting was being convened, the drastic tempering that was beginning to occur of the earlier, one-sided celebration of "Africa's second liberation" in the face of the persistence of authoritarian forms/structures of governance had certainly created a strong intellectual case for a systematic review of the experience of the political opposition. "In this respect, the Accra conference represented a timely intervention aimed at filling an important gap in the ongoing debate about the democratisation process in Africa. Naturally, no comprehensive discussion of the experience of opposition political parties could be undertaken without attention being paid to their links with other sources and forces of opposition, including civil society groups. Indeed, several of the case studies presented in this volume focus attention on developments within civil society in the framework of the changing environment of politics associated with the transitional process specific to the different countries.

The eight chapters that make up much of this book were among the eleven papers that were originally commissioned for the Accra conference. In their revised form, they tackle an interesting mix of issues, ranging from a critique of multiparty/opposition politics in the context of the continuing economic decline in much of Africa to an assessment of the efforts made by the opposition to establish an effective presence under extremely difficult circumstances. The contributors to the book also draw attention to the many internal organisational /leadership problems that have contributed as much to the weaknesses of the opposition as the machinations of the ruling parties and the activities of *agents provocateurs*. The poor interface between the oppositional elements in political society and pro-democracy activists in civil society, and the consequences of this failure to sustain and consolidate the links between civil society-based pressures for reform and opposition political party bids for change are discussed in the context of the experiences of transitional politics in the diverse set of countries, namely, Kenya, Niger, Nigeria, Senegal, South Africa, Uganda and Zimbabwe, that serve as the case materials for the analyses presented in this book. In several instances, ethnicity, religion, and regionalism are identified as crucial, additional factors militating against the opposition. On the whole, the issues tackled, the positions taken and the options discussed in this book are broadly reflective of the diversity and richness of the discussions that took place at the Accra conference; in many respects, they also capture the state of the debate within Africa on the continent's political future. It is our hope that readers will find the contributions engaging.

At this stage, I would like to thank my colleagues whose revised papers have been included in this publication for their cooperation in making this venture a success. Thanks are also due to Clive Napier and his colleagues on the editorial board of *Politeia* who, earlier on, encouraged us to contribute four of the papers from the Accra conference to a special issue of their journal that was published in 1996. Furthermore, I would like to acknowledge the contributions of Solveig Hauser and Kajsa Övergaard, respectively the present research and administrative assistant for the Nordic Africa Institute's programme on *The Political and Social Context of Structural Adjustment in Sub-Saharan Africa* and her immediate predecessor, for all the hard work which they put into the preparation of the Accra conference and the production of this publication. Ms Övergaard has also compiled a consolidated bibliography, covering relevant books and articles available at the NAI library, for inclusion in the special issue of *Politeia*. Ms Hauser, for her part, has compiled a directory of parties and elections in contemporary Africa for the benefit of readers who want a quick reference source on the transition to multiparty politics on the continent. The Accra meeting itself was co-hosted with the Department of Political Science at the University of Ghana, Legon, Accra and we are grateful to the staff of the Department for their support. In particular, I would like to single out for mention, Dr Joseph Ayee, the Head of the Department of Political Science, and Professor J.R. Anquandah, the Dean of the Faculty of Social Science, for all that they did to make the conference the success that it was.

Finally, one member of the NAI research network on political change in Africa who was unable to participate in the Accra conference was Dr Norbert Tengende of the Department of Political and Administrative Studies, University of Zimbabwe. Barely a few days prior to the meeting, he was compelled to withdraw on account of ill-health. Unfortunately, it was an illness from which he did not recover and during the course of 1996, he died. It is to Norbert Tengende's memory that we dedicate this book.

Adebayo Olukoshi
Uppsala, November 1997

Chapter 1

Economic Crisis, Multipartyism, and Opposition Politics in Contemporary Africa

Adebayo O. Olukoshi

AFRICAN SELF-DETERMINATION

The period since the end of the 1980s has witnessed a series of developments on the African continent suggesting a massive return to liberalised forms of politics. These developments have largely centred around the dismantling of many constitutional or *de facto* one-party regimes, the termination of a number of military-led or -dominated governments, the embrace of a multiparty political framework, the abolition, formally at least, of many life presidencies, the convening of sovereign national conferences (especially in Francophone Africa), the licensing of private, including opposition/independent news and information media, the restoration of some basic freedoms to the citizenry, and the convening, under the watchful eyes of an assortment of international observers, of multiparty elections. These changes, taking place as they did in virtually all parts of the continent, led some commentators to advance the position that they signalled the beginning of Africa's "second liberation". If the first liberation was from the scourge of colonialism, the second was from the clutches of the different types of political tyranny associated with the increasing monopolisation and personalisation of power in post-colonial Africa (Legum, 1990).

The popular pressures for democratisation which gripped many African countries towards the end of the 1980s took place within two important contexts. The first context relates to the experience of acute economic crisis and structural adjustment which virtually all African countries were already undergoing at the time when local demands began to build up for an opening up of the national political space to opposing political views and organisations (Havnevik, 1987; Gibbon et al., 1992). The second context centres around the far-reaching changes that were taking place in the international system, changes which were dramatically captured by the collapse in 1989 of the Berlin Wall, the subsequent re-unification of Germany, the collapse of the Warsaw Pact in the framework of the overthrow of the monopoly on power enjoyed by the ruling communist parties of eastern and central Europe, the severe weakening and eventual dissolution of the Soviet Union and the birth of many new countries out of the old Soviet federation, the spread, all over the former Soviet bloc, of multiparty political forms, and the embrace by many of the hitherto centrally-planned socialist economies of market-based economic strategies. These dramatic developments signalled the end of the super-power Cold War as we once knew it and, in so doing, undermined a crucial basis on which many regimes in Africa rested, namely, the almost unconditional propping up of unrepresentative and unaccountable African governments by the Cold War rivals as part of their strategy for maximising their global advantages.

In pursuit of their global geo-political strategies, the Western and Eastern bloc countries in the forefront of the Cold War were not only prepared to ignore the domestic political records of their "clients" in Africa, they also actively tried to prevent the crystallisation of internal pressures for change in the guise of preventing "counter-revolution" or "containing communism". In this fundamental sense, the Cold War represented a major source of obstruction to the development of representative and accountable government in Africa. The end of the Cold War and the spread of multiparty politics associated with it created an international climate that was far more conducive to and tolerant of internal political reforms in Africa than at any time since African countries won their independence in the 1960s. Thus, when domestic pressures for change began to build up in various African countries, pressures which took the form of massive and sustained public protests, they dovetailed with an emerging post-Cold War international mood that had become far more accommodating of internal political dissent and change. Indeed, some Western countries were to go so far as to embrace "political conditionality" as a new instrument in their dealings with African countries in the post-Cold War period (Gibbon et al., 1992; Olukoshi and Wohlgemuth, 1995; Olukoshi, 1996).

As a consequence of the widespread domestic pressure for reform, for which the changing international political environment was conducive, the political map of Africa, defined in terms of the regime type that was in place, underwent a radical change. Whereas in 1989, when the Berlin Wall collapsed, 38 out of the 45 states in sub-Saharan Africa were under one-party or military rule, by 1990, well over half of them had promised to hold multiparty elections (*Guardian* (London), 11 September, 1990). Between 1990 and 1994, 31 out of the 42 sub-Saharan African countries that did not already have a multiparty political framework embraced one variant or the other of the system and held competitive elections on the basis of the new arrangement. Of the 31 competitive elections that were held, 14 resulted in the defeat of incumbent governments, some of them dominated by people who had been in power since their countries attained independence and who had erected elaborate structures for preserving their political power (Bratton,

1995). Of course, several incumbent governments, in places as diverse and as far apart as Kenya, Mozambique, Guinea Bissau, Seychelles, Ghana, Cameroon, and Côte d'Ivoire managed, one way or another, to hold on to power in the elections that they convened but even here, the ruling parties had to fight hard for their victories amidst vociferous charges from the opposition that they had abused their incumbency to ensure that they were returned to power.

Only in countries like Nigeria and Algeria were elections that produced outcomes that incumbent governments did not like annulled and military rule maintained either directly or through civilian proxies. In the case of Nigeria, which is discussed more extensively in chapter eight of this volume, the 1993 presidential elections were annulled by the military junta led by General Babangida once it became clear that Moshood Abiola was heading for an emphatic victory. In Algeria, the annulment of the elections was prompted by the huge electoral success which the Islamic party, FIS, had obtained on a platform which promised to transform the country into an Islamic republic. In the Gambia, the military toppled the government of the long-ruling Dawda Jawara. The same happened in Sierra Leone where the military overthrew the discredited government of J.S. Momoh as the ruling All Peoples' Congress (APC) grudgingly moved the country towards constitutional reforms preparatory to multiparty elections. In all, the wind of change that swept across Africa in the late 1980s and early 1990s blew forcefully, even if unevenly, in favour of political reforms; no incumbent regime was able to ignore the widespread agitation for change although some tried to stop it (Legum, 1990; Olukoshi and Wohlgemuth, 1995). The apparent change in the African political landscape encouraged by popular domestic pressure and the end of the Cold War was boosted by the demise of apartheid in South Africa and the inauguration of Nelson Mandela as the first president popularly elected by South Africans of all races.

Yet, for all the apparent strides which have been taken in Africa towards a pluralistic political framework, and these should not be underestimated or underplayed, questions have persisted not just about the vitality, "quality" and relevance of the kind of democratic transition that is taking place but also about its sustainability and the prospects for consolidation/institutionalisation of the reforms that have been put in place. The themes of the relevance of the political reform type that has pervaded the African landscape since the late 1980s and its sustainability have increasingly dominated the discourse about the future of democracy in Africa. Whereas some argue that the excessive focus on multiparty/competitive elections in the current African democratic practice and discourse is both too narrow and limiting, others take the view that the acid test of Africa's democratic transition lies in the way succession politics is conducted as evidenced by the manner in which future elections are handled and victory and defeat managed. The latter concern is beginning to spurn studies devoted to an assessment of "second elections". The view has also been advocated that Africa's effort at the institutionalisation of formal democratic politics cannot be sustained unless they are accompanied with measures aimed at ensuring that popular participation in the political process is encouraged. According to this position, although the embrace of the formal rules of democratic politics and constitutionalism is an important step forward in Africa's movement towards political reforms, this development is not, in and of itself, a sufficient basis for "democratic consolidation" on the continent. For democracy to endure, the embrace of the formal rules and processes of liberal political pluralism would have to be anchored in mechanisms for enforcing popular sovereignty in the political system (*Africa Demos*, 1995; Shivji, 1988; 1989; Ake, 1992, 1996).

Other contributors to the debate on the problems of and prospects for the promotion of political reform in Africa have emphasised the importance of focusing on ways of infusing democratic values into the political and social practices of various groups as the chief challenge of the quest for an enduring African democratic transition. Concern has also been expressed about the unsettling consequences for the African democratic project of the resurgence of "chauvinistic" ethnic, regionalist, and religious identities in most African countries that have opened up their political spaces (Young, 1995). The dangers posed to the democratic project and, indeed, the nation-state itself by ethnic and religious identities are increasingly being debated as the euphoria that greeted the "second liberation" begins to die down (Young, 1995; UNRISD 1995; Beckman 1993; Olukoshi and Laakso, 1996). Much of the discussion which has taken place on the political opposition has been carried out within the context of attempts at understanding how opposition groups are linked to the resurgence that has been occurring in ethnic and religious forms of mobilisation. Many commentators have pointed to the attempts by opposition elements to tap ethnic and religious resentments as part of their struggles against the *ancien régime* which they are keen to replace.

This essay is, very broadly, concerned to assess the experience in Africa at promoting multiparty politics in general and opposition political activity in particular in a context that is marked by a continuing problem of economic stagnation which over 15 years of structural adjustment has failed to reverse, with far-reaching social and political consequences. The domestic economic context of the political reforms which have been undertaken in Africa since the late 1980s is one which has mainly been influenced by the neo-liberal market ideology. Since the late 1970s, African countries have, one after the other, under sustained donor pressure and conditionality, had to adopt the neo-liberal-inspired programme of structural adjustment designed by the International Monetary Fund (IMF) and the World Bank, to tackle their rapidly dwindling economic fortunes. The adoption of market-based economic reforms in Africa took place in the context of the rapid spread, on

a global scale, of neo-liberal monetarist ideas even as socialist central planning and Keynesian welfarism went into a sharp decline and began to be
dismantled (Ghai, 1991; Gibbon et al., 1992).

As far as Africa is concerned, the rise of global neo-liberalism not only
meant that domestic political change was inaugurated in the context of continuing economic decline and structural adjustment but also that elected
governments could hardly ignore the hegemonic political forces in the international system that had themselves taken on board the neo-liberal ideology
of the market in their dealings with the countries of the Third World in general and Africa in particular. The emergence in the post-Cold War international system of conditions favouring political reforms in Africa did not
simultaneously produce conditions for the reversal, or even tempering, of
neo-liberalism or structural adjustment. Nor did the post-Cold War order
produce a greater freedom of choice of economic policy direction for the
countries of the Third World. Indeed, there is a sense in which the Group of
Seven (G-7) countries, and the multilateral/international financial institutions that were increasingly reduced to being instruments for the promotion
of their policy preferences, saw or tried to forge a positive correlation
between liberal democracy and the neo-liberal version of the market.
Africa's elected governments, the so-called new democracies (re-)established
in the late 1980s or early 1990s, therefore, willy-nilly had to adhere to
IMF/World Bank structural adjustment programmes as the main framework
for searching for national economic recovery in what Mkandawire has described as "choiceless democracies" (Mkandawire, 1996).

We argue in this essay that the complications created by the continuing
implementation of domestically unpopular structural adjustment programmes, which, over a decade and a half after their introduction, have
failed to reverse economic decline on the continent even as they continue to
exact huge social and political costs, represent one of the greatest sources of
threat to the current democratic project in Africa. Matters are not helped by
the generally uninspiring experience of opposition political activity on the
continent which, among other things, has mostly been weakened by elitism,
factionalism, ethnocentrism, and systematic obstruction by incumbents.
Thus, most African countries today are operating "democratic" transitions
without an effective and coherent political opposition that is seen by the
generality of the populace as constituting a credible alternative to the discredited incumbents which they seek to replace. As voter apathy and disillusionment spread, attention is, once more, being focused on the potential for
the revitalisation of the forces of civil society with an interest in the promotion of democratic change. The question which is posed in this regard is
sometimes cast in terms of whether what Africa needs is the "thickening" of
civil society or its "politicisation" (Gibbon, 1993; Gibbon and Olukoshi,
1996). We take the position that pro-democracy civil society groups and
those forces in political society interested in promoting a reform agenda

need to build organic linkages in order to enhance the prospects for democratic governance on the continent. In seeking to develop this argument, we consider the prevalent views in the literature on the relationship between economic development and democracy and on the role of the opposition in the democratisation process, the effects of economic crisis and structural adjustment on the quest for democratisation in Africa, and the experiences, since the late 1980s, of political liberalisation in the context of neo-liberal economic reforms.

Given that widespread opposition to structural adjustment implementation fed into the local agitation for political reforms in most African countries, and given that most of the governments that were elected as a consequence of the successful campaign for political change have simply intensified implementation of orthodox structural adjustment policies, it is not difficult to see the myriad of problems which are posed for the deepening of the democratic process in Africa. This is all the more so as the objective reality of economic deprivation and hardship combines with the authoritarianism which structural adjustment implementation elicits to undermine the consolidation of the democratic transition of African countries. We argue the position, in concluding the chapter, that what the current conjuncture in Africa calls for is a developmentally-oriented state with a fully re-vamped constitutional basis which is sensitive to the demands of rational economic policy-making, the social welfare of the populace, and the goals of electoral pluralism and political liberalisation. It is important to state at once, lest we are misunderstood, that "rationality", as employed here, is not solely a function of economic considerations nor the preserve of technocrats; it necessarily includes measures aimed at cementing state and regime legitimacy and involves complex processes of political bargaining, consensus-building, and consent-generation. Blind adherence to orthodox structural adjustment, with the authoritarian political and repressive socio-economic costs which it carries, will do more harm than good to the cause of democratisation in Africa.

ECONOMIC DEVELOPMENT AND DEMOCRATISATION

The debate on the correlation, if any, that exists between economic development and democracy is a long-standing one which is as old as political theory itself. During this century, especially after the Bolshevik Revolution of 1917, the debate assumed a sharp and openly ideological dimension with some scholars arguing that "democracy" can only thrive under conditions of market capitalism while others insisted that "real" democracy that has meaning for the majority of the people can only thrive when capitalist social relations have been overthrown and the construction of a socialist order is embarked upon. Following the onset of the East–West Cold War, the ideological thrust of the debate increased as various academic partisans, depending on where their loyalties were, attempted to show that democracy is the flipside of either capitalism or socialism. Following the end of the Cold War and the spread of an air of Western triumphalism, the position that capitalism and the "free" market are but two sides of the same coin started to be re-asserted with even greater conviction and certitude by the high priests of neo-liberalism. In the light of the historical evidence, however, it is clear that both postulations equating democracy either with capitalism or with socialism are too simplistic and reductionist to be accepted as a basis for serious analysis (Dahl, 1985; Diamond et al., 1988; Duncan, 1989; Fukuyama, 1992).

Although the arrival of the capitalist era brought about important socio-economic and political changes that represented a qualitative advancement for human kind, it has neither been the ultimate harbinger of democracy nor did it banish authoritarianism for good. This is why some critics have insisted, with justification, that democracy and capitalism are different projects in the history of the modern world, a position which rules out the kinds of automatic, organic correlation which ideologues of neo-liberalism attempt to make between the two. Thus, the experiments in democratisation, with all of their limitations, undertaken by the Greek city states occurred without a capitalist system. On the other hand, capitalism, both in its early and monopoly stages of development, has displayed a capacity to produce highly repressive and anti-democratic political and administrative tendencies, including fascism in the period after the First World War. The authoritarian structures and processes associated with early and late capitalism have generated/elicited intense struggles of resistance which produced broad political and work place reforms. Thus, it is not capitalism *per se* that is inherently democratic; the hidden and open, sometimes bitter, struggles against its repressive tendencies and instincts have been central to the production of some of the reforms that are today the hallmark of liberal democracy (Markoff, 1997; Bangura, 1992; Duncan, 1989; Keane, 1988). It is instructive to note, in this regard, that not only has democracy, locally and internationally, developed in uneven waves, but also that the content and meaning of democracy are the subjects of constant negotiation and re-negotiation among the different players in society and between them and the state (Markoff, 1997).

Just as in capitalism democracy is not given, so also in socialism it cannot be taken for granted as an automatic outcome of a collectivised system of property relations. For although the capitalist and socialist revolutions that have taken place in the course of recent world history may be reflective of intense popular aspirations for a more representative government and meaningful socio-economic and cultural existence for the majority of the people, they are not, by themselves, tantamount to the establishment of a democratic order, however defined. The experience recorded in the various socialist countries that emerged in the period from 1917 was one in which far-reaching social improvements in the lives of most people were cancelled out by the gradual decay of the social movements that led the struggle for socialism and the increasing repression of individual political liberties, the opposite of the situation in most capitalist countries where individual political liberties were more or less recognised but economic and social inequalities remained widespread, thereby limiting the capacity of many to enjoy and/or enforce their formal political rights. "Socialist democracy", in the way it was defined and operationalised, entailed the constriction of individual rights and liberties as well as political pluralism in the framework of efforts at collectivising production by a state that enjoyed a monopoly on power. "Liberal" democracy, on the other hand separated individual political liberties from socio-economic rights and tended to place the interests of property owners over those of other groups in society (Ake, 1996). It is little wonder then that both in the "liberal" and "socialist" democracies, struggles continue to be waged for systemic reform as individuals and groups attempt to counter the erosion of their rights and concerns as citizens and extend the boundaries of their liberties and entitlements.

Clearly, democratisation is a process without a finite limit and whose content and vitality at any one point in time are reflective of the balance of social forces in a given social system. What this means is that there can be phases in the democratisation process characterised by setbacks as well as advances. There is, thus, no such thing as a "full" or "pure" democracy since the democratic process is constantly being renewed on local and global scales. Static notions/models of democracy against which all other processes of democratisation are measured, therefore, serve little other than an ideological-political end. Yet, it is such static notions of democracy that underlie much of the attempt to understand the contemporary African experience of transition politics. For, in critiquing the African reform project, many scholars approach the subject with idealised, as opposed to dialectical notions/interpretations of "Western" democracy and then proceed to catalogue how and why Africa falls short of the ideal. It does not occur to them to first establish that their idealised notions of democracy exist in the West. Invariably, what we get is the kind of unhelpful duality that celebrates "social capital" in one context and berates broadly similar relations and networks as "neo-patrimonialism" and "rent-seeking" in another. Clearly, there is no "complete" democratic system in existence nor is it possible to arrive at one so long as unequal power relations continue to underpin social interaction and exchanges. That is why reversals in the process of democratisation are possibilities which have also occurred in concrete historical contexts. The rise of fascism in the thick of the inter-war depression years may only be an extreme example; it is not, however, exceptional as changing socio-economic conditions bring about new political permutations that, potentially at least, could negate principles and practice of democratic governance (Bangura, 1992; Keane, 1988).

One aspect of the debate on democratisation which is particularly relevant to Africa relates to the level of economic development and what it means for the democratic prospects of countries. This question is especially relevant for Africa mainly because of the widespread state of economic underdevelopment on the continent. Africa lags behind most of the rest of the world on the basis of most indicators of economic and social development—gross domestic product, gross national product, per capita income, life expectancy, rate of mortality, the level of foreign exchange reserves maintained, literacy and school enrolment levels, per capita health provisioning, balance of payments position, the volume of exports, the continent's share of world trade and per capita consumption, among others (UNDP, 1994). On top of these, the huge debt burden which the countries of the continent carry has exacted considerable financial and social costs with which many governments have found it hard to cope. There are, of course, several contending explanations for the state of underdevelopment and prolonged economic crisis in Africa but these need not detain us here as they have been extensively presented elsewhere (Mkandawire, 1988; Mkandawire and Olukoshi, 1995; Gibbon and Olukoshi, 1996; Lensink, 1996; Tarp, 1993). The really crucial question is the implication of this situation of underdevelopment for the prospects for the initiation and sustenance of democratic political reform on the continent (Widner, 1994; Ottaway, 1997).

The widespread state of economic underdevelopment in Africa has led some scholars, on the left and on the right, to argue that the democratic prospects for the continent are very bleak precisely because the existing level of economic development cannot sustain democratic forms of politics. On the contrary, the low level of accumulation in most African countries can only produce/reinforce authoritarian economic, political and social practices. This position has sometimes been extended to include discussions about the alleged failure of the accumulation process to transform the values and practices of African peoples; the persistence of "tribalism", and the "relations of affection" woven around it, have tended to reinforce the authoritarian impulse that inheres in the accumulation process and underline the urgent necessity to move Africa towards a "proper" capitalist revolution that will simultaneously remove all existing/"traditional" impediments to democracy. In other instances, particularly among those working within the neo-liberal "political economy"/public choice approach, the view has been taken that the immersion of a vast array of African social forces, which in other political contexts might be the bearers of a durable struggle for democratic reform, in structures and processes of "neo-patrimonialism", "clientelism", "rent-seeking" , and corruption, means that the domestic impetus for meaningful change is weak. Matters are not helped in this regard by the context of decaying economies, itself an outcome of "neo-patrimonial" state interventionism, and the mediating influence of ethnicity which is manipulated to prevent far-reaching reform (Hydén, 1983; see especially, Bates in Widner, 1994; Ottaway, 1997). The suggestion has also been made that the absence/weakness of a strong bourgeoisie/middle class and the low level of per capita income hardly provide an auspicious setting for the emergence and triumph of democracy.

The chief weakness of most of the studies that have been carried out on Africa's democratic prospects in the context of its economic underdevelopment is their excessive determinism and economism. This is quite apart from the increasing vacuousness of such notions as "neo-patrimonialism" and "rent-seeking" which have the dubious status of being the ubiquitous explanatory variables for any and everything that is wrong with Africa and, therefore, ultimately explain nothing. Democratic struggles may be the result of the material interests of the forces that bear them; these material interests are, however, not solely or narrowly economic but could, and oftentimes do embody social and political concerns and considerations. In any case, as Markoff (1997) reminds us in his reflection on the transition to liberal democracy in Latin America and Europe, democratic outcomes were never, initially at least, the self-conscious products of actors aiming to promote democracy. Oftentimes, measures that were later to carry a huge democratic import were initially adopted precisely in order to contain democratic change. The determinism that has been prevalent in the literature has, more often than not, translated into a neglect of the important distinction that exists between democratic struggles and "democratic consolidation", the former being a prevalent feature of politics in many African countries as various social groups struggle to create, re-create and expand the space within which they must reproduce themselves economically, politically, and socially (Beckman, 1992, Bangura, 1992; *Africa Demos*, 1995). Thus, although the level of economic development and the dynamics of the accumulation process do have direct implications for democratic struggles and consolidation, these cannot be fully grasped within a framework that is determinist and which, therefore, treats the politics of accumulation in a manner that suggests that its outcome in underdeveloped countries is a foregone conclusion. In this instance, determinism and economism reinforce each other as non-economic sources of democratic change hardly feature in the explanatory framework that predominates in the debate on the reform process in Africa.

The contestation of the authoritarian practices associated with economic underdevelopment or primitive accumulation have, historically, opened democratic possibilities whose consolidation may have been difficult (not necessarily impossible) but which have clear implications for that process of accumulation. This pattern of democratic politics is no less significant in its historical/specific context than the forms of democratic struggle associated with advanced capitalist societies. Moreover, as we noted earlier, it is not particularly helpful to the development of proper analytic insights merely to equate "democracy" with a particular mode/level of economic production and castigate other modes, and the values associated with them as inherently and irredeemably "undemocratic". In this regard, the tendency to reduce all the internal political processes in Africa to the "rent-seeking", "neo-patrimonialist" logic which neo-liberal "political economists"/public choice theorists have elevated to the status of an explanatory *deus ex machina* and posited as a syndrome beyond which all of the potential forces for political reform are unable to rise, is extremely unhelpful as it creates a self-fulfilling prophecy of one-sided doom and gloom that is bereft of history and a sense of process in all of its contradictoriness. We need a much more dynamic, less simplistic understanding of the politics of democratisation (Bangura, 1992; Rudebeck, 1992). Furthermore, suggestions that the existence of a strong middle class is a pre-requisite for the emergence of democracy assume that, in the specific African historical context, the middle class, by definition, has an automatic interest in the promotion of democracy. Empirical studies can be cited to suggest the contrary, namely, that this class could in fact champion the cause of authoritarianism as the specific circumstances demand (Liabes, 1995; Olukoshi, 1995; Mkandawire, 1996).

Reflecting on the linkage between the level of economic development and the prospects for democratization, Bangura notes, correctly, that:

> ... the establishment of stable and sustainable democracy requires substantial changes in the forms of accumulation; the promotion of an acceptable level of welfare that will allow the majority of the people to have confidence in the capacity of democratic institutions to manage economic, social, and political conflicts; and the resolution of the contradictions between authoritarian relations that are dominant in the political sphere and nascent liberal pressures that are to be found in civil society" (Bangura, 1992).

Thus, although economic underdevelopment may not necessarily be fundamentally inimical to democratisation, it could pose problems for its consolidation especially where it inhibits the operationalisation of a social contract. Yet, it should not be taken for granted that economic advancement will necessarily lead to the automatic consolidation of democracy. As the example of many of the Asian tigers shows, advancement can go hand-in-hand with the persistence of different variants of political authoritarianism. Also, as we noted earlier, the reversal of the democratic process, however temporarily, has been part of the experience of some of the developed capitalist countries as evidenced by the growth of fascism in the inter-war years. In both advanced and underdeveloped economies, therefore, the struggles of various social groups are crucial to the initiation, sustenance and consolidation of the democratic project in all of its ramifications (O'Donnell, 1986; Nyong'o 1987).

When it comes to the role which the opposition could play in the democratisation process, the view which is prevalent in the literature is one which insists that the existence of an effective opposition in the context of a multi-party arrangement is absolutely indispensable to the emergence and consolidation of a stable democratic order. This represents a total reversal of an earlier wisdom in and about Africa which treated formal opposition as being potentially obstructive, if not outrightly divisive, not in the African "spirit" and the African way of doing things, inhibitive of the nation-building project and of the prospects for rapid national economic development (Olukoshi and Laakso, 1996; Wiseman, 1996). It also represented a radical modification of the main intellectual assumptions which informed most notions of the "vanguard" party associated with the former Soviet bloc and the practice of Marxism-Leninism in several African countries (Cohen and Goulbourne, 1991). As Africa began to experience pressures for domestic political reform from the late 1980s onwards, political theories, mostly liberal, on the place of the opposition in the democratisation process began to be revived. A few studies attempted to define the nature of the oppositional forces pushing the African political reform process and the factors that shape their capacity and determine the impact which they are able to make in their struggle for power and influence (Widner, 1994; Ottaway, 1997).

At the heart of the liberal theories is the assumption that no political order can be democratic which does not rest on the right of citizens who are entitled to a suffrage to vote in or vote out the highest officials of government. The political party is the most effective vehicle for mobilising voter support in the competition for electoral office. The institutionalisation of a multiparty system is, therefore, indispensable to the principle and practice of democracy. This way, the quest for political pluralism is reduced, in practice, to multipartyism. The opposition parties have to be distinct from and autonomous of the ruling party. The rules of the political system have to be such that they allow freedom of organisation by the parties on a level playing field and in a framework that allows the rotation of power based on the "free" choice of the electorate. The opposition parties would, in the interval between one election and the next, serve as the formal, institutionalised watch-dog within and outside parliament, to keep the ruling party in check. At election time, the opposition will provide the electorate with choice, politically and ideologically. It is this broad liberal political framework for understanding the role and place of the of the opposition that has informed the quest for the promotion of reform in Africa from the late 1980s onwards (Widner, 1994; Wiseman, 1996; Ottaway, 1997). But as we will see later, opposition political activity in much of Africa has been bedevilled by a host of problems whose overall implications suggest that the opposition is not able to play the role assigned to it in liberal theories.

ECONOMIC CRISIS, STRUCTURAL ADJUSTMENT AND DEMOCRATISATION IN AFRICA

The first and second oil "shocks" of the 1970s created the immediate context within which most African countries slid into economic crisis which, almost invariably, initially manifested itself in the form of balance of payments problems. By the early 1980s, virtually all African economies were mired in crisis, including those of them, like Nigeria, which enjoyed a revenue boom from the oil price increases of the 1970s. The African economic crisis took place in the context of the decline of the post-colonial model of accumulation which mixed a strong dose of state interventionism with state-supported social and welfare provisioning. The failure of the revenue receipts of most governments to match the rate of growth in the demand for social and welfare services combined with declining economic growth rates, diminishing terms of trade, and growing corruption and bureaucratic bottlenecks to gradually undermine the foundations of the post-colonial "social contract" on the basis of which much of Africa was ushered into independence (Bangura, 1992; Olukoshi, 1992). Prior to the 1980s, struggles were already being actively waged in various African countries aimed at defending and expanding the welfare gains of independence on the basis of which the legitimacy of the post-colonial state was partially constructed. In many parts of Africa, these struggles constituted the key elements of the quest for democratisation as various groups attempted to defend their socio-economic and welfare gains in the face of dwindling state revenues, declining economic growth rates, and growing corruption.

The economic crisis of the 1980s and the sharp decline in public revenues which it implied led to further attacks on the social and welfare expenditure of most African states as governments adopted a variety of austerity policies aimed at coping with their worsening economic position. The crisis situation resulted in a strengthening of the authoritarian reflexes of the post-colonial African state in part because its diminishing ability to meet the welfare needs of the citizenry translated into a deepening legitimacy crisis but also because the austerity measures adopted by governments often provoked strikes and riots which were for the most part brutally suppressed. Thus, even as the social expenditure of the state fell in real terms (and, in some cases, in nominal terms as well), the resources devoted to defence and security matters either maintained their share of the public expenditure or even grew. The authoritarianism of the state became increasingly associated with a sharp diminution in its ability to meet the welfare needs and aspirations of the populace. Struggles against this gradual dissolution of the post-colonial "social contract" intensified with mixed results. In many cases, governments became pre-occupied with repressing all opposition to their rule; security increasingly became the essence of governance and it was defined in naked terms that aimed to allow as little room as possible for independent political action and the promotion of human and peoples' rights/civil liberties (Bangura, 1992; Mustapha, 1988).

With the embrace by one African state after the other of IMF/World Bank structural adjustment programmes during the course of the 1980s, whatever was left of the post-colonial "social contract" was dealt more systematic and sustained blows. The entire structural adjustment model was premised on a single-minded anti-statism which included direct and indirect attacks on the social expenditure of the state. Cost recovery measures, user charges, food subsidy withdrawals, efforts at the overall curtailment of public expenditures, the de-control of prices, the commercialisation and privatisation of public enterprises, the deliberate holding down of wages even as inflation spiralled and local currencies were repeatedly devalued, and the retrenchment, on a massive scale, of public sector employees were just a few of the policies associated with structural adjustment which struck at the heart of what was left of the post-colonial "social contract". In spite of all protestations to the contrary, structural adjustment, in design and logic, was not only meant to exact huge social costs but also to undermine the social policy orientation and expenditure programme of the post-colonial state. The programmes for the mitigation of the social costs of adjustment which were later introduced were little more than "add ons" that did little to change the essential anti-social sector thrust of the neo-liberal market reform project whilst appearing to take account of growing international concerns about the adverse social consequences of the reform process.

If the post-colonial "social contract" was integral to an accumulation model which drew inspiration from Keynesian economic thinking, and if its development was undertaken with state interventionism at the centre, structural adjustment aimed to overthrow the entire post-colonial African economic development model and bring the "free" market to the centre of the resource and value allocation processes. The neo-liberal, monetarist thrust of the adjustment model, with its emphasis on a zero-sum market approach, was one which, from the outset, carried huge social costs. Not surprisingly, resistance to the implementation of the adjustment program-mes not only among the popular social groups that are the biggest losers from its adoption but also among the more privileged groups that profited from the efforts at economic liberalisation, was widespread and spirited in various parts of Africa. A common feature of the early 1980s in various adjusting countries were the "IMF riots" that occurred, sometimes sponta-neously, to protest the huge costs of market-based economic reforms (Mkandawire and Olukoshi, 1995; Bangura, 1992; Beckman, 1992; Gibbon et al., 1992; Sidell, 1988).

What has structural adjustment meant for the struggle for democratisa-tion in Africa? When the programme initially made its entry into the eco-nomic crisis management process of African countries, one early proposition that was deployed in its support centred around the view that it would help to produce a market-based bourgeoisie which, minimally connected to the state, will in turn promote a dual project of proper capitalist transformation and liberal democracy. According to this view, the mainstream African eco-nomic elite is mired in rent-seeking activities that involve a network of patron-clientelist relations in the state and society. These relations not only

slow down the capitalist development process, they also subvert the prospects for democratic governance on the continent. Structural adjustment,
with its strong market orientation would not only roll back the frontiers of
the state but also discipline the African economic elite to the rigours of the
market. Thus purified, the new bourgeoisie will, in turn, become the stan-
dard bearer for the democratisation of Africa on the basis of a market
economy that would have put paid to "patron-clientelism", "neo-patrimonialism", "prebendalism", the political economy of "affection", and the political economy of the "belly", among other allegedly peculiar ills that define
and bedevil African politics (Diamond, 1988; Nelson, 1989, 1990; Sandbrook,
1985; Widner, 1994; Ottaway, 1997).

Another proposition, related to the foregoing and also emphasising the
view that structural adjustment would strengthen Africa's democratic prospects, focused on the alleged liberating effects of the market reform process
for civil society. There are various dimensions/perspectives to this proposition but, in summary, most of its advocates opine that the state interventionism of the post-colonial years in Africa obstructed, even stifled the
development of the continent's civil society. Since it is at the level of civil
society, with its complexity of interest groups and associational life, that the
process of democratisation crystallises, its liberation from the "dead-weight"
of state interventionism would simultaneously result in a boost for Africa's
democratic prospects. In support of this position, some scholars have pointed to the flowering of civic associations in Africa as an increasing number of
countries embraced structural adjustment. Others have pointed to a process
of massive "disengagement" from the state as individuals and groups,
unable any longer to gain or retain access to the state and the resources it
controls, join the tide of informalisation as the underwriters of the parallel
economy and the "new" democratic seeds germinating in civil society
(Azarya and Chazan, 1987; Azarya, 1988; Bratton, 1989; Ottaway, 1997).

In sharp disagreement with the position that structural adjustment
would strengthen the democratic prospects of African countries, a host of
scholars has pointed to both the authoritarianism that inheres in the neo-
liberal market reform model as well as its authoritarian consequences for the
conduct of politics. In the view of these critics, not only is authoritarianism a
property which inheres in the adjustment model itself, its implementation
also reinforces the authoritarian political structures and practices of the post-
colonial state. For one, the anti-state, public sector-retrenching thrust of the
programme is one which carries an in-built authoritarian political load
directed against public sector interests that are denigrated in the neo-liberal
model as "self-serving" "rent-seekers". Within such a framework, undemocratic actions taken in the name of structural adjustment against supposedly
"self-serving" "rent-seekers" almost become self-justifying. For another, the
implementation of the adjustment programme with its strong dose of
austerity which, additionally, aims to overturn the entire basis of the post-

colonial model of accumulation, including cutting back severely on public sector social provisioning, requires a "strong" authoritarian state which will be prepared to ride roughshod over public opinion as well as suppress interest group opposition. In using conditionality as an instrument for pressurising African governments to stay the course of adjustment in the face of popular domestic disquiet, the authors of the adjustment programmes wittingly or unwittingly encourage local policy makers and state officials to employ repressive measures in their dealings with the opposition.

Furthermore, the conditionality clauses attached to the adjustment package are such that they promote accountability by African governments only to bilateral and multilateral donors even as local opposition is, at best, ignored and, at worst, suppressed. This deficit of accountability to the local population of the adjusting countries is reinforced by the absence of popular participation in the reform process in part because the adjustment programme was introduced in most cases as an external imposition but also because its content (initially at least), sequencing and implementation were shrouded in secrecy and mystery. The World Bank itself, as part of its involvement in the internal politics of structural adjustment implementation in Africa was to come up with Machiavellian formulations, aimed at "insulating" technocrats from popular pressure, wrong-footing the opposition to the market reform process, gaining surprise advantages for the adjusting governments, and strengthening "winners" from the reform process against "losers" (Mkandawire and Olukoshi, 1995; Beckman, 1992; Olukoshi, 1992; Gibbon et al., 1992; Bangura, 1992).

Given the fact that the economic and social thrusts of the adjustment programmes have the effect of further lowering the living conditions of the majority of the peoples of the adjusting countries of Africa, it should not be surprising that they have tended to reinforce the overall authoritarianism of African governments. If struggles for democratisation still remained a prominent feature of the African political landscape in the 1980s and early 1990s, it is not because of the alleged liberating effects of structural adjustment but because of the popular struggles which have crystallised against the neo-liberal market reform programme in various countries. In other words, it is opposition to structural adjustment rather than the adjustment programme itself that has served as the main domestic impetus for the democratic struggles of the 1980s and early 1990s in Africa (Beckman, 1992). Against the proponents of structural adjustment who expected the emergence of a purified, market-based bourgeoisie that would lead the democratic struggle, critics of the programme pointed to its adverse consequences for local productive activities, especially manufacturing production. Not surprisingly, the fabled bourgeoisie whose emergence was forecast has failed to appear whilst many sections of the existing dominant classes have been undermined. Moreover, the spread of market reforms, far from eliminating the rent-seeking behaviour that is supposed to be at the heart of public policy in Africa, merely re-located it from much of the state to the market, especially the deregulated financial sector where speculators enjoyed a field day (Olukoshi, 1992; Ghai, 1991; Onimode, 1989).

As to the alleged liberating effects of structural adjustment implementation on civil society in Africa, critics of the programme have noted that precisely because the leading forces in that arena are also the main actors/ actresses in the struggle against the neo-liberal market reform project, the state has made spirited efforts to stifle its democratic potentials. African regimes have been supported in this by the World Bank which has set itself the task of intervening in the civic arena through a programme of support to non-governmental organisations (NGOs) targeted at groups that are thought likely to back the neo-liberal project and, in so doing, counter-balance or neutralise the opposition. In the context of the Machiavellianism of the World Bank and the repressive interventionism of the state, the sharp decline in the living conditions of the groups that are the most active in the civil society of African countries, namely labour, the professionals, and students/youths, has acted to rob many activists of the economic and social autonomy required for them to sustain long-term democratic struggles. In several African countries, commentators were to express alarm at the emergence of what looked like a "culture of silence" as people's living and working conditions collapsed and state authoritarianism and repression intensified. It was only in the second half of the 1980s that this "culture" began to be broken as various groups once again found their voices and rediscovered their capacity to resist unpopular economic policies and the political authoritarianism/repression associated with their implementation. But as the Kenyan case-study in this book notes, this revival of the culture of opposition may already be withering as livelihood considerations associated with the pains of the prolonged adjustment process have tended to encourage individuals and communities to defect from the opposition back to the ruling party.

One of the most important forms by which opposition to increasing economic austerity and political authoritarianism was expressed was through direct attacks on the one-party or military-dominated state. Popular agitations were mounted for the dismantling of the political monopoly of the incumbent elite and for free, open elections to be convened. Street demonstrations and public rallies were accompanied in many cases with the launching of various fora for opposition activists and the publication of opposition/independent newspapers. In several of the Francophone and Lusophone countries of Africa, the opposition forces were able to force through their proposals for a sovereign national conferences; in other countries, constitutional clauses preventing the existence of parties other than the ruling one were repealed to allow for the new parties that were launched. In all cases, the opposition activists were united by their shared distrust of and disdain for the ruling party or oligarchy (Wiseman, 1996). As we will argue later, and as Kenyan and South African experiences that are analysed in chapters two and seven respectively show, this source of unity was to evaporate once the opposition activists were allowed to register their parties to contest elections. Furthermore, the period leading up to the recognition by incumbent regimes of the inevitability of multipartyism was characterised by a close unity of purpose between the forces for democratisation in civil society and those in political society. This relationship was to founder in the run-up to elections and after. In some cases, as is argued by Neocosmos in chapter seven of this book, civil society simply began to be depoliticised. In other cases, as is shown by Kanyinga in chapter two and Ibrahim and Niandou in chapter five, civil and political society forces simply drifted in their different, uncoordinated directions.

THE QUEST FOR POLITICAL LIBERALISATION IN THE CONTEXT OF STRUCTURAL ADJUSTMENT

Political Reforms and the Politics of Economic Liberalisation

The main achievements of the sustained and widespread agitation for political reforms in Africa during the late 1980s and early 1990s include the dismantling of many one-party and military regimes, the liberalisation, to varying degrees and depths, of the local political space in order to permit open political competition and freedom of association, the convening of multiparty elections that resulted in the defeat of several incumbent governments, the open advocacy of the obligation of governments to respect the human rights of the populace, some measure of political decentralisation in a number of countries, and the pluralisation of the sources of news and information as private and oppositional media were licensed to operate side by side with government-controlled news organs. One thing though which did not change is the framework within which the quest for African economic recovery is being pursued. Almost without exception, and irrespective of the political/ideological colouration of the new or re-elected governments that emerged, structural adjustment, with its neo-liberal thrust, remains the economic model through which African economies are being reformed. This is as true for countries where technocrats connected to the World Bank came to power (Benin Republic, for example) as for countries like Mozambique (nominally on the ideological left) and Kenya (professing an ideological right position) and in places like Zambia where a trade unionist came to power on the crest of popular opposition to structural adjustment and the repressiveness of the United National Independence Party (UNIP) of Kenneth Kaunda. In the majority of African countries where incumbent regimes were able to hold on to power, they simply continued with the adjustment measures which they had previously followed under donor pressure/supervision.

Given that the resistance to and struggles against the extreme hardship associated with structural adjustment and the increasingly authoritarian record of African governments were among, although they were not solely, the main triggers for the onset of the popular agitations for democratic reform that were witnessed in various parts of the continent during the late 1980s and early 1990s, it is clear that persistence with the neo-liberal market reform programme of the multilateral donors is bound to exact political costs which the new or re-elected governments would have to deal with. This is all the more so as the record of achievement of some 15 years of structural adjustment implementation has, on almost all scores, fallen well below the expectations and projections of even its authors. In most sectors of African economies, with the partial exception of financial services and real estate where speculation is rife, and tourism where massive currency devaluations have created a mini-boom of some sort, stagnation and decline are in evidence. This is especially true for the productive sectors. For most Africans, individual and corporate, life has been reduced to a daily struggle for subsistence as formal structures go into decline and informalisation spreads. In the perception of many (and perceptions influence political choices and action as much as anything else), structural adjustment is the direct cause of their dwindling economic fortunes; persistence with it without any tangible results to show after so many years of its implementation definitely has dire implications for the African political reform process (Mkandawire, 1996).

Sympathetic critics of the World Bank and IMF market reform project in Africa, examining the prospects for a successful programme of simultaneous political and economic re-structuring, argue that the process of the implementation of market economic reforms by elected (African) governments enjoying popular support is likely to be far more successful than implementation by un-elected and unrepresentative governments (Haggard and Webb, 1994). In this line of thinking, the bane of earlier attempts at reform implementation in Africa lay mainly in the fact that the task was entrusted to un-elected, unrepresentative and increasingly illegitimate governments that made little or no effort to persuade their populace of the need for adjustment. According to these sympathetic critics, most of them working within the public choice/neo-liberal "political economy" school, the legitimacy enjoyed by elected governments and the fact that they would be more willing to engage parliament, the opposition, and the wider populace in debates and consultations about the economic future of their countries would not only increase the chances for successful reform implementation but also simultaneously help to deepen the roots of the nascent democratic transition in Africa.

The tragedy of the optimistic assessment of the public choice school however centres on the fact that in many cases, on account of donor conditionality and leverage, the economic recovery model which governments are implementing is often not open to internal negotiation with the local opposition, at least not in its essence. What most governments have tried to push is a ready-made blueprint approved by donors, led by the IMF and the World Bank, and implemented on the basis of pre-agreed targets. This is a process which hardly allows for any systematic consultation; in most cases, it seeks to by-pass the elected legislature or to sideline it from the essential elements of the reform programme. In any case, the fact that any recovery programme that is the product of internal dialogue and consultation which deviates from neo-liberal orthodoxy will not only be opposed but also boycotted by the multilateral donors has served as a dis-incentive to newly elected governments that might otherwise have promoted local debates on the economic options available to their countries. The multilateral donors have left no doubt that support for local consultation and dialogue will be forthcoming only where the result favours structural adjustment the way they define it. In sum, the experience in most of Africa since the early 1990s, has been of elected governments promoting economic reforms in a manner that does little to enhance the local democratic process in their countries. Yet, few will deny that regimes that are able to generate consent are the ones that enjoy the greatest benefits in terms of their stock of legitimacy.

If elected African governments have, willy-nilly, stuck to the neo-liberal project of economic reforms (some, like Chiluba's government in Zambia have even attempted to push through the reforms much more vigorously than their predecessor in office), they have done so without concurrent political and social programmes aimed at safeguarding the democratic transition of their countries or stemming the precipitous decline in the social conditions of their populace. Often resorting to arm-twisting and increasingly authoritarian ways in order to push their views through, many of these governments have not shown themselves to be different from the discredited politicians whom they replaced. Taken together with rampant corruption among senior state officials, even as the majority of the people are subjected to fresh or renewed austerity, it should not be surprising that the impression in many parts of Africa today is one of *plus ça change, plus c'est la même chose* or even worse. The only people applauding this state of affairs, whilst simultaneously attempting to move with the barometer of international opinion, are the main multilateral donors; within African countries themselves, in some of the worst cases, as people come to terms with the dashed hopes of their attempt at a democratic transition, an unfortunate, if inevitable nostalgia for the *ancien regime* is being expressed. A clear example in this regard is Benin where Matthew Kerekou has been returned to power. In Zambia, profound disillusionment with the MMD government of Chiluba is translating in some quarters into pro-Kaunda/UNIP sentiments. Feeling threatened by this backlash, the Chiluba regime has not only adopted more nakedly authoritarian modes of governance, it also adopted controversial legislation aimed at eliminating Kaunda from the presidential elections that took place in November 1996 (Olukoshi and Laakso, 1996).

But beyond the fact that elected governments implementing orthodox structural adjustment reforms under donor pressure have neither shown themselves to have superior democratic credentials to their predecessors nor overcome the authoritarian impulses that the political management of an economic crisis situation produces, there is a growing problem of popular de-participation in the political process of most African countries. In some places, this has translated into a generalised distrust of the entire political process; in others, it has taken the form of the withdrawal of people on a massive scale from the electoral process so soon after an earlier round of enthusiastic participation (see Appendix 1 in this book for participation levels in some of the recent elections). Against the background of the mass sense of alienation which is evident in many African countries, communalist, religious, ethnic and regionalist identities have mushroomed, a process reinforced by the worsening economic and social situation in the continent. Thus, even as the optimism of the African democratic transition fades away, several states on the continent are faced with direct domestic challenges some of which carry potential implications for their integrity. Lacking faith in the political process, disaffected groups in places as far apart as Niger and Mali on the one hand and Lesotho in Southern Africa have resorted to extra-constitutional, extra-legal means of seeking and winning redress. The fragility of the democratic transition itself, underlined by the diminishing legitimacy of the newly or recently installed governments and the environment of continuing economic decline, has, in turn, led leaders to resort to the use of force to address rising disaffection. As the tragic examples of Liberia, Somalia, and Rwanda show, such resort to force only hardens positions and makes political problems much more difficult to resolve.

That the continuing context of economic stagnation within which attempts at democratising Africa has far-reaching adverse consequences for the sustainability and extension of the political reforms introduced should not be surprising. If some 15 years of structural adjustment have simply meant a continuation or worsening of austerity for a majority of the populace, it should not be shocking that a process of mass de-participation has crept into the political landscape of countries which only a few a years earlier were gripped by popular campaigns for reform. For, the democratic dynamic is also a highly, though not exclusively instrumentalist one. Social forces put their political weight behind a project of democratisation mainly if it helps to protect their advantages or minimise their disadvantages. The failures of the governments elected as part of the current quest for democratisation in Africa to effectively address the socio-economic concerns of the populace largely on account of their donor-induced commitment to structural adjustment has, not unexpectedly, translated into a growing disillusionment with politics generally and "democratic" politics in particular. The danger which this represents for the immediate future of democracy in Africa will be fully appreciated if it is realised that although, formally, democracy is concerned with open political competition and participatory governance, its capacity to survive, let alone flourish, depends on the extent to which it embodies social and economic characteristics that are relevant to the aspirations of the majority of the people (Bangura,1992). It is these socio-economic issues that increasingly underline the failures of the African democratic transition of the late 1980s and early 1990s. Even as the process of political reforms gathered pace on the continent, more Africans were sliding into absolute poverty than ever before and in the perception of many, structural adjustment has a key part to play in this (Cornia et al., 1992; UNRISD,1995).

The Weaknesses of Africa's Opposition Parties

It is bad enough that the potential gains to the peoples of Africa from the liberal-isation of their national political spaces have been undermined by the exigencies of the politics of market reform implementation. Matters appear to have been worsened by the fact that in most African countries, the promise which the opposition once represented as the bearer of the hopes and aspirations of the generality of the people has substantially faded away. Indeed, in a number of cases, the opposition parties are severely discredited before the populace and do not present a viable alternative to the electorate. There are several factors which would appear to have acted together to weaken and, in some cases, discredit the opposition in much of Africa's on-going experience with multiparty politics. In several countries, the opposition was faced with recalcitrant incumbents who only very reluctantly conceded a multiparty framework but stopped at nothing to obstruct, weaken, harass, and divide the opposition. Kenya, which is discussed in detail in chapter two of this book, and Zaire are salutary examples in this regard but they are by no means exceptional. Also, as part of the strategy employed by incumbent regimes to weaken the opposition, public sector patronage was withdrawn from private sector business organisations that were sympathetic to or identified with the opposition. This acted to weaken the financial base of the opposition parties and, in so doing, limited their organisational capacity even as incumbents freely availed themselves of state resources to finance their bids for remaining in power. In Zimbabwe, as Nkiwane points out in chapter three of this volume, the ruling party went so far as to make a provision for itself in the annual expenditure programme of the state.

Clearly, in most countries, the opposition did not enjoy a level playing field with the incumbents against whom they contested. Official, publicly-funded media organisations as well as the various arms/apparatuses of the state, including especially the security services, were deployed against opposition parties and their activists. Incumbents did not lose much opportunity to rig elections both structurally (by loading the rules of the game against the opposition, blacking them out of the official media, and altering constituency boundaries, for example) and physically (by stuffing ballot boxes or altering actual votes cast wherever possible) in spite of the "watchful" presence of international and local observers. Thus, not surprisingly, none of Africa's multiparty elections has gone unchallenged by the opposition on the grounds that the outcome was rigged by the winning party. The use of the boycott weapon by the opposition to protest the absence of a level playing field has also been widespread. Furthermore, in several documented cases, ruling parties infiltrated *agents provocateurs* into the main opposition parties to cause disruptions for them from within and, thus, limit the actual and potential challenges which they pose to the incumbent. The activities of *agents provocateurs* has certainly been a factor, although not the only explanation, for the factionalisation and splits that have characterised opposition politics across Africa. Electoral boundaries were also frequently drawn and re-drawn by incumbents to maximise their advantage. In the case of Uganda which is analysed in chapter six of this book, opposition parties, already faced with a formidable incumbent, are not allowed to mobilise support as political parties. In all, the environment within which the opposition operated was a tough one indeed.

With many of the parties relying on a handful of patrons, usually also their leaders/founders, for the finances they needed for maintaining their activities, they increasingly became susceptible to attempts at building cults of personality and internal structures of patronage. Many of the opposition parties were themselves launched as vehicles for key individuals to achieve power. Most of the individuals who founded/helped to found the new parties were disaffected members of the single party or ruling military oligarchy; some were badly tainted by their past associations and actions. In many instances, the opposition leaders carried their personal rivalries into the opposition parties they helped to found; a great deal of energy and time was spent by them staking rival claims which prevented collective action even when the circumstances indicated that that was the most viable course of action open to them. Individual rivalries were reinforced by lingering or resuscitated ethno-regional/religious competition and suspicion. In this context, internal party democracy was hardly given priority by the main opposition elements except as an instrument in their struggle for individual and group advantage. As factionalism took hold and the prospects of life in opposition looked too uninviting, some of the prominent opposition elements were to jump ship and trace their roots back to the ruling party from which they defected in the first place. Kenya and Zaire are once again two of the countries in Africa where this has been rife; it has acted to demoralise the opposition and weaken popular interest in democratic politics.

There is no doubt that the electoral system operated in most African countries, namely the British first-past-the-post, winner-take-all model worked to the detriment of the opposition. The number of seats which the opposition won in most countries was not proportionate to its share of the vote. Thus, in a lot of instances, it became easy for the winning party to rule without direct reference to the opposition and to seek, on the one hand, to isolate and intimidate opposition members of parliament and, on the other hand, attempt to lure them with the carrot of state patronage. Pressure on the opposition was also exerted by the ruling party through the freezing of all public, developmental projects in the constituencies that voted for opposition politicians. Since voting often took on distinct ethno-regional patterns corresponding to the perceived ethno-regional character of the parties, such punitive measures implemented by the ruling group acted, at one level, to reinforce popular ethnic and religious identities and, at another level, to pressure individual opposition politicians to make peace with the party of government. In this environment, the quality of the public political discourse did little to enhance the popular interest in the struggle for meaningful political change.

In articulating their demands for multiparty politics, many opposition elements were too quick to allow themselves to be hurried by incumbents into elections without first insisting on the implementation of the far-reaching constitutional changes that were necessary for governing post-electoral political activity. The only exceptions in this regard were the hand-ful of Francophone and Lusophone countries that held conclusive sovereign national conferences. But even here, it is necessary to distinguish between the sovereign national conferences which were the unavoidable result of sustained pressures from below (Niger, Madagascar and Benin, for example) and those that were organised from above as part of pre-emptive steps to contain the opposition (Chad and Gabon, for example). In most countries, including especially Kenya, Tanzania, Ghana, Cameroon, Guinea, and others, the opposition appeared content that multipartyism had been intro-duced, a contentment that was partly reflective of the (excessive) confidence which some of them had in their chances for defeating the incumbent party. Thus it was that crucial questions regarding the manner in which the transi-tion to multiparty politics would be governed and by whom were side-stepped. Rules regulating the rights of political associations to convene rallies or organise protests were virtually ignored until the opposition fell foul of them after the dust of electioneering had settled.

In several African countries, opposition political activity came to depend heavily on donor/external (financial) support for its sustenance. Certainly, external support was useful in getting some of the parties established; it, however, sometimes resulted in the neglect of the local avenues that were available for tapping finance and, more importantly, building a strong and national membership base. Furthermore, it lay some of the opposition elements open to nationalistic attacks which, though self-serving, struck a chord with some sections of the local population that are sensitive to external domination of the African political-economic space. Indeed, not too infrequently, incumbents who had themselves taken IMF/World Bank loans, pointed opportunistically to the dependence of their opponents on "foreign money" in a bid to undermine their nationalist/ patriotic credentials. On the whole, the "donorisation" of aspects of opposition party politics fed into the elitism that was a defining feature of the parties. Few indeed were the opposition parties that entered elections as mass movements even if the period immediately following their founding suggested they enjoyed an initial mass appeal. Perhaps the most notable or best known exception in this regard is the MMD in Zambia. It is, of course, a different question altogether whether the MMD, after gaining political power, has been able to remain a mass organisation with a mass appeal that cuts across ethnic and regional divisions in Zambia.

It is important to note that most opposition political activists were very effective at mobilising opinion and following in the main urban centres but were extremely weak when it came to reaching out to people in the rural areas where the bulk of the population—and of the voters are concentrated. Yet, it was precisely in the rural areas that the ruling parties concentrated most of their attention. Unlike the opposition parties, they had solid organisational structures on the ground in the rural areas and were able, in spite of multipartyism, to retain their influence as the only/leading political force known to the rural populace. Of course this advantage owed a lot to the long monopoly on power which the ruling oligarchy enjoyed; little systematic attempt was made by the opposition forces to break this grip. In certain instances (Senegal, Côte d'Ivoire, and, to some extent Kenya to cite three examples) the ruling party practically abandoned the urban vote to the opposition and concentrated on the rural vote. The voting pattern in some countries showed clear rural-urban divisions, with the rural areas largely controlled by the ruling party and the urban vote going to the opposition. The presence and influence of "traditional" chiefs, provincial and local government officials, and religious officials were freely deployed in the rural areas to bolster support for the ruling party. Chapter four of this volume which details the experience of the Senegalese opposition contains references to the pronouncements of the leaders of the highly influential mouridic sects giving explicit and open instructions to vote for the ruling party. In the case of Kenya, the ruling party always resorted to using local government officials to block opposition parties from organising in the rural areas. This process is graphically described in chapter two.

With the programmes of most of the opposition parties not inspiring and retaining much national interest and confidence, the connection which many of them initially had with civil society groups, especially those in the forefront of the human rights struggle, simply unravelled. In places like Kenya, even before the elections, a disconnection between the opposition parties and the civic/professional associations that campaigned long and hard for reforms was already in evidence. Today, the party political opposition is in a state of crisis and disintegration in the majority of those countries where it did not manage to unseat the incumbent regime. This crisis is taking place in the context of the weakening of secular, national territorial forms of politics brought about by changing popular identities that have resulted in the resurgence of ethnic, regional, and religious associations and the generalised decline of traditional vehicles of national mobilisation like the trade and students' unions as well as professional associations. This obviously has adverse implications for the quest for democratisation in Africa; in many countries on the continent, the ruling parties have conducted themselves in a manner which suggests that multipartyism in the way in which it has unfolded means little for the practice of governance. Even in countries like Zambia where the opposition came to power, it has conducted itself like the erstwhile single ruling party which it replaced. In the case of Niger which is discussed in detail in chapter five, the opposition alliance that won the first multiparty elections simply disintegrated and in so doing, facilitated the staging of a military *coup d'état* whose leader then enacted one of the most blatantly rigged elections in post-colonial Africa in order to transform himself into a civilian president.

TOWARDS A DEVELOPMENTAL DEMOCRACY AND CONSTITUTIONAL REFORMS IN AFRICA

It is clear that at the root of the difficulties that currently bedevil the quest for democratisation in Africa is the growing disconnection between the political forces produced by the wave of agitation for political reform and the social forces that were at the forefront of the struggle. There is a sense in which the increasing trend towards popular alienation and demobilisation which is being witnessed on the continent replicates aspects of the early post-independence experience in Africa when there was a rupture in the links between the nationalist politicians who took over the reins of state power and the popular social movements that were central to the anti-colonial struggle (Mamdani et al., 1988). A crucial element in the current process of demobilisation is the continuing economic and social crisis on the continent which structural adjustment has done a lot to exacerbate and complicate. Given that the well-being of the majority of the people is crucial to the consolidation of the democratic process, it should not be surprising that disaffection is deepening against governments which were (re-)elected with a fanfare but have been unable to give concrete meaning to the democracy project. The distinct danger that disillusionment will develop to a level which questions the very essence of a democratic political system is one which confronts us and which needs to be addressed urgently (Mkandawire,

1996). The disarray that has tended to characterise the opposition in most countries after elections have been held has not helped matters in this regard. Unable to win power, many opposition parties have simply splintered into factions and/or faded into irrelevance. Some have been weakened by crippling financial problems; others were the victims of the short-term perspective which their founders had.

In order for popular confidence to be restored in the democratic process, it is necessary for several things to happen. At one level, African countries need to move rapidly towards a new "social contract" within the framework of a developmental democracy which, in addition to jettisoning the zero-sum market approach of the neo-liberals will also restore a long-term developmental perspective to the state. As part of this perspective, the requirements of the social welfare of the people will have to be given a central place rather than being treated as a peripheral after-thought to be conveniently attached to a programme of economic reform for the purpose of marketing that programme. No programme of economic reform can be meaningful which wipes out the social and welfare gains of the populace. Politically, processes and structures of democratic governance which reinforce political and cultural pluralism, give a high premium to democratic accountability and guarantee the protection of human and peoples' rights will have to be instituted as part of this new "social contract". Societies recovering from war or a long history of conflict or those that are faced with the danger of conflict and disintegration need, additionally, to work towards political decentralisation and power sharing in order to ensure that competing interests are represented in the political process. Of course, a programme of decentralisation and power-sharing which is not preceded by a systematic effort at democratising power by disciplining it to the popular prescriptions specified by the populace could easily amount to an exercise in nullity. A democratic core, therefore, has to be the hub around which the project of decentralisation and power-sharing are organised.

At another level, those countries where serious steps have not been taken to carry out open and far-reaching constitutional reforms will have to be pressured by local social movements to do so. In many respects, the vitality which the opposition in general, as opposed to party political opposition specifically, still has in many countries is the result of the work which various "civil society" associations are carrying out in defence of the freedom of association, human rights and the freedom of the press. It is these associations that, under appropriate conditions, could lead the campaign for the far-reaching constitutional reforms that have eluded many countries. The increasing "(re-)politicisation" of these associations through their direct intervention in the political arena is, therefore, a process which should be encouraged. The failure to drastically reform the constitutional basis of the state in Africa as part and parcel of the quest for democratic political reform is an important omission for which the opposition parties—and the generality of the citizenry too have paid dearly. One of the most important elements of any constitutional reform will have to be a bill of rights which, additionally, should be justiceable. Such a bill could, at least, provide a platform through which members of civil and political society could make democratic demands on the state and in so doing, curtail political arbitrariness and a resurgent authoritarianism.

As readers will observe, several of the issues which we have raised in an overview fashion in this chapter are pursued and illustrated in greater depth in the essays that follow. The country-cases which are analysed present an interesting mix that offers useful insights into various aspects of opposition politics in general and party political opposition in general. It is worth underlining that not all African countries entered or re-entered multiparty politics from exactly the same background context: questions of the form of the pre-existing state, the internal coherence of the ruling party that monopolised/dominated political power, the nature of the civil society that was in place, including the scope for interest group mobilisation and articulation, the history of political society, the domestic resource base of the country, and the patterns of interaction between the local political economy and the international system are some of the factors that explain the specificities of each country and offer a basis for comparative analysis of the different national cases. On the basis of these parameters, readers will find that the seven countries—Kenya, Niger, Nigeria, Senegal, South Africa, Uganda, and Zimbabwe—whose experiences of opposition politics are discussed in the volume have as much in common as what separates them from one another. For instance, three of the countries—Niger, Nigeria and Uganda—have had a history of military rule; Niger was only ushered into multiparty politics for the first time in its history in the early 1990s, an experience which contrasts sharply with that of Senegal and Zimbabwe that have operated as *de jure* multiparty systems, or Nigeria and Uganda that have had short episodes of multiparty politics interspersed with long experiences of unelected, mostly military or military-backed government. Kenya, Zimbabwe and, in a sense, South Africa had experiences of white settler rule which elicited armed resistance from the black majority; Uganda was also to undergo armed resistance against post-independence political authoritarianism. Of the seven countries, Nigeria and Uganda are not currently operating multiparty regimes, the latter being, officially, a no-party system, the former still under military rule. To slightly varying degrees, each of the countries, with the exception of Nigeria, is presently ruled by one dominant party, with the opposition movement consisting of relatively much smaller parties. In Kenya, Senegal, South Africa and Zimbabwe, the dominant party of government in each country has managed to hold on to power since independence, or in the case of South Africa, since the demise of apartheid. Museveni and his NRM have also had a prolonged stay in power. The list of similarities and differences that can be drawn is endless. In the end though, the key question which emerges out of the different experiences centres on the issue of how power can be re-organised in order to ensure popular democratic participation on the basis of an open system of political pluralism that is underpinned by a sustainable social contract.

BIBLIOGRAPHY

Africa Demos, 1995, Vol. III, No. 4, March 1995, "Issue on The Promise of Democracy"

Ake, C.,1996, *Democracy and Development*. Washington, D.C.: Brookings Institution.

Ake, C., 1992, "The Feasibility of Democracy in Africa". Mimeo. Ibadan.

Azarya, V., 1988, "Re-ordering State-Society Relations: Incorporation and Disengagement", in D. Rothchild and N. Chazan (eds.), *The Precarious Balance: State and Society in Africa*. Boulder: Westview.

Azarya, V. and N. Chazan, 1987, "Disengagement from the State in Africa: Reflections on the Experience of Ghana and Guinea", *Comparative Studies in Society and History*, 29,1.

Bangura, Y., 1992, "Authoritarian Rule and Democracy in Africa: A Theoretical Discourse", in P. Gibbon et al. (eds.), 1992.

Beckman, B., 1993, "Economic Reform and National Disintegration". Mimeo. Stockholm.

Beckman, B., 1992, "Empowerment or Repression? The World Bank and the Politics of African Adjustment", in P. Gibbon et al. (eds.), 1992.

Bratton, M., 1995, "Are Competitive Elections Enough?", *Africa Demos*, III, 4.

Bratton, M., 1989, "Beyond the State: Civil Society and Associational Life in Africa", *World Politics*, XLI, 3.

Cohen, R. and H. Goulbourne (eds.), 1991, *Democracy and Socialism in Africa*. Boulder: Westview Press.

Cornia, G.A. et al. (eds.), 1992, *Africa's Recovery in the 1990s: From Stagnation and Adjustment to Human Development*. Florence: UNICEF.

Dahl, R., 1985, *A Preface to Economic Democracy* . California: University Press.

Diamond, L. et al. (eds.), 1988, *Democracy in Developing Countries, Vol. 2, Africa*. Boulder: Lynne Rienner.

Diamond, L., 1988, "Roots of Failure, Seeds of Hope", in L. Diamond et al. (Eds.), 1988.

Duncan, G. (ed.), 1989, *Democracy and the Capitalist State*. Cambridge: Cambridge University Press.

Fukuyama, F., 1992, *The End of History and the Last Man*. London: Penguin.

Ghai. D. (ed.), 1991, *IMF and the South: Social Impact of Crisis and Adjustment*. London: Zed Books.

Gibbon, P. et al. (eds.), 1992, *Authoritarianism, Democracy and Adjustment: The Politics of Economic Reform in Africa*. Uppsala: Nordiska Afrikainstitutet.

Gibbon, P., 1993, "Civil Society and Political Change, with Special Reference to Developmentalist States". Mimeo. Uppsala.

Gibbon, P. and A. Olukoshi, 1996, *Structural Adjustment and Socio-Economic Change in Sub-Saharan Africa*. Research Report No. 102. Uppsala: Nordiska Afrikainstituet.

Haggard, S. and S. Webb (Eds.), 1994, *Voting for Reform: Democracy, Political Liberalization and Economic Adjustment*. Oxford: Oxford University Press.

Havnevik, K. (ed.), 1987, *The IMF and the World Bank in Africa: Conditionality, Impact and Alternatives*. Uppsala: Nordiska Afrikainstitutet.

Hydén, G., 1983, *No Shortcuts to Progress: African Development Management in Perspective* . London: Heinemann.

Keane, J., 1988, *Democracy and Civil Society*. London: Verso.

Legum, C., 1990, "The Coming of Africa's Second Independence", *The Washington Quarterly*, Winter Issue.

Lensink, R., 1996, *Structural Adjustment in Sub-Saharan Africa*. London: Longman.

Liabes, D., 1995, "Entrepreneurs, Privatisation and Liberation: The Pro-Democracy Movement in Algeria", in Mahmood Mamdani and Ernest Wamba-dia-Wamba (eds.), *African Studies in Social Movements and Democracy*. Dakar: CODESRIA Books.

Mamdani, M. et al., 1988, *Social Movements, Social Transformation and the Struggle for Democracy in Africa*. Dakar: CODESRIA.

Markoff, J., 1997, "Really Existing Democracy: Learning from Latin America in the Late 1990s", *New Left Review*, No. 223, May/June.

Mkandawire, T., 1988, "The Road to Crisis, Adjustment and De-industrialisation: The African Case", *Africa Development*. Vol. XIII, No.3.

Mkandawire, T., 1996, "Economic Policy-Making and the Consolidation of Democratic Institutions in Africa", in K. Havnevik and B. van Arkadie (eds.), *Domination or Dialogue: Experiences and Prospects for African Development Cooperation*. Uppsala: Nordiska Afrikainstitutet

Mkandawire, T. and A. Olukoshi (eds.), 1995, *Between Liberalisation and Repression: The Politics of Structural Adjustment in Africa*. Dakar: CODESRIA Books.

Mustapha, A.R., 1988, "Ever-Decreasing Circles: Democratic Rights in Nigeria, 1978–1988". Mimeo. Oxford.

Nelson, J. (ed.), 1990, *Economic Crisis and Policy Choice: No Politics of Economic Adjustment in the Third World*. Princeton: Princeton University Press.

Nelson, J. (ed.), 1989, *Fragile Coalitions: The Politics of Economic Adjustment*. Oxford: Transaction Books.

Nyong'o, P.A. (ed.), 1987, *Popular Struggles for Democracy in Africa*. London: Zed Books.

O'Donnell, G., 1986, *Transitions from Authoritarian Rule: Prospects for Democracy*. Baltimore: John Hopkins University Press.

Olukoshi, A. (ed.), 1992, *The Politics of Structural Adjustment in Nigeria*. London: James Currey.

Olukoshi, A., 1995, "Bourgeois Social Movements and the Struggle for Democracy: An Inquiry into the "Kaduna Mafia", in Mahmood Mamdani and Ernest Wamba-dia-Wamba (eds.), *African Studies in Social Movements and Democracy*. Dakar: CODESRIA Books.

Olukoshi, A., 1997, "The Elusive Prince of Denmark: Structural Adjustment and the Crisis of Governance in Africa". Mimeo. Uppsala.

Olukoshi, A. and L. Wohlgemuth (eds.), 1995, *A Road to Development: Africa in the 21st Century*. Uppsala: Nordiska Afrikainstitutet.

Olukoshi, A. and L. Laakso (eds.), 1996, *Challenges to the Nation-State in Africa*. Uppsala: Nordiska Afrikainstitutet.

Onimode, B. (1989, *The IMF, the World Bank and the Africa Debt*. 2 Vols. London: Zed Books.

Ottaway, M. (ed.), 1997, *Democracy in Africa: The Hard Road ahead*. Boulder: Lynne Rienner.

Rudebeck, L. (ed.), 1992, *When Democracy Makes Sense: Studies in the Democratic Pattern of Third World Popular Movements*. Uppsala: AKUT, Uppsala University.

Sandbrook, R., 1985, *The Politics of Africa's Economic Stagnation*. Cambridge: Cambridge University Press.

Shivji, I., 1989, "The Pitfalls of the Democracy Debate", *CODESRIA Bulletin*, No. 2 &3.

Shivji, I., 1988, *Fight My Beloved Continent: New Democracy in Africa*. Harare: SAPES.

Sidell, S.R., 1988, *The IMF and Third World Instability: Is there a Connection?* London: St. Martins.

Tarp, F., 1993, Stabilization and Structural Adjustment: *Macroeconomic Frameworks for Analysing the Crisis in Sub-Saharan Africa*. London: RKP.

UNDP, 1994, *Human Development Report 1994*. Oxford: Oxford University Press.

UNRISD, 1995, *States of Disarray: The Social Effects of Globalization*. Geneva: UNRISD.

Widner, J., (ed.), 1994, *Economic Change and Political Liberalisation in Sub-Saharan Africa*. Baltimore: Johns Hopkins University Press.

Wiseman, J. A., 1996, *The New Struggle for Democracy in Africa*. Aldershot: Avebury.

Young, C., 1995, "Democracy and the Ethnic Question", *Africa Demos*, III, 4.

Chapter 2

Contestation over Political Space: The State and the Demobilisation of Opposition Politics in Kenya

Karuti Kanyinga

INTRODUCTION: BETWEEN LIBERAL AND POPULAR DEMOCRACY

The period since the mid-1980s has witnessed an increased interest among students of Africa in the potential for the institutionalisation of democracy on the continent. Among scholars working within the liberal/neo-liberal framework, the main pre-occupation has been with studying the inter-connections that are thought to link Africa's "weak" civil society to the different processes and institutions of "neo-patrimonialism" and a variety of problematic developmental outcomes. The view soon gained ground among this category of scholars that the combination of "neo-patrimonialism" and "weak" civil societies within a politico-institutional framework that negated pluralism was responsible for the onset and/or persistence of Africa's economic and political crises (Jackson and Rosberg, 1982; Sandbrook, 1985; Chazan et al., 1992, Hydén and Bratton, 1992; Bratton and van de Walle, 1994). The discussions that took place on how Africa might democratise and overcome its crisis gave rise to a civil society perspective which saw in the retrenchment of the state or the disengagement of civil institutions from it, the possibilities for the emergence of a "liberated" civil society that could provide a sound basis for political pluralism and democracy (Azarya, 1988; Bayart, 1985; Bratton, 1994).

Alongside the flowering of liberal/neo-liberal thinking on the politics of contemporary Africa was the emergence of another approach, the popular politics school, which developed to focus scholarly attention on the promise and limitations of indigenous social/popular movements for Africa's democratic transition. If the neo-liberals were pre-occupied in their studies with the promotion of a one-sided anti-state ideology, the popular politics school also saw post-colonial statism, and the logic of accumulation from above which was associated with it, as being highly obstructive of Africa's socio-economic and political development. The state bourgeoisie for whom the project of accumulation from above functions is seen by most of the students working within the popular politics approach as being averse to popular democratic politics. Still, pressures from below have consistently built up in African countries, reflective of popular yearnings for a participatory and accountable model of development. Needless to add, such struggles for popular democracy are seen in a negative light by the local bourgeoisie (Nyong'o, 1987 and 1988; Mamdani et al., 1988; Shivji, 1992; Neocosmos, 1993).[1]

Although the neo-liberal and popular politics approaches to under-standing contemporary African political realities are united in their shared perception that the state/post-colonial statism, in one way or another, is central to the severe political, economic, and social crises facing the conti-nent, they differ sharply in their agenda for remedial action. Whereas the neo-liberal analysts emphasise the need for the retrenchment of the state side by side with the liberation of civil society and the forces of the market within an institutional-political framework that is pluralistic and based on multiparty politics, the popular politics approach insists mainly on a far-reaching reform of the state not with a view to crippling/jettisoning it but in order to make it more responsive to popular aspirations from below. Moreover, the popular politics approach is far less celebratory of the market and civil society and cautions against the equation of the inauguration of a multiparty political system with democracy.

The political reform process which has been witnessed in Africa since the late 1980s has been marked primarily by the reinstatement by various gov-ernments of competitive politics in the framework of pre-existing attempts, dating back to the early 1980s, at liberalising markets. But the extent to which the programmes of political and economic liberalisation which gov-ernments felt compelled to embark upon corresponded to the aspirations of the popular classes of Africa is highly debatable. It is apparent, from the evidence that is available, that in the rush to undertake political and eco-nomic reforms in order, partly, to conform with donor expectations, the popular demands and aspirations of the people have tended to be glossed over or robbed of any meaningful content. Not surprisingly, the main win-ners from the reform processes have been the very elites who profited from the pre-reform models of politics and economic development. These elites, in their attempts to demobilise local popular movements for democracy and limit the substantive implications of political reforms, have resorted to the mobilisation of ethnic and religious identities in a manner that has tended to undermine the liberatory import of pressures from below.

---

[1] See also the debate in Africa Development, Vol. XIII, Nos. 3 and 4, 1988, in which P. A. Nyong'o, S. Gutto and T. Mkandawire discuss the question of democracy and political instability in Africa.

Against the background of the foregoing, it is little wonder that questions are now being asked across Africa if, indeed, the fact of the existence of a multiparty political system constructed from above is, by itself, sufficient to lay the basis for an enduring transition to democracy on the continent. For some, the weakness of Africa's current effort at democratic reform lies in the persistence of neo-patrimonialism in the institutions and processes of politics on the continent. For others, the crucial matter for concern is the way in which the struggles of popular forces for deep-rooted reforms in local power relations have been so easily hijacked and defeated by the elite. Whatever the view we may hold of the on-going experience of multiparty politics, our discourses inevitably lead us into a systematic assessment of the role and place of the opposition in the political process. Indeed, an appraisal of the experience of the opposition is indispensable to a proper understanding of the limitations and possibilities of the on-going efforts at political reform in Africa.

This chapter is devoted to a critique of the experience of opposition politics in Kenya within the framework of the country's return to multiparty politics. In undertaking this task, the approach which we take is a historical one, starting from a review of the way in which, from the colonial period, elite politics in Kenya was structured not only to preclude the crystallisation of popular democratic demands but also to factionalise opposition to the ruling political elite. We argue that an understanding of this historical background is indispensable to a fuller appreciation of the march, soon after independence to the one-party state, and the current crisis that has bedevilled oppositional political activity following the restoration, in the early 1990s, of a multiparty political system. The deepening socio-economic crisis which Kenya has been confronted with since the mid-1980s has hardly provided an auspicious setting for the construction of a coherent and enduring opposition platform that could serve as an alternative to the ruling party. In fact, on the basis of the evidence available to us, it would seem that party politics in general and oppositional political activity in particular are in danger of undergoing a severe decline on account of deepening popular disillusionment.

DECONSTRUCTING THE COLONIAL STATE AND ITS POLITICAL ECONOMY

Nationalism in Colonial Kenya

In much of sub-Saharan Africa, the colonial state developed as an instrument of control, oppression and the domination of society. It also served as the principal framework for accumulation by the colonial elite and its African loyalists. In the specific Kenyan context, the process of accumulation via the state began with the expropriation of land and the institutionalisation of "extra-economic coercion". This was accompanied by spirited efforts at a massive restructuring and re-orientation of existing social relations with a view to replacing them with a new order that was more attuned to the needs of colonial capitalism. Colonial capitalism was built on a system of deep socio-economic inequalities that functioned to the benefit of the groups, consisting mainly of white settlers, that were allied to the state. These groups depended for their accumulation strategies on the framework for extra-economic coercion established by the state, coercion which include highly exploitative labour regimes and intense political oppression (Mamdani, 1990; Berman and Lonsdale, 1992).

In time, the dynamic of deepening economic inequalities and widening social differentiation on which colonialism was built ignited local resistance and popular pressures for decolonisation and democratisation. Out of those struggles was born a host of political organisations dedicated to the termination of colonial rule and the associated colonial mode of accumulation. The first such political associations to be established were the East African Association (EAA), Kikuyu Central Association (KCA) and Kenya African Union (KAU). The first two were formed in the early 1920s while KAU emerged towards the end of the Second World War. These organisations had radical factions which pressed for a complete revolutionisation of colonial economic and political relations. The radicals relied for support on the increasing numbers of workers and peasants who had entered the arena of organised political activity. It should be noted, however, that by this time, there had also developed a nascent Kikuyu capitalist class whose political activism was inspired by the need to gain greater access to and support from the state and, in so doing, expand its spheres of accumulation in order to be better able to compete favourably with the white settler economic elite (Maloba, 1993; Kanogo, 1987; Throup, 1987).

The period between 1945 and 1952 witnessed the proliferation of quasi-nationalist social movements, several of them religious, and set up with the declared or implicit objective of countering colonial political domination. Examples of such movements include the *Dini ya Msambwa* in Western Kenya, the *Nomia Church* in Luo Nyanza, and the *Dini ya Kaggia* as well as a host of other independent churches in Central Kenya. These groups emerged as protest movements against both the colonial state and the Church Missionary Society (CMS) which, under official patronage, had assumed the status of a state church.

It is clear from the foregoing that nationalism germinated in a terrain that had a rich history of social protest, protests which soon crystallised into social movements around which different social groups tried to mobilise against the colonial mode of domination. It was these movements which prepared the ground for the emergence of nationalist political groups, some of which were later to become political parties. Mainly constructed in response to popular pressures from below, these social movements had one ideal around which they rallied the populace: democracy and decolonization. Within the framework of this ideal, they attempted to articulate the collective grievances of different social groups against the colonial order: the return of expropriated land, the equalisation of political and economic opportunities, and unrestricted access to education and other basic necessities, among others. The Mau Mau movement which was later to emerge became the best organised expression of the demands of the colonised.

The violent contestation by the Mau Mau of the colonial political and socio-economic order led to a decision by the colonial state to proscribe all the political organisations of the colonised; local political activists, both elite and popular, were also arrested and detained. Subsequently, the state attempted to establish a firmer control over socio-political events in the colony by prohibiting pan-territorial political mobilisation except that which was accountable to it and/or organised by its loyalists and the bureaucratic elite. As a result of this development, encouragement was only given to district-based groups to operate, the sole exception being Central Kenya where political activity of any kind was completely prohibited. In restricting organised socio-political activity to the district level, the colonial state argued that district associations would encourage a simple and orderly development of African political life and opinion (Gertzel et al., 1972:106); in reality, the objective was to undermine the development of pan-territorial radical nationalism. Not surprisingly, with active encouragement from the colonial authorities, several new and some pre-existing social welfare organisations, such as the Kavirondo Tax Payers Welfare Association, were steered in a direction that was aimed at undermining the social bases of radical political organisations.

The colonial state's objective of attempting to undermine local pan-territorial mobilisation and political pluralism was itself made difficult to sustain because of the exploitative and oppressive socio-economic conditions under which most of the colonised lived, conditions which proved to be fertile grounds for the articulation of political demands. Thus, in spite of the spirited effort it made to repress the Mau Mau movement, the state was compelled, nonetheless, to give in to pressures emanating from its activities and set in motion, a process for granting Kenya independence. Yet, negotiations over independence excluded the vast majority of Mau Mau activists because most were still in the forests or in detention. This generated a host of contradictions that continue to agitate the Kenyan political terrain to this day. Perhaps the most important of these contradictions is the Land Question which, in the first place, was the primary reason for the onset of the Mau Mau but which was not conclusively resolved. Also significant is the fact that the "independence question", which, thanks to the colonial authorities, gradually carried ethnic connotations with it, became the basis upon which political parties were formed and demobilised. The framework that exists in Kenya today for the operationalisation of party politics has roots in the

"ethnicised" politics of independence and the related issue of land ownership.

The Crisis of Popular Politics in Late Colonial Kenya

Both elite and popular forces played a critical role in the Kenyan decolonization process. KAU, for example, was established with a populist tradition
which was also relevant to the interests of the emerging local elite. It drew
its main following from among the Kikuyu in Central Kenya but trans-ethnic
support for its activities was to expand with the growth of militancy against
the colonial establishment. In the same period, Oginga Odinga formed the
Luo Thrift and Trading Corporation to help build a credible economic base
for opposition among the Luo to the colonial establishment. In concert with
other groups such as the North Kavirondo Central Association (NKCA)
which was active among the Kakamega Luhya, the Ukamba Members Association, and the Taita Hills Association, these organisations helped to keep
the struggle for decolonisation alive and, in so doing, contributed to the
weakening of the colonial state.

In response to the gathering pace of the local anti-colonial struggle, the
colonial state declared a state of emergency in 1952 during which KAU was
proscribed and its leaders detained for associating with the Mau Mau. In
response, the Mau Mau intensified their struggles against the colonial state.
The activities of other nationalist movements were severely restricted by the
state but trade unions filled the emerging lacuna in the urban areas while
discrete Mau Mau activities further undermined state capacity in the rural
areas. Realising that reforms were inevitable, the colonial authorities proceeded to outline a framework which, whilst taking on board such local
concerns as would be sufficient for preventing a backlash against the colo-
nial/settler economic and bureaucratic elite, was also decisively aimed at
preventing popular forces from taking power or claiming ownership of the
reform project.

The political component of the reform programme which the colonial
state undertook was best captured by the Lyttelton constitution which was
introduced in 1954. That constitution set out a framework for African political development in the form of a limited multi-racial government. In conso-
nance with the programme, the government relaxed the ban on political
associations, but afraid that colony-wide parties would further the aims of
the Mau Mau, confined their formation and activities to the district level. In
response, several associations, formed under the leadership of a generation
of young, educated Africans, emerged. These associations were mostly
established along "tribal" lines and tried to advance parochial community
interests. They were, therefore, an impediment to the development and

advancement of colony-wide popular struggles against colonial domination.[1]

The Lyttelton plan for a multi-racial government resulted in the convening of the first ever elections in which Africans participated both as voters and candidates. These elections were for delegates to the Legislative Council (Legco) and they were held in March 1957. But the new African Legco members had no national organisational platform on which to aggregate and articulate African interests since the state had prevented the formation of such pan-territorial associations. From the beginning, therefore, and as dictated by the logic of the colonial state's political design, the African Legco group was beset with serious leadership problems. The group, nonetheless, still pressed for more political reforms in Kenya and even turned down ministerial appointments (Gertzel, 1970).

Some hope that it might still be possible to forge a united national political platform was raised when, in 1958, "district tribal leaders" initiated proposals for the formation of a national alliance that could serve as a forum/ convention for all African associations. It was also hoped that through the alliance/convention, it would be possible to foster greater unity of action between the districts and elected members of the Legco. The initiative was, however, blocked by the colonial state which refused to register the alliance on the basis of its pre-existing policy of prohibiting colony-wide political movements. Failing to gain legal recognition, the alliance's problems were further complicated by a host of latent internal organisational problems which increasingly came out into the open and undermined it. Many of the disputes originated from or were fuelled by such factors as personality and leadership rivalries, ethnic considerations, differing levels of ethnic political awareness, and infiltration by partisan white settler interests.

The divisions among the African members of the Legco took a dramatic turn in July 1959 when they split into two factions, one supporting urban interests and the other supporting rural interests. The urban group, represented by the Kikuyu and Luo members of the Council, was the more militant and uncompromising in its demands. As to the rural group, it was made up of the representatives of the numerically smaller ethnic groups (the Kalenjin represented by Moi and Towett; the Baluhya-Bukusu by Muliro, and the coastal groups by Ngala). The rural faction was driven mainly by its resentment of the influence and power of urban nationalism whose potential for reaching out to and dominating the minority areas was also a source of fear for them. For the members of the rural faction, the challenge, as they saw it, was to prevent the urban group from usurping their entrenched positions in the minority areas (Gertzel et al., 1972:108).

---

[1] Examples include the Nairobi District African Congress (NADC) set up in 1956, the Nairobi People's Convention Party (a splinter group of the NADC), the Mombassa African Democratic Union, the Nakuru African Progressive Party, and the Taita African Democratic Union. See Gertzel, 1970.

The division among the Legco members soon crystallised into distinct political formations: the Kenya National Party (KNP) representing the rural group and Kenya Independence Movement (KIM) representing the urban faction. However, as the first Lancaster House Conference to discuss constitutional and independence arrangements for Kenya got underway, the two groups made an effort to submerge their differences by agreeing to the establishment of a joint "political community" through which they would articulate a common nationalist front at the conference (Wasserman, 1976: 63). This effort at forging a united front was, however, short-lived. The same factors that impeded the earlier initiative on a national convention resurfaced and polarised the group once again, but this time concretising the division into actual political parties with colony-wide support. The KIM, following conferences which it held in Kiambu in March and May 1960, changed its name and transformed itself into a mass organisation that came to be known as the Kenya African National Union (KANU). It drew the bulk of its support from the members of the old KAU and, more specifically, from the Kikuyu and Luo ethnic groups in the rural and urban areas of Kenya. The organisation also elected, in absentia, two members of the rival KNP, Moi and Ngala, into its executive in the hope that they and their party members could still be persuaded to join KANU in forging a united African front against the colonial state and the settlers.

The formation of KANU represented a direct threat to the KNP. Although Moi and Ngala (representing Kalenjin and Coast interests respectively) were elected in absentia into national positions in KANU, they spurned the gesture that was made to them and began in earnest to organise their own ethnically-based parties to counter KANU's advances. Moi mobilised his Kalenjin ethnic group into the Kalenjin Political Alliance (KPA), resolving to make a generalised claim on Kalenjin ownership and control of land in the Rift Valley as well as campaigning to stop future Kikuyu "advances" in the area. The KPA was adamant that it would not join KANU; instead, it invited others to join it in moulding a new national party. Among the other prominent non-KANU politicians associated with the KPA, Ngala formed the Coast African People's Union (CAPU) while Muliro rallied the Bukusu-Luhya around the Kenya African People's Party (KAPP). The Maasai, led by Justus Ole Tipis, formed Maasai United Front (MUF) which, like the KPA, was equally concerned about the future of Maasai land in the Rift Valley and what it saw as systematic Kikuyu encroachment and take over.

Before long, Kikuyu-phobia gained ground and became the primary basis for the mobilisation of the minority communities. This pattern of ethnic mobilisation was deliberately encouraged and expedited by the colonial state's propaganda against the Kikuyu during the Mau Mau period and the urgent desire among the white settlers to support alternative social and political movements to those dominated by the land-poor/hungry Kikuyu.

For the settlers, the task of creating such an alternative was defined as being indispensable to the protection of their interests. As a result of this favourable setting, the minority groups were able to found a party of their own without difficulty. The groups convened a meeting in Ngong in June 1960 and agreed to merge together to form the Kenyan African Democratic Union (KADU). The meeting was also attended by the Somali National Association (SNA), an organisation which was set up to champion the greater Somali unification project, and which, therefore, attended the meeting in the hope that its secessionist agenda would receive backing from the anti-Kikuyu/KANU groups that had assembled at Ngong.

Clearly, the formation of both KANU and KADU occurred in a manner which fed into the political machinations of the colonial state and the settler leadership. Both parties were also the products of elite negotiations. KANU drew its leadership mainly from the growing class of proto-capitalist Kikuyu farmers and businessmen and the educated Luo elite. Its membership included radical revolutionaries who wanted nothing less than the complete destruction of the colonial political economy and moderates/liberals who did not want further disruption of the system by the militant Mau Mau and their sympathisers. Clearly absent from the core of the KANU leadership were the Mau Mau "freedom fighters": they were either still incarcerated by the colonial authorities or were considered to be too "illiterate" by the party to be trusted with national leadership. KANU elites did not hide their preference for the exclusion of the "freedom fighters" from the party because of a concern that their inclusion might put the negotiations for the release from prison of Kenyatta and other KAU leaders in jeopardy. Moreover, the elites did not want anything that could prevent them from claiming full ownership of the independence project.

As with KANU, no radical nationalists were represented in the leadership of KADU. Consumed by their suspicion of the Kikuyu, the leaders of the party were more concerned about how to handle the presence of Kikuyu farmers and residents in the Rift Valley. While some in the leadership opted for the outright eviction of "immigrants" (a euphemism for the Kikuyu and, to a lesser extent, the Luo), others made the case for the status quo with regard to landholding to be maintained. It is interesting to observe, in this context, that both KANU and KADU were formed in a political framework that had been shaped by the Mau Mau nationalists, namely, the struggle against landlessness and colonial exploitation. Yet, none of the main nationalist parties made an effort to address or even include in their agenda, problems suffered by the Mau Mau in the course of the resistance against the colonial state. Torture and loss of life in detention stood out as the main complaint by the Mau Mau activists, yet none of the parties gave primacy to these grievances in their programme of demands.

Thus it was that in the run up to independence, popular forces, their organisations and concerns were increasingly pushed aside as elite nationalism took centre stage. That nationalism was, itself, divided and segmented along the lines of ethnicity and regionalism, with personality and leadership rivalries adding some spice. Local politics came gradually to be reduced to the promotion of ethnic and (individual/group) elite interests within the colonial state or boundaries defined by it. Systematically engineered by the colonial state as a means of blunting the effectiveness of local opposition to colonialism and de-radicalising the nationalist movement, political faction-alisation and ethnic polarisation soon became an integral element of local and national politics. It was on this basis that the politics of independence was played out; the post-independence crisis of party politics has its histori-cal roots in this colonially-constructed structure of polarisation and frag-mentation.

PARTY POLITICS AFTER INDEPENDENCE

The polarisation that developed within the nationalist movement during the late 1950s deepened as discussions on the kind of constitutional framework that would be appropriate for launching Kenya into independence pro-gressed. Each of the groups involved in the negotiations developed its posi-tion based on the arrangement which it thought would best serve the inter-ests of its members. Central to the definition of positions was the Land Question. Indeed, depending on what the different groups thought was their stake with regard to the land issue, they decided on that basis to develop their affiliation to or support for one or the other of the dominant political parties that had emerged (Bates, 1989; Gertzel, 1970; Kanyinga, 1996).

Within KANU, there existed a radical group that articulated a popular position on land similar to the demands put forward by the Mau Mau. This radical group included within its ranks such figures as Oginga Odinga and Bildad Kaggia. Like the Kenya Land and Freedom Army (KLFA) that was formed to give politico-military teeth to the demands of the Mau Mau on land reform, the radical group set itself the task of ensuring that KANU did not deviate from this primary element of the nationalist agenda. Not unex-pectedly, its position was countered by the relatively liberal wing of KANU led by Kenyatta and Tom Mboya. Both Kenyatta and Mboya, together with their supporters, were determined to prevent the crystallisation of latent demands for revolutionary land reforms and, for this reason, were prepared to jettison the Mau Mau whose militants they now derogatively referred to as *imaramari* (a Kikuyu word for idlers and criminals) (Berman and Lonsdale 1992).

As to KADU which, as we noted earlier, was mainly made up of people drawn from the numerically small ethnic groups of Kenya, the principal demand which they put forward centred around the necessity for a *Majimbo* or federal system of government. This demand was driven by their convic-tion that only such an arrangement could enable them to check what the leaders of the party often referred to as the Kikuyu "advancement" in the Rift Valley. However, soon after Kenya's formal independence in 1963, KADU's position on the land question was weakened by the withdrawal of the Luhya from the "KADU political community" on account of a disagreement among the leaders of the party over whether Trans Nzoia should fall into Western Kenya or the Rift Valley Province (Throup 1987).

Having failed in their attempt to gain control of the apparatuses of government, the leaders of KADU soon began to negotiate for incorporation into the state. Several of them were allocated settler farms and/or appointed into cabinet positions in the KANU independence government led by Kenyatta. By 1964, KADU had lost its vigour as a party and its leaders, anxious to protect their personal class interests, no longer had the appetite for oppositional politics. That same year, KADU put a motion before the parliament to wind itself up and, in so doing, "promote" national unity and stability. Thus it was that the official opposition was dissolved once its leaders were assured that they would all be "catered" for under KANU. In reward for their action, KADU's leaders were incorporated into the state, some through ministerial appointments.

Meanwhile, within KANU, although the liberals were able to sideline the radicals in the struggle for the control of the party and its programmes, the divisions within the organisation continued to widen due to the heightening intra-Luo rivalry that pitched Oginga Odinga against Tom Mboya. The rivalry had as much to do with a clash of material interests between them as with their genuine ideological differences over the way the task of post-colonial nation-building in Kenya was to proceed. There was also the issue of which of the two of them was going to assume political leadership of the Luo (Kenya's second largest ethnic group) and, in so doing, take up the number two position (that of the vice president) in the KANU/Kikuyu-Luo coalition that came to power at independence.

The intensity of the Odinga–Mboya rivalry was soon to lead to a formal split within KANU when, in early 1966, the party's delegates' conference was convened by Mboya against opposition from trade unionists and the parliamentary radicals who saw the step as an attempt to create a forum for the "eviction" of Odinga and his associates from the organisation. As was widely predicted, the delegates' conference abolished Odinga's position as National Vice President of the party and, instead, created six new positions of Provincial Vice Presidents. Odinga and his supporters were not appointed to any of the new positions; predictably, Odinga decided to resign both from the government and the party. He then established a new political party, the Kenyan People's Union (KPU), which drew massive support from the Luo of Nyanza, Odinga's home area. Several other KANU officials and parliamentarians defected and joined the KPU.

However, because of systematic state-sponsored intimidation and massive electoral manipulation, several of those who had joined Odinga in defecting from KANU were unable to win back their seats in the elections that followed. The pressure on the KPU was to be reinforced when Mboya and some of the other KANU liberals urged the government to undertake a thorough scrutiny of the party with a view to ascertaining its loyalty to the state. In this regard, they stressed that the party represented only one "tribe" and that it seemed to have subversive intentions that could not be tolerated (Gertzel, 1970:145). It was under these difficult conditions, characterised by continuous harassment and intimidation, that the KPU tried to operate until October 1969 when it was proscribed for allegedly being disdainful of the president.

By the end of the 1960s, therefore, on account of the dispute between KANU radicals and liberals, a dispute which was laced with intra-Luo rivalries and personality rifts, the Kenyan political terrain was, once again, transformed into a *de facto* single party one. Like the first *de facto* single party experience which was the product of an economically-driven decision (expressed in terms of the Land Question) by the leaders of KADU and other parties to fold up and join KANU, the second phase was occasioned by disagreements over how the Land Question should be tackled. But unlike KADU which voluntarily dissolved itself, the KPU was proscribed by the state partly because of the popular appeal which its radical position on the Land Question conferred on it and also because of the open and bold confrontations which Odinga regularly had with Kenyatta. With the proscription of the KPU, Kenya was systematically put through a regime of statism from above. Indeed, it can be argued that between 1969 and 1991, as multiparty politics went into decline, statism was intensified.

THE RISE OF THE SINGLE PARTY STATE: FROM *KAMALIZA*[1] TO *NYAYO*[2]

The proscription of the KPU in October 1969 came shortly after the assassination, in July 1969, of Tom Mboya. Mboya's killing had been preceded a few years earlier by the murder of Pio Gama Pinto, Odinga's top political aid, who met his brutal end in 1966 during the early, formative stages of the KPU. The immediate factor that precipitated the proscription of the KPU was the confrontation which Odinga had in 1969 with Kenyatta in Kisumu in the Luo heartland. Kenyatta had gone to Kisumu on a visit after Mboya's assassination but the tour was disrupted when his motorcade was stoned

---

[1] *Kamaliza* is a Kiswahili word for an "exterminator" and is used here to refer to a leader who destroys everything in his path that he perceives as being obstructive of his political interests. Kenyatta was given this nickname by ordinary Kenyans after the assassination of Tom Mboya and the murders of Kungu Karumba and J.M. Kariuki.

[2] *Nyayo* is a Kiswahili word for footsteps. Moi assumed the presidency and promised to follow Kenyatta's footsteps or political course.

and rioting broke out in which several people died. Kenyatta held Odinga and the KPU responsible for the crisis; what followed next was the announcement of the decision to proscribe the KPU. Following his experience in Kisumu, Kenyatta never set foot again in Nyanza Province, leaving it to his new vice president, Moi, to play the role of his political errand boy in the area.

For the Luo, Kenyatta's decision to boycott them spelt something of a political doom since what came after was the setting in motion of a process deliberately and systematically aimed at dismantling the historical alliance that linked them to the Kikuyu. This alliance dated back to the period around the First World War and its dissolution began at a time when access to the state and state patronage were becoming ever more salient factors in the livelihood strategies of communities and individuals. The push for the dissolution of the alliance occurred with the blessing of Kenyatta and the members of his entourage. That entourage was itself to witness the entry of new players, most of them Kikuyu loyalists, who were disdainful of radical nationalism, and therefore, of Odinga, and who gained access to Kenyatta's bailiwick in order also to establish for themselves, a framework for personal and group accumulation as well as political patronage.

For his part, Kenyatta showed his appreciation to the loyalists in his inner circle by marrying into their families, building an unbridgeable distance between himself and the Mau Mau radicals, and working out a compromise with the colonial/white settler economic elite (Throup, 1987). Among the most prominent members of Kenyatta's inner cabal were those liberal Kikuyu elites who had publicly and vociferously distanced themselves from the radical-populist stance that Kaggia and Odinga had tried to promote within KANU in the period from 1963 to 1966. They included prominent (Kikuyu) power brokers such as Mbiyu Koinange (Minister of State), James Gichuru (Minister of Defence), Njoroge Mungai (Minister of Foreign Affairs) and Charles Njonjo (Attorney General). These men spared no effort to ensure that the state house was fenced off from other Kikuyu elites; they also actively prevented the Mau Mau radicals from playing a role in central state politics and from gaining access to the presidency.

Furthermore, the members of Kenyatta's inner circle tried, in the name of the president and KANU, to dominate political and civil society in Kenya. At one level, this led them into attempts at "exterminating" all autonomous political associations and popular movements associated with anti-colonial nationalism. Second, the group mobilised political and economic resources to prevent the re-birth of radical politics in the country, especially with regard to issues of land ownership and the loses suffered by Mau Mau "freedom fighters". Radical elements who attempted to pursue the latter were mercilessly repressed, even exterminated. The high profile example of J. M. Kariuki, or J.M. as he was popularly known, is perhaps the best illustration we can offer of the determination of the members of the Kenyatta entourage to snuff out all autonomous and radical political activity.

Kariuki had used the parliamentary platform that was available to him as an MP to reactivate the radical nationalist position on the Land Question and to challenge the private, often corrupt appropriation of the "white high-lands" by the members of Kenyatta's inner cabal. His campaigns struck a chord with a wide cross-section of Kenyans, to the chagrin of the government. He was murdered in early 1975 in circumstances which directly implicated the state generally and Kenyatta's inner cabal in particular. The fate that befell Kariuki, together with the increasing transformation of post-colonial Kenya into a security police state by Kenyatta and his cabal of advisers, led to a lull in radical politics. It was the era of the *Kamaliza* in post-colonial Kenyan politics.

In time, the only politically vibrant association that was left in Kenya other than KANU itself was the Gikuyu, Embu, Meru Association (GEMA) in which members of the Kenyatta inner cabal were active. Other associations such as the Luo Union and Abaluhya Union were compelled to confine themselves to welfare activities and eschew any overt political role. More than KANU, GEMA became the forum where key decisions affecting the country were taken before they were rubber-stamped by the party and implemented by the government. This shift in the institutional locus of power was demonstrated by the chain of events that occurred as it became increasingly clear that Kenyatta was nearing the end of his life.

Alarmed by Kenyatta's faltering health which old age did little to assuage, GEMA began to construct a succession project which would best suit the interests of the dying president's inner circle. In 1976, the GEMA elite canvassed the idea of a constitutional amendment which was aimed at blocking the incumbent vice president, Daniel Arap Moi, from succeeding Kenyatta in the event of his death in office. It took Kenyatta's personal intervention to block this plan. The members of the GEMA group then decided to stick to the existing constitutional provision which would mean a Moi succession but they also let it be known that even if that happened, it would only be a passing cloud. How to deal with and contain this game plan became a key foundation of politics in the *Nyayo* state.

THE *NYAYO* SINGLE PARTY STATE

The construction of the *Nyayo* state began immediately after the burial of Kenyatta and it involved its authors in a thorough re-appraisal of the prevailing political context in Kenya generally and with regard to the operation of GEMA in particular. In his attempt to build a foundation where *Nyayo* hegemony could take root, Moi began by initially taking on board certain key members of the Kikuyu elite and "entrusting" the day-to-day management of the affairs of the state to them. He also embarked on a charm offensive designed to boost his profile with the Kenyan public; indeed, his popularity was to rise on account of this offensive which included anti-corruption pronouncements and gestures. It was on this platform that Moi began systematically to dismantle those aspects of Kenyatta's legacy which did not suit his own agenda. Bureaucratic and political elites who owed their positions to Kenyatta were gradually removed to be replaced with Moi appointees whose loyalty to him was not in doubt (Nyong'o 1987; Throup 1987; Kanyinga 1995).

The attempts at building *Nyayo* hegemony were, over time, reinforced by a deepening system of authoritarianism and *étatisation* which necessitated the simultaneous remoulding and revival of KANU both to serve Moi's objectives and recover ground which the party had lost to GEMA during the latter half of the Kenyatta years. The hitherto moribund KANU was, therefore, reinvigorated at the same time as the provincial administrations began to exercise more control and extend their repressive reach. Thus, through the provincial administrative structure and the local agents of the ruling party, the state engaged in a spirited effort to control and channel civil society activism in the directions it wanted. As part of this project, *Harambee* (self-help) groups, cooperatives, and associations operating in the voluntary sector were infiltrated by agents of the party and the state and their activities increasingly undermined where they were thought to be unacceptable to the Moi government.

It is little wonder then that shortly after Moi's rise to power, all the structures of dissent and avenues for articulating differing views which had survived Kenyatta's authoritarian rule were vigorously attacked and dismantled. The arrest and detention of the activists of dissenting groups became commonplace. Members of the political elite who were not in favour under the new order or who expressed misgivings about the trends in the country were systematically excluded from the party and its related organs, including those for organising development initiatives. In brief, the reinvigorated KANU assumed a totalitarian image, operating, with Moi's blessing, with absolute power and unprecedented latitude. Not even parliament had the kind of powers that the party came to enjoy.

The consolidation of KANU's grip over the Kenyan national political terrain was taken one step further when in early 1986, the party established a Disciplinary Committee charged with enforcing loyalty to the president. As part of their attempt to rise to the demands of their assignment, the committee members visited China in order to "study organisation of the Chinese Communist Party". On their return, they got the KANU leadership to try to establish branches of the party in all public institutions. In addition, the party demanded that senior civil servants take out a life membership in KANU. The Central Organisation of Trade Unions (COTU) and *Maendeleo ya Wanawake* were also co-opted into KANU as were several other civil society organisations (see Ngunyi and Gathiaka, 1993).

Furthermore, rules governing elections to KANU and for general elections in the country were changed in order to ensure that Moi and the
emerging cabal around him would be directly able to influence the choice of
candidates. This was a central element in their effort to bring more actors
who owed their loyalty solely to Moi into the political arena. The party also
took steps to institutionalise the inheritance of electoral seats by the relatives
of politicians loyal to KANU.[1] Election by secret ballot was abolished and, in
its place, the so-called *Mlolongo* (queue) model was introduced.[2] That model
further strengthened the hands of Moi and his closest advisers/business
partners to hand-pick those individuals whom they felt would owe allegiance to them rather than the electorate. Consequently, the 1988 parliament
was mostly composed of members who were personally loyal to Moi. Some
of those elected either got in unopposed or were assisted to intimidate their
opponents in order to be able to get more than seventy per cent of the votes
cast and thus qualify to be declared outright winners. This turn of events
generated unprecedented domestic protest, some of it of an underground
nature, and other in the open, although very subtle. It was this domestic
pressure for change that gradually built up and which, together with external (donor) pressure eventually compelled the state to concede the introduction of multipartyism.

There is no doubt that the growth in the level of political protests and the
subsequent re-emergence of multiparty politics in Kenya were a direct result
of Moi's power maximising stratagem. Particularly responsible for the rise of
the protests was the intensification of popular disappointment with the
president's failure to match his early "populist" pronouncements with
action that was relevant to the aspirations of the generality of the people.
Added to this was growing dissatisfaction with the ruthless way in which
the clique around Moi and Moi himself acted to "disengage" people who
were seen as legitimate leaders of their communities or interest groups from
the epicentre of political power. The political circuit which Moi perfected of
moulding personalities, then very quickly disengaging/disgracing them as
they began to enjoy their high profile, only later to recycle them back into
high office dated from 1983 and was successful in assisting him to replace
the Kenyatta oligarchy with his own cabal; it, however, became a source of

---

[1] Prominent and loyal politicians who died in office had their party and parliamentary positions "inherited" by their sons or immediate relatives. The party simply
obstructed candidates other than the relatives of the deceased loyalist from contesting the seat. Examples of this kind of "inheritance" include the university
undergraduate Vincent M'Maitsi (Hamsi constituency) and Musalia Mudavadi
(Sabatia constituency) who obtained their parliamentary seats in 1988 and 1989
respectively.

[2] Under this system, people were required to line up behind the candidate of their
choice or the agent of their candidate. The winner was the candidate who was able
to muster 70 per cent of the total votes cast. If no candidate was able to fulfil this
requirement, all the contestants moved on to the next phase.

increasing disaffection as was the partisan and selective appointment of individuals to the leadership of strategic and resource-rich parastatals.[1]

If the extreme politicisation of appointments to the top leadership of parastatals had the effect of weakening their operational effectiveness and making them the victims of high profile corruption, for the cabal around the president, the importance of that strategy lay in the fact that the corporations could be transformed into "prebendal altars" from which resources were systematically siphoned and channelled into Moi's network of political patronage. Some of the leading beneficiaries of this patronage system were commercial and bureaucratic elites drawn from Moi's Kalenjin ethnic group. Indeed, with the assistance of Asian capital, a concerted effort was made to promote the emergence and consolidation of a Kalenjin bourgeoisie that would also be capable of articulating the economic and political interests of Moi and his inner circle. This was a development to which the Kikuyu economic and political elite was compelled to respond (See Kanyinga, 1995).

In sum, the *Nyayo* one party state, once it consolidated, was marked by the further narrowing of the space for civil society activism, increased political repression that bordered on tyranny, the severe constriction of popular participation in the political process, and intensified corruption. Considering that all of these features were also present in varying degrees during the Kenyatta years, it is not too difficult to see the feeling of frustration which many felt about the direction in which the country was headed. The feeling of disappointment was intensified by the disappointment of popular optimism which Moi's accession to the presidency initially generated. Little wonder then that various social forces concluded that a programme of mass mobilisation had become necessary in order to take Kenya back to the path of competitive politics. That was the immediate internal context for the onset of the campaign for the return of multiparty politics in Kenya. It was a development which profited from re-alignments that had occurred or which were still unfolding in the international system.

THE RE-BIRTH OF COMPETITIVE PARTY POLITICS

Dissatisfaction with, and dissent against the *Nyayo* state was not the monopoly of any one social or ethnic group or region; as the 1980s wore on and the Moi agenda unfolded more clearly, every group in Kenya realised that it had something to protest against. Soon, a variety of groups, mainly comprising moderate civil society institutions such as the churches, the asso-

---

[1] This refers to Moi's strategy of picking and using a politician to accomplish a specific objective and then dumping him immediately or soon after. The same politician might be recycled through the system for another mission. For an elaboration, see Kanyinga, 1995.

ciations of professionals, and the "progressive" print media[1] began to agitate for the re-introduction of multiparty politics in line with what was happening internationally following the end of the Cold War and the dissolution of the Soviet Union. The campaign mounted by civil society organisations was complemented by agitations from various groups and/or individuals who felt that they had been involuntarily excluded from the *Nyayo* state and were thus exposed to economic and/or political marginalisation.

The specific arguments which were developed in favour of political reforms differed slightly among the different groups that were agitating for change. This was partly a function of the differences in the ways the groups felt that they had been affected by the *Nyayo* state. For the Kikuyu economic elite which felt deliberately excluded from the economic opportunities associated with the *Nyayo* state project, and which interpreted its exclusion as being for the benefit of an ascendant Kalenjin bourgeoisie, the promise of political liberalisation was seen as residing in the opportunity it would offer for a weakening of the social bases of Moi's support as a first step towards getting him removed from the presidency.

As for the Luhya and Luo elites, their disillusionment arose out of the unfulfilled expectation which they had that they would be included in the *Nyayo* state project after Moi's rise to power. Like the Kikuyu, they too felt they had been dispensed with by an up and coming Kalenjin bourgeoisie which, together with Asian capital, had managed to penetrate deep into the state and exclude others. The peasantry and the working class were similarly disillusioned with a government and party which failed to honour the populist promises it made shortly after Moi's rise to power. The generality of ordinary Kenyans were soon to realise that the primary burden for the provision of basic services and amenities was going to rest more and more on their shoulders as promises of full state support went unfulfilled.

At the same time as domestic discontent was brewing, relations between the government and several of the country's main financial donors also began to sour. This was quite a significant development as, until the late 1980s/early 1990s, most donors considered Kenya, very uncritically, to be an island of peace and economic prosperity in a continent wracked by conflict and poverty. Of particular importance in the shift of donor attitude and strategy was the cruel murder of Robert Ouko, the Minister for Foreign Affairs and International Cooperation, in February 1990.[2] and the arrest and detention in June 1990 of Messrs Kenneth Matiba, Charles Rubia, Raila

[1] Notable here were the National Council of Churches of Kenya (NCCK), the Catholic Episcopal Conference of Bishops, and the Law Society of Kenya (LSK). The alternative print media that informed on sensitive issues included *Society*, *Law Monthly*, and *Finance*.

[2] Robert Ouku, Minister for Foreign Affairs and International Cooperation, was murdered in February 1990. The state hurriedly dissolved the commission after several senior politicians and civil servants were implicated in the murder by witnesses.

Odinga and several lawyers who were in the vanguard of the struggle for multipartyism. These actions incensed the donor community and resulted in a decision to press the government to undertake reforms if it expected continued international support (Chege, 1994).

The depth of disillusionment against the *Nyayo* state and the intense personalisation of power associated with it was such that it was sufficient to encourage the variety of social forces rooting for reform to (temporarily at least) set their particular differences—class, ethnic, regional, religious—aside and unite under the umbrella of one organisation to collectively fight against Moi's version of statism. This opposition/reform organisation rapidly crystallised into the Forum for Restoration of Democracy (FORD), a popular movement which brought together radical as well as liberal/moderate, bourgeois and non-bourgeois social forces in a common effort get Moi and KANU out of political power. For these different groups, Moi and KANU had become synonymous with authoritarianism and their removal had become necessary if the task of resuscitating a project of democratisation in Kenya was to be realised.

KANU as a party and Moi as a person resisted the local and donor pressures for political liberalisation for as long as possible. In the end, however, they gave in to the popular demands for reform and amended the constitution by repealing the clause that named KANU the sole, recognised party in the country. Thus it was that the country was returned to the path of multiparty politics and once this happened, the differences within the opposition which, hitherto, had been suppressed by the common desire to win concessions from the government burst into the open. Very quickly, divisions began to emerge within FORD and these conflicts soon resulted in a veritable fragmentation of the opposition. The two factions that initially emerged out of the FORD alliance were the FORD-Kenya and FORD-Asili.[1] At the same time as FORD was splitting up, several other parties were also being formed by various opposition elements. The most important of these other opposition parties were the Democratic Party of Kenya (DP), the Kenya National Congress (KNC), the Kenya Social Congress (KSC), and Islamic Party of Kenya (IPK).[2]

If the split in the ranks of the opposition was a source of dismay for many of the people who were involved as foot soldiers in the struggle for multipartyism, even more disconcerting was the fact that most of the political parties that constituted the opposition to KANU drew their membership and support along distinct ethnic lines. Predictably, the votes which they

---

[1] *Asili* is a Kiswahili word meaning "genuine" or "original". The Matiba faction adopted the name *Asili* in order to convey the message that the group had the founder-members and progressive forces associated with the original FORD in its ranks.

[2] The state refused to register IPK. The members of the party subsequently sought accommodation in FORD-Kenya.

garnered in the multiparty elections that followed displayed distinct ethno-regional patterns: candidates and parties mostly won in their home districts and on the basis of their ethnic affiliation. Interestingly, KANU, drawing most of its votes from the Kalenjin and a number of other ethnic minorities, received immense electoral support in those regions where the defunct KADU was dominant in the early 1960s while the opposition was supported mostly in those areas that were the original strongholds of KANU in the lead up to and immediately after independence.

After the 1992 multiparty elections, several significant developments in the organisation of Kenyan party politics began to unfold. At one level, some opposition leaders began to decamp to the state party, KANU. At another level, the state itself began increasingly to tie its development assistance to communities and districts to the level of electoral support which they pro-vided to Moi and KANU; in effect, state patronage was now blatantly ethni-cally based with expenditure outlay in different parts of the country tied ever more closely to the support which the different ethnic groups and regions gave to the ruling party in the 1992 elections. This domestic "developmental conditionality" meant effectively that opposition areas could not expect (new) government activities and projects unless their lead-ers switched allegiance and declared support for KANU. Among the oppo-sition parties themselves, a trend developed whereby they engaged in fratri-cidal power struggles which also involved them undermining one another's support base. While this situation unfolded, Moi cocooned himself in the presidency of the country, watching the opposition tear itself apart and stoking the fire of division as dictated by KANU's own plan for consolidat-ing itself in power.

THE DISINTEGRATING POLITICAL CONJUNCTURE

FORD, when it emerged, was the product of a combination of interests and processes. At one level, the organisation was the beneficiary of initiatives both from below and above. At another level, the initiatives that emanated from above encapsulated latent rivalries between the economic and political elites who were active in the opposition movement. The struggle for the leadership of the organisation therefore reflected, initially at least, the com-bination of elite and popular interests. The six founder-members of FORD—Messrs Oginga Odinga, Masinde Muliro, Martin Shikuku, Ahmed Bamahariz, George Nthenge, and Philip Gachoka—generally identified themselves with the popular groups in Kenyan society and their demands. As a consequence, the movement received tremendous support among urban workers, rural peasants, students, and those segments of the elite that had disengaged or had been involuntarily disengaged from the *Nyayo* state.

The popular social groups that rallied to FORD saw in Oginga Odinga, an opportunity to revive the radical nationalist struggles which he championed in the 1960s for distributive justice, a struggle which led first to his ostracisation by the KANU elite and then to the marginalisation of the Luo, and finally to the state-led assault on all autonomous and radical/popular forms of political mobilisation/activism. The appeal of FORD to popular social forces was bolstered by the credible credentials of many of its other frontline leaders/founder-members. Thus, Martin Shikuku, much like Odinga, was also seen as a "people's watchman" for his steadfast criticism of the state and the bureaucratic elite throughout his political and parliamentary career.[1] Masinde Muliro too had endeared himself to the generality of the people for his defence of the *mwanainchi*,[2] a stance which cost him his ministerial position in 1975 when he gave his support to the parliamentary probe committee established by a number of maverick back benchers intent on getting to the bottom of J.M. Kariuki's murder. Clearly, with the exception of Philip Gachoka who was seen as a proxy for Kenneth Matiba,[3] all the other founder-members of FORD were individuals who had a great deal of experience in local and national politics. They became the rallying points in the national opposition movement and tried to insulate it both from ethnicisation and massive elitisation.

The entry into the movement of the so-called "Young Turks", made up of a team of relatively young and combative professionals who had helped the "old guard" in its legal and political battles with the state, set in motion a number of contradictions that marked the onset of divisions within FORD. Lawyers Gitobu Imanyara, Paul Muite, James Orengo, and other Young Turks got into FORD to play key roles in the same way that they had done in championing the campaign for the re-introduction of multipartyism in Kenya. Significantly too, other political elites who had been disengaged from the *Nyayo* state also began to formulate an agenda for inclusion in FORD, their hope being that if the opposition was able to win against KANU, their interests would be accommodated. But as many of these elites were joining the opposition belatedly, they resorted to the mobilisation of ethnic and regional support which they tried to use as a bargaining tool for inclusion in FORD and its future government if it won the election.

---

[1] Shikuku has been in parliament since early 1950s save for the period after the 1988 elections when he lost at the *Mlolongo* stage. He always won the seat with huge majorities. He was to recapture the seat in the 1992 elections.

[2] *Mwanainchi* is a Kiwahili word for citizen but often used in reference to the ordinary people in general.

[3] Philip Gachoka, a Kikuyu from Matiba's Murang'a district, represented his interests in FORD on understanding that once Matiba was discharged from hospital where he was recuperating from a stroke suffered while in detention, Gachoka would step aside for him. Gachoka's position was also interpreted as a Kikuyu membership of FORD since the party knew that it required the support of the Kikuyu, Kenya's largest ethnic group, in order to have a chance of displacing KANU from power.

Although ethnicity did not appear to be a significant issue when FORD was founded, it was bound to become a key factor which the organisation would have to reckon with as it developed. Not long after it had established itself as a major force on the Kenyan political scene, and in spite of the best efforts of some of its leaders, FORD was to find itself struggling to prevent ethnic factors from tearing it apart. In the end, ethnicity was the main lynchpin around which the organisation's fragmentation occurred. Central to this development was the calculation by many Kikuyu elites that given the saliency of ethnicity in the changing political conjuncture in the country, and given the demographic advantage which the Kikuyu had as the most populous ethnic group in the country, they had a chance of successfully pushing Kenneth Matiba forward as a candidate for the leadership of FORD, and, therefore, of the country if the party won the upcoming elections.[1] Odinga and the Young Turks tried to avoid the pressures that were emanating from sections of the Kikuyu elite, insisting that the most immediate task before FORD was to settle a number of constitutional questions which were critical to the transition to multiparty politics. They also argued that all other organisational issues could be settled through elections within the party. But while all of this was going on, Luo pressure also began to mount on Odinga not to give in to Matiba's quest for the leadership of FORD since, as it was seen in Luo-land, it was now their turn to be supported by the Kikuyu to aspire to the presidency of the country.

As acrimony deepened within the movement and spilled over into public arguments, Odinga scheduled elections within the party for August 1992. Matiba and his supporters rejected this and, instead, convened a steering committee to set a different date for the party elections and nullify the date that had earlier been announced by Odinga. The deepening lack of trust among the different groups in the movement which played itself out in terms of a lack of consensus on how to conduct elections within the organisation finally led to its fragmentation. Matiba, supported by five of FORD's founder-members (only Odinga himself was not in this group) set up a rival camp at Muthithi House, their argument being that the Agip House from where FORD had hitherto operated before the split was also the office for Odinga's private business concerns. However, Odinga and the Young Turks who were loyal to him remained at Agip house.

The split in FORD came as a great relief to KANU which, until then, had been thrown into disarray by the sheer popularity which the movement enjoyed across the country. Both the Muthithi and Agip factions applied for

---

[1] For instance, Kimani Wanjoike had called on the Kikuyu to ensure that they played a prominent role in the opposition parties. Others visited Matiba in the hospital to press him to announce his candidacy for the leadership of FORD and the presidency of the country. Matiba, in turn, accepted to vie for the positions and emphasised that his candidacy was not likely to lead to a split along ethnic lines in the party since ethnicity was, supposedly, no longer an issue in Kenyan politics. For details, see the editions of the *Weekly Review* for the month of February, 1992.

registration and were registered in October 1992 as different political parties, the one known as FORD-Asili and the other known as FORD-Kenya. FORD-Asili was made up of members of the Muthithi faction led by Matiba, with the backing of several of the founder-members of the pre-split FORD and many Kikuyu economic and political elites. As to FORD-Kenya, its core consisted of the members of the Agip faction led by Oginga Odinga with the backing of the Young Turks and Luo politicians.

The other opposition parties that came into existence were not immediately faced with the kinds of pressures towards fragmentation which FORD had to be deal with, but then they were also much smaller in size and their membership/ support base was much narrower than that of FORD before its split. The Democratic Party (DP), for example, was easily united around the elitist project which it tried to pursue; its public rallies were marked by a display of wealth and elitism. Other parties such as the Kenya National Congress (KNC), Kenya Social Congress (KSC), and Social Democratic Party (SDP) were formed by their founders either as vehicles for enabling them to gain entry to the parliamentary contest or as a stop-gap measure pending a decision to join one or the other of the main warring factions.

Although the DP was established as a party for safeguarding the interests of a section of the Kikuyu economic and political elite, it also tried to market itself as a credible representative of the interests of economic elites from other ethnic groups. For this purpose, it made a special effort to reach out to the people from the other communities in its target group. Thus it was that John Keen (a Maasai), Eliud Mwamunga (a Taita), Samuel Arap Ngeny (a Kalenjin) and Mohammed Jahazi (Coast) emerged as notable members of the party from other ethnic groups. Most of the frontline followers of the DP were individuals who had been marginalised from Moi's political project but who, all the same, had used the state framework to accumulate wealth and capital. A majority of them were individuals who had lost face after the highly contested primaries which KANU held preparatory to the 1988 elections. Those primaries witnessed a great deal of manipulation and rigging directed from KANU's central office against those who had lost favour with Moi and his entourage.[1]

Despite the split which occurred in FORD and the proliferation in the number of opposition parties that occurred, efforts continued to be made to forge a common action programme for pressing the government to implement further reforms in the political system and the internal security regime. These efforts were, however, always attended by a great deal of difficulty.

---

[1] Njenga Karume was allegedly defeated by a peasant coffee farmer at the sub-locational level while, at the district level, Kuria Kanyingi was set up against Muhoho. See Kanyinga, 1995, for details. The state had also supervised the political humiliation of several other politicians who were later to become founder-members of the DP. They cited the humiliation which they suffered in the 1988 primaries as one reason for leaving KANU.

To cite some examples: as early as February 1992—barely two months after the registration of parties—the DP refused to back FORD's call for a national strike to force the government to release all political prisoners. Also, in November 1992, after the split of FORD, FORD-Asili and the DP failed to support FORD-Kenya's call for a massive boycott of the voter registration exercise, a campaign which Odinga and the Young Turks had organised in order to press the government into releasing identify cards to people, mostly opposition supporters, who did not have one. The possession of an identity card was a precondition for voter eligibility and registration.

In most of its activities, the DP preferred to take a rather moderate approach and this extended to its response to most of the issues that came up on the national political scene. Its approach was in contrast to that of FORD which, given the fact that it was composed of a mixture of forces and the circumstances of its birth, inevitably took on a belligerent attitude in its relationship to the *Nyayo* state. Even when the party split, the groups that made up the two factions still adopted an aggressive position towards the state, although this was slightly more pronounced and frequent in FORD-Kenya than in FORD-Asili because of the presence and prominence of the Young Turks in the former. Mass support for FORD-Kenya and FORD-Asili relative to the other opposition parties, had to do, in part, with the street-level perception which people had that they were the two parties that had members who had the courage and capacity to get Moi and KANU out of office. Thus, among those who supported FORD-Asili, a key argument was the view that Matiba was a very courageous individual who could stand up to Moi. The Young Turks in FORD-Kenya were, likewise, seen by the party's supporters as "boys" who had the requisite courage and determination to force Moi out of political power (Kanyinga, 1995).

That the DP opted for a path of moderation should not, as we noted earlier, be surprising: its frontline members, being elites who had accumulated through the state—and KANU—were not very keen to undo the state or support a radical programme of reform because this would jeopardise their economic interests. Moreover, the establishment of the party very late in the day by individuals who were once key players in the onset of the *de jure* single party state required that it tread softly while trying to study the changing political space. Its moderation, together with the circumstances of its formation by erstwhile KANU stalwarts, aroused suspicion that it had connections to "dissidents" within KANU, the so-called KANU (B). It was on account of this that the DP was described by its critics in both FORD factions as a "branch" of KANU set up explicitly to spoil the chances of the opposition.

The Demobilisation of the Opposition after the 1992 Elections

With the opposition as badly divided as it was, it did not come as too much of a surprise that KANU and Moi emerged victorious in the 1992 multiparty elections. The period following the elections was to witness a deepening of the crisis of oppositional politics in Kenya. Defections from the opposition to KANU, the ability of KANU to re-assert its presence and even strive for dominance in the local political space, and the highly divisive intra-party rivalries that occurred among opposition elements were salient features of the post–1992 political conjuncture. There were many factors responsible for the weakening of the social base of opposition politics but one of the most important centres on the disillusionment caused by its unsuccessful attempt in 1992 to gain control of the state generally and the state house in particular. Let us elaborate on this a little more.

Some of the actors who went into the opposition did so because of the expectation they had that the struggle for democratic reforms would offer them new and/or enhanced opportunities for accumulation through greater access to or control of the state. This category of actors also included ambitious elements who saw in party politics, a vehicle for gaining political power for themselves and/or their ethnic or sub-ethnic groups. And since some of them had been sidelined by the *Kamaliza* and/or *Nyayo* state(s), they saw political pluralism as a long-awaited breakthrough that would enable them to take over the reins of power and, thus, open up/expand opportunities for accumulation from above. Some of the actors also carried over into the multiparty era, old political rivalries that dated back to the period of *de facto* and *de jure* single party politics. Thus, in several constituencies across the country, political competition generally and the 1992 elections in particular became little more than a replay of the intra-elite rivalries that wracked KANU in the 1980s. Some of the socio-political forces who were active in the intra-party squabbles of the 1980s simply transformed themselves into actors for different political parties in the 1990s and, in doing so, carried all the baggage of KANU politics during the 1980s with them.

The problems that were faced by the opposition parties were not mitigated by the differential reading which they had, and held rigidly to, of the challenges ahead of them. Some of the leading opposition figures, for example, took a position that it was necessary to make a distinction between KANU and Moi and this view was developed against the argument of those who saw in that party and its leader, an inseparable line, even a fused relationship. For those who insisted on separating the party from its leader, the key problem as they saw it was that Moi had replaced the original principles of KANU—which were laudable—with those of KADU from which he joined the ruling party in the 1960s. The main motivation for Moi in doing so was his insatiable desire for political security and for the ascendancy of the cabal around him. The challenge, therefore, was how to achieve a KANU without Moi so that the party could be brought back on course.

Among the most ardent advocates of the position that Moi and the ruling party could be separated were first generation KANU leaders who had participated in the decolonisation struggle and played a part in the organisation of KANU in early 1960s. Several of them, in fact, had senior, though not always active positions in the party during the Kenyatta years. They included politicians such as Paul Ngei, Jeremiah Nyaga, and Mwai Kibaki all of whom had served in different capacities in the Kenyatta and Moi administrations. In pushing this position, they were also not unmindful of the limited influence which they could have over the opposition but their position was reinforced by some Kikuyu elites who saw KANU as a political project of the Kikuyu and, therefore, argued for the party to be purged of KADU elements rather than abandoned to them.

Beyond the underlying and explicit differences in judgement, ideal and goals which led to the fracturing of the opposition, the point also ought to be emphasised that the opponents of KANU and Moi did not enjoy level ground on which to compete with the ruling party and the president. KANU never hesitated for one moment to use the apparatuses of the state as well as its material resources to weaken the opposition parties. The security agencies were also frequently used by the government to intimidate supporters and members of the opposition parties; efforts by the opposition leaders themselves to rally their constituencies or consult with activists working for them were regularly disrupted. The provincial administrative apparatus played a key part in the campaign of intimidation and disruption which KANU and the government directed against the opposition, especially in those areas where the opposition was strongest.

Furthermore, and this was a point which we noted earlier in passing, the state withdrew, or openly threatened to withdraw resources and patronage from those parts of the country where the opposition parties enjoyed popular support. This was a strategy that was clearly designed to weaken the support base of the opposition and to compel the leaders of the opposition parties to seek accommodation with KANU in order to prevent the marginalisation of their people. The threat of sanctions by the government and KANU was most effective in the agriculturally-poor areas of Kenya, especially in those places where reliance on relief supplied by the state during famine and drought was great. In those areas, politicians knew that the prospects for their re-election were closely tied to their capacity to attract government relief to families that needed it. Not surprisingly, several opposition figures from these areas felt compelled to switch over to KANU as a measure aimed at meeting demands from below. Others who did not outrightly defect had to "befriend" the state by showing open support to KANU while being inactive in the opposition.

KANU also perfected a strategy of "buying" some opposition leaders either with a view to forcing them to defect to its ranks or to become "moles" for the party within the opposition movement generally or their own specific parties. Thus, for instance, some opposition leaders who had received loans from state financial institutions were brought under severe pressure and compelled either to succumb to KANU by defecting or by withdrawing their support for oppositional activities; they had to play the game according to KANU's wishes if their loans were not to be suddenly recalled or the collateral they submitted confiscated.[1] Remarkably though, for all of KANU's success in prompting defections from the opposition, it did not manage to win any of the by-elections that occurred in the Central and Nyanza provinces as a result of seats vacated by those who left their parties to join it. Only in the Eastern Province, dominated by the DP, was KANU able to profit from the defections that occurred and from its manipulation of famine and drought relief as well as the gerrymandering associated with the creation of new districts.

A discourse, directed at minority ethnic groups, on the need for a concerted resistance against internal domination was another strategy that was used by KANU to garner support from sub-ethnic groups located in areas dominated by the opposition. This discourse was backed up after 1992 with a vigorous programme of gerrymandering involving the creation of new administrative districts. This strategy also had the effect of reinforcing sub-ethnic and ethnic consciousness as well as socio-political differentiation among peoples who had lived in the same administrative jurisdiction since the colonial period. Numerically small groups were urged by KANU and the government to demand "independence" from domination by larger groups. For instance, Mbere district, carved out of the old Embu district, was a product of the defection of the MP representing the area, Ireri Ndwiga, from the KNC to KANU. Following Ndwiga's defection, a by-election was called and KANU's main campaign message was that if the Mbere people, who were the dominant group in the constituency, voted for it, the government would create a district of their own for them and, in so doing, free them from "domination" by the rival Embu people. This line of campaigning was aimed at playing up the complaint of the Mbere that the Embu had not only dominated them for too long within the existing district but that the latter also considered them to be an inferior group. It did not come as too much of a surprise when KANU won the by-election even though the area was previously an opposition stronghold.

The policy which KANU embarked upon of creating more districts had one additional advantage, that of providing the central government with many repressive provincial administrations that could enable it to more

---

[1] Kiruhi Kimondo, a Nairobi (Stahere) Ford-Asili Member of Parliament defected to KANU in mid-1995 after failing to get financial assistance from Matiba to service his loans. The opposition also saw the defection of Charles Owino (FORD-Kenya, Migori), Julius Njoroge (FORD-Asili, Makuyu), Ochola Ogur (FORD-Kenya, Nyatike), and Tom Obondo (FORD-Kenya, Ndhiwa) as having been financially induced by KANU.

tightly control events at the local level. The creation of a new district always involved the establishment of new divisions, locations, and sub-locations as essential, integral administrative units. Since the highly repressive Chiefs Authority Act that dates from the colonial period has never been amended, this exercise in decentralisation effectively amounted to little more than an attempt at bringing political repression closer to the people. No wonder then that opposition politicians vigorously contested the so-called administrative decentralisation programme of the government, pointing out that it was aimed by KANU at co-opting all segments of the population so that the party could more easily control the political space and contain the spread/consolidation of opposition politics. The opposition also pointed out that the new districts were essentially an economic and political burden to the local communities since residents themselves had to pay for the physical infra-structure necessary for the new administrative set up to begin operations.

The views articulated by the opposition in critique of the new districts that were created were echoed by many other Kenyans. The opinion was widespread that the creation of new districts was preparatory to the re-introduction of the *Majimbo* form of government to which Moi had been committed during the early stages of his political career but which was shelved in 1964 when he and his other associates dissolved KADU and joined KANU. There was also widespread conviction that the keen interest shown by KANU and Moi in the establishment of new districts was part of a strategy for increasing the number of parliamentary units that would enable the ruling party to consolidate its absolute majority in parliament.

In all, life in the opposition has been extremely difficult, not least on account of the machinations of the ruling party. The opposition itself has been wracked by intra-elite rivalries and the attendant factionalism which has meant the increased fragmentation of the social support base of the opponents of KANU. Ethnic/regional suspicion has played as much a part in the internal problems of the opposition as class factors and external manipulation emanating from KANU. Some of the opposition leaders have further deepened the problems faced by their parties by attempting to build a personality cult; others have simply reduced their parties to instruments for advancing their personal cause or the interests of their ethnic group. A close scrutiny of each of the main parties, such as we attempt below, will reveal that elitism, together with their failure to gain access to the state, have also been central to the decline of opposition party politics. Through a close discussion of the experiences of each of the main parties, we are able to show just how counter-productive the ethnic factors that influenced the genesis of some of them have been for the development of the opposition.

The DP's Atrophy: The Young Rival the Old

In the initial stages of its formation, the DP was widely seen as having something of an organic relationship with KANU. This was because, as we noted earlier in a different context, a majority of the party's founder-members had served Moi's government in one capacity or the other and only deserted it after the re-introduction of multipartyism. Some of them also held senior party positions in KANU and, in addition, were members of Kenyatta's GEMA cabal. Mwai Kibaki, for instance, had served as Finance Minister in Kenyatta's government and as Moi's Vice-President for a short period; Njenga Karume was GEMA's chairman and Assistant Minister for Cooperative Development in Moi's government; Eliud Mwamunga and John Keen also served both the Kenyatta and Moi governments as ministers. Two of Kenyatta's kin, George Muhoho and Ngengi Muigai, who were founder-members of the DP, had also been ministers in Moi's government.

Given their antecedents, it is not surprising that the founder-members of the DP were individuals who had accumulated massive political and economic capital through their long period of engagement with the state. Their reason for forming the DP centred partly on their disaffection with the Moi presidency but also partly because of their desire to insulate their economic gains from any adverse fall-out from the transition to multiparty politics. Although their influence waned under Moi, the DP founder-members, as KANU insiders, felt that they had something to fear from a possible political backlash that might flow from a FORD victory at the polls. This was why although the party was set up in opposition to KANU, it was never at ease with the radical activism of FORD militants and deliberately tried to cultivate a moderate outlook that enabled it to strategically straddle KANU and the core opposition. It is on account of this that its senior members came to be seen/described as "fence-sitters", "indecisive", and "yellow-bellied" politicians. The party, unlike the two FORD factions, never took a radical position against KANU.

The failure of the DP as a party to gain control of the state after the 1992 elections occasioned atrophy in the organisation. It was the first party to lose an elected member to KANU—by way of a defection which prompted a by-election that the party also lost. Protus Momanyi's defection in March 1993 to KANU was followed by a series of other losses: several councillors in Momanyi's Kisii district also defected to KANU and the majority won the subsequent by-elections that were held. Other defections soon occurred, this time involving a number of the party's founder-members who returned to KANU in order to negotiate an accommodation within the ruling party to which they once belonged.

The party was also wracked by intra-elite rivalries. These rivalries began with the 1993 party national elections in which ethnic balancing in the distribution of national party positions took precedence over all other factors. Once the elections were over, it became clear that no Meru had been put into any significant position. John Keen, the party's Secretary General at the time, pointed out that this was not a serious problem because the Kikuyu are the "cousins" of the Meru and would, therefore, represent Meru interests in the party. This incensed the Meru elites in the party; they responded by observing that the "Kikuyu" had begun once again to exclude them from the spoils of office even though they had both fought equally for the gains which the party made in the 1992 elections. They expressed their complete dissatisfaction with what they considered a Kikuyu stratagem to "use and dump" them as happened during the height of GEMA's influence.

In furtherance of the protest by the Meru, the DP MP for Tigania, Benjamin Ndubai, threatened to organise either a massive Meru walk out from the party or a mass rebellion by the general party membership against Kibaki (the Chairman) and the Kikuyu in general. Other Meru elites supported Ndubai's position by stressing that the Meru were not prepared to be used as a stepping stone by the Kikuyu for getting into higher office.[1] Thus, what was supposed to be an election to send out signals that the party was a strong and united entity turned into an exercise that tore apart its ethnic membrane.

Dissent within the DP deepened following the land clashes that occurred in the Rift Valley and which led to some of the party's founder-members, especially those of them who were former GEMA officials, entering into talks with their Kalenjin counterparts. The GEMA-KAMATUSA talks,[2] as they came to be known, took place in August 1996 and immediately opened new lines of disagreement within the DP as some party members questioned the relevance of the dialogue in the light of widespread suggestions that Kalenjin elites were involved in provoking the Rift Valley clashes. Critics of the DP's participation in the discussions with the Kalenjin elite saw little benefit for the party in the exercise other than that it represented an effort by some of its founder-members to revive GEMA. In doing so, however, the section of the Kikuyu elite that participated in the dialogue was also, unwittingly perhaps, contributing to the strengthening of the Kalenjin-dominated KAMATUSA coalition.

Some of the DP founder-members who were sympathetic to the idea of the dialogue had suggested that it was aimed at forestalling further conflicts in the Rift Valley. From the point of view of KANU, however, the talks fed into a wider strategy aimed at neutralising the presence of the opposition in the Rift Valley. They also had the added benefit of enabling Moi to, as it were, weigh the state of Kikuyu political opinion about himself and KANU. Furthermore, there was some hope expressed by KANU strategists close to Moi that the talks might serve as a platform on which the party could launch

---

[1] Meru district KANU politicians supported Ndubai in this regard.

[2] The talks were organised by elites from the Kikuyu and KAMATUSA communities ostensibly to "heal the wounds from the land clashes". The GEMA team was led by Njenga Karume while Nicholas Biwott led the KAMATUSA group.

an effort to win back Central Kenya, the Kikuyu heartland. As part of this broad objective of bringing the Kikuyu back into KANU on terms that were acceptable to KAMATUSA, it was hoped that elements within the DP could be constructively engaged side by side with the moulding of new personalities who could be presented as community leaders. This entire strategy however unravelled following the failure of KANU to win a by-election in the Kikuyu-dominated Kipipiri constituency, an outcome which was considered by the KAMATUSA group to be so disappointing as to lead to the discontinuation of the dialogue with the GEMA/DP group by the Kalenjin elites and their strategists within KANU.[1]

The younger generation of DP leaders, comprising Benjamin Ndubai, Kennedy Kiliku, and Ngengi Muigai, had argued forcefully and vociferously against the decision by their party to enter into the talks with KAMATUSA. They insisted that the solution to the problems that had developed in the Rift Valley, the ostensible reason for the dialogue, lay not in the negotiation of informal pacts but in far-reaching constitutional reforms to which KANU was completely opposed. Other opposition parties were similarly critical of the talks and were in agreement with the DP's younger leaders that the answers to the clashes in the Rift Valley lay in the constitution of a national convention to discuss the country's future. Kijana Wamalwa, the successor to Oginga Odinga as leader of FORD-Kenya, observed, for instance, that the talks were "nothing but a strategy to woo the opposition to KANU".[2] This tallied with the views of some of the elements within the DP that the talks appeared to be aimed at building a bridge for the "GEMA elders" to be individually accommodated within the highly influential Nicholas Biwott-Moi axis within KANU.

It is interesting to note that although the talks were supposedly about their future, the members of the Kikuyu Diaspora in the Rift Valley did not play a prominent role either in the organisation of the dialogue or in the actual discussions once they got off the ground. This lent further credence to the view that the talks were simply being used by a section of the Kikuyu elite to negotiate an accommodation with or within KANU that would safeguard their interests, interests that had been jeopardised by Kikuyu opposition to Moi during the 1992 elections. As for the Kalenjin elite, the talks offered an opportunity to try to win back the Kikuyu Diaspora since the latter's political and economic capital was a function of the character of its relationship to the Kalenjin elite in the Rift Valley and to the organisation of opposition politics in general.

Disagreements within the DP over the modalities for addressing the land clashes in the Rift Valley fed into wider issues of party leadership. The

---

[1] This was a pointer to the fact that politically the Kalenjin had the upper hand in the organisation of the talks because Moi was involved.

[2] See the *Daily Nation*, 1 August 1995.

younger generation accused the old guard of selling the DP to the KAMATUSA elite despite the suffering which many ordinary Kikuyu workers and peasant farmers had undergone during the clashes. They also accused the old guard of weakening the party through actions that occasioned or facilitated defections to KANU. Moreover, according to the younger generation, the old guard had failed signally to activate the local level branches of the party, a fact which appeared to justify suggestions that the founder-members were happy with the *status quo* in Kenya and were not prepared to be aggressive in the struggle against KANU. In the meantime, the party was bleeding from the loss of some of its key members, including Mohammed Jahazi, Eliud Mwamunga (National Treasurer) and John Keen (Secretary General), who all defected to KANU. The defectors cited the inability of the opposition to organise a common agenda as being the principal reason for their decision to quit the DP. Agnes Ndetei, the MP for Kibwezi, also defected to KANU, citing pressure from her constituents.

In view of all of the foregoing, it is not surprising that the contest for the leadership of the DP pitched the younger members against the old guard. The younger generation of leaders within the party consisted mainly of individuals who entered politics during the early period of *Nyayo*. They also included professionals who were ushered into politics following the expansion in the local political space created by struggles for liberalisation that took place in the late 1980s and early 1990s. This generation of leaders within the DP may, correctly, be referred to as the party's Young Turks, although unlike their counterparts in FORD-Kenya, they were not as belligerent and/or volatile in their disposition.

The main similarity between the younger members of the DP and the old guard, and what brought them together in the first place, was their common interest as business persons or individuals interested in advancing private business. However, the alliance between them began to crack when their party failed to gain access to the state and its resources after the 1992 elections. Matters were not helped by the fact that several of the party's leaders had close business relations and/or interests with people who were in KANU, and with elements of the emerging Kalenjin bourgeoisie as well. This was a reason why a section of the party started in earnest to bargain for accommodation with/within KANU. This development was rejected by the younger members of the party who both disowned the negotiations and insisted that the project amounted to a betrayal of the Kikuyu community.

Disillusioned with the direction their party was taking, some of the younger leaders began to call for the convening of the party's annual delegates' conference with a view to creating avenues for excluding the old guard. This deepened the fissures in the party, with the members of the old guard conducting elections at the delegates' conference that they convened. During the conference and the elections, the members of the old guard mustered all the influence at their disposal to effect the defeat of all of the younger leaders opposed to their policies. Most prominent among those who lost their positions were Kiliku, Muigai and Ndubai who were among the most vociferous critics of the old guard. The forces of the *status quo* had prevailed over their critics within the organisation but it was not enough to stop the party's atrophy.

Split in FORD-Kenya: Inter- and Intra-Ethnic Rivalry

While he was still alive, Oginga Odinga's towering figure, together with his patronage of FORD-Kenya, helped, for a short time at least, to conceal several latent lines of division within the party. However, following the death, in early 1994, of the opposition veteran, the differences which his presence had largely helped to conceal came out forcefully into the open. These differences, as much on ideology as on style, personality, and approach pitted one section of the Young Turks against the other. The intensity of the conflicts and the absence of an effective internal mechanism for managing them were to hurt the party badly and lead to splits within its ranks.

Shortly before Odinga's death, the basis had been laid for the internal divisions among the Young Turks that were later to undermine FORD-Kenya. The divisions bore directly on the question of the succession to the ailing Odinga and over how the fight against state-led economic corruption and the misappropriation of public resources was to be conducted. The immediate factor that brought the divisions out sharply was the revelation by Odinga that he had, on behalf of FORD-Kenya, received financial assistance from Kamleshi Patni, the Asian businessman who was at the centre of the Goldenberg corruption scam under which export compensation was paid for fake gold exports. This revelation was extremely disquieting for many party members. Some of the Young Turks immediately pointed out that the action of their party leader was improper. This was all the more so as he was, in his capacity as the leader of the parliamentary opposition, also the chair of the Public Accounts Committee which was investigating the scam. Having soiled his hands and tainted the party by accepting money from Patni, Odinga's critics within the party felt that he could not continue to chair the parliamentary committee that was investigating Goldenberg and Patni.

The position of the FORD-Kenya Young Turks who were critical of Odinga was countered by others, notably James Orengo, who observed that Odinga had come out up front and openly on the matter and that those within the party who were against his actions and chairmanship of the investigation process wanted to force a *coup* and assume party leadership. The Young Turks, such as Gitobu Imanyara, (the party Secretary General), Paul Muite (the first Vice Chairman), Kiraitu Murungi (Secretary for Parliamentary Affairs), and Farah Maalim (Shadow Minister for Energy), who were critical of Odinga responded by "walking out" of the party but they did not resign their parliamentary seats.[1] Wamalwa Kijana (a Luhya) and Munywa Waiyaki (a Kikuyu) were swiftly appointed into the position of first Vice Chairman and Secretary General respectively while James Orengo assumed the position in the executive committee of the party which Wamalwa had vacated. Raila Odinga remained the party's deputy director of elections.

The death of Odinga in February 1994 opened a new wave of struggles in the party centring on the succession to the leadership position which he occupied. These struggles were soon transformed into a generalised leadership rivalry that eventually took on ethnic undertones and finally split the party into two factions. Initially cast as an intra-Luo rivalry for the leadership of the Luo bloc in the party, and therefore, for the representation of the Luo voice in national level politics, the conflicts quickly assumed inter-ethnic dimensions.

At the level of the intra-Luo rivalries, two distinct factions emerged to claim Odinga's mantle. One faction, led by Odinga's son, Raila, mobilised around radical concerns in the same way as Odinga had done for decades. The faction was also concerned with what it considered to be the systematic marginalisation of the Luo community by KANU. It placed emphasis on issues of unemployment among the youth and lack of a governmental development agenda for the Luo region. The other faction, led by James Orengo, was elitist and drew the bulk of its support from the majority of the party's MPs and the Luo elite. The faction was particularly keen to thwart what it saw as Raila's attempts to ascend to FORD-Kenya's leadership. Thus, the Orengo camp, in its campaigns, kept observing that Nyanzaland was not a monarchy and had no room for political inheritance. The faction initially had enormous support from the politicians of South Nyanza who saw the rivalry as an opportunity to resist "political domination" by Siaya Luo from where the Odingas come. The prominence which the Siaya enjoyed over other Luo districts dated from the colonial period.

Raila's faction, initially comprising Luo urban working class elements and radical or hardline professionals, presented itself as being engaged in a

---

[1] The group later formed a development trust—Mwangaza—to help provide development in opposition areas where the government had vowed not to provide "development" unless the electorate switched back to the ruling party. The government de-registered Mwangaza and the organisation responded by transforming itself into a party named SAFINA, a Kiswahili word for the biblical Noah's Ark. SAFINA drew support from the broad citizenry, including the teeming population of Kenyans who were disillusioned with the unhealthy and counter-productive rivalry among the opposition elites. It should be noted however that although SAFINA offered a potential alternative to the mode of organisation of the opposition, it was itself divided over the issue of its leadership. The fact that the interim leadership of the party was conferred on Richard Leakey, a white Kenyan, provided KANU with a racial weapon with which to mobilise against it and weaken its support base. The government also tenaciously refused to register the party and, in so doing, precipitated its decline.

struggle which pitted "Luo popular forces" against the Luo elite represented by Orengo's group. Raila's campaign struck a chord with the young, especially as he appeared to articulate their concerns and those of the Luo in general. The fact that Raila had previously been detained by Moi boosted his leadership credentials further among many ordinary Luo; his experience also won him the sympathy of those who thought that, just like his father, he had made immense personal sacrifices for the restoration of democracy to the country. The activists of Raila's faction tried to build on this popular perception by packaging an image of him as a fearless leader qualified on his personal merit to inherit Oginga Odinga's political cloak. They took a hardline position against their opponents and spared no opportunity to dislodge Orengo's faction from Nyanzaland.

Although the Orengo faction enjoyed some initial sympathy in parts of Luo-land for its insistence that there was a need to prevent the domination of Luo politics by one family, the alliance which its members forged with FORD-Kenya's Luhya fraternity led by Wamalwa made their task of building a base among the Luo much more complicated. It also made the crisis within the party more difficult and complex as both Luo factions tried to build a broader support base within the party such that what initially looked like an Orengo-Raila rivalry became quickly transformed into a Raila-Wamalwa rivalry. This latter rivalry spilled over into the fabric of the party organisation and caused even more polarisation. The decision of Wamalwa to give his support to Orengo pitted Raila's supporters in the party against him.

In the party elections that were held in February 1994, Orengo was elected the first Vice Chairman of FORD-Kenya. Those allied to him and Wamalwa also emerged as the holders of all the key positions in the party. Raila's supporters were completely blocked out, an outcome which immediately led them to cry foul. They claimed that the elections had been rigged in favour of Orengo's faction. They also argued that KANU had infiltrated the party through the Wamalwa-Orengo faction with a view to undermining Raila personally, and the Luo in general. Furthermore, Raila's supporters blamed their defeat on Wamalwa over his open support for Orengo's ascendancy to vice-chairmanship of the party.

With his faction interpreting his poor showing in the party elections as evidence of an attempt to get him out of the party mainstream/leadership and, in so doing, hinder him from becoming the leading figure in Luo politics, Raila was encouraged by his supporters to directly take on Wamalwa. For them, the position adopted by the Wamalwa faction was at variance with their interpretation of the popular wishes and concerns of the Luo and for that reason, Wamalwa had to be fought and removed. As the battle lines were drawn, the Wamalwa faction based the locus for its activities in the parliamentary buildings, using the office of the leader of the opposition. They were later to move to Oginga Odinga House where they set up camp.

As to the Raila faction, their operational base became the famous Agip House. It was from here that Raila perfected his plan for holding "grass-roots" elections on the argument that Wamalwa had failed to carry out the task. Predictably, the Wamalwa group described the proposed elections as illegal and a nullity.

Feeling that their kinsman had been unjustly attacked by the Raila faction, the Luhya members of FORD-Kenya who were also active in the Wamalwa-Orengo faction began to mobilise Luhya support behind Wamalwa on the argument that the time had come for one of their own, who was now a major party leader, to have a shot at the presidency of the country. In this interpretation of the conflicts taking place within the party, the hardline position which Raila had become associated with, and which had been backed up by Luo "fundamentalists", amounted to an attempt to convert FORD-Kenya into a Luo Party. This view was countered by Raila's supporters who argued that FORD-Kenya was indeed a Luo party and that if the Luhya felt unhappy about it or the prospects of Raila's leadership, they were free to leave and start their own party. They also argued that, after all, the Luo had more FORD-Kenya MPs than the Luhya, and that it was the Luhya who had paved the way for KANU to make in-roads into opposition strongholds by their defections. Furthermore, they emphasised the point that Wamalwa had not managed to capture any seat for FORD-Kenya in all of the bye-elections that were prompted by the defection of several Luhya MPs to KANU. The Luhya, therefore, had a duty to "lie low" to Luo leadership in the party.

In the meantime, the rise of a distinct Luhya faction within FORD-Kenya caused trepidation in KANU because it had the potential of eroding the ruling party's gains in Western Kenya. KANU's concerns were intensified by the announcement that the Wamalwa faction and the DP were negotiating a united opposition platform with a view to endorsing a single presidential candidate for the next elections. KANU decided to embark on an active programme of campaigning and mobilisation in the Western Province in order to check the rising profile of the "Wamalwa FORD-Kenya" in the area. As part of this programme, KANU Luhya elites organised public meetings where they urged the people to support KANU because the Luo would not dump one of their own, namely Raila, just to support a Luhya, Wamalwa.

The April 1996 party elections provided yet another occasion for the further deepening of the polarisation of FORD-Kenya along ethnic lines. These elections had been necessitated by the court ruling that the "grassroots" elections which the Raila faction was planning to hold should be discontinued. The faction agreed, following arbitration, that it would participate in fresh party elections provided a neutral umpire acceptable to it and the Wamalwa group was appointed to supervise the voting. As it turned out, it was easier for both factions to accept the terms of the judicial arbitration than to live with the results of the first attempt at implementing them. The party primaries that were held as a first stage in the election of leaders were attended by a great deal of controversy, with the Raila faction accusing Wamalwa and his group of fraud and the latter accusing Raila of orchestrating the violence that made it difficult to conduct the primaries everywhere. The two factions also publicly bickered over the venue for the party's National Congress before finally settling for a location in Thika, on the outskirts of Nairobi. But when the Congress was finally held, it served little purpose more than to confirm the split within the party. Both factions disagreed over voter eligibility, thereby forcing the independent umpire to withdraw. Each faction then held its own national elections and subsequently applied to the registrar of organisations as the authentic, legitimate FORD-Kenya, complete with a new list of office bearers. Thus it was that FORD-Kenya was thrown into disarray.

FORD-Asili: Party Ownership and Personality Cult

FORD-Asili, as we noted before, was established by five of the six founder-members of FORD who were key players in the struggle for power and influence that resulted in the split of 1992. There were a variety of factors influencing the decision of the five founder-members to establish FORD-Asili: their opposition to the heavy influence and frontline role of the Young Turks, the strong influence which the Young Turks appeared to have over Oginga Odinga, the desire on the part of sections of the Kikuyu elite to take the leading role in the party, a resentment of what was seen as an emerging cult of the personality whereby Oginga Odinga was equated with FORD, and a desire on the part of those who became the leaders of FORD-Asili to prevent their marginalisation from the new multiparty dispensation in Kenya. Following the split in FORD, Kenneth Matiba became, as widely expected, the Chairman of FORD-Asili with Martin Shikuku as its Secretary General.

It was not long after the 1992 elections that FORD-Asili began to face serious internal crises of its own, crises which were to lead to its decline. Several factors were responsible for the crises and decline which the party faced. They include: the virtual breakdown of the Luhya-Kikuyu alliance that underpinned the party, especially after its failure to win the presidency of the country in the 1992 elections; Matiba's intransigence as a party leader; and the party's complacency. Although these different factors acted to reinforce one another in propelling FORD-Asili towards its decline, Luhya disenchantment was perhaps the most significant of them. In this regard, in spite of the fact that the party's presidential candidate, Kenneth Matiba, emerged second to Moi in the share of votes received in the presidential elections of 1992, the Luhya segment was to become quickly disillusioned by the party's failure to gain control of the state house.

The disillusionment felt by the Luhya group within FORD-Asili was made all the more unavoidable by the fact that the pattern of voting in the 1992 elections showed a three-way split in which some sections of that ethnic group voted for KANU, others voted for FORD-Kenya, and the remainder voted for FORD-Asili. Pressure mounted on the FORD-Asili Luhya group to devise strategies for minimising their individual political risks and the losses that might be suffered by their constituents who voted for them against KANU. The way most of them responded to the pressures took the form of defections to KANU, defections which were presented by KANU as being part of a process of the return to its fold of all Luhya sub-groups, with the exception of the Bukusu who were represented in FORD-Kenya.

Between August 1993 and August 1994, the party lost five Luhya MPs and several councillors to KANU. The first to defect was Nicodemus Khaniri (August 1993) followed by Apili Wawire (November 1993). Japheth Shamalla (Shinyalu), Ben Magwagwa (Ikolomani) and Sifuna Wawire (Lugari) defected as a group in mid-1994. Evidence that the defections were closely co-ordinated as part of a KANU onslaught to regain a strong foot-hold in Luhya areas was provided by the fact that President Moi personally campaigned for the re-election of the defectors under their new KANU ticket; the ruling party won all the bye-elections. It is worth noting that the defectors, in seeking to justify their actions, stated that they felt frustrated by the fact that Matiba had no time for the opinions of other people within FORD-Asili and party officials were simply expected to follow his orders without any question.

Furthermore, the defectors stated that they were concerned about the personalisation of the party by Matiba and put off by his presidential behaviour—long motorcades and a battery of aides and security agents—which made it hard for senior party colleagues and officials to relate to him as equals or close associates. As a result of the defections, FORD-Asili's clout in parliament dwindled with the number of MPs on its benches falling sharply from a total of 31 at the beginning of 1993 to only 23 by June 1996.

As if the defections of many of its Luhya MPs and councillors were not enough, the party also lost a number of bye-elections in areas which were once considered FORD-Asili/Matiba strongholds. For instance, in a bye-election marked by profound voter apathy and serious complacency on the part of FORD-Asili, the party lost the contest for the constituency of Starehe, Nairobi, following the resignation of its MP, Steve Mwangi. Mwangi's decision to resign his parliamentary seat was widely seen as having been induced by patronage which KANU offered him. Indeed, immediately after leaving his seat, he participated in the organisation of a visit by Moi to his rural home in Gatundu. The area's councillor (who was, until then, an opposition activist) defected to KANU during the presidential visit, although, in this particular case, he lost the bye-election that followed his action. FORD-

Asili also lost to KANU in several other bye-elections in Kiambu and Murang'a districts, the two areas where the party considered itself indomitable.

Matiba's ambition for personal rule and his little regard for other party officials immensely contributed to the decline of FORD-Asili. The attempts made by some of the founder-members to reconcile the different wings of the party were treated by him with contempt and levity. Indeed, Matiba was to boast repeatedly that many of the party officials and leaders, including the founder-members, would not have been in parliament had it not been for him. For their part, the founder-members, led by Martin Shikuku, the party's Secretary General, reminded Matiba that he only came on board the political train after they had made enormous sacrifices in the struggle for the re-introduction of multipartyism in Kenya; indeed, they noted that Matiba made an insignificant contribution both to the struggle against colonialism and post-colonial authoritarianism during the Kenyatta and Moi years. Instead, he had used the state to acquire "immense" personal wealth that had now become the basis for his "arrogant" disregard of internal party democracy. The divisions within the party soon developed into a full-blown rivalry for its control and actual ownership, a rivalry that resulted in the birth of two factions, one led by Matiba and the other by Martin Shikuku.

As was the case with the other opposition parties, the attempt to conduct internal party elections in the context of divisions that were developing provided the framework for the actual split that finally ripped FORD-Asili apart. Disagreements over the modalities for conducting the party's grass-roots elections pitched Matiba's faction against that of the founder-members. The latter, made up of most of FORD-Asili's senior officials, claimed that since they had control over the party machinery and were also founder-members, their actions as well as the programme they had for the elections were legitimate. This position was contested by the Matiba faction which emphasised that its leader was responsible for the party's financing, and thus survival; this fact alone was sufficient to confer on Matiba, the right to control the party, a right which, moreover, was bolstered by the massive electoral support which Matiba's presidential bid enjoyed in 1992.

Thus, while both party factions agreed to the convening of internal elections as a means of resolving the impasse that had developed, they could not agree on the modalities for realising this goal. As a result, in June 1995, Matiba decided to lock the founders-members out of the Muthithi House offices of the party. He also moved important party documents out of the building to his personal residence outside the city. The founder-members responded by opening another party office at Nyanja House, a building owned by a member of the faction. These events confirmed the split in the party into the Matiba and Shikuku (founder-members) factions.

The Matiba faction decided to go ahead and organise party elections on its own. These elections were held in February 1996 and in March of the same year, Matiba constituted a new shadow cabinet which excluded all members of the Shikuku faction. Although this shadow cabinet attempted to replicate the Kikuyu-Luhya alliance that underpinned the party before the defections and split it suffered, the team which Matiba assembled was distinguished mainly by the fact that it consisted of people with relatively very little practical experience in high politics; they were all second generation politicians.[1] Matiba's action was immediately challenged by the Shikuku faction which declared the elections he organised illegal and insisted that it was the authentic FORD-Asili.

On the whole, the view is widely shared among local political commentators in Kenya that Matiba, in the way he played his politics, had a lot to answer for not only in relation to the crisis in his party but also with regard to the issue of the lack of unity among the opposition parties. He always spurned approaches made to him and FORD-Asili on the forging of a common opposition front; he had, in 1992, rejected the suggestion that the opposition should have a common presidential candidate in part because he believed that the demographic size of the Kikuyu gave him a fair chance of winning on his own. Thus, although it was always his style to tell his fellow politicians to "let the people decide", there was a constant, if implicit assumption on his part that they would decide in his favour, failing which he took disruptive steps that often undermined confidence-building within his party and the broader opposition movement. Yet, at the same time as his approach made the task of developing a common, minimum opposition platform difficult (the so-called United Alliance proposal, for example), it did not contribute to the enhancement of his political support base.

Indeed, Matiba's frequent resort to the issuing of ultimatums to KANU and Moi, together with his "technical" appearances in parliament, while initially popular with the urban/peri-urban lumpen elements who constituted the bulk of his supporters in the slums of Nairobi, soon alienated informed opinion in civil society. Thus, even as he adopted a belligerent attitude towards other opposition parties, his style of confronting KANU was increasingly seen as being little more than empty rhetoric. Critics saw his style as smacking of arrogance and wondered why he opted for the "technical" appearances that enabled him to have the minimum required number of attendances necessary for him to keep his seat instead of using the parliamentary platform as an effective instrument for tackling KANU. Furthermore, popular perception of his effectiveness as a serious political player was dented by an image of him that emerged as a sick person who

---

[1] The shadow cabinet list excluded Matiba's critics, a majority of whom were MPs allied to the Shikuku faction. The list was mainly made up of those Kikuyu politicians who supported Matiba plus some Luhya members and a sprinkling of people identified as representing other ethnic groups. The inclusion of the non-Kikuyu politicians was meant to give the shadow cabinet a semblance of a national outlook. See *Daily Nation*, 3 May, 1996.

had not fully recovered from the stroke he suffered while in detention. Thus, the decline of FORD-Asili was the result of factors that, in part, had to do with the leadership weaknesses of its leader.

THE DECLINE OF PARTY POLITICS: THREE LOCAL LEVEL CASE STUDIES

Uasin Gishu: Sub-Ethnic Rivalry and Disintegration of KANU

Uasin Gishu District is in the former White Highlands in the Rift Valley Province. The majority of the inhabitants of the district are the Nandi and the Keiyo Kalenjin sub-ethnic groups. They settled in the area prior to the establishment of the colonial state and after pushing the Maasai further down the Rift Valley. The area also has a significant number of Kikuyu inhabitants whose settlement in the district dates from the establishment of the colonial settler economy. Their numbers were boosted by the post-independence land settlement programmes that were undertaken by the Kenyatta regime during the 1960s and the 1970s.

The land clashes that occurred just before the 1992 elections resulted in the ethnic polarisation of the district, with the Kalenjin, who are the demographic majority supporting KANU, and the Kikuyu, who are a minority in the area, throwing their weight behind the opposition. Although the ethnic clashes were consciously orchestrated by KANU politicians desperate for electoral advantage, it is also important to emphasise that there were structural bases to the ethnic polarisation that occurred. Of particular importance in this regard is the question of the control and ownership of land in the district. The Kalenjin re-activated their latent resentment of the settlement programmes that were implemented in the 1960s and 1970s, claiming that what took place was little more than the allocation of their ancestral land to Kikuyu "immigrants". This was, of course, rejected by the Kikuyu. The ensuing clashes that took place served a dual purpose: the eviction, as expected by those who orchestrated the fighting, of the Kikuyu from the district and the largely unanticipated establishment of a basis for emergence of a crack in the Kalenjin coalition that is central to the workings of the *Nyayo* state.

There was a widespread recognition in Uasin Gishu that the land clashes were triggered off by local political and economic elites with a vested interest in land matters. The clashes enabled the ruling party to make a concerted effort at undermining the social bases of the opposition in the area; for the local elites, there was hope that those who were well connected among them would use the opportunity to appropriate the lands abandoned by the non-Kalenjin who either deserted the district or were the victims of eviction from the area.[1] Although the land clashes did succeed in considerably under-mining opposition politics in Uasin Gishu, they also, ironically, opened up contradictions among the Kalenjin with members of the Nandi sub-ethnic group complaining that their youth had been "used" in executing the clashes while the Keiyo sub-ethnic group was reaping most of the benefits from the incumbency of Moi in the state house. Indeed, after the clashes, Nandi complaints that the Keiyo were enjoying a disproportionate political and economic dominance over them in Uasin Gishu became more vocifer-ous. A former Uasin Gishu councillor, for instance, lamented that the Keiyo had "colonised" the Nandi and, in doing so, used the state house and the presidency to facilitate their ascendancy. While Biwott and other officials used their proximity to Moi and the state house to advance Keiyo interests, they cared little about others, except the Tugen sub-group of the president himself.[2]

Nandi political leaders and elites were keen to emphasise after the 1992 elections that not all Kalenjins had benefited from the presidency of Moi. Indeed, one Nandi school teacher whom we interviewed stated categorically that "... the Keiyo and the Tugen have drawn more benefits from the gov-ernment than any other Kalenjin or KAMATUSA sub-group". The respon-dent added that this outcome was "... made possible by the fact that the Keiyo and the Tugen have their sons (Moi and Nicholas Biwott) located inside State House which is the distribution centre of everything" (Inter-view, 25 February 1996). Some of the Nandi respondents we discussed with also argued that their community had been subjected to relative political marginalisation from the time Moi rose to power in part because during the 1960s, the main person who consistently rivalled Moi for the leadership of the Kalenjin, Jean Marie Seroney, was a Nandi. After Moi ascended to the presidency, he, according to this line of thinking, tried to settle old scores with the Nandi for their support of Seroney.

Nandi elites were also concerned to distance themselves from the organi-sation of the land clashes and the distribution of rewards that was associated with the conflict. Some of the Nandi emphasised that "it was not the entire Kalenjin community that was involved in the land clashes but the Keiyo and the Tugen elites who were motivated by the urge to dominate everybody in the district" (Interview, 25 February, 1996). This observation by a local school teacher was corroborated by a group of Nandi youth who told us that "... it was the Keiyo who were deeply involved in this thing: they promised their youth that once the Kikuyu are evicted, all warriors will be allocated five acres each of the Kikuyu land".[3] What the Kalenjin leaders who

---

[1] Interview with a local primary school teacher in Kuinet, Moiben division, 23 Febru-ary, 1996.

[2] Interview with a former Councillor in Kiplombe location, 16 March, 1996.

[3] Interview with a group of youth in Olare location, Ainabkoi division, 12 March, 1996.

orchestrated the clashes did not anticipate was that their actions would not only result in the undermining of the Kenyan opposition but, also, of the Kalenjin coalition.

The decision by the Nandi to distance themselves from the clashes also led them towards the embrace of some form of opposition politics, although this opposition was articulated within KANU. The Nandi faction within the Uasin Gishu district branch of KANU often referred to itself as KANU-B; it drew its support from the lumpen elements as well as political elites in the area who felt disengaged from the *Nyayo* state or the dominant Tugen-Keiyo axis. The main complaint of the faction was that although, like other Kalenjin groups, the Nandis had provided full political support to Moi since his ascendancy to power in 1978, they had gained little or nothing in return. Instead, employment opportunities and loans for business were awarded to the Tugen and the Keiyo despite their low numbers in the district. Some Nandi also felt disenchanted with the decision to continue the construction of the controversial Eldoret International Airport,[1] a project which they saw as primarily benefiting only rich Tugen and Keiyo businessmen (a veiled reference to Moi and Biwott) who wanted to use it to market their horticultural products.

At the forefront of the Nandi opposition within KANU were the party's Uasin Gishu district chairman, Wilson Kibor, and Kipruto Arap Kirwa, representing the Nandi Diaspora. They attracted massive political support from disenchanted Nandi economic and political elites as well as the youth. Particularly appreciated by their supporters was their courage in attempting publicly to articulate and advance the cause of the Nandi in order to prevent their erosion by the Tugen and Keiyo. Their political stature increased considerably as a result of what was seen as their "hardline" stand in promoting the Nandi struggle against marginalisation by both the president and his Tugen-Keiyo cabal. Not surprisingly, the challenge posed by Kibor and Kirwa was to attract angry attention at the headquarters of KANU. Kibor was suspended as branch chairman of KANU at the urging of Moi; in the subsequent election that was held to choose a new chairman, the Nandi rallied their forces to ensure Kibor was re-elected. The results of the elections were then annulled by the party headquarters and Kibor suspended from KANU. These actions, according to the Nandi, were clear pieces of evidence that the contest was not simply one between Kibor and his local rival, Lang'at, but between the Nandi and the Tugen-Keiyo groups.

The fact that the Tugen-Keiyo axis was unable to effect the defeat of Kibor in the district party elections ordered by KANU headquarters forced Moi to adopt new strategies for handling the challenge from the Nandi. This

---

[1] Opposition parties were against the construction of the airport because it did not have the approval of the parliament. The government proceeded with the project, but scaled it down in the face of concerted pressure from the opposition and donors.

was especially so as Kibor's suspension from KANU appeared to deepen resentment among Nandi elites who moved even closer to the KANU-B opposition within the ruling party. Cherangani MP, Kipruto Arap Kirwa, rose to the challenge of becoming the principal representative of Nandi concerns, publicly pointing out that a systematic political marginalisation of the Nandi, complemented by a campaign of intimidation carried out by the provincial administration, was being implemented by the ruling party. Indeed, Kirwa went so far as to suggest that Moi was personally involved in the design of schemes aimed at creating economic and political problems for the Nandi. This attempt to undermine the Nandi went back, according to Kirwa, to Moi's days as Kenya's Vice-President. He also publicly stated that Moi seemed to have a great deal of difficulty transcending his "majority phobia" syndrome, instinctively opting to pursue policies aimed at ensuring that any community that was numerically stronger than his own was "cut down to size". For the Nandi, matters were not helped by the fact that Moi's main Kalenjin rival, the late Seroney, was a Nandi.[1]

Kirwa received effusive support from several Nandi politicians and the youth. KANU officials loyal to the Moi-Biwott faction within the party attempted to organise demonstrations against him and Kibor in Uasin Gishu but soon realised that the people they were able to rally were the supporters of the two leading Nandi activists. On one occasion, KANU youth leaders openly declared their support for Kirwa and called on the party leadership to respond to the variety of issues he had raised in criticism of Moi and party managers. Several Nandi youths also confessed to having been "used" as fighters in the land clashes; in addition, they made public pledges never to allow themselves to be "misused" again by senior politicians.

It is clear that intra-Kalenjin rivalry in Uasin Gishu was related to two important events: the dynamics of the land clashes in the Rift Valley and the lop-sided distribution of *Nyayo* benefits among the different Kalenjin groups. The Nandi were concerned that they had been "used" to fight other ethnic groups so as to pave the way for Tugen-Keiyo domination in the district. This was made all the more irritating to them by the fact they felt that they had received few benefits from the Moi presidency, unlike the Tugen and Keiyo who were very close to the centre of power in Nairobi. As the 1990s progressed, the Nandi elite began to distance themselves from the politically powerful Keiyo and Tugen and, in doing so, moved closer to the forces of opposition to the Moi-Biwott axis within KANU. Thus it was that the land clashes became a source of threat to the Kalenjin coalition in KANU. While the Nandi elite drifted towards KANU-B, the Tugen-Keiyo group was the core of Kanu-A loyalists. So deep were the suspicions between the two groups that membership recruitment meetings in the district were halted for fear of factional problems.

---

[1] See the *Daily Nation*, 29 March, 1996 and *Finance*, May 1996.

Nyambene: Personality Feud in Place of Party Politics

Nyambene District was carved out of Meru in 1993 and comprised three parliamentary constituencies: Tigania, Igembe, and Ntonyiri. The parliamentary units had boundaries corresponding to those of the administrative units (with similar names) but with the creation of the district, the number of divisions, locations and sub-locations was increased considerably. Respondents interviewed in the area generally viewed the creation of Nyambene district as a political reward to the Meru community for their support to Moi in the 1992 elections despite the influence that the DP and Kibaki enjoyed in Meru. Several of those interviewed noted that the decision to create Nyambene district had already been made as part of a bargain between Moi and Meru elites when the latter held a meeting with him a few months before the 1992 elections. As part of the bargain, the Meru elite disavowed their relationship with the Kikuyu and GEMA. They specifically underlined that the Meru benefited the least from the Kenyatta state, and, therefore, that the community was happy to identify with Moi and KANU. Moi appreciated their concerns and promised to reward them with a district if they voted for him and KANU.[1]

In the 1992 elections, KANU won the Igembe, Imenti Central and Tharaka parliamentary seats although the DP's influence was also widespread as indicated by the amount of votes the party got in the civic and the presidential polling. Furthermore, although KANU candidates won the three seats mentioned earlier, Moi got less votes than the number received by his party's parliamentary candidates, except in Igembe. This has been interpreted as suggesting that what the electorate was concerned with was personalities and not party politics.[2] All the same, the fact that KANU was able to establish a footing in an area that was widely seen as part of the DP heartland encouraged him to live up to his promise of rewarding the Meru with a district. Arguably, therefore, Nyambene was also created as part of a bigger project to weaken the GEMA coalition by providing a framework for the construction of a distinct Meru identity.

The Nyambene project was, however, to have negative consequences for local politics in Meru in the sense that it unleashed an intense and unhealthy socio-political rivalry between the Igembe and the Tigania, the two dominant sub-ethnic groups in the area. That bitter rivalry, in turn, eroded the social bases of party politics. Political competition in the area came to be defined more by narrow intra-community rivalry and personality conflicts than by party identities and policy issues. The Igembe (including Ntonyiri)

[1] Personal communication with a local politician who attended the meeting.

[2] Moi had fewer votes than the KANU parliamentary candidates in these constituencies. For instance, in Tharaka, Moi had 4,873 compared to Kagwima, the KANU parliamentary candidate, who polled 10,065 votes. In Tigania, Karauri got 10,553 votes compared to the 8,297 received by Moi. For further details, see the *Weekly Review*, 6 January, 1993.

were backed in their rivalry with the Tigania by a powerful minister of state in the Office of the President, Jackson Kalweo, who recaptured the Igembe seat in 1992 after a long period in the political cold. Like several other associates of Charles Njonjo, Kalweo lost his seat to Joseph Muturia in the 1983 snap general elections because he had been named in parliament as Charles Njonjo's "political harbinger".

As to the Tigania, their cause was projected by a former assistant minister, Mathews Karauri, who lost his seat in 1992 to a DP candidate, Benjamin Ndubai. The rivalry between the Igembe and Tigania also carried elements of a competition for influence and dominance between Kalweo and Karauri, with the former striving hard to re-establish himself as a major force to be reckoned with after the setback he suffered during his years in the political wilderness. The defeat which Karauri and another of his rivals, Muturia, suffered provided Kalweo with the opportunity he thought he needed to establish a commanding dominance in the district. He saw the party elections that were to be held for the new district as providing the framework for the concretisation of his plans for dominance. Kalweo's insistence that KANU headquarters should schedule party elections in the district irritated Karauri and Muturia who were already acting branch chairman and secretary respectively because they were officials of the Meru branch of the party before the establishment of Nyambene as a separate district. The two officials, therefore, mobilised their own forces with a view to checking Kalweo's ambitions to achieve dominance. With the battle lines drawn, the two rival groups began to trade accusations about alleged plans to commit electoral fraud. The tensions that built up compelled the KANU headquarters to postpone the elections indefinitely. Rifts emerged and factionalism spilt over.

By the time KANU took the decision to postpone the party elections, Nyambene had become bitterly divided between the Igembe (represented by Kalweo) and the Tigania (by Karauri). Support was mobilised on the grounds that what was at stake was the exercise of control over the politics and economic resources of the new district. The price of victory would not only be the domination of the local party structure but also the other levers of power and influence in the area. The debate was not, therefore, one about how the new district might be developed but about which sub-ethnic group and personalities would emerge as power brokers. Being the minister in charge of provincial administration and internal security, Kalweo was obviously in some position of strength vis-à-vis his opponents and he had, as part of his bid for dominance, established a patronage network at the head of which he sat dispensing money, employment opportunities in the civil service, and other largesse to his supporters who included not-so-well-educated but rich businessmen, chiefs, and local civil servants. So strong were the benefits of being associated with Kalweo that some members of the rival faction were tempted to move closer to him.

Although the Karauri-Muturia group did not have anything like the largesse which the Kalweo faction had available to it, many in the Tigania community still felt an affinity to it because it was seen as being engaged in a fight to prevent their domination by the Igembe. For many in the Tigania community, the Karauri-Kalweo "fight" was seen as a struggle between the Igembe and the Tigania. This interpretation of the struggle made it relatively easy for those from the Igembe group who were in the Karauri-Muturia faction to withdraw their membership and line up behind Kalweo. They argued that Muturia (an Igembe) was being used by Karauri to pave the way for the domination of the Tigania. These sub-ethnic sentiments considerably weakened Muturia's support base among the Igembe and polarised the district even more.

In the meantime, even as the conflicts in the local KANU branch were raging, opposition parties also found themselves increasingly losing support among the residents of the area. Although the DP once enjoyed a huge advantage in the district, its popularity subsided considerably after 1992 and several of its councillors decamped to KANU. Several of the people whom we interviewed pointed out that the party began to lose support in the area because of the creation of a separate Nyambene district which meant "independence" from the Imenti people who had dominated the Tigania and Igembe for a long time. Others emphasised that DP activists and MPs went "under" after the 1992 elections.[1]

KANU too had added pressure to the opposition by dispensing patronage to those areas that voted for it in the 1992 elections. For instance, the Igembe were rewarded with the appointment of Kalweo as a cabinet minister; throughout the Kenyatta years, the only ministerial appointments from the area always went to the Imenti. Kalweo buttressed KANU's use of patronage by employing his influence to ensure that various infrastructural facilities in Igembe areas were improved considerably. Indeed, it was evidence of the patronage which association with KANU yielded that lured several opposition councillors to defect to KANU. Once they defected, they were aided by the ruling party and Kalweo with the financial and other resources which they needed for regaining their seats.

If the DP was widely supported in 1992 in the area that later became Nyambene district, it was because the people wanted to vote for a party led by a former Vice-President and Minister for Finance—Mwai Kibaki—and whose founder-members were the Kikuyu, cultural cousins of the Meru. The view was, however, widespread at the time we visited the district that those reasons were no longer going to be valid as a basis for support to the party. Although, in the run up to 1992, people genuinely wanted change and to be rid of Moi and KANU, the fact that both emerged victorious soon created a

---

[1] Some of the people interviewed told us that the residents of the area were disenchanted with the failure of opposition politicians to organise development projects and with their "absence" in the area.

new environment which encouraged many to return to the ruling party in order to avoid personal and group reprisals from the government. Thus, opposition eventually came to be organised around the Karauri-Muturia faction in what some have referred to as the new "FORD-KANU" in the area to reflect the fact that the faction was mainly supported by excluded KANU elites keen to contain the influence of Kalweo and his entourage. But because of the intimidation which they suffered and general restrictions placed on their activities by the provincial administration, the opposition was only able to win one council seat—Thangatha in Tigania—after the defection of the DP councillor to KANU. The constituency where the election took place was in Karauri's stronghold and the fact that it was a FORD-Kenya (or "FORD-KANU") candidate who won the by-election with a landslide majority gave a pointer to the depth of Tigania resentment of Kalweo's efforts to dominate the local political terrain. The ruling party took its defeat badly and the government instigated the interdiction of a chief and an assistant chief for their inability to prevent KANU's loss to the opposition.

Interestingly, a majority of the former supporters of the DP rallied around the Kalweo faction after their defection to KANU. The Karauri group continued to draw most of its support from those forces who gave their backing to KANU in the 1992 elections but who were opposed to Kalweo before and during the 1992 elections. The factionalism that characterised local KANU politics in the area, therefore, had roots in the intra-KANU rivalries that pre-dated 1992. The same factions that competed for political power in the area during the heyday of single party rule were also the ones that came to compete for position and influence during the era of multiparty politics, this time mobilising sub-ethnic forces to back their cause.

Kilifi: Past in the Present and the Loss of the Market for Opposition

Kilifi, in the Coast Province, is inhabited by members of the Miji Kenda sub-ethnic group. The area also has a minority group of Kikuyu, Kamba, and Taita residents scattered in several parts of the district and involved in small-scale agricultural farming (the district has a low agrarian potential) and/or the provision of labour to the district's tourist economy. It is also worth noting that KADU's first president, Ronald Ngala, came from the district, a fact which had a significant influence on the organisation of politics in the area.

Two factors shaped the character of the 1992 elections in the district. One was the Ngala factor which inspired the local population to support KANU on the argument that KANU was led by friends of Ngala and, specifically, people with whom Ngala had formed KADU to advance the interests of the ethnic minorities of Kenya. Local KANU politicians tried to buttress this line of thinking by reiterating to the people of the area that the opposition was mainly made up of "up-country people" or "outsiders" (a euphemism for the Kikuyu) "who have been dominating and exploiting the Coast since the Kenyatta era".[1] The view was also widely held in the area that those in the opposition were not credible enough and, therefore, could not effectively market the opposition parties to a population dominated by an ethnic minority group that is politically conservative and averse to political change. The local KANU elite spared no effort to ensure that the growth of opposition parties in Kilifi was stunted.

The second factor which influenced the 1992 elections in Kilifi was the issue of land ownership. This factor contributed to the weakness of the opposition in the area. The early discovery of the district's high potential for tourism resulted in an increased exploitation of the coastline by national political elites acting through the local elite. The pattern which this politics of land grabbing took involved national elites, with the assistance of their local collaborators, identifying beach plots for allocation by the Ministry of Lands in Nairobi (sometimes with the consent of the president), obtaining the necessary allocation and/or development permits, and then selling the papers to Asian and European hoteliers. So sought after were the beachlands among KANU national leaders that the local elite tended to be overshadowed by the national elite. This increasingly became a source of discontent among the local political elite who did not have any control over this form of accumulation despite the fact that local government regulations and those of the District Development Committees (DDCs) required the allotees to also obtain local council approval. KANU responded to this simmering discontent by getting the government and the provincial administration to allocate land to the local elite and urging them to help persuade the *wanainchi* that their problems would be looked into. Thus it was that the local political elite came to be sandwiched between pressures from below (as evidenced by the demands of the landless poor) and pressures from above (as represented by the demands of the national elite operating from/through Nairobi).

How then did it happen that in spite of the fact that the national political elite, especially those operating within KANU, had denied the majority of the local residents of Kilifi access to the most prized land and settlement in the area, a significant proportion of the populace still voted KANU? The interviews which we conducted in Kilifi suggest that among the Miji Kenda who constitute the majority of the population of the area, the predominant perception was that it was the "up country" people (that is, the Kikuyu) who bought the bulk of the arable land in the area during the Kenyatta years and after; the "up country" people, now openly in opposition after the re-intro-

---

[1] Interview conducted on 5 January, 1996 with two "immigrant" respondents (a businessman and a school teacher) in Kilifi. Both stressed that the ordinary people are not against the "up-country" people since inter-marriages were quite common among them. They emphasised that it was the politicians who incited the Giriama against the "up-country" residents.

duction of multiparty politics, were also seen as dominating the local tourist economy. The local political elite, in responding to pressures from their constituents, played on this prevalent perception to blame landlessness on "outsiders". This is how the view came to be widespread among the Miji Kenda that their land problems were the fault of unscrupulous "up-country" groups and not of their local elites who continued to be seen as struggling to advance/protect the interests of the community.

It was against the background described above that ethnic clashes surfaced in Kilifi District in May 1994, about a year and half after the 1992 multiparty elections. The clashes developed immediately after a local politician had held a series of meetings urging the Miji Kenda to be wary of "outsiders" dominating their economic activities and acquiring their beach plots. KANU politicians also played the local population against the provincial administration by targeting messages at the Miji Kenda to the effect that the District Commissioners (DCs) and District Officers (DOs) had failed to take care of their interests in the coastline; some of the messages went so far as to suggest that it was appropriate for the Miji Kenda to take steps to evict the "up-country" people so as to sensitise the government to the local land question. Thereafter, "up-country" people living in the Mtondia settlement scheme and doing business in Kilifi town had their houses torched in what was clearly a well-coordinated bid to evict them from the area. The clashes also seemed to increase the popularity of KANU among the Miji Kenda; that appeared to have been the intention of the KANU partisans who did all they could to inflame the local passions that generated the conflicts.

CONCLUSION: THE WITHERING OF PARTY POLITICS?

The struggle for the decolonization of Kenya led to the formation of political parties around which a variety of interests aggregated. The clash of elite and popular demands occasioned the cracks that occurred first in the nationalist movement and later in the political parties. Ethnic identities increasingly became the bases for mobilising political support by the two dominant, rival parties, namely, KADU and KANU, that occupied the Kenyan political space. The polarisation that resulted has continued to inform and animate Kenya's political situation to date. The discussion in this chapter has shown that Kenya's political history is replete with attempts by both the state and the political elite to hijack, co-opt or polarise the struggles of the popular forces in society. Thus, what initially begins as a popular initiative is immediately hijacked by "forces from above" who promptly attempt to place their class and ethnic imprint on it. It is on account of this development that the potential of popular groups to undermine authoritarianism in Kenya has suffered repeated reversals.

While the return to political pluralism in Kenya represented a concrete effort at the expansion of the local space for action, the oppositional forces who have sought to play within the space have enjoyed only a limited capacity to check the state and, in so doing, insulate the citizenry from the political excesses of the state itself. The political parties that were formed as part of the return to multiparty politics have had their potential punctured by contradictions internal to their various organisations: elite factionalism and leadership rivalry spiced with ethnic and regional consideration have, in the main, been the factors responsible for their decline and for their inability to serve as credible bearers of popular demands. The weaknesses of the opposition were reinforced by the selective administration of governmental patronage by the ruling party. This entailed the allocation of projects and resources to those areas of the country that voted for KANU and the penalisation of opposition strongholds through the denial/withdrawal of governmental patronage.

The pressure on the opposition which the policy of selectively distributing state patronage implied was exacerbated by the environment of economic crisis and structural adjustment in which Kenya has been steeped for some time. Economic decline and structural adjustment appeared to weaken the capacity of individuals and communities to resist the pressures exerted on them by KANU through the discriminatory disbursement of economic benefits. As Kenya prepared for the next round of general elections in 1997, the opposition appeared to be in a state of complete disarray, causing widespread disillusionment among ordinary Kenyans as they wondered if they would not have to take on the task themselves of pressurising KANU and the government to implement the kinds of far-reaching reforms that would enable democracy to have a greater meaning to their daily lives. As opposition party politics went into disarray, opinion among civil society activists increasingly moved in the direction of campaigns for the convening of a constitutional forum to debate and reform the legal-political foundations of the post-colonial Kenyan state. As with the campaign for the return to multiparty politics, the leadership position in this campaign is being taken mainly by civil society activists.

REFERENCES

Azarya, V., 1988, "Re-ordering State-Society Relationships: Incorporation and Disengagement", in N. Chazan and D. Rothchild (eds.), *The Precarious Balance: State Society in Africa*, Boulder: Westview Press.
Bates, R., 1989, *Beyond the Miracle of the Markets: The Politics of Agrarian Change in Kenya*. Cambridge: Cambridge University Press.
Bayart, J., 1986, "Civil Society in Africa", in P. Chabal (ed.), *Political Domination in Africa*. Cambridge: Cambridge University Press.
Berman, B. and J. Lonsdale, 1992, *Unhappy Valley: Conflict in Kenya and Africa*. London: James Currey.
Bratton, M., 1994, "Civil Society and Political Transition in Africa", in J. Harbeson, D. Rothchild, and N. Chazan (eds.), *Civil Society and the State in Africa*. Boulder, Co: Lynne Rienner.

Bratton, M. and N. van de Walle, 1994, "Neo-Patrimonial Regimes and Political Transition in Africa", *World Politics*, pp. 453–489.

Chazan, N., R. Mortimer, J. Ravenhill, and D. Rothchild, 1988, *Politics and Society in Contemporary Africa*. Boulder, Co.: Lynne Rienner Publishers.

Chege, M., 1994, "The Return of Multiparty Politics", in J.D. Barkan (ed.), *Beyond Capitalism vs. Socialism in Kenya and Tanzania*. Nairobi: East African Educational Publishers.

Gertzel, C., 1970, *The Politics of Independent Kenya, 1963–1968*. Nairobi: East African Publishing House.

Gertzel, C., J. Goldschmidt and D. Rothchild, 1972, *Government and Politics in Kenya*. Nairobi: East African Publishing House.

Hydén, G. and M. Bratton, 1992, *Governance and Politics in Africa*. Boulder, Lynne Rienner Publishers.

Jackson, R. and C. Rosberg, 1982, *Personal Rule in Black Africa*. Los Angeles: University of California Press.

Kanogo, T., 1987, *Squatters and Roots of Mau Mau, 1905–1963*. Nairobi: Heinemann.

Kanyinga, K., 1995, "The Changing Development Space in Kenya: Socio-Political Change and Voluntary Development Activities", in P. Gibbon (ed.), *Markets, Civil Society, and Democracy in Kenya*. Uppsala: Nordiska Afrikainstitutet.

Kanyinga, K., 1996, *Struggles of Access to Land: The Land Question, Accumulation, and Changing Politics in Kenya*. Working Paper No. 504. Nairobi: IDS, Univ. of Nairobi.

Maloba, W.O., 1993, *Mau Mau and Kenya: An Analysis of a Peasant Revolt*. Indianapolis: Indiana University Press.

Mamdani, M., E. Wamba-dia-Wamba and T. Mkandawire, 1988, *Social Movements, Social Transformation and the Struggle for Democracy*. CODESRIA Working Paper No. 1. Dakar.

Mamdani, M., 1990, "State and Civil Society in Contemporary Africa: Reconceptualizing the Birth of State Nationalism and the Defeat of Popular Movements", *Africa Development*, Vol. XV, Nos. 3 and 4.

Mkandawire, T., 1988, "Comments on Democracy and Political Instability", *Africa Development*, Vol. XIII, No. 3.

Neocosmos, M., 1993, *The Agrarian Question in Southern Africa and Accumulation from Below: Economics and Politics in the Struggle for Democracy*. Research Report No. 93. Uppsala: Nordiska Afrikainstitutet.

Ngunyi, M. and K Gathiaka, 1993, "State-Civil Institutions Relations in Kenya in the 80s", in P. Gibbon (ed.), *Social Change and Economic Reform in Africa*. Uppsala: Nordiska Afrikainstitutet.

Nyong'o, P.A. (ed.), 1987, *Popular Struggles for Democracy in Africa*. London: Zed Books.

Nyong'o, P.A, 1988, "A Rejoinder to the Comments on Democracy and Political Instability", *Africa Development*, Vol. XIII, No. 3.

Nyong'o, P.A., 1989, "State and Society in Kenya: The Disintegration of the Nationalist Coalitions and the Rise of Presidential Authoritarianism, 1963–78", *African Affairs*, No. 351, April.

Sandbrook, R., 1985, *The Politics of Africa's Economic Stagnation*. Cambridge: Cambridge University Press.

Shivji, I.G., 1992, *Fight My Beloved Continent: New Democracy in Africa*. Harare: SAPES Trust.

Throup, D., 1987, "The Construction and Destruction of the Kenyatta State", in M. Swatzberg (ed.), *The Political Economy of Kenya*. New York: Praeger.

Wasserman, G., 1976, *Politics of Decolonization: Kenyan Europeans and the Land Issue, 1960–1965*.Cambridge: Cambridge University Press.

Chapter 3

Opposition Politics in Zimbabwe: The Struggle within the Struggle

Tandeka C. Nkiwane

INTRODUCTION

One of the more critical debates on the African continent in recent times surrounds the issue of the increasingly stalled multiparty agenda that the "third wave" of democratisation was supposed to have ushered in. The political optimism that accompanied the dawn of the post-Cold War era has yet to realise its full potential, and scholars are faced with the onerous task of analysing why nominal multipartyism has not translated into concrete democratic gains. Claude Ake set the stage for this debate by drawing attention to "the crude simplicity of multiparty elections ... whose relevance ... is problematic at best, and at worst prone to engender contradictions that tend to derail or trivialise democratisation in Africa" (Ake, 1996). The multiparty agenda of the late 1980s and early 1990s has, increasingly, been criticised for failing to address, in a sustainable and concrete way, deeper questions of democratic change and consolidation in Africa. There are, however, some scholars who have countered the growing concerns about the "emptiness" of multipartyism by asserting that the renewed interest shown in many African countries in pluralistic democracy is useful simply as an end in itself, as opposed to serving only as a means towards a desired end. As Guy Hermet so succinctly put it, "real democracy cannot exist without formal democracy" (Hermet, 1991), and, therefore, the dialogue concerning the formalistic components of what we understand by "democracy" is as important as anything else.

Although questions surrounding the entrenchment of civil liberties, the regulation of elections, and the freedom of the press have been the subjects of extensive analysis in the literature on transition politics, the problematique of the institutionalisation of political pluralism/multipartyism in contemporary Africa is, perhaps, the single most prominent issue in the current phase of the debate on democratisation on the continent. The experience of Zimbabwe, which gained independence on 18 April, 1980, has not been exempt from consideration in this debate. Indeed, it has been one of the focal points in the discussion concerning opposition politics and the prospects for (liberal) democracy in Africa. This is so particularly because Zimbabwe is often described as a *de facto* one-party state, although, paradoxically, it is also a functional (nominal) multiparty system. Therefore, the problems of and prospects for the development and sustenance of oppositional political activity in the African context are poignantly displayed in the political theatre of Zimbabwe. This chapter examines, in very broad terms, the experience of opposition politics in Zimbabwe. In undertaking this task, we focus, at one level, on the formally-established opposition political parties in the country. At another level, we attempt to relate to the implications, actual and potential, of the emergence of an "opposition" from within the ranks of the ruling party, ZANU(PF). In concluding the chapter, we pose a number of questions regarding post-Mugabe politics in Zimbabwe, with a view to exploring the potential for the birth of an opposition force that is capable of becoming a viable participant in the on-going struggle for the deepening of democracy in the country.

CONTEXTUALISING OPPOSITION POLITICS IN ZIMBABWE

New Opposition Parties and Conscientious Objectors

Although opposition political parties have always formally existed in Zimbabwe since the country attained its independence in 1980, it was only from about 1989 onwards, after the signing of the "Unity Accord" between the ruling Zimbabwean African National Union (ZANU-PF) and the Zimbabwe African People's Union (PF-ZAPU), that a set of new groupings emerged with the potential to seriously challenge the political monopoly of Robert Mugabe and his colleagues in the ruling party. Interestingly enough, these opposition parties were formed at a time when, deriving from the logic of the ZANU-ZAPU "Unity Accord", Mugabe and the ZANU hierarchy were openly contemplating making Zimbabwe a *de jure* one party state. In a sense, this was the next logical step that was open to them since the only really effective opponent they had until then, namely, ZAPU and its leader, Joshua Nkomo, had given up opposition and agreed to be dissolved and fused into ZANU.

ZAPU had grown increasingly weary of the prolonged and costly war in its stronghold of Matabeleland. The war pitched the militants and supporters of ZAPU against ZANU and the Zimbabwe army. The people, economy and politics of Matabeleland were to pay a huge price for the conflict; the pain associated with the war was heightened by the sheer brutality of the special North Korean-trained Fifth Brigade of the army that was deployed to "pacify" the area and "flush out" armed dissidents. It was against the background of the rising costs of the war that ZAPU decided, for all intents and purposes, to dissolve itself and "unite" with ZANU in government. For ZANU, the accord eliminated the thorniest source of opposition to its rule; the formal imposition of one-party rule would be a logical step in the totalisation of its domination of the country's politics.

Yet, at about the same time as ZANU was contemplating formalising one-party rule, a confluence of external and internal factors came into play to effectively undermine its plans and force the ruling party to maintain Zimbabwe as a formal multiparty political system. This confluence of events resulted in the emergence of a new set of opposition parties with a serious potential to challenge the hegemony of the ruling party. At the external level, the parties benefited from the push for multipartyism by the international community following the fall of the socialist regimes of Eastern Europe in the late 1980s. This external pressure, resulting from the demonstration effect of the events that were unfolding in Eastern Europe, was complemented by the decision of several donor governments and international financial institutions to promote (multiparty) political reforms in Africa under the broad theme of "good governance". The World Bank, for instance, declared in its 1989 report, *Sub-Saharan Africa: From Crisis to Sustainable Growth*, that "good governance" had become an area for legitimate concern in development circles. African governments, dependent as they were on donors, were compelled to at least take cognisance of these pressures and of the winds of change that were blowing across the world.

The pressures for political reform did not only emanate from outside. Internally, across Africa in general and in Zimbabwe in particular, local pressures for a more inclusive and participatory political system developed in the form of popular agitation for reform. In all the corners of the country, various components of civil society began a campaign for inclusion in the political process. Non-governmental organisations, advocacy groups, the university community, students, and a plethora of other groups and individuals began to demand accountability from the government. The tone and tempo of these demands increased during the course of the late 1980s as the promise of independence and black majority rule began to exhaust itself and a crisis of expectations started to take hold. By 1988, university students in their historic anti-corruption demonstration, dared to ask why the emperor had no clothes. The pressures created by the demonstration led to the formation of the Sandura Commission of Inquiry into the Distribution of Motor Vehicles, and the subsequent resignation of several prominent government ministers. By 1989, when the Zimbabwe Unity Movement (ZUM) was formed, the prolonged post-independence honeymoon between the government and the people was all but over. As the government became increasingly detached from popular aspirations, the people, for their part, demanded a more open and accountable form of governance that would enable them to impose their own democratic prescriptions on the ruling elite. The post-Cold War political parties which were formed in Zimbabwe were mostly headed by prominent political figures with a history dating back to the days of the liberation war.

In addition to the new political parties that emerged, the terrain of opposition politics in Zimbabwe was also to witness the growth of the phenomenon of "independents", that is, politicians who chose to navigate a path that does not involve formal affiliation to any of the political parties, although they constitute part of the broad opposition to the ruling party. These independent candidates are essentially conscientious objectors who were once active within the ranks of ZANU(PF) but who quit the party for one reason or the other. They have increasingly made in-roads in both local and national politics, aided no doubt by their decision to distance themselves from the ruling party. The phenomenon of independents is both reflective of the incapacity of ZANU(PF) to tolerate and sustain criticism within the party, and an indictment of the new opposition parties which largely failed to attract disaffected prominent members of ZANU(PF) into their fold. These independents, rightly or wrongly, have often been characterised as those who attempted to ensure that the ruling party lived up to its founding principles, and were marginalised or even expelled for this form of dissent.

National Liberation and Opposition Politics

Any analysis of the politics of opposition in Zimbabwe must necessarily begin with a review, however brief, of the war of liberation against white settler colonialism and racism. The experience of settler colonialism and the prolonged, bloody war of liberation that was fought by the black majority have weighed heavily on politics in post-colonial Zimbabwe and it is important to bear this in mind as it has had implications for the nature of, and scope for, oppositional activity. Moreover, it should be stated that it is not a mere accident that many of the personalities who were prominent during the liberation war have also been the people who have been dominant in the post-colonial political terrain whether as stalwarts or opponents of the ruling party. Indeed, as we shall see later, especially as disaffection grew within ZANU(PF), some of these figures were also to be the ones who emerged to form the leadership and membership core of several of the post-independence opposition parties and movements.

In 1961, after the banning of the Southern Rhodesia African National Congress (ANC) and the National Democratic Party (NDP) by the ruling White settler minority government, the Zimbabwe African People's Union (ZAPU) was formed, under the leadership of Joshua Nkomo, as the new umbrella organisation for articulation and promotion of the nationalist aspirations of the black majority. ZAPU's subsequent banning in 1962 led to the exile of the liberation movement to Zambia. In exile, ZAPU was wracked by internal conflicts which resulted in a split. This split was formalised in 1963 when Ndabaningi Sithole led a splinter faction which ultimately formed the Zimbabwe African National Union (ZANU), following differences over approach and the direction of the liberation struggle (Dabengwa, 1994). ZAPU and ZANU remained the two dominant movements pre-occupied with the liberation of the black majority and, until the signing of the Lancaster House constitution in 1979, carried out most of their political operations from their exile bases whilst launching military campaigns within the country.

Both ZAPU and ZANU went through periods of intense political discord driven by internal power struggles and factionalism. ZAPU's internal discord was associated with a number of political figures, including James Chikerema, and lasted from 1968 until 1972. While ZAPU was emerging from its internal conflicts which, in the 1970s, claimed the lives, through assassinations, of Jason Moyo and Nikita Mangena, ZANU plunged into factional in-fighting which led to the ousting of Ndabaningi Sithole from the movement's helm in 1975 and his replacement by Robert Mugabe. There were also the assassination of a number of prominent political figures from within the ranks of ZANU, including Herbert Chitepo and Josiah Tongogara who was killed after the signing of the Lancaster House settlement that paved the way for black majority rule (Dabengwa, 1994; Sithole, 1997). This inter- and intra-party factional fighting, characteristic of the liberation movements, was also symptomatic of a political culture of violence which, to this day, still pervades Zimbabwean politics. During the 1970s, ZANU and ZAPU, for a brief period between 1976 and 1979, formed a loose coalition known as the Patriotic Front (PF). It was also during the 1970s that the United African National Council (UANC) gained prominence within Southern Rhodesia, under the leadership of Abel Muzorewa.

THE 1979, 1980, AND 1985 ELECTIONS

Zimbabwe has held regular general elections at five yearly intervals since its independence in 1980, and this fact is significant in terms of formal process. All the elections have been contested by numerous political parties, although in the case of the earlier elections, two parties were predominant, these being ZANU(PF) and PF-ZAPU. The first one person/one vote elections were held in the short-lived Republic of Zimbabwe-Rhodesia in 1979. These elections are popularly known as the internal settlement elections, and did not include the two liberation movement parties. The main significant elements of the 1979 elections were the establishment of an Electoral Supervisory Commission (ESC) and the usage of proportional representation in determining the allocation of seats in the parliament (Sithole, 1986).

The Distribution of Parliamentary Seats

Following the signing of the Lancaster House constitution in 1979, general elections including ZANU(PF) and PF-ZAPU were scheduled for 27–29 March, 1980. The House of Assembly, comprised of 100 seats, had 20 of these seats reserved constitutionally for 10 years for whites, all won by the Rhodesian Front (RF). These elections also used the proportional representation system, and of the remaining 80 seats, ZANU(PF) won 57, PF-ZAPU 20, and UANC 3. The 1985 elections, although following a broadly similar pattern in terms of delivering a ZANU(PF) victory, were also significantly different. Unlike the 1979 and 1980 elections, the 1985 exercise was based on the plurality, first-past-the-post electoral system under single member districts (SMD). This election secured the victory of ZANU(PF) by 64 seats, as compared to 15 seats for PF-ZAPU, and 1 for ZANU (Sithole).

From the point of view of our concern in this chapter, the first set of elections held in Zimbabwe were instructive in several respects. First, the elections clearly established the predominance of ZANU(PF) as the political party of choice for most Zimbabweans. Masipula Sithole and others have argued, with some justification, that it is no coincidence that the proportion of the popular vote accrued by ZANU(PF) corresponded neatly to Zimbabwe's ethnic composition. ZANU(PF) was victorious in the areas of Zimbabwe predominantly populated by the Shona ethnic group, which comprises approximately 80 per cent of the population. Similarly, PF-ZAPU was victorious in areas predominantly populated by the Ndebele ethnic group, which comprises approximately 20 per cent of the population (Sithole, 1986).

Second, as Giovanni Sartori has argued, electoral systems are "the most specific manipulative instrument of politics" (Sartori, 1968) and the switch from the proportional representation system to the plurality, first-past-the-post system had a significant, adverse impact on the possibility for the opposition to increase its share of the parliamentary seats available. There is a broad consensus in the literature on electoral systems that the proportional representation system yields greater proportionality and minority representation, whereas the plurality system promotes both two-party systems and one-party executives. In adopting a majoritarian (plurality) system over a consensus (proportional representation) system, the Zimbabwe government limited the potential for opposition gains in terms of parliamentary seats.

Third, the elections were characterised by patterns of violence towards the opposition which led to several fatalities, particularly in the larger urban centres. The level of violence, although not high enough to bring the total validity of the elections into question, clearly entrenched a culture involving the use of force, in particular between ZANU(PF) and PF-ZAPU, in the political process. The worst incidences of violence occurred in Matabeleland. As we pointed out earlier, low intensity warfare was declared in the area with the knowledge that it was also the main PF-ZAPU stronghold in the country. The execution of this warfare involved the use of the machinery of the state, including the army and a specially-trained unit known as the Fifth Brigade, in a determined effort to crush the social basis of political opposition to the government from that part of the country. This violence, most recently documented in a report by the Catholic Commission for Justice and Peace and the Legal Resources Foundation entitled *Breaking the Silence, Building True Peace: A Report on the Disturbances in Matabeleland and the Midlands 1980–1988,*[1] revealed a plethora of human rights abuses, including well over 3000 extra-judicial killings. The violence was only arrested subsequent to the signing, on 22 December, 1987, of the "Unity Accord" between ZANU(PF) and PF-ZAPU, an accord which resulted in the establishment of a united ZANU(PF).

Fourth, the extremely high voter turnout in the early elections confirmed the existence in Zimbabwe of a politicised and mobilised electorate, which, however, various opposition parties failed or were unable to capitalise on. Although nine political parties contested the 1980 general elections, for example, it was only ZANU(PF) and PF-ZAPU which made any significant impact on the electorate, with voter turnout estimated at over 94 per cent of those eligible to participate.

THE EMERGENCE OF A POST-INDEPENDENCE OPPOSITION: THE ONE-PARTY STATE DEBATE AND THE ZUM RESPONSE

As we noted earlier, following the signing of the "Unity Accord" of 1987 and the alteration of the constitution in order to form an executive presidency, the united ZANU(PF) clearly enunciated a policy for the establishment of a one-party state in Zimbabwe. This policy objective, arguably, was the proverbial straw which broke the camel's back, in terms of the emergence of a voice of dissent from within the ranks of ZANU(PF). While the world appeared to be moving away from the one-party state concept in the late 1980s, the apparatniks of the post "Unity Accord" ZANU(PF) felt that Zimbabwe could balk the trend and provide a local fertile ground for the consolidation of a single party system. They were grossly mistaken.

ZANU(PF) members of parliament such as Edgar Tekere, Byron Hove, and Sydney Malunga who were elected in 1985, began to lend their voices to those of what was left of the opposition and the resurgent forces of civil society in criticism of the proposals from the ruling party for the establishment of a *de jure* one-party state in Zimbabwe (Sachikonye, 1991). The views of these ZANU(PF) members of parliament was in direct contrast to the offi-

---

[1] This report was published in March 1997 and after a period of controversy over its availability to the public, it was published by the *Mail and Guardian* on the Internet in May 1997.

cially stated position of their party which had also been backed publicly by President Mugabe, among other senior state and party officials. This open vocalisation of opposition to the one-party state led to the expulsion of Tekere from ZANU(PF) and his subsequent decision to form Zimbabwe's first post-independence opposition party, the Zimbabwe Unity Movement (ZUM), in 1989.

As has already been mentioned, although opposition parties were in existence throughout the 1980s, their constituencies and credibility were severely limited. The UANC, under the leadership of Muzorewa, for example, was perpetually hamstrung by the fact that Muzorewa was the Prime Minister of the unrecognised Zimbabwe-Rhodesia and, in the eyes of most Zimbabweans, he was seen as being little more than a puppet of the white minority regime of Ian Smith. ZANU (Sithole) faced broadly similar criticisms as the UANC for its association with Zimbabwe-Rhodesia; its already bad case was not helped by the self-imposed exile of its leader, Ndabaningi Sithole, who spent most of the 1980s in the United States.

ZUM, when it was established, therefore, filled a major gap in Zimbabwean politics, and it aspired to a national agenda, as opposed to the particularistic constituencies which many of the smaller political parties represented/appealed to. ZUM was also assisted by the fact that its leader had strong and credible credentials as a "revolutionary", being well-respected as a former Secretary-General of ZANU(PF) in exile. Indeed, with Tekere at its head, the issue of ZUM's credibility, so crucial in the Zimbabwean political environment, was immediately rendered a non-issue. ZANU(PF) itself realised the potential damage which Tekere and ZUM could do to its hold on power; its concerns were heightened by the sheer enormity of popular support which was expressed for the new party and its leader. Incapable of simply dismissing Tekere and ZUM, ZANU(PF) was forced to address the challenge which its formation posed as something that was representative of discontent from a number of quarters both within and outside the ruling party.

The 1990 general elections were significant in two senses. First, the provision for 20 reserved white seats was removed from the constitution, and, therefore, an expanded 120 seat parliament with no racial barriers was entrenched. Second, this was the first election in which a post-independence political party, namely, ZUM, contested against ZANU(PF) in most constituencies. ZUM fielded candidates in 107 of the 120 constituencies in the March 28–30, 1990 general elections, posing the most formidable challenge to the ruling party emanating from within. Although ZUM only managed to win two parliamentary seats (but a significant 23 per cent of the popular vote), and approximately 22 per cent of the popular vote in the separate presidential elections, its impact nationally laid the groundwork for the emergence of new opposition voices, and, in particular, presented ZANU(PF) "insiders" who were unhappy with the ruling party with the possibility of an alternative political route or platform. Jonathan Moyo notes as well that had the 1990 elections been held under a proportional representation system, the opposition could have won at least 23 parliamentary seats (Moyo, 1992).

In its 23-page electoral manifesto entitled *Towards a Democratic Zimbabwe*, ZUM clearly enunciated a policy primarily opposed to the establishment of a one-party state and for a transition towards a more accountable system of governance (ZUM, 1989). These policies provided a national rallying point at a time of immense disaffection among Zimbabwean voters. The establishment of ZUM not only opened up the political space for the emergence of several other political parties with differing agendas and constituencies, it also reinvigorated pre-existing parties like those of Sithole and Muzorewa that, hitherto, had appeared for all intents and purposes to be moribund.

MULTIPARTY COMPETITION FOR THE ZIMBABWEAN POLITICAL SPACE

Many opposition political parties exist in Zimbabwe, with the vast majority of these appearing and disappearing around the period of general elections. The most prominent of the opposition parties are:

i) United African National Council (UANC)/ United Parties (UP)

The UANC was formed in 1971 under the leadership of Abel Muzorewa, and continues to function, although under the larger umbrella of the United Parties (UP). The UANC/UP's political impact was at its peak in 1980 when it managed to win three parliamentary seats. Since then, its impact has been negligible.

The UP has drawn most of its support from the ranks of the United Methodist Church, of which Muzorewa is Bishop, as well as from those who subscribe to the Bishop's personal political agenda. Indeed, like most political parties in Zimbabwe, both opposition and ruling, the highly personalised character of the party in relation to its leadership is a function of both its history and the kind of political culture which the elite have tried to promote in order to ensure their grip on the organisations which they lead. Muzorewa opted to contest the presidential elections of March 16–17, 1996, but then dramatically decided to pull out of the race just hours before voting was due to start. The UP had attempted to have the elections postponed until the Supreme Court could make a ruling on whether sections of the Electoral Act and Political Parties (Finance) Act were constitutional. After the failure of the application, the UP pulled out of the race, but the Registrar General's office insisted that Muzorewa's name should remain on the ballot because he had missed the 21-day deadline for declared candidates to withdraw from the race. The votes cast under these circumstances gave

Muzorewa approximately 4.8 per cent of the popular vote, in second place behind Mugabe.[1]

ii) Zimbabwe African National Union (Ndonga)

ZANU (Ndonga), led by Ndabaningi Sithole, a reverend and academic, is, as we noted earlier, essentially an off-shoot of the intra-ZANU factional fighting which occurred during the 1970s. ZANU (Ndonga) was, as of 1996, the only opposition party with parliamentary seats, the two seats it held being from Chipinge, the home area of Sithole and his ethnic group, the Ndau (a sub-group of the Shona). The formidable presence and strength of ZANU (Ndonga) and its leadership in Chipinge has led political observers to describe the area as a "one-party state" in and of itself; it is the only area in Zimbabwe where ZANU(PF) has been incapable of penetrating with a view to dislodging the opposition. This was particularly so after the return of Sithole from self-imposed exile in the United States in December 1992. Sithole was the third contestant in the 1996 presidential elections, and although he also pulled out of the race approximately two weeks before the election, he still received 2.4 per cent of the popular vote.[2]

The strength of ZANU (Ndonga) locally has been its Achilles heel nationally, with the party unable to make any significant inroads in other constituencies outside Chipinge. Perception is often at least as important as reality in politics, and although Sithole, for example, unlike both Mugabe and Muzorewa, is perfectly bilingual and was able to campaign nationally in Shona and Ndebele, the two dominant languages among the black majority, the perception that ZANU (Ndonga) is representative of a specific sub-ethnic group and a narrow geographical area has led to the localisation of its political impact.

Additionally, ZANU (Ndonga)'s policies have not been clearly enunciated and differentiated from those of other parties, including the ruling party. It campaigned on a platform promoting free enterprise but did not elaborate upon the mechanisms and modalities to be utilised for the realisation of its vision of a *laissez-fairist* Zimbabwe. ZANU (Ndonga) also campaigned on the controversial issue of land redistribution. The Zimbabwe version of "40 acres and a mule" was enunciated by the party when it advocated that every Zimbabwean family should have 15 acres of land and some start-up cash.[3] These policies, designed to win the hearts and minds of the populace, only served to provoke more questions than the leadership of the party was prepared or able to answer.

---

[1] See "Mugabe Declared Winner" in *The Herald* (Harare), March 20, 1996, for further details about the electoral results.

[2] See "Mugabe Declared Winner" in *The Herald* (Harare), March 20, 1996. Again, the 21-day deadline was used to keep Sithole on the ballot.

[3] See "Sithole on Zimbabwe" in *The Village Voice*, April 1992.

iii) The Democratic Party (DP)

After the 1990 general elections, ZUM as a political party began to factional-ise as it failed to consolidate its popularity, particularly in the larger urban centres of Zimbabwe. One of the factions, led by Emmanuel Magoche, a medical doctor, seceded and formed the Democratic Party of Zimbabwe (DP) in 1991. This development was almost inevitable, for ZUM was formed on the basis of a very strong dose of Tekere's personal convictions which, sooner or later, was bound to create problems. At the time of the founding of ZUM, Tekere had stated:

> I am very scared here in Zimbabwe with the trend of things, and this is why I am very outspoken these days. And I say, and I am repeating it, that in Zimbabwe today, democracy is in the intensive care unit.[1]

Once relations started to sour within ZUM, Tekere's critics began to question his style, conviction and apparent personalisation of the party. Indeed, the DP's inaugural document described him as "self-appointed" and ZUM's manifesto as being "loaded with democratic niceties that later proved too ambitious and too sophisticated for its rogue leader to understand" (Democratic Party, 1991).

The Democratic Party, in terms of process, appears to be one of the better organised opposition political parties. The party frequently distributes information pamphlets and documents to the public and holds internal meetings and elections with seeming regularity. The problem with the DP, though, is its target constituency. Much of the party's aims and objectives are designed to appeal to the intelligentsia, and the urban-based middle-class, a social category which economic structural adjustment is, in practice, rendering on the verge of extinction. Coupled with the objective reality that the majority of Zimbabwe's population lives in the rural areas, the mobilisation strategy of the DP has clearly been misplaced, and it is not surprising that the DP has yet to produce a parliamentarian or even one local government official. The DP also appears to be lacking in original and innovative policies which could touch the populace as a whole.

iv) Front/Movement for Popular Democracy (FPD or MPD)

The FPD (or MPD), founded in 1993 by the academic, Austin Chakaodza, has suffered the same fate as the DP, in terms of its target constituency, and the "high level" approach which it adopts to politics. Perhaps the FPD's only unique contribution to the political debate in Zimbabwe was its clearly enunciated stance in opposition to the World Bank/International Monetary Fund (IMF) Economic Structural Adjustment Programme (ESAP) for the

---

[1] Excerpt from an interview with Edgar Tekere by the author, August 11, 1988, just prior to his expulsion from ZANU(PF), and reproduced as an appendix to Nkiwane, 1990.

country. The FPD, in its opposition to structural adjustment, took the bold position of questioning the rationale for the programme and the systematic denial by the state and the international financial institutions of opportunities for the articulation of local alternative reform strategies. The party also poured scorn on claims made by the ruling party on the "successes" derived from the programme.

Much of the FPD's platform, specifically designed in anticipation of the 1995 general elections, addressed economic questions and concerns, in addition to the issue of the democratisation of the political system (MPD, 1993). But the party failed to translate most of the legitimate issues of concern which it raised into something tangible and concrete that could appeal to the general population. We recall the now famous tenet that people cannot eat democracy, and what the FPD did not lack in ideas, it lacked in realism. In this sense, its fate was similar to that of the Democratic Party. Unlike the DP, though, the FPD appeared to be lacking in the organisational and public relations skills that are so necessary for a sustainable political programme.

v) Forum Party of Zimbabwe (Forum)

Subsequent to the splintering of ZUM, the second political party with the potential for a national impact was the Forum Party of Zimbabwe, formed in 1993 and led by Enoch Dumbutshena, former Chief Justice of the Supreme Court. Forum was the product of a merger between the Forum for Democratic Reform (Trust), of which he was patron, and the Open Forum, formed a year earlier in 1992. The party was designed to pose a challenge to ZANU(PF) in the 1995 general elections. At the time it emerged, it was viewed by political analysts as a serious and credible threat to ZANU(PF), and like ZUM before it, managed to group together a core of committed and well-known figures, including Justice Washington Sansole, who is currently Forum's Acting President. Indeed, much of its core support came from high-level ZUM defections, including Gweru businessman Patrick Kombayi. Dumbutshena, Forum's very reluctant leader, became an attractive enigma for the Zimbabwean public: a well-respected former Chief Justice who, after 13 years of *de facto* one-party rule by ZANU(PF), offered the people the prospect of a change in the leadership of the country.

Forum, as a political party, enjoyed a broad-based appeal both for what it represented and who its leader was. Instead of a manifesto, the party's launch in Zimbabwe's second largest city of Bulawayo was accompanied by a set of "policy papers". Forum's main economic policy focused on reduced government spending, as well as land redistribution, and the elimination of government monopolies in a variety of areas (Forum Party of Zimbabwe, 1993). It was also the only political party with a clearly enunciated policy on gender equality. Its broad appeal enabled it to attract support from both the white and black communities within both its leadership and among the rank and file membership, and it was, perhaps, this factor, more than any other, which led both to in-fighting and the party's very rapid loss of popularity and credibility in the period prior to the general elections of 1995. ZANU(PF) as well as other opposition parties accused Forum of having "sold out", and the impression that was created that the party was a bearer of white interests quickly led to the emergence of internal discord. Shortly before the April 8–10, 1995 general elections, Forum split into two parties, with the splinter faction calling itself the Forum Party for Democracy.

Severely weakened, Forum was only able to present candidates in 27 constituencies for the 1995 elections. Not surprisingly, it did not win a single parliamentary seat. The party received approximately only 5.9 per cent of the popular vote. It decided to boycott the 1996 presidential elections, citing electoral irregularities for its action. Since its electoral defeat, the party has remained active through the court system, challenging the validity of a variety of electoral laws and provisions. Significantly, in May of 1996, it won the nullification of the municipal elections for the position of Executive Mayor in Masvingo, Bulawayo and Harare.

THE PHENOMENON OF "INDEPENDENT" CANDIDATES

One of the most interesting phenomena in recent years in Zimbabwe, in particular since the 1990 general election, has been the emergence of "independents". These are usually ZANU(PF) members, who are either suspended, expelled, or blocked from running for political office, and who, therefore, proceed to run (and, sometimes, win) on their own ticket. These independents do not identify strongly enough with any of the existing opposition parties to seek full membership with them; at the same time, their relationship with the ruling party is so sour that they feel unable to maintain their loyalty to it.

ZANU(PF) began to hold primary elections in 1990, in order to enable the party's members at the constituency level to have a say in the selection of the candidate who would then proceed to run as the official ZANU(PF) candidate in the general election. In run up to the 1990 and 1995 general elections, these intra-ruling party primaries were, indeed, more hotly contested than the general inter-party elections. Although this initial screening process that the primaries amounted to was supposed to be a transparent and open process, it was severely criticised as being subject to abuse by the contestants, vote-buying by rival candidates, and even interference from members of the ruling party's highest organ, the Politburo.[1]

The first glimpse we had of the "independent" phenomenon was in 1993 when 16 members of ZANU(PF) were dissatisfied with the way they lost in

---

[1] See "Primary Polls Ticklish Problem for ZANU(PF)" in The Herald (Harare), June 30, 1993.

the primary elections for the rural district councils in Masvingo province. They contested as independents, and won. In 1995, the former ZANU(PF) Member of Parliament for Harare East, Margaret Dongo, contested in the primary elections for the new constituency of Harare South, and lost to Vivian Mwashita, who then became the ruling party's candidate. Dongo alleged gross irregularities in the primary elections and announced her candidature as an independent, a move which led to her suspension and subsequent expulsion from ZANU(PF). After a fiercely contested general election held in early April 1995, Dongo lost, and again alleged irregularities, particularly with regard to the voters' roll. This time, she took her case to the high court.

On August 9, 1995, the high court, in consultation with the Attorney-General, nullified the election result, and called for a fresh by-election in Harare South. The by-election was re-scheduled for November 1996 and it saw a re-match between Dongo and Mwashita, as well as intense campaigning by the political heavyweights in ZANU(PF) on behalf of Mwashita. Dongo won the by-election, and was duly installed as the Member of Parliament for Harare South, becoming only the third parliamentarian (the other two being ZANU (Ndonga) candidates, one of whom is Ndabaningi Sithole) who is not from the ruling ZANU(PF).

The significance of Margaret Dongo's victory cannot be overstated. First, the constituency of Harare South is one of the most strategic, located in the heart of the capital city. Many political heavyweights, including President Mugabe, put their reputations on the line, by publicly denouncing Dongo and backing Mwashita, a move that would, under normal circumstances, ensure a ZANU(PF) victory. But these were unusual times with an equally unusual candidate.

Dongo had the added advantage that she was a former member of the Central Intelligence Organisation (CIO), and, therefore, knew many of the "dirty tricks" employed by ZANU(PF) in carrying out what she termed "irregularities"; she was, thus, able to provide evidence of these when she argued her case in court. Dongo also had her revolutionary credentials as an ex-combatant from the ranks of ZANLA (the military wing of ZANU), and she was in very close touch with her constituents, in particular the female constituents who form the bulk of eligible voters. Dongo to date claims that she belongs to "the old ZANU(PF) and not the present one which is full of egotistical opportunists".[1]

Dongo's victory propelled her both to national and international fame, which has caused analysts to review the traditional approach which states that only members of a particular political party with a party machinery to back them can make a difference. Dongo's victory has also caused many to question the hegemony of ZANU(PF), and to examine the possibilities for

---

[1] See *Horizon* Magazine, December 1995, p. 12.

strategic cleavages within the ruling party as one route towards eroding its virtual monopoly of power.

In a similar case, during the elections for Executive Mayor of the city of Mutare, Lawrence Mudehwe, a former Mutare mayor, contested and lost in the ZANU(PF) primary elections. Mudehwe cried foul and contested as an independent, winning the mayoral elections held October 28–29, 1995. Again, the victory of Mudehwe calls into question the whole discussion surrounding the strategy of the opposition, and how to win political office from outside the ranks of the ruling party.

The success of the independents is an indictment of ZANU(PF). It is indicative of a party which has failed to use appropriate carrots, and not just sticks, in order to maintain a semblance of unity and stability. The success of the independents is equally an indictment of the opposition parties, for failing to offer an appropriate platform for disaffected ZANU(PF) members to join them.

FACTORS THAT UNDERLIE THE WEAKNESSES OF
THE ZIMBABWEAN OPPOSITION

i) Neglect of the Rural Vote

There has been much debate in Zimbabwe over the inability of the opposition to make significant in-roads into the hegemony of the ruling ZANU(PF). As has been illustrated earlier in this chapter, the question of leadership has been insufficiently addressed in a number of the opposition political parties. Equally, the "issues" and/or ideologies separating the political parties are not so significant as to swing the vote/electorate one way or the other. But perhaps the greatest area of weakness characteristic of the opposition movement in Zimbabwe, has been its lack of identification with the rural population. The strategy by the opposition movement of concentrating on the urban centres, and of using the more traditional forms of political campaigning often associated with the West, has only served to widen the gulf between the potential voters and the newly emergent political parties.

In contrast to the opposition, the ruling party has perfected the art of cultivating the rural population and promoting political organisation in the rural areas. Some have argued, in attempting to account for the solidity of the rural support for ZANU(PF), that the ruling party, far from being appreciated in the rural areas, is rather feared. The party has also been accused of resorting to blackmail and coercion in order to win the rural vote.[1] While, to

---

[1] The Classic case in the 1995 general election was that rural villagers were informed that drought relief was a "gift" from ZANU(PF) in general, and, more specifically, Mugabe, as opposed to being products financed with state funds that came from taxation. Similarly, rural villagers were informed that this "gift" could be removed as easily as it was given, should they not vote for ZANU(PF).

the extent that evidence which has been collected, particularly by non-governmental organisations, suggests that there is some weight to this argument, it ought also to be conceded that among the political organisations in the country, only the ruling party has a presence in all areas, including especially the rural areas. The opposition parties could certainly have made a greater effort to penetrate the rural areas; they, instead, chose the easier option of staying in the urban areas to preach to the already converted in the comfort of the large cities. The question then becomes: who does the opposition aspire to represent?

ii) Ethnicity: Permanent Majorities?

The question of ethnicity in Zimbabwean politics is a crucial one, in particular because of the experience gained from the elections that were held prior to the "Unity Accord". ZANU's majority was always guaranteed as long as it was able to continue to tap, as it did, the votes of Zimbabwe's majority Shona ethnic group. Supported mainly in the Matabeleland area from which its key leaders were drawn, there was never a chance that PF-ZAPU would ever be able to win a majority because its Ndebele backers are an ethnic minority in the country. Zimbabwe's political terrain was, for all intents and purposes, therefore, underpinned by permanent majorities (ZANU/Shona) and permanent minorities (PF-ZAPU/Ndebele). Flowing from this, it has been suggested that if, indeed, there are permanent majorities and permanent minorities in Zimbabwe, then perhaps there is very little or no room for a vibrant opposition in the country. Equally too, there is no room for any opposition movement or party to make a significant impact nationally.

There is no doubt that the ethnic factor is one which has to be reckoned with in any attempt to construct an effective opposition in Zimbabwe. This is all the more so in times of economic, political and social crises, such as Zimbabwe began to experience during the late 1980s onwards. At such times, the ethnic card becomes one of the easiest to play. Yet, the experience of ZUM and Forum in particular, also suggests that there is a window of opportunity available to those political aspirants/organisations that wish to transcend ethnicity. The success of ZUM and Forum in Bulawayo urban, for example, indicates that the generality of the people are prepared to support parties that offer a genuine hope for national transformation and do not always simply vote blindly according to kinship. This is not to say that such parties can afford to ignore ethnicity completely; rather, it is to argue that ethnicity, important though it is, is not the only consideration that underpins political choice.

iii) Lack of Internal Party Democracy

Another generalisation that we can make from our examination of the various opposition parties relates to the lack of internal democracy from which they suffer. This lack of internal democracy is, of course, not limited to the opposition as the phenomenon of the independent candidates so aptly demonstrates, but it is worthy of mention that in a variety of cases, an autocratic form of leadership coupled with the absence of formal rules and procedures has led to internal squabbles and splits within opposition political parties.

Some have argued, and again with some credence, that the splits in the opposition are due to infiltration by ruling party *agents provocateurs* or CIO personnel, rather than being the products of genuine differences in policy within the parties. While we acknowledge the disruptive role that *agents provocateurs* can play in politics and how they may have affected the fortunes of the Zimbabwean opposition, it is also true that the absence of due process has led, often unnecessarily, or at least avoidably, to the disintegration of many opposition parties.

iv) Voter Apathy

A total of 54 per cent of eligible voters cast their ballot in the 1990 election. By the time the 1995 elections took place, only an estimated 40 per cent of eligible voters bothered to cast their votes. The decline in voter turnout seems to be indicative of two things. First, the low voter turnout, as opposed to the extremely high voter turnout in the first two post-independence general elections that were held in the 1980s, would seem to indicate a trend towards voter apathy and increasing disaffection with the present electoral arrangement. In situations of rising voter apathy, those who stay away from the polls usually include a high proportion of people who could have supported a viable opposition party. Second, and this is where there is a cause for concern for the opposition, voters seem not to have found a worthy opponent in the opposition movement, and, therefore, have also not bothered to cast their ballot in a different direction. This argument is equally true with respect to the 1996 presidential aspirants. If it is true that people vote with their feet, then the massive stay-away in the Zimbabwe context speaks volumes.

v) Political Violence

As was discussed earlier, Zimbabwean political culture has always been characterised by violence towards any form of opposition, this practice dating back to the days of the liberation struggle in exile. The earlier elections witnessed the outbreak of violence between ZANU(PF) and PF-ZAPU. Violence also characterised ZANU(PF)/ZUM relations, particularly during the 1990 general elections. This violence was symbolised by the shooting of

Patrick Kombayi who, at the time, was the National Organising Secretary for ZUM. On March 24, 1990, a few days before voting in the Gweru Central constituency, in which Kombayi was contesting against Vice President Simon Muzenda, he was the victim of shots which were deliberately fired at him (Ncube, 1991). The independent candidates whose experiences we discussed earlier were also the victims of constant threats as were members of opposition parties contesting against ZANU(PF). In October of 1995, Ndabaningi Sithole and other ZANU (Ndonga) members were arrested on allegations of treason and attempting to assassinate President Mugabe. The case against Sithole has yet to be presented formally by the state, and the conventional wisdom in Zimbabwe that the arrest was a ploy designed to intimidate would appear to have strong merit.[1]

vi) Negative or Positive Unity?

Unlike the case of Zambia, for example, where a political coalition of different interest groups was created in 1991 and named the Movement for Multiparty Democracy (MMD) in order to enable the opposition to topple the incumbent government on an anti-UNIP platform, Zimbabweans have never been renowned for their unity, even in the hardest of times. Although attempts have been made to promote discussions on the establishment of a common platform among them, the post-independence opposition parties of Zimbabwe have always failed to introduce a united front that could bring them together under an umbrella body as part of their strategy for ousting ZANU(PF). This situation has not been helped much by the fact that there has been very little common ground among the different opposition parties.

An attempt to forge a common opposition platform was first made in September, 1992, when the United Front was established. The United Front brought together ZUM, UANC, ZANU (Ndonga), and the white Conservative Alliance of Zimbabwe (CAZ) led by former Rhodesian Prime Minister Ian Smith. The United Front had a short shelf-life, partially because the grouping was very diverse in composition. Several discussions focusing on unity between a variety of parties, led to a second short-lived alliance between ZUM and the UANC under the name, the United Parties, in which Tekere and Muzorewa were co-presidents. Tekere pulled out of this alliance shortly after its formation.

These types of "negative" unity, or efforts at unity that are not connected to the forging of common programmes but which rather serve as expedients for quick advantage, have not proved successful in the Zimbabwean context,

---

[1] Sithole also had a large farm confiscated by the government in 1994. The argument cited by the government in attempting to justify its action was that the farm constituted a health risk. 3,877 families were evicted from the farm, and in an out-of-court settlement, Sithole was compensated for the loss and damages he suffered to the tune of approximately 3 million dollars.

and in all likelihood will not be a useful electoral strategy for the opposition. This is true in part because of the very personalised nature of the opposition parties which we commented on earlier in the chapter. The vast majority of opposition parties, both pre- and post-independence are led by the old nationalist guard, with a complicated and distrustful relationship between and amongst the various leaderships. The strategy of "positive" unity, or uniting due to commonalties, is an equally implausible strategy in present-day Zimbabwe because of the lack of common ground between the opposition parties and in some cases the absence of a concrete agenda or programme.

In the case of the independents, it is clear that they have made a strategic impact and have dented the armour of ZANU(PF), but the existence of a small and similarly diverse grouping of independent candidates cannot be a prescription for wresting power from the ruling party or running the machinery of government. In the absence of any formalised procedures or methods of accountability to specific constituencies, it is difficult to view independents as lasting components of the Zimbabwe political terrain. The independent phenomenon, therefore, is useful only in the sense that it expresses a protest vote, but still fails to offer a comprehensive sense of a coherent political future for Zimbabwe. The recently-formed Movement for Independent Candidates, led by Margaret Dongo, though noble in objective, will, in the near future, be forced by political circumstances to re-strategise its long-term vision if it is to survive at all, let alone play a meaningful role in the political process.

THE COURTS AND CONSTITUTIONAL ISSUES

The court system of Zimbabwe has been one of the avenues that the opposition movement, both political parties and individuals, has found useful in its fight to level the playing field politically. As has already been mentioned, the high court has, on several occasions, nullified the results of various elections in favour of the opposition. The confidence inspired by several of the afore-mentioned court victories has led to the emergence of one area where the opposition share a united voice: the call for a constitutional conference and the review of laws pertaining to the electoral process. In particular, the opposition has targeted the Political Parties (Finance) Act of 1992, which allocates 30 million dollars from the taxpayers to any political party with 15 or more parliamentary seats. This law, in effect, allows the use of public funds for the financing of the operations of ZANU(PF). Other Acts of Parliament under scrutiny have included the Official Secrets Act, the Privileges and Immunities Act, and the Defence Act.

The opposition parties have also questioned the impartiality of the Electoral Supervisory Commission, the Delimitation Commission, and the Election Directorate, all appointed by the President. The role and impartiality of the Registrar General's office has also been subject to much scrutiny, particularly after the victory of Margaret Dongo clearly showed that the voters' roll was improperly prepared.[1] Furthermore, the opposition has boycotted a number of polls, although not in a united fashion. For example, ZUM, Forum, DP, and the FPD boycotted the 1996 presidential elections, while UANC and ZANU (Ndonga) stayed in the contest until the last minute. Although UANC and ZANU (Ndonga) did eventually boycott the poll at the eleventh hour, the lack of a united strategy which their initial decision to participate implied, rendered the entire opposition boycott action ineffective.

Finally, the opposition movement including the independents have called for a constitutional conference, similar to what occurred in a number of Francophone countries in the late 1980s and early 1990s. The Lancaster House constitution, negotiated in 1979, was designed to be a temporary and transitional document, with a review expected to have occurred in 1990. The opposition movement has, therefore, latched on to this to call for a comprehensive review of the constitution, with the intention of making it a truly representative and Zimbabwean constitution. These calls, though, have fallen upon deaf ears, with the government and ruling party unwilling to re-open the constitutional question. With the organisational weakness of the opposition so glaring, it has been unable to mobilise enough national support in order to compel the government to host a constitutional conference.

CONCLUDING REFLECTIONS: ZIMBABWEAN POLITICS AFTER MUGABE

It has often been argued that politics in Zimbabwe will become interesting only after President Mugabe retires from the political scene. ZANU(PF), unlike the monolithic and homogenous party that some political analysts have portrayed it to be, is in reality a loose and fragmented coalition party, held together by the persona of Mugabe. This coalition brings together a diverse grouping of classes, ethnic and sub-ethnic groups, and interest groups, in a very unnatural and uneasy alliance.

As the experience of other political parties and the phenomenon of the independents has illustrated, ZANU(PF) has the potential for splits and cleavages, and without the leadership of the "old guard", there is much speculation as to whether the party will be able to continue as a united, if fragile coalition. The succession question has been deferred from discussion within ZANU(PF), and it is perhaps the result of the succession debate

---

[1] See Press Statement by the Attorney-General, dated 9 August, 1995 and entitled Margaret Dongo vs. Vivian Mwashita and Others. In this statement, the Attorney-General concedes that persons not resident in the constituency and dead persons were registered as voters, along with many other irregularities that necessitated the nullification of the poll.

which, more than anything else, will determine the direction of opposition politics in Zimbabwe. Will ZANU(PF) splinter into several contesting factions, or will a leader emerge from within the ranks of ZANU(PF) with the substance and form to hold the party together? Will the opposition be able to capitalise on the fragility of ZANU(PF) and exploit its cleavages, or perhaps join ranks with other disillusioned members? More importantly, will the opposition be able to present a serious alternative platform in Zimbabwe with a mass appeal? What is clear is that any opposition platform, for it to be successful, will of necessity have to include a leadership that is national in character, appeal, and aspiration, and which, moreover, has staying-power.

The record of the formal opposition in Zimbabwe has not been a very encouraging one, and in the face of the disunity and in-fighting that has characterised the opposition parties, it is doubtful that they can serve as an enduring source of hope in a post-Mugabe era. In the end, we are compelled to pay closer attention to the internal dynamics of ZANU(PF). For, suffering as it is from its own internal cleavages and the possibility that conflicts which are presently latent within it are likely to boil over after Mugabe leaves the scene, it is to the party that we must look for sources of opposition that could offer a chance for the severe denting, if not complete overturning of the monopoly on power which it has so far enjoyed. This is what we mean when we speak of the struggle within the struggle; it is to suggest that although the justling that will be associated with the post-Mugabe era leaves the possibilities for political change open-ended, there is no doubt that whatever happens, opposition politics in Zimbabwe will continue to be coloured and informed by the politics and personalities of the ruling ZANU(PF).

In many senses, Claude Ake was correct in arguing that the mere existence of opposition parties does not necessarily contribute to the promotion of democratisation, and the Zimbabwe example amply demonstrates the plethora of problems associated with an opposition without popular sustenance and, in some cases, without a clear cause. Opposition politics in Zimbabwe is a struggle within a struggle and will continue to be so well into the period of the next general and presidential elections, scheduled for the years 2000 and 2002 respectively. The steady increase of voter apathy in Zimbabwe exposes a gap yearning to be filled. To fill this gap, though, the population demands and deserves an opposition with the clarity, resoluteness, and mass appeal that can help to reactivate the interest of Zimbabweans in the electoral process. Thus far, this has not been the case at the national level, although some individual candidates, most notably Dongo, have managed to mobilise constituencies proving that when seriously motivated, people will stand up and be counted. Traditionally, the opposition movement has blamed the machinations of ZANU(PF) for its limited impact. While there is some validity in this claim, and while there is no doubt that ZANU(PF) has used its incumbency to advantage, the problems of the opposition have also been compounded by the many internal organisational weaknesses of the parties themselves. Overcoming these problems, or at least bringing them into manageable proportions, is a basic pre-requisite for any chance the opposition might have to profit from the squabbles that could accompany the arrival of the post-Mugabe era in Zimbabwean politics.

BIBLIOGRAPHY

Ake, Claude, 1996, *Democracy and Development in Africa*, Washington, D.C.: The Brookings Institution,

Dabengwa, Dumiso, 1994, "The Early Period in the History of the History of the Liberation Struggle", paper prepared for ZANU(PF) Seminar on the *History Project of the Liberation Movement*, June 30–July 3.

Hermet, Guy, 1991, "Introduction: The Age of Democracy", *International Social Science Journal*, Vol. 128, May.

Moyo, Jonathan, 1992, *Voting for Democracy: A Study of Electoral Politics in Zimbabwe.* Harare: University of Zimbabwe Publications.

Ncube, Welshman, 1991, "Report on the 1990 General and Presidential Elections: Midlands, Mashonaland West, and Mashonaland East Provinces", *Election Studies Project Occasional Paper Series*, Vol. 1, No. 2. Harare: University of Zimbabwe, Department of Political and Administrative Studies.

Nkiwane, Tandeka, 1990, *The One-Party State in Southern Africa: The State of the Debate.* B.Sc. (Hons) dissertation, University of Zimbabwe.

Sachikonye, Lloyd, 1991, "The Context of the Democracy Debate," in I. Mandaza and L. Sachikonye (eds.), *The One-Party State and Democracy.* Harare: SAPES Books.

Sartori, Giovanni, 1968, "Political Development and Political Engineering", *Public Policy*, Vol. 17, p. 273. Cambridge: Harvard University Press.

Sithole, Masipula, 1997, "Zimbabwe's Eroding Authoritarianism", *Journal of Democracy*, Vol. 8, No. 1, January.

Sithole, Masipula, 1993, "Is Zimbabwe Poised on a Liberal Path? The State and Prospects of the Parties", *Issue: A Journal of Opinion*, Vol. XXI, Nos. 1 and 2, 1993.

Sithole, Masipula, 1986, "The General Elections 1979–1985," in I. Mandaza (ed.), *Zimbabwe: The Political Economy of Transition*, Dakar: CODESRIA.

Newspapers and periodicals

The Herald
Horizon
The Village Voice
The Financial Gazette

Political Party Manifestos

Zimbabwe Unity Movement (ZUM), *The Manifesto: Towards a Democratic Zimbabwe.* November 26, 1989.

Democratic Party, *Inaugural Statement.* September 28, 1991.

Forum Party of Zimbabwe, *Policy Papers from the National Conference in Bulawayo.* March 27–28, 1993.

Movement for Popular Democracy (MPD), *Blueprint for MPD Party*, reprinted in *The Insider*, No. 31, September 1993.

Chapter 4

The Senegalese Opposition and its Quest for Power

Aminata Diaw and Mamadou Diouf

INTRODUCTION

If, in several important respects, Senegal has generally been considered by observers as constituting something of a model in a continent which, for a long time, was dominated by one-party regimes, the wave of national conferences which was experienced across Africa between 1989 and 1992 has also served to expose the limits of the country's democratic experience. In fact, its early and apparently steadfast embrace of formal multipartyism has, in no way, succeeded in making its official system of democracy (more) effective for or meaningful to the majority of the Senegalese people. There are ample reasons for wondering if the notion of democracy in Senegal has not been an illusion, especially as the country seems so incapable of achieving one of the conditions which would allow its claim to being fully democratic to stand the test of objective scrutiny, namely, the institution of a system for ensuring that political power alternates between competing political parties according to constitutionally-established procedures and the wishes of the citizenry. In the light of the Senegalese experience, it is legitimate to ask: might multipartyism be little more than an instrument for holding democracy captive? The import of this question is that it shifts the focus of analysis away from the state and towards the opposition.

This chapter is concerned with undertaking a critical assessment of the Senegalese opposition's quest for power and influence within the framework of the formal multiparty political system which the country has been operating for some time. In addressing this task, we analyse the path taken by the opposition since the country's independence with a view to identifying the weak points in its strategy and the obstacles it has encountered in the course of its struggle for power. Furthermore, in the context of a broad discussion of some of the questions posed by Senegal's accession to national sovereignty, we will attempt to assess what the lot of the opposition has been from the perspective of nation-building. More precisely, our objective will be to determine what the opposition's strategies for gaining power have been within the framework of the nationalist paradigm and then point to the limits of these strategies in terms of their failure to deliver a change of political power. The challenges posed for the opposition in its struggle for greater relevance and political power will also be discussed in the chapter within the framework of a wider reflection on the future of democracy in Senegal following the 1993 elections. Much of the analysis in the chapter covers the post-colonial political history of Senegal in the period up to the 1993 presidential and parliamentary elections.

FORGING A UNITED OPPOSITION IN SENEGAL: DIFFICULTIES POSED BY THE IMMEDIATE POST-INDEPENDENCE CONTEXT

The post-independence unity project that was pursued in Senegal, as elsewhere in much of Africa, had two main objectives: nation-building and, related to this, development. These two objectives were defined as constituting the practical function of the state, a function which, because it was legitimated by a discourse concerned with the evolution of a national identity, and thus also with unity, led, almost inexorably, to an unceasing quest for a unifying party of government and, thus, the one-party system. The unifying/umbrella/consensus party came to be defined as the exclusive bearer of the project of national unity, the success of which was also seen as a *sine qua non* for the attainment of national development. By tapping the financial and institutional instruments of the state, the single party was able to extend and exert its influence over the country in a process which also undermined political pluralism and the multiplicity of places in which discourses could be held. At the same time as pluralism was eroded, a public space was engineered which the ideological legitimation of the state invested with official myths such as development, national identity, and national unity, among others. In assuming responsibility for the imperative of consensus, to use Momar Coumba Diop's expression, the state became intolerant of any other centre of power. Thus, one-party rule in Senegal, as elsewhere in Africa, was no historical accident; its existence, or rather the necessity for its existence, arose from the failure to break away from the colonial legacy, the opposition itself also continuing to be determined by this colonial paradigm.

In the face of the concerted push, after independence, for all Senegalese to embrace a state-led project of national unity and political unanimity, with all of the attendant consequences, the opposition was faced with two alternatives: either to be integrated into the ruling Senghorian Socialist Party, the UPS, an option which some elements in the opposition chose and which ended in the formation of a united party in 1966, or to go underground, as was the option chosen by the Marxist opposition that was not prepared to submit to the political logic which Léopold Sedar Senghor was attempting to foist on the country. It was this framework that structured the workings of the Senegalese opposition at least until 1974 and it also explains, to a degree, why it is not possible fully to understand the opposition and oppositional politics without taking full account of the trade union and student movements which, together, in the face of the totalising, authoritarian tendencies of the state and the UPS, carried and reflected the democratic aspirations of those sections of society which were opposed to subordination in the interests of imperialism.

The splits which emerged within the opposition on how to relate to the Senghorian political project arose, originally, from the differing attitudes which the different parties had to the struggle for and prospects of national independence. The differences persisted even after Senegal achieved national sovereignty, a fact which is attested to by the municipal and regional elections which took place in June 1960 amidst the expression of renewed opposition by the PRA and the African Independence Party (PAI), and in the context of protests in Saint-Louis that led to the PAI's dissolution by the authorities. The PAI continued actively to operate from underground, even from 1962 onwards, holding meetings of the Executive Council of Bamako, with Majmouth Diop confirmed as Secretary-General and Babacar Niang and Seydou Cissoko emerging as his right-hand men. Under Diop's leadership, the PAI defined its role as consisting of the radicalisation of the independence struggle, an objective which did not escape the notice of the ruling powers in Senegal.

The sequence of events which occurred between 1963 and 1966 was important in the evolution of the PAI as it exposed the party's "directional crises" and the inappropriate character of some of its tactical options, options which were justified on the grounds that the situation was deemed "revolutionary" and was affected, above all, by the dramatic disintegration of the Mali Federation and the crisis in the highest echelons of the state that occurred in 1962. However "revolutionary" it was, this situation did not prevent the defeat of the guerrillas, nor the harsh repression which was visited on the PAI militants. The decision taken by the party in 1963 to exclude certain of its highest ranking members, such as Babacar Niang and Tidiane Baïdy Ly, and the dismissal of the Secretary-General, Majmouth Diop, who was held personally responsible for the situation in which the party found itself, indicate the depth of the crisis faced by the PAI. The crisis in the party was further confirmed by the neutralisation of its Dakar cells and by the "first split in Senegalese Marxism" that followed the creation in 1965 by Landing Savané of a pro-Chinese communist party.

The discovery by the authorities of the PAI's underground apparatus in March 1966, the arrest of several of its members for allegedly posing a threat to Senegal's internal and external security, the prolonged and orchestrated denunciation which it suffered, and the high profile defections of some of its members (in particular, Ousmane Camara's, because of the repressive consequences it had), all undoubtedly contributed to the weakening of the party. The congress of rectification which the PAI held in 1967 had little success in injecting a new dynamic into the struggles it was intent on waging. Matters were not made easier for the party by the fact that the conditions that defined the context within which it had to work were becoming harder and harder and were marked, at the political level, by the conclusion of a unification deal that resulted in the integration of PRA-Senegal with the UPS in 1966, and, at the legal and institutional level, by the constitutional reforms of 1967 which effectively enshrined the presidential system in Senegal. It is also certain that operating underground contributed to the party's increasing weakness by accentuating the ideological differences between the militants that were in exile and those who stayed in the country.

For the PAI, the homogenisation of the leadership (culminating in the dismissal of Majmouth Diop and the nomination of Seydou Cissoko as his successor) was seen as an essential means of putting a brake on the party's ideological drift and internal troubles. To this imperative was added the crucial task of identifying the gaps and weaknesses in the functioning of the party and of defining the activities which needed to be undertaken in order to re-launch it as a key player on the Senegal political scene. These challenges constituted the backdrop to the 1972 congress which, on the one hand, resulted in the establishment of a core leadership group within the party, and, on the other hand, issued a call to the Senegalese people on the necessity for a regrouping of all the country's political forces in order to create a government of national unity.

It is necessary for us at this stage to come back to the question of the PAI's strategy of operating underground in order to underline one particular fact, namely that, to perceive its underground nature as merely being an accident of circumstances is to misunderstand what we have described elsewhere as the impossible proposition of being an effective opposition built on democratic postulates in a context defined by the fiction of a unity project that functions like a matrix in the nationalist discourse—a discourse that is both about identity and unity (Diaw, 1994:2). The alternatives open to the opposition, namely, those of either joining forces with the ruling party or operating underground, were informed by the workings of this impossible proposition built into Senegalese post-independence politics. The ruling party's plans for hegemony could only be achieved if it was able to secure the active assistance of an opposition which was prepared to operate without any competing, alternative project of its own.

Thus, not surprisingly, no real challenge to the ruling party could be expressed within a legal framework for a long time (Hesseling, 1985:257). The affirmation or confirmation of an ideological anchorage in Marxism-Leninism, especially in the context of the Cold War, made it fairly obvious that unless the PAI renounced this ideological identity, it constituted an irreducible element which could not be taken be taken on board as a partner by the local guardians of neo-colonial power. The building and consolidation of state power through the taming of the diverse social forces (the youths, trade unions, and the student movement, among others) which the PAI relied upon for its political mobilisation efforts bore witness to the readiness of the ruling party to embark on a negation of rights, both in theory and in practice, in order to achieve its objective of dominating the local political space. This behaviour entailed the muzzling of democratic freedoms and, in a sense, led to a dynamic of integration with parties such as the PRA-Senegal.

Such is the logic which informed the politics of consensus, unification and integration articulated by the Senghorian ruling bloc, especially with regard to the PRA-Senegal which, as Abdoulaye Ly has pointed out, "arose out of a split specifically about the demand for independence" (Ly, 1992:304). Negotiations with the PRA-Senegal first began in December 1962 on the possibility of, and terms for, its integration with the UPS only to be put on the back burner in 1963 with the referendum on constitutional law which enshrined the presidential system and on which the PRA-Senegal, as always convinced of the necessity of unity, allowed its members a free vote. The breakdown of negotiations on 6 April, 1963 was instigated by the UPS, despite the fact that there were no profound differences of opinion at the doctrinal or the programmatic level. In fact, the only real point of disagreement related to the division of political and governmental offices and responsibilities, and this would also lead to a split within the PRA-Senegal. The dissident faction of the PRA-Senegal, which took the name of PRA-Renovation, opted to undertake a quick merger with the UPS in 1964.

The parliamentary elections which were held in December 1963—the first after independence—dealt a mortal blow to what was left of the PRA-Senegal and, in so doing, accelerated a process of decline which appeared to be unstoppable. Indeed, the PRA-Senegal's "call to the people" that "the ... elections must mark the end of an era ... (and) ... herald the dawn of a new era in our national history and in the life of our society" (Ly, 1992:433) underlined their historic significance from the point of view of the opposition. With a manifesto that was tagged "Democracy and Unity in Senegal", the opposition initiated a united campaign of action under the patronage of the PRA-Senegal. This brought together not only the members of the PRA-Senegal but also the *Diaistes* (i.e. supporters of Mamadou Dia), activists of the (still underground) PAI, former friends of the marabout *tijaan*, Cheikh Tidiane Sy (organised under the umbrella of the Senegalese People's Party, PSS), students, activists of the defunct Coalition of Senegalese Masses (BMS), and the Senegalese National Front (FNS) of Cheikh Anta Diop, among others.

Arguing that the taking of responsibility nationally was the most urgent and neglected task facing the country, the opposition manifesto also drew attention to what it considered as the "anti-democratic, anti-national and anti-popular nature" of the Senghorian regime and denounced the elections in advance as a fraud and a masquerade. The climate of violence in which the elections were held (arrests, arson or attempted arson targeted at the buildings of political parties, mass demonstrations, and pitched battles between the supporters and opponents of the regime in power) fed into the generalised situation of social tension in the country. The government of Léopold Senghor, faced with concerted protests, decided to put the army and the gendarmerie on the alert; numerous opposition activists, including, most notably, Abdoulaye Ly, Secretary-General of the PRA, were placed under preventive arrest. These arrests, which mainly took place in Dakar, were to be fatal to the PRA-Senegal, paralysing and asphyxiating it and depriving it of any possibility of organising a systematic reaction or response.

The second attempt at a *rapprochement* between the Senghorian regime on the one hand and the PRA-Senegal on the other hand began with a reprieve for Abdoulaye Ly, and resulted in the laying of the foundations for the weaknesses of the opposition during the historical sequence that unfolded from 1960 to 1974. In fact, the *rapprochement* ultimately resulted in the integration of PRA-Senegal with the UPS, and this was sanctioned by the ministerial shuffle of 15 June 1966. The politics of unification was completed with this integration into the UPS of the radical nationalists who had broken away in 1958 in order to be able to choose immediate independence: the UPS became a unified party, and, effectively, the only party in the country even though multipartyism has always been guaranteed by the constitution. What lessons can be drawn from this?

Clearly the politics of "divide and rule" was put into practice by the Senghorian oligarchy in a very efficient way: the ruling power bloc employed every means possible to prevent the consolidation of the legal opposition in order to facilitate its integration into the UPS. To a certain extent, this explains the difficulties of consolidation that were at the very heart of the experience of the political opposition. The establishment by Cheikh Anta Diop of the Coalition of Senegalese Masses (BMS) on 15 September 1961, and the subsequent creation by the same Cheikh Anta Diop of the Senegalese National Front (FNS), is illustrative of the view that the opposition was bedevilled by serious problems of organisation, coherence, and strategy which the ruling party lost no opportunity to exploit. In fact, even over-riding the legendary rivalry between Senghor and Cheikh Anta Diop, was an underlying logic which meant that the BMS, in the same way as PRA-Senegal after it, would be the victim of a split that occurred on the back of negotiations that were underway between it and the UPS. This split facilitated the integration of the BMS into the UPS. The integration of the dissident faction of the BMS led by Boubacar Guèye with the UPS was facilitated by the dialogue begun between the two parties, with the active support of the Caliph of the Mourids, in October 1963. It was also made easy by the fact that numerous members of the BMS were former UPS members, being individuals who once professed socialism. Thus it was that the ruling party was simply able to dissolve the BMS.

The hard core of the BMS which contested the integration with the UPS re-emerged in November 1963 as the Senegalese National Front (FNS) with Cheikh Anta Diop as its leader. The FNS itself was to be dissolved on 17 December 1963 on the grounds of the authority of prior judgement (Zuccarelli, 1988:95). It is worth noting that the FNS itself, which included former supporters of Mamadou Dia, was also beset by serious internal conflicts. PRA-Senegal, therefore, seemed to be the only legal opposition party left. It was unable to benefit from the existence of the PAI because of the path the latter had taken, namely, to operate underground. However, even before the PAI went underground, the history of cooperation between the two parties—which were naturally drawn together by their decision to opt for immediate independence and, in so doing, reject the proposal from Paris for the creation of a French Community—failed to produce any formal agreement between them because of the suspicion aroused by the alleged alliance between the PRA-Senegal and the PSS. The PAI's requirement that the PRA-Senegal refuse integration was the final cause of the break between the two parties. As in the case of the PRA-Senegal's parting of ways with the PAI, the BMS, whilst it was still united under Cheikh Diop's leadership, opposed the PRA-Senegal's integrationist proposal for a unified and democratic party until it also suffered a split. Thus, while the ruling party was able to promote integration as a strategy for consolidating itself, the opposition's experience was marked by the repeated splits and divisions that became the order of the day.

With Senegalese politics characterised by a dual dynamic of integration, alliances and unification on one side, and exclusion and marginalisation on the other, the UPS was able to strengthen its position by appointing many new and younger political personnel into the party and government while, at the same time, systematically neutralising the articulation of an alternative project by the opposition. This process, loaded as it was in favour of the ruling party, was facilitated by the systematic alienation of rural society from politics. As Momar Coumba Diop has emphasised:

> ... the *marabout* network prevents forces hostile to the ruling class from infiltrating the rural domain and upsetting the rules of the political game (Diop, 1992).

Thus the opposition found itself weakened (almost to the point of annihilation) by its inability to find any real anchorage in Senegalese rural society. It was a victim of its "urbanity" and its petit bourgeois and intellectual associations.

No discussion of the weaknesses of the opposition would be complete without an acknowledgement of the opposition parties' own share of responsibility for the numerous problems that confronted them. As Abdoulaye Ly has noted, with considerable courage, in an official statement which he made, "It's an irrefutable fact that we [the opposition] were not up to [the challenges of] fulfilling the hopes of the people". For Ly, and quite correctly too, the main source of the responsibility borne by the political class of this period, including the opposition, resides in its mistaken belief that bourgeois democratic reforms without national independence could be transformed into a popular national democratic revolution anchored in the people. An inadequate understanding of the true class positions that underpinned the nationalist movement facilitated the process, above all because the essential political determinant was always the concern with the content of inter-national relations.

As to the Marxist opposition, its weaknesses were not only a function of its relationship with the ruling power bloc, which was one of exclusion, but also of its nature which was closely tied to its inability to transcend the par-ticular historical context of the struggle for independence to which it appeared to be irretrievably subordinated. These weaknesses were exacer-bated by the ambiguity of the PAI as a political organisation: on the one hand, it was the party of the *Momsarew*[1] which, by its logic, meant advocacy of consensus politics and, on the other hand, it remained solidly anchored in its Marxist-Leninist origins which made it the most radical wing of the nationalist movement.[2] Thus, this party which, from an ideological per-spective, should have been the party of the working class remained essen-tially dependent on petit bourgeois elements at a time of major social and political flux.

Commenting on what he has called the "disaster of the Marxists", François Zuccarelli rejects the suggestion that their problems were mainly external in origin, linked to state repression. Important though this may be as an explanation, a more profound reason for the problems of the marxist opposition had to do with factors that were internal to the movement itself. According to him,

> They lacked minimal popular support, having cut themselves off from it by an ideological construction and quarrels between the cells which are totally obscure to their fellow citizens (Zuccarelli, 1988:94).

Undoubtedly, what we find here are the effects of the original ambiguity mentioned above, which raises the question of whether in the specific his-torical context within which it found itself, the Marxist movement had really worked out a relevant theoretical framework with regard to the conditions that were necessary for the establishment of a Marxist-Leninist party, the requirements for meeting those conditions, and the structures that needed to be created.

---

[1] *Momsarew*, literally to "own one's country", means independence and sovereignty.

[2] Even as the most radical section of the nationalist movement, the PAI proved unable to resist the unity logic as is evidenced by the unproductive contacts which it had with such parties as the PSS, PRA-Senegal, and the UPS.

In a sense, the lack of minimal popular support for the Marxist movement also arose from what the Senegalese sociologist Momar Coumba Diop, borrowing the term from Bianchini, has called the inaccessibility of society in a context characterised by "the absolute grip that Islam has on the ordinary people" and, therefore, "the problem of access to the peasantry, the numerical weakness of the working class, etc." The imperative of decolonisation seems to have rendered problematic any explicit class and ideological project in the sense that it imposed on the parties a heterogeneous social content, a heterogeneous sociological composition. Abdoulaye Ly's characterisation of the political parties during this historical sequence of events is particularly pertinent: he saw them as "structured movements of a national type, targeting imperialist domination but always under the control of a petite bourgeoisie of colonial origin" (Ly, 1992:304). The fundamental consequence of this, which is important in that it affected the direction taken by the political parties, is the following: the primary contradiction, posed in terms of the dominated versus colonialism, supplanted the contradictions associated with internal social differentiation but in a manner which did not succeed in eliminating them. The lines of political and social demarcation were blurred because of the increasing contradiction between the actual experience of independence and the expectations of certain social forces. Thus, the logic of unification was unable to prevent the major socio-political crises which confronted Senegal in May 1968 and in 1989, and on other occasions.

The strategy of unifying the political space, which came to an end in 1966 with the integration of the PRA-Senegal with the ruling party, did not itself imply the pacification of the social space despite the peaceful elections that were held in June of that year. Paradoxically, and contrary to the anticipated effect, the unification strategy exacerbated domestic social contradictions, and in so doing showed that the colonial economic logic had survived independence. The barrenness of the 1966–1967 campaign and the simultaneous ending of the policy of a fixed price for groundnuts, following the establishment of the Common Market in Europe, caused anxiety among the peasantry. The groundnut crisis saw people in rural society unable to honour the payments due on equipment they had purchased; the immediate consequence was an increase in the rural exodus. Agriculture was not the only sector affected; in the industrial sector, the recession increased unemployment but above all aggravated what Abdoulaye Bathily has called "the frustration of the economic operators" (Bathily, 1992:22), referring to the severe indictment of France's interference in the constitutional assembly of the Union Nationale des Groupements Economiques du Sénégal (UNIGES)/the National Union of Senegalese Economic Associations. The freezing of salaries that dated back to 1958, the decline in consumer purchasing power, and the rise in the cost of living all contributed in nurturing

hostile feelings towards France for its tight control over the local bureaucracy and the wheels of government.

This exacerbation of social contradictions which the logic of unification
was not able to prevent had an echo in the re-emergence, even radicalisation,
of the trade union movement, enabled, ironically, by the unification project
that occurred within the movement itself. After integrating with the UPS, the
PRA-Senegal called on its trade union allies, the USTS, to do the same with
the UNTS, the allies in the trade union movement of the UPS. The illegal
opposition, represented by the PAI, was not left behind. Trade unions such
as the SPAS and SITS which represented intellectuals/professionals, and the
physicians' and pharmacists' union, SUEL, completed the task of widening
the base of the UNTS by integrating with it. They were assisted in this by the
CTS, the CNTCS, the CGTS and the Confederal Labour Alliance (Cartel
Confédéral du Travail). This process, which had a direct effect on the orientation of the UNTS, began in April 1967: in opening its doors to labour
activists who were not members of the UPS, the UNTS experienced pressures from the grassroots to denounce cooperation by the trade union
movement with the ruling UPS. Little wonder then that on account of the re-
orientation which its opening created, the UNTS took on a central role in the
crises of 1968 and 1969, a fact which led the ruling power bloc to clamp
down on it and create a new central body, the CNTS, headed by Doudou
Ngom, for the trade union movement. By the time of its dissolution, the
UNTS was considered by the state as being excessively under the influence
of the PAI. The statutes of the ruling party were, thereafter, modified in line
with those of the regional unions in order to integrate the CNTS.

As Boubacar Diop has emphasised, "this radicalisation of the trade union
movement was to create fertile ground for the protests of school and college
students from March 1968 onwards" (Diop, 1992:485). Without going into a
detailed discussion of the events of May 1968 which have already been
impressively analysed by A. Bathily, it is still appropriate to recall one of his
conclusions, namely, that May 1968 was the manifestation of a profound
internal crisis. When the root causes are examined, May 1968 surely sym-
bolises the failure of the Senghorian attempts at integration. The logic of
unification, by rendering impossible any legal expression of a political alternative, ended up radicalising one sector of society, namely the trade union
movement, in its opposition to the neo-colonial state.

By virtue of its social and cultural stake in national life and its role in the
training of the elites, the University—which was hitherto "completely in the
hands of France" (Bathily, 1992:36)—also became a terrain for vigorous contestation, the place where subordination to the interests of imperialism was
denounced. Thus it was the "natural" place for the left to articulate its opposition to the construction of ruling class, neo-colonial hegemony. As a space
where there was academic freedom, it was the only place where protest was
allowed both generally and in the formulation of demands for democracy.

But the harshness of the repression unleashed on it by the state demonstrated, if proof was needed, that campus protest went beyond the pedagogical domain: it attacked the very foundations of the ruling power bloc by demanding the reform of the political system and the content of education as well the adaptation of the latter to national and continental realities. Thus Momar Coumba Diop was able to conclude, as R. Fatton before him, that May 1968 represents the proof that independence had not lived up to the hopes of the mass of the population (Diop and Diouf, 1990:444).

Even if members of the PAI were heavily involved in the organisation of the events that produced the crises of 1968 and 1969, it is not correct to talk, as the ruling power bloc did, of a project of opposition by proxy: the internal crisis that was going on within the PAI constitutes an objective proof in this respect. The necessity of defusing the crisis arising from the failure of the political management strategies of the single party, a crisis which neither the repressive politics of the regime nor the attempt to impose state control on the unions proved able to contain, brought about a change of personnel in the ruling party, a deconcentration of power with the amendment of the constitution in 1970, and, above all, a democratic opening in 1974.

THE OPPOSITION AND THE MODIFICATION OF THE SYSTEM OF CONTROLLED DEMOCRACY IN SENEGAL FROM THE MID-1970S

The new political map of Senegal which began to be drawn after 1974 brought the country more closely in line with its formal constitutional norm: the merging of parties and climate of repression which had been dominant features of the pre-1974 period had ended up clearing a legal space for the opposition to operate in. Persistent upheavals involving several sections of Senegalese society, upheavals which resulted in the banning by the state of the country's students' unions (UDES and UED) in 1971, the dissolution of the teachers' union, the SES, in 1973, an increased number of workers' strikes, and growing anxiety among the peasantry, especially following the severe drought of 1973, demonstrated clearly that, except in a very formal legal sense, the ruling power bloc no longer had control over the political terrain, and this had already been evident since 1968. Admittedly, viewed solely from the official results of the 1973 elections, the full import of the social and political tension that had gripped the country would be hard to discern. But beyond the official results, there was no doubt that Senegal was confronted with a serious crisis. Thus, Abdoulaye Bathily was to note that the participation rate in the elections stood at a mere 17 per cent while Mar Fall, without giving any figures, spoke about the largely untenable character of the elections: "How does one explain that the country was to find itself on the verge of civil war a few weeks after [the elections]?" (Fall, 1986:16).

In addition to the upheavals which we mentioned above, the ruling power bloc also had to face up to its own internal contradictions. The crisis of the state and its apparatus (the CNTS) which necessitated the widening of the social base of the regime, showed that the UPS/PS no longer had the upper hand in the political terrain. By the early 1970s, in contrast to what was the norm during the first decade of independence, its actions increasingly took on the form of reactive measures. The initiative seemed to lie more with the various groups in society that were in the forefront of the agitations for the enthronement of the people's democratic aspirations. In response to the popular demands that built up from below, the ruling power bloc resorted to "legalistic, technical means, ... persuasion, pressure and lawsuits" (Hesseling, 1985:271). But would the process of liberalisation or decompression as a response to the organic crisis really prevent the onset of a revolutionary crisis? How was the opposition to profit from this latent revolution? These were the questions that were posed by the situation that prevailed in the early 1970s and the way in which they were resolved resulted, yet again, in the wrong-footing of the opposition.

In the first place, the amendment of the constitution in 1976, together with the introduction of the "law of the three trends" under which only three ideological-political trends were recognised in the country, had the effect of determining the nature of the opposition acceptable to the Senghorian oligarchy. Under the law, all political parties, including those in the opposition, could only claim to believe in liberal democracy, social democracy (a niche already occupied by the party in power) or communism/Marxism-Leninism. This selective recognition was to again divide the Senegalese opposition into two: the legal opposition which consisted of those parties that were able to find a place within the political framework authorised by the ruling oligarchy and the illegal opposition which continued with a policy of non-cooperation in the face of the attempt by the state to control/strait-jacket political thinking and expression in the country.

The years 1974–1981 saw the terrain that was reserved for the legal opposition exclusively controlled by the Senegalese Democratic Party (PDS), with the PAI playing the role of an accessory. It is important to note, however, that, because of their ideological position and the historical situation in which they found themselves, the two recognised parties were incapable of challenging the hegemonic politics of the ruling power bloc despite the contradictions in the basis of its power and authority. In fact, after achieving recognition, the PAI was, by 1976, a severely weakened party whose secretary-general was dismissed by the original PAI. Thus this party, which purported to be the representative of Marxist ideology, saw its legitimacy contested by those who continued to claim legitimacy on the basis of the 1972 congress and who, for this reason, positioned themselves as the PAI-Senegal or the orthodox PAI. As clear evidence of the fact that the PAI would be unable to represent the entire Senegalese Marxist movement objectively, it is also pertinent to recall that it had already featured prominently in a split that occurred in April 1975 at the time of the meeting of the General Union of (Senegalese) Students, Pupils and Probationary Teachers in Europe. The dissident faction, in order to shift the balance of power in favour of the proletariat, denounced the politics of the Democratic Front in 1972 and sought to mobilise Marxist against moderate opponents so as to bring down the Senghorian ruling party. From this split was to emerge the radical left front which we know today as the Democratic League/Workers' Party (LD/MPT).

These splits and disputes over legitimacy give a clear picture of a PAI that was legally recognised by the state but which, in truth, was only a pale reflection of the historical PAI. Politically and ideologically, this so-called reconstructed PAI (some were to call it the revisionist faction) did not seem to have measured up to the challenge of gaining influence in the political arena in spite of its claim to being the rallying point for the *Momsarew* and its resort to the distribution of political tracts. Its status as the official Marxist opposition was, therefore, an exaggerated one and, in the hands of Senghor, served as the decisive argument for the refusal to recognise the "illegal" Marxist opposition. For all intents and purposes, therefore, the formally sanctioned terrain for the legal opposition was mainly controlled by the PDS. It was helped in this regard by the fact that its Secretary-General had a legal training.

In its confrontation with the ruling power bloc, the PDS rested several of its challenges on the issue of political rights, insisting that the government should embrace and respect the principles of democracy as a *sine qua non* for the development of a framework for healthy politics. It called on the supreme court to declare the presidential elections of 1978 illegal because of what it claimed were the fraudulent manoeuvrings of the PS, and protested about the unequal television time given to the various parties. It also protested against the failure of the government to respect Article 2 of the constitution concerning the secret ballot. This juridico-political battle, combined with a campaign of information and recruitment, became a source of confirmation of the existence of the PDS's public voice on the Senegalese political scene, a voice relayed through the party's journal, *Le Democrat*, through the Union of Free Workers of Senegal (UTLS) which the PDS helped to create, and, above all, through the party's parliamentary presence after the elections of 1978 (with 18 MPs out of 100).

In his interpretation of the results of the 1978 elections, Mar Fall notes that:

> ... these election results, although representing something of a defeat for the strategy of Senghor's party, do not, however, spare the PDS or Majmouth Diop's PAI, which had warned against the limitations imposed by the prevailing political trends in the country. They inform us on the crisis of nationalism in terms of its objective limits and incapacity of the opposition to mount a response that is organised to exploit its full potential.

While there is some validity in Fall's critique, it is necessary to pay greater attention to the significance of the PDS's political presence given the context within which it had to function. The resurgence of extremely partisan political action by the PS and the government, the high rate of voter abstention in the elections, and Abdoulaye Wade's score in the presidential election (17.4 per cent) despite the absence of a common opposition front should, all things considered, be interpreted as being reflective of the PDS's presence in the Senegalese political arena. The strong showing which Wade made in several of the politico-administrative departments in the country—in Oussouye (50 per cent of the votes cast), in the communes of Louga (46.3 per cent), in Meckhé (49.5 per cent), and in the departments of Vélingara, Gossas, Nioro du Rip, Bambey and Thiès (between 30 and 40 per cent)— showed the diversity of his support base and the extent to which Wade's party had gained a hold. Although the only commune the PDS won was that of Oussouye, the result was nonetheless still very significant because that area is in the Casamance, the centre of opposition to the state.

The very nature of the PDS played a part in its relative success: in defining itself as the party of opposition, in seeking to win "democratic but not systematic power", the PDS was able to coopt all the disaffected (moderates) from the Senghorian camp. Besides, in the opening speech he made at the first national conference of his party, Wade made an explicit appeal to the UPS leaders:

> I earnestly hope that UPS leaders who feel constrained, confined and limited in their party by political feudalism and corrupt structures, will come to the PDS so as to free their creative energy and participate in the great task of genuine nation-building.

There is, however, also a sense in which it can be argued that the soundness of the PS's political logic in initiating reforms in the mid-1970s and acquiring the capacity for controlling the limited reforms were dependent on the existence of a relatively strong PDS. This hypothesis deserves attention particularly because with the emergence of the PDS as the main pillar of the opposition in Senegal, the power equation within the political class now consisted of shifting to the ideological right (in the bid to be a credible party of government) or farther to the left (in order to be a credible opposition). The departure of Senghor from office and the arrival of Abdou Diouf did not appear to weaken this argument, at least not in the short-term. But for all that, the experiment in controlled democracy which Senghor started was momentarily jeopardised by Cheikh Anta Diop's RND. The five long years for which it had to wait for recognition did not prevent the RND from making its activities highly visible or having a public voice through its journals, *Siggi* and *Taxaw*, despite the fact that it lacked legal existence. The nationalist ideology and, in particular, Cheikh Anta Diop's great moral and intellectual aura, had succeeded in attracting many intellectuals, especially among those on the left.

The success of the RND, which contributed to the social ostracisation of the ruling power bloc, should not, however, conceal the fact that there was an absence of agreement within the party on a practical programme or ideology. The crisis of the RND when it came, and the split that inevitably followed and which gave rise to the PLP, were symptomatic of the crisis of post-colonial nationalism in general and, more particularly, of the failure of the opposition to convert popular discontent into a programme of action. The political configuration in the country, initiated as it was by the ruling UPS/PS, accepted by the PDS and PAI for the reasons already explained, and jeopardised by the RND, was rejected by the leftist opposition but the reality on the ground was that, overall, the logic of unity which had been constructed during the first decade of independence with the process of unification/integration/consensus-building did not seem to have been completely removed from the Senegalese political domain. The opposition, recognised and authorised by Senghor, and enshrined in its official role, did not fundamentally challenge this logic. The plurality of discourse which was now tolerated did not allow the emergence into the political domain of the logic of competition or a logic of autonomous projects which could serve as a basis for popular mobilisation.

Against the background of the foregoing, the crisis that occurred at the university and in a number of technical colleges and secondary schools, the reorganisation of the trade unions in the teaching profession, the termination of the affiliation of the CNTS to the PS, and the creation of the UTLS and its network of cells through the Maoist movement, accounted for the continuing unrest in the society and, above all, conveyed an idea of the tense climate in which the struggle for recognition was waged. Given the framework of the opposition's struggle for recognition, it is important to make the following point: the ruling power bloc's self-appointed prerogative to accept only certain political ideologies was not extended to attempts at rigidly controlling the freedom of expression. The reason for this was not so much that there was total freedom of expression as that the ruling power bloc knew for a fact that so long as the language of protest remained the written word and the French language, a natural limit was imposed on the size of the receptive public.

Taking up Bathily's argument, it can be said that the press, together with a circumscribed multiparty system and the control exerted over economic actors, was one of the three factors that enabled the partial liberalisation of the Senegalese political domain during the 1970s. That period was marked by the appearance and/or flourishing of several journals such as *Le Démocrate* (PDS), *Siggi* (the RND journal which Moussa Paye remembers for its "Homeric linguistic jousts" between Pathé Diagne, Cheikh Anta Diop and Senghor, and its replacement by *Taxaw*), *Momsarew* (PAI-Revolution and PAI-Sengal both publishing their own editions), *Le Militant* (LD), *L'Educateur*

Sénégalais (SUDES), *Liberté* (UTLS) and *Le Politicien*, a satirical magazine which very quickly became popular with the Senegalese reading public.

The section of the press that supported the opposition made strenuous efforts to provide a critical evaluation of the government's role in the deepening political crisis facing Senegal and subsequently in the movement towards full multipartyism. The best example is provided by the monthly journal, *Andë Sopi* (Unite for Change), founded in 1977 by Mamadou Dia, Maguette Thiam and Samba Dioulдé Thiam (the latter two being militants from PAI-Senegal). This journal can be considered the main symbol of the new sense of unity that, for a period at least, caused excitement in the opposition. The relevance of, and opportunity for the emergence of a unified opposition strategy to discredit once and for all, the law of controlled democracy that Senghor developed was one which the journal encouraged the opposition parties to embrace. In doing so, they managed to change the Senegalese political landscape somewhat, especially after the formation in 1978 of the Association of Senegalese Democrats. This movement, which called itself apolitical but whose objectives included a firm reiteration of the opposition's demand for full democracy, numbered among its founder-members Abdoulaye Bathily, Mamadou Dia, Babacar Sané, and Abdoulaye Ly, among others. The ruling power bloc, for its part, showed that it was not unaware of the identity of these men when it threatened the organisation with prosecution under the law on seditious associations.

Driven by the same dynamic of striving for unity, the Coordinating Association for the Unified Senegalese Opposition (COSU) was also created in 1978, articulating demands for greater democracy, the departure of French troops stationed in Dakar and an improved quality of life for the mass of the people. The principle of pushing for unity which was adopted by the opposition as part of its strategy for achieving greater recognition and impact did not, paradoxically, obscure the fact that some of the key political forces in the formally-recognised opposition were crumbling. The Marxist opposition, despite its attempts at *rapprochement*, remained divided by the parameters of radical left international politics, thus reflecting the unbridgeable gap between the pro-Soviet pole and the Maoist pole. The bitter struggles at the heart of SUDES which resulted in Mamadou Ndoye (LD) succeeding Maguette Thiam provide further ample illustration of this reality. But more than this, the cause of unity among the forces of opposition suffered from two problems: the absence of the PDS from the various efforts and, perhaps more significantly, the lack of discipline and cohesion among the cooperating elements.

The fragmentation of the opposition was to become greater still with the arrival of Abdou Diouf in the presidency and the establishment of a fuller, unrestricted version of multiparty politics. By doing away with the "law of the three trends" and recognising all the opposition parties, the ruling power bloc was able, initially at least, to weaken them as they struggled to find their footing under the new dispensation. Since each party was called upon to prove its oppositional status by defining its particular ideology, the areas of discourse were multiplied. The ensuing cacophony did not allow the emergence of a strong alternative programme of action to that on offer from the government, a situation which was not helped by the problematique of the need for a national consensus which was increasingly posed by the ruling party. The problematique of a government of national unity which was underpinned by the ideology of the national leap forward suggests clearly that the ruling power bloc wished to continue to control democracy even if the means and the context for doing so had fundamentally changed. The immediate consequence was the displacement of the dividing line between the ruling power's space and that of the opposition.

The critical potential of the RND was the first to be undermined and defused by this new political deal for reasons which we adduced earlier. The party excluded itself from the increasing campaign for unity and also abstained from the 1983 elections. The political realignment which was unleashed by the rise to power of Abdou Diouf also diverted attention from the activities of an anti-imperialist action front, *Suxxali Reewmi* (Save the Country), which rejected any alliance with the ruling power bloc and adopted the following objectives:

> ... to fight for an end to the PS regime and foreign domination, for the holding of free and democratic elections, for the electing of a sovereign national assembly, and a government responsible to this assembly and charged with implementing a new political programme that breaks away from imperialist and neo-colonial domination in order to satisfy the demands of the working masses.

Within this front which formed around Mamadou Dia were to be found the League of Communist Workers (LCT), the Popular Democratic Movement (MDP), the African Independence Party (PAI), and the Senegalese Peoples' Party (PPS). On the opposite side of this front was a new grouping which began to take shape, consisting, on the one hand, of the PDS, preaching "the idea of a government of rectification" which could include the PS (and indeed had to do so), and, on the other hand, of PAI-Senegal or PIT, which in a sense simply abided by the 1972 option. The PDS was subsequently to suffer a double split: the Secretary-General of the UTLS left with some of his supporters to create the UDS-R, and in 1987, the MP, Serigne Diop, left to create PDS-Renovation. However, the radicalisation of the PDS which saw it participate in the formation of the Senegalese Democratic Alliance (ADS)—regrouping the LD, And-Jeff, the OST and the UDP, and led by A. Bathily—was perhaps not unconnected with the technocratic approach adopted by the new political class in command, the impact of the private press which reinforced the notion that it was possible to take power through the ballot box and, above all, the ever-increasing popular discontent that was a result of the implementation by the government of a programme of structural adjustment. All in all, the radicalisation of the PDS came from a combination of circumstances. In the end, however, the demand of the ADS for opposition participation in the 1988 elections to be made conditional on the reform of the electoral system was, in fact, jeopardised by Wade's party.

On the eve of the 1988 elections, the Senegalese opposition had still not resolved the tasks, especially of uniting around a minimum platform, which it had set itself or which the ruling power bloc's strategy for retaining office had imposed on it. While being aware of the necessity for unity—as the various attempts at achieving it prove—it nevertheless always let itself be enclosed by the PS which spared no effort to separate the opposition political class from society and, in so doing, locked it in a sterile confrontation with the ruling power elite. The possibility of the opposition being in a position to effect a change of political power in Senegal clearly resided in the deconstruction of this approach in order to assure the accessibility of society to the opposition. From this viewpoint, the structural adjustment programmes, by allowing unprecedented modes of political expression, could be seen as offering the Senegalese opposition an opportunity to think in a different way and form itself in a different way. For the time being, it seemed that a change of government was reduced to a mirage, and this was all the more the case because the PDS remained as strong and also as mobile as ever among the various opposition parties.

CONTESTING THE CONTENT OF SENEGAL'S DEMOCRACY: OPPORTUNITIES WON AND LOST BY THE OPPOSITION DURING THE DIOUF YEARS

The sequence of events which began with the post-election riots of 1988 and which were followed by intermittent waves of violence, together with *Set Setal's* campaigns and the return of the government to power with an increased majority for the president, altered the Senegalese political scene in a way never before experienced. The elections took place in a context that was totally new. The PS was only able, with considerable difficulty, to manage the political repercussions that flowed from the changes imposed by Diouf on the national and local administrative machinery as well as on the mode of managing the regime's political and economic clientele. Several of the leading elements in the leadership group experienced serious difficulties in getting into step with the new president and his style. This factor, together with the president's technique of controlling the party through a policy of supporting one or the other of the factions which were tearing themselves apart at all organisational levels, and the extraordinary vitality of the opposition parties, in particular the PDS, opened up spaces which, at one level, attested to the weakening of the PS and, at another level, indicated the instability of the regime and of the ruling class.

In the wake of the 1983 elections—which confirmed him as head of state after two years of exercising power as Senghor's heir—Abdou Diouf undertook a major politico-administrative shake-up that saw him abolishing the post of Prime Minister (April 1983) and pensioning-off the barons of the Senghor era. The occasion for the purging of the barons was the PS Congress which was held in January 1984. Following the Congress, the supporters of the new president took control of the party and Jean Collin, a minister of state, quickly emerged as the key player in the new regime and around Diouf. He was to remain the central figure in the government during the first decade of the Diouf years (Diop and Diouf, 1990:101–114). But the new position of influence occupied by Collin did not go uncontested within the party. Indeed, the assumption of control over the party and administrative machinery by this apparently all-powerful minister provoked many internal clashes between his supporters and opponents as well as among those who were indifferent to him. Collin thus became the focus of political hatred, fear, and suspicion on a scale which has not been equalled since.

The extraordinary confidence which the Senegalese president reposed in Collin allowed him to rise above all his rivals: in 1984, Habib Thiam, a personal friend of Diouf and his prime minister from 1981 to 1983, was eliminated after a manoeuvre by the minister of state to reduce the term of office of the President of the National Assembly, a post held by Thiam, to one year, simultaneously creating an instability which allowed the minister of state to put his long-term rival's position in constant danger. In protest against this manoeuvre, Thiam resigned from the PS and the government. The same year, on account of manoeuvrings emanating from Collin, the minister of foreign affairs was forced to resign after an altercation with the minister of information, Djibo Kâ, during a meeting of the PS Political Bureau that was held in the presence of Abdou Diouf.

The emerging picture of a ruling power in total crisis was reinforced by the social consequences of the structural adjustment policies which the Diouf government was implementing. Increasingly ruthless struggles for position within the PS caused great disillusionment within the party and led to a large number of party members resigning to join the opposition PDS. The feeling of disillusionment was not assuaged by the neo-liberal economic policies of the government. Amidst the rising social costs of adjustment, a growing proportion of the Senegalese people lost their faith in the capacity of the ruling party to reform the Senegalese economy and society. At the same time, the PDS's credentials as a competent and coherent political organisation were growing. The combative nature of the journal, *Sopi*, which contained the serious, informed and competent economic analysis of Abdoulaye Wade, together with the aggressive diatribes of Jean Paul Dias and the sarcastic "Pèle Mêle" column which furnished minute details of "embezzlement, skulduggery and small and large state secrets" to the reading public succeeded in convincing a growing number of people that the PDS possessed competent leaders who could ensure that it had access to the state's most closely guarded secrets. The PDS was to extend its offensive against the PS to the international level where it targeted the political and financial backers of the ruling party with its message that it represented a credible alternative.

At the same time as the PDS was attempting to build its credibility as a potential party of government, the Marxist opposition tightened its hold on the sectors of society from where it had traditionally mobilised support, namely, the teaching profession, students, skilled technicians and engineers. The capacity of the radical left—as opposed to the liberal left that organised around Wade—to mobilise popular support was made manifest by the strikes at the university (involving lecturers and students) and in the schools (also involving teachers and students) which began in March 1984 and continued for another decade. This was also the moment that the Movement of Democratic Forces of Casamance (MFDC) chose to renew its guerrilla operations which mainly took the form of attacks on government targets and people from the northern part of the country (Fall, 1986:78–82).

The increasing social turbulence which gripped Senegal created a fertile context for the emergence of a multitude of associations which were, to a greater or lesser extent, mostly political in character. Of these associations, perhaps one of the most important was the one that brought together qualified but unemployed teachers who had been trained for positions in the higher education sector. The intensification of the social crisis in the country coincided with a deepening national political crisis. In responding to the crises, the government resorted to the systematic use of repressive measures. This repression worsened with the decision of the opposition parties to boycott the municipal and rural elections that were scheduled for November 1984. Thus it was that a march against apartheid organised by Abdoulaye Bathily, leader of the LD/MPT, and Abdoulaye Wade was violently broken up by the internal security authorities and the two principal organisers of that event arrested and thrown into prison in August 1985. At the same time as this, the government employed an administrative measure to prevent the formation of an electoral coalition by one section of the opposition called the Senegalese Democratic Alliance (ADS).

The context of crisis and repression in which Senegal was enveloped precluded the possibility of a lull in the hostilities between the Senegalese opposition, whether radical or liberal, and the PS, despite the appeals for unity and consensus-building made by President Diouf in 1986 and 1987. The opposition's refusal to cooperate—at least as far as dialogue was concerned—was motivated by the government's failure to satisfy its principal demand, namely, a full-scale reform of the electoral system which was considered to be biased in favour of the ruling power bloc. Thus confrontation between the ruling party and the government on one side and the opposition parties and their supporters on the other side, became inevitable. It was in this highly threatening situation that the two most serious crises of the first decade of Abdou Diouf's presidency exploded: the strike by university and school students which began on the eve of presidential and legislative elections and led to the first *année blanche*/lost year in the history of the Senegalese educational system, and the strike which took place after the police broke up a demonstration following the sentencing to a term of imprisonment of police officers accused of having beaten a prisoner to death. President Diouf reacted swiftly and vigorously to this situation by laying off the entire Senegalese police force after appointing Jean Collin as the head of the ministry of the interior, a post which he had previously occupied for a term during the presidency of Senghor (Diop and Diouf, 1990:285–293).

The privately-owned print media, most notably *Sud Magazine, Wal Fadjri,* and *Le Cafard Libéré* made their own contribution to the opposition-led attempt to uproot the hegemony of the PS. For this, they were labelled by PS devotees as a "certain kind of press" "... [which] tends to devote itself to defamation, intoxicating and upsetting the morale of the nation and dis-crediting the institutions of the republic" (Paye, 1992:373). These journals reported the disputes between the opposition and ruling parties and acted as a tribunal on the issues raised by political parties and social movements. In so doing, they were able to break the regime's monopoly on information and at the same time expose the partial and partisan nature of a regime which had always claimed to be beyond reproach. The rumours which were intro-duced/fanned by this section of the press about the ways in which national affairs were being conducted, the daily revelations which they published about innumerable cases of corruption and misappropriation of public funds, and the attempt which they made to raise moral standards in public life may have been interpreted as evidence that they took sides with the opposition or, at least, were rooting for a democratic change of power. Whatever the case may have been, there can be no doubt that their activities placed the PS in an increasingly defensive position. In March 1988, on the eve of the elections, the publishers of *Sud Magazine* brought out a daily en-titled *Sud Hebdo;* this development had been preceded by the decision, taken at the end of 1987, of the publishers of *Wal Fadjri* to transform the publica-tion from an Islamic weekly into a general information journal. *Wal Fadjri* declared itself to be engaged in the same fight "on the side of *Sud Hebdo* and *Le Cafard Libéré*" (Paye, 1992:370).

With the stage fully set and the politicians geared up for the legislative and presidential elections of February 1988, the PS found itself shaken by internal crises and the disputes raging in the society as a whole. It was buffeted by the increasingly sharp attacks made by the opposition and the independent press and became defensive economically, politically and socially. Not surprisingly, even before the official opening of the election campaign, the main players had begun vigorously to unfold their strategies with a view to out-manoeuvring their rivals. As C. Young and B. Kanté recount:

President Diouf had worked out a prolonged and carefully elaborated schedule
of official visits in the three important regions, areas where plenty of promises
of local development were made. In the months preceding the campaign, the
opposition adopted a strategy of systematic harassment of the government,
filing a series of cases in the courts which challenged certain provisions of the
electoral system, as well as using other means (1992:95).

The strategy of harassing the PS and the government at the juridico-
administrative level was primarily the handiwork of the PDS which, in
taking such actions, wanted to demonstrate the opposition's capacity for
initiating a new form of political intervention that was based on rules and
procedures which are universally accepted as democratic. If the strategy
succeeded, it would have the added bonus of confirming to the generality of
Senegalese that the PDS was responsible and could engage in the legal business of the state, the legal-judicial domain being, *par excellence,* an important
symbol of the Senegalese struggle for democracy. For its part, the radical
opposition—as if the task of destabilising the PS had been carefully shared
out between it and the PDS—took on the role of social mobilisation, including the encouragement of various groups to agitate for concessions from a
regime which was faced with an electoral battle which it knew was going to
be very difficult.

The increasingly repressive measures adopted by the government, its
refusal to negotiate a reform of the electoral system, the profound social
malaise provoked by the effects of structural adjustment programmes (the
retrenchment of the state and of public/parastatal enterprises, growing
(youth) unemployment, particularly among university and high school
graduates, and repeated strikes in the school and university sectors to protest the harsh austerity policies of the government), and the signs of organised discontent among police officers who had been laid off combined to
give the opposition a space in which to voice its complaints, mobilise an
increasingly disaffected citizenry, and denounce the government for its
incapacity to resolve the country's many serious problems. Moreover, for the
first time, the PDS had a new political style which established it as a credible
opposition.

Employing methods of recruitment and operation similar to those of the
PS, possessing an extraordinary capacity to make the radical opposition
dance to its own tune, and often to subordinate the latter's strategy to its
own as required by its status as a populist party which the population could
believe in, the PDS proved its expertise in its use of a political idiom which
could activate the electorate and young people. *Sopi* (change) became the
rallying cry of the opponents of the regime, and it captured the diversity of
their grievances. Sarcastically twisting the regime's political campaign
slogans to poke fun at the PS and Diouf, the opposition also simultaneously
mobilised the citizenry to agitate for the lowering of the price of rice and
support the proposal for a televised Diouf/Wade debate. Predictably, Diouf
opposed the idea of a televised debate but that did not stop the PDS and the

opposition in general from popularising the notion that a change of political power could be achieved through the ballot box. For the first time in the history of Senegal, the principal player in the political game of the opposition was neither a Marxist nor a historically radical nationalist but a person who, initially at least, cut his teeth as a liberal nationalist.

However, the overall extraordinary vitality of the opposition masked the profound divisions that ran through it, divisions that were both ideological and personal. From the time of the 1983 elections to the eve of the election campaign of 1988, the opposition sought in vain to achieve a unified framework strong enough to bring it to power. On issues such as the forging of a united action programme by the parties, the adoption of a single candidacy in order to strengthen their position, and the formulation of a common platform on crucial questions, the Senegalese opposition never succeeded in creating a common ground on which it could intervene as an organised group. Instead, its failed manoeuvres on these issues and its violent quarrels about leadership simply reproduced a history of splits, excommunications and denunciations that had always characterised the Senegalese opposition. The public demonstrations of love and fraternity displayed by the different opposition parties, usually following on well publicised quarrels that were often tinged with insults, both confused the electorate and profoundly undermined the long-term credibility of the opposition. The ruling party lost no opportunity to seize on the love-hate relationship within the opposition; the polemic of the PS and Diouf was often laced with references to the "irresponsible" political opposition.

Failing to agree on basics after all the mileage which it had covered, the opposition ended up going into the 1988 elections in a state of disarray. Four candidates stood for the presidential elections: Abdou Diouf (PS), Landing Savané (AJ/PADS, supported by the MSU), Abdoulaye Wade (PDS, supported by the LD/MPT and PIT) and Babacar Niang (PLP). In the legislative elections, these parties and the PDS/R put candidates forward. By far the most credible challenger to Diouf and the PS in terms of his potential capacity to inflict serious political damage was Abdoulaye Wade. Conscious of this fact, he organised enormous political meetings in the towns of Senegal, meetings which attracted all the disaffected people in the areas he visited. The youth were particularly visible at his rallies; indeed they took on the role of "storm troopers" for Wade. Thus, the meetings of the PS were routinely disrupted and forcefully dispersed by those whom the partisans of the PS saw as "young hooligans manipulated by the opposition's highwaymen". Violence reached an unprecedented level three days before the elections during a meeting at Thiès addressed by a PS candidate who promised that exemplary punishment would be meted out to the leaders of the opposition once the ruling party's victory was confirmed.

The election results that were officially declared gave victory to the PS and Diouf. This was immediately rejected by the opposition and a fairly significant proportion of the urban population; there is no doubt that the outcome did not conform with their expectations and the general impression which they had formed of the election campaign. The feeling was widely held that the PS had cheated at the expense of the PDS. The immediate popular reaction to the official results was very serious rioting in the working-class areas of Dakar (Diop and Diouf, 1990). The absence of any concrete gestures from the PS inflamed passions further as did the declaration by the PDS of its intention to publish what it described as the "true" results of the elections. It was against this background that President Diouf took a decision to proclaim a state of emergency and arrest the principal leaders of the opposition, including Wade. Wade and the frontline members of his party were tried swiftly and sentenced to various terms of imprisonment. This action further inflamed passions and had the unintended consequence of mobilising the urban population against the government. The tense and volatile situation in the country forced the PS and its leader to resort to dialogue with the opposition by convening round table talks to discuss the political situation (Diop and Diouf, 1990:362–368). The negotiations failed to yield positive results, with the opposition using the forum to rehearse its main complaints against the ruling party and the government and the PS attempting to use the fact of the dialogue to once again remobilise and renew themselves. The result was an impasse which persisted side by side with increasingly frequent crises in the schools and universities and an intensification of state repression directed at the critics and opponents of the regime.

The post-election crisis launched a number of new actors onto the Senegalese political scene. Because the crisis mostly unfolded in the main urban centres and resulted in violence, which most people associated with *Sopi*, it was not surprising that most of the new players brought to the fore were young people the majority of whom were growing up with the feeling of being excluded from the economic, social and political system. The crisis was also indicative of the failure of the country's political institutions. Furthermore, the fact that the 1988 elections failed to produce a change of government left many ordinary Senegalese deeply disappointed. The most highly mobile and politicised sectors of the population opted out of the formal political framework and attached themselves to autonomous organisations, such as associations of women, professionals, and young people as well as minority ethnic groupings. For them, the formal political framework had become a minefield. Two songs released during this period by the famous Senegalese musician, Youssou Ndour, namely, *Set* (Clean up) and *Douma combine beré* (I'm opposed to phoney/pre-arranged contests; I don't cheat) very aptly captured the mood of the country.

What was to be done now that the strongest mobilisation ever waged against the PS regime by the opposition had failed to deliver a change of government and ruling party in the country? This was a question which pre-occupied various sectors of Senegalese society. The response in the towns was the almost spontaneous launching of the *Set Setal*, a movement dedicated to bringing physical, moral and aesthetic order to a situation of urban disorder and the PS' record of bad governance. The birth of the movement was a testament to the fact that the country was beset by a profound malaise; it also revealed the feeling of confusion that was rife among the youth. Furthermore, the *Set Setal* marked the end of the illusion which many held that power could change hands through the ballot box, a prospect which had stirred thousands of young people and women into action. The movement was also a contestation of the institutional framework for political expression, whether as represented by the majority or the opposition.

The profound malaise that beset the young people of Senegal found another, more brutal outlet following the onset of the Senegalo-Mauritanian crisis of 1989. As M. Diouf has pointed out,

> ... the failure to overturn the [PS] regime under the impetus of *Sopi* and the vicissitudes of the confrontation between the government and a greatly divided opposition led to new forms of protest organised principally by the urban youth but also by lawyers, journalists of the so-called independent press, and school and university students. In a wider sense, one can argue that they adopted new practices which, as a response to Diouf's strategy of fragmentation, reinterpreted the process of achieving democracy as one requiring various collective strategies (Dioup and Diouf, 1990:273).

The withdrawal of the populace into activities organised outside the framework of party politics compelled the opposition to re-define its strategies. The demise of *Sopi*, the Senegalo-Mauritanian crisis, and the increasingly difficult relations between "Senegal and her neighbours" (Diop and Lavergne, 1994) buried once and for all, the political project for a possible change of power which Wade and the PDS had hoped to achieve. In 1991, after being pressurised by "friendly countries", including France, to hold secret talks, the PDS, together with the PIT, rejoined the government set up by Abdou Diouf and run by a freshly rehabilitated Habib Thiam.

THE RECOMPOSITION OF POWER, POLITICS, AND RELIGION
DURING THE DIOUF YEARS

The transformation that was taking place in the country's politics naturally had implications for the *marabout* (Islamic religious leader) component of the Senegalese political configuration. This configuration was redrawn as much by political changes unleashed by the extension of the democratic space, first by Senghor (following his decision in 1974 to effect a political opening on the basis of a democracy initially limited to three and then to four parties), and then by Abdou Diouf who launched a programme of complete political liberalisation. Also relevant for the process of political re-configuration were the series of demonstrations that were organised across the country at different stages of its recent political history, the appearance of new actors in the public arena, the increasing visibility of Islamic movements, the persistence of irredentist and secessionist demonstrations in the Casamance, and increasingly violent social movements nourished by the economic crisis that gripped the country.

Several studies, such as those by J. Copans (1980), D. Cruise O'Brien (1975, 1977, 1989), C. Coulon (1981, 1984), L. Creevy-Berham (1977), I.L. Markowitz (1970), R. Fatton (1985, 1987) and M. C. Diop and M. Diouf (1990) have attempted to capture the role and place of the *marabout* factor in contemporary Senegalese politics. The studies have placed particular emphasis on the political arrangements that have been worked out between the *marabouts* and politicians, arrangements which are generally thought to lie at the centre of Senegal's "quite remarkable success story". To use the words of Cruise O'Brien and Coulon:

> This success was attributed to the emergence of an authentic national political culture, to relatively viable linkages between the communities (local, religious or ethnic) and the state. The success is manifest in the capacity of the governmental party as an effective political machine. The quality of political leadership made the Senegalese state a "uniquely effective political apparatus", and an instrument of stability although still unable to initiate effective development policy. The state in Senegal at least was not a political "artefact" working in a void, without effective links with society at large (1988:145).

The extraordinary manner in which the general caliph of the Mouridic brotherhood chose to express his support for Abdou Diouf, and his party, the PS, during the presidential and legislative elections in 1988 had multiple consequences for the Senegalese political scene. Unlike on previous occasions, the Mouridic leader did not in 1988 simply confine himself to delivering the customary *ndigël* that has always been his practice at the time of every election since independence, namely that, every *taalibe* (disciple) who regarded himself a true member of the confraternity had a duty to vote for the PS and its presidential candidate. Instead, he proclaimed loudly and clearly that "anyone who fails to vote for Diouf and his party is betraying the message and teaching of the founder of the brotherhood, Ahmadou Bamba Mbacké". No *ndigël* had ever been more forcefully delivered. The highly pointed nature of the 1988 declaration prompted a great deal of discussion regarding the reasons for the unprecedented tone that was adopted by the grand caliph. It was the first time that the authority of the brotherhood's most venerated saint, Ahmadou Bamba Mbacké, had ever been invoked in support of a partisan political cause.

Among the different interpretations that have been ventured is one which suggests that the declaration reflects the total capture of the brotherhood by the state and the ruling oligarchy. This was all the more so as members of the *maraboutic* hierarchy were engaged in economic and financial operations which required state protection and guarantees of continued access to credit. This reality meant that the *marabouts* would henceforth be under some sort of obligation to the politicians of the ruling PS (M. C. Diop and M. Diouf:1990). For other commentators, including Cruise O'Brien and Coulon, the question that was posed was whether, at the end of the 1980s, Senegal was confronted with a local Islamic peril:

> President Abdou Diouf has said repeatedly that there is no Muslim funda-mentalist offensive in Senegal; but to stay just a few days in Dakar is to realise that the tranquil and moderate Islam which has long prevailed in this country is now in question. One finds in Senegal the atmosphere of Islamic agitation which marked the early years of colonial rule, a period when the economic, social and political upheavals introduced by the European presence produced large scale religious movements such as gave birth, for example, to the Mouridism of Ahmadou Bamba (1989:156).

The interpretation offered by these two authors emphasises the economic and social transformations of the 1980s and their repercussions on the social movements and political arrangements linking various social actors. In their retrospective analysis of the period, they suggest that the "groundnut *marabouts*"

> ... were more concerned for their plantations and their businesses than for "Islamic revolution". First the colonial administration and then the Senegalese government itself supported their agricultural activities and set up these relig-ious notables as local bosses and political inter-mediaries. Clientelism prevailed and services were mutually rendered. The *marabouts* exercised a sort of indirect administration over an entire section of the population and favoured the devel-opment of groundnut cultivation. The politicians acknowledged the heads of the brotherhoods as "chiefs of the hinterland" and linked up with them in order to recruit followers and voters. Everything seemed to be for the best in the Islamic and patrimonial worlds (1989:156).

According to these authors, what changed in the course of the 1980s, with the economic crisis, was the appearance of reformist Islamic movements in Senegal. These movements were formed by a host of new Islamic associa-tions which not only demanded a key autonomous role for Islam in Senegal but also proceeded progressively to try to construct it. Naturally, this auton-omy was asserted in relation to the state and the ruling class and also in relation to the brotherhoods which they accused of subordinating Islam to political causes. Does this, therefore, mean that Abdou Lahat Mbacké's dec-laration which we cited earlier represented an attempt by the Mouridic *marabouts* to exert control over the reformist pressures that were building up both within and outside the brotherhoods by reaffirming their historic alli-ance with the ruling class? Or was it simply the case that the Mouridic *marabout* was, with greater solemnity, reaffirming an alliance that was threatened by the diversity of political activities taking place at the heart of the brotherhoods, a diversity brought about by full-scale multipartyism? Whatever the answer to these questions may be, it seems absolutely clear that Abdou Lahat Mbacké's stipulation reflected both a malaise about how to control the political activities of the *marabouts* and the *taalibe* in each brotherhood and a tension between the autonomy of the brotherhood and collaboration and subordination in relation to the political elite—an elite that was now increasingly distributed among the different parties on the political chess-board, of which the two most important were the PS and the PDS.

Paradoxically, the caliph's words also reflected the deepening fragmentation that was taking place within the hierarchies of the brotherhoods. This process of fragmentation was, in part at least, a function of the increasing competition within and among the brotherhoods for access to state sinecures and financial, commercial and economic support, resources which were shrinking because of the worsening economic crisis in the country and the new austerity policies of the government. In the familial and private domain of the *marabouts*, the violent nature of the conflicts that developed between sections and strands, but also between brothers, called into question the image of homogeneity and unity of purpose as well as of action for which the brotherhoods were reputed. Thus it was that the long-held practice of obedience which enabled the brotherhoods to present a disciplined public front and which, therefore, assured the brotherhoods of a secure presence in the public arena, was gradually eroded. Quarrels over succession, especially in the *tijaan* brotherhood, added to the conflicts (Villalon, 1995:124–129).

The crisis confronting the maraboutic establishment was made all the more serious by the fact that the *taalibe* were increasingly less able to make donations of any significant size to them; indeed, many were the *taalibe* who were propelled by their political activities towards struggles requiring increasing support from the trade unions and decreasing *maraboutic* patronage. The formation of the union for Sandaga market traders, dominated by the Mourids and the National Union of Senegalese Traders, a development which was important in mobilising against the monopolistic advantages granted by the state to its principal clients in industry, commerce and various parastatal organisations, is indicative of the changes taking place and the gradual formalisation of relations between traders and the managing elite. This process of formalisation had the effect of shrinking, if not eliminating the intermediary position of the *marabouts* who were beginning, progressively, to lose their strategic position as protectors of economic entrepreneurs whose principal commercial activities were sustained by fraud and the non-payment of taxes.

The post-election upheavals that took place in the country in 1988, the growing culture of political and domestic violence that was enveloping Senegal, and, to some extent, the death of Abdou Lahat were the main contextual reasons for the retreat of the leaders of the brotherhoods from the political field. Not surprisingly, they did not give any orders to their followers on how they should vote in the presidential and legislative elections of 1993. They retreated into a deafening silence, thus enabling the worldly *marabouts*—those among the heads of *maraboutic* families who were still engaged in the political and economic game—to speak out. The retreat of many *marabouts* had one signal effect: a space was opened up as much for those who were actively supporting the ruling party/oligarchy as for those who were strongly opposed to it. Those *marabouts* who insisted on an open political role, especially those of them who were politicians, had no option other than to enter directly into the arena. In so doing, they lost their aura as *marabouts* and became activists who from then on received a political salary.

CONCLUDING REFLECTIONS

The new political situation in which Senegal found itself after the 1988 elections confirmed the end of the logic of integration that had, for long, characterised Senegalese politics; it also opened up a new form of political alliance, that of cohabitation among the different political forces vying for power and influence in the country, each with its own personality and able to express its opposition to the views of the government. This political/ governmental set-up was to have multiple consequences for the configuration of the political space and the character of the Senegalese political game. It became the central axis around which politics operated (Diaw, 1994). As cohabitation was put into practice, so too was the popular hope for change placed on the back burner. *Sopi* was inherited by the radical opposition and the ordinary people were left with nothing. Wade and the PAS negotiated a reform of the constitution creating the position of vice-president. That constitutional amendment represented the final death blow for the prospects for a democratic change of power. The project of cohabitation also failed to benefit the supporters of radical change. The attempt by the AJ/PADS to remobilise the people against a "government that divided up the national cake" did not meet with much popular enthusiasm.

The alliance between the PDS and the PIT did not deter the Marxist opposition from ploughing ahead with its own campaigns; the belief among the marxists was that from now on, the struggle against a single rightist party (the operational slogan was that the PS=the PDS) would give it greater opportunities to mobilise the populace for radical change. There were even hopes that the changed situation brought about by the decision of the PDS to join the PS in cohabitation would, at last, make it possible to build lasting left unity around the LD/MPT and AJ/PADS. The litmus test came in 1993 as the elections scheduled for that year approached and, as it turned out, these parties were unable to produce a common list of candidates for the legislative elections or to agree on a common candidate for the presidential elections. In the meantime, Wade resigned from the government and remobilised his party in order to take part in the elections. Abdoulaye Bathily (LD/MPT) and Landing Savané (AJ/PADS) emerged as great mobilisers during the election campaigns. They attracted so many people to their meetings that the illusion was created that one of them might successfully insert himself between Diouf and Wade.

When the results were announced, Wade and Diouf and their respective parties were the victors; the radical opposition performed poorly. The possibility of a change of power in Senegalese politics became even more remote. Wade had done better in 1993 than in 1988 despite being part of the government. From now on, in the relations between the PS and the PDS, partnership replaced confrontation. But at what price? It was around this critical question that conflicts developed within the PS and the PDS between the supporters and the opponents of cohabitation. The post-election upheavals that occurred and the arrest, once again, of Wade after the assassination of one of the judges on the Constitutional Council, simply bore witness to the shifting contours of the political battles that were taking place within the ruling coalition. Between the time of the declaration of the results and the arrest of Wade, the LD/MPT, drawing its own conclusions from the experience it had during the 1993 election campaign and the fact that the position of the PDS was strengthened despite its association with the government, decided to rejoin the PDS in the cohabitation arrangement with the PS. An electorally-based change of political power in Senegal was, thus, made to seem even more remote as the third party among the most important parties in the country dramatically changed its strategy and entered the government. While the LD/MPT was making its way into the government, the PDS waited in the ante-chamber of power and then decided to rejoin the government fully once the legal problems of certain of its leaders were over. Opposition politics in Senegal will probably never be the same again for a long time to come.

BIBLIOGRAPHY

Bathily, Abdoulaye, 1992, *Mai 68 ou la Révolte Universitaire et la Démocratie*. Paris: Editions Chaka/Afrique Contemporaine.

Copans, Jean, 1980, *Les Marabouts de l'Arachide*. Paris: Le Sycomore.

Coulon, Christian, 1981, *Le Marabout et le Prince*. Paris: Pédone.

Coulon, Christian, 1984, "L'Etat et l'Islam au Sénégal: Divorce ou Nouveau Rapport de Force", *Année Africaine*. Paris: Pédone.

Creevy-Berham, Lucy, 1977, "Muslim Politics and Development in Senegal", *Journal of Modern African Studies*, Vol. 24, No. 2.

Cruise O'Brien, Donal, 1975, *Saints and Politicians: Essays in the Organization of an Islamic Brotherhood*. Cambridge: Cambridge University Press.

Cruise O'Brien, Donal, 1977, "A Versatile Charisma: The Mourid Brotherhood 1975–76", *Archives Européennes de Sociologie*, Vol. 18, No. 1, p. 84–106.

Cruise O'Brien, Donal and Christian Coulon (eds.), 1988, *Charisma and Brotherhood in African Islam*. Oxford: Oxford University Press.

Cruise O'Brien, Donal, J. Dunn and R. Rathbone (eds.), 1989, *Contemporary West African States*. Cambridge: Cambridge University Press.

Diaw, Aminata, 1994, *Démocratisation et Logiques Identitaires en Acte: L'Invention de la Politique en Afrique*. Dakar: CODESRIA.

Diop, Momar C. and Mamadou Diouf, 1990, *Le Sénégal sous Abdou Diouf*. Paris: Karthala.

Diop, Momar C. (ed.), 1992, *Sénégal: Trajectoires d'un Etat*. Dakar: CODESRIA.

Diop, Momar C. and Real Lavergne (eds.), 1994, *Regional Integration in West Africa: Proceedings of the International Conference organized by IDRC in Dakar, Senegal, 11–15 Jan 1993*. Ottawa: IDRC.

Fall, Mar, 1986, *Sénégal: L'Etat sous Abdou Diouf ou le Temps des Incertitudes*. Paris: Harmattan.

Fatton, Robert, 1985, "Organic Crisis, Organic Intellectuals and the Senegalese Passive Revolution", 28th Annual Meeting of the African Studies Association, New Orleans, Nov. 1985.

Fatton, Robert, 1987, *The Making of a Liberal Democracy: Senegal's Passive Revolution 1975–85*. Boulder: Lynne Rienner.

Hesseling, Gerti, 1985, *Histoire Politique du Sénégal*. Paris: Karthala.

Ly, Abdoulaye, 1992, *Les regroupements politiques au Sénégal 1956–1970*, Dakar: CODESRIA.

Markowitz, I.L., 1970, "Traditional Social Structures: The Islamic Brotherhood and Political Development", *Journal of Modern African Studies*, 8, 1, (April).

Paye, Moussa, 1992, "La Presse et le Pouvoir" in M.C. Diop (ed.), *Sénégal: Trajetoires d'un Etat*. Dakar: CODESRIA.

Villalon, Leonardo A., 1995, *Islamic Society and State Power in Senegal: Disciples and Citizens in Fatick*. Cambridge: Cambridge University Press.

Young, C. and B. Kanté, 1992, "Governance, Democracy and the Senegalese" in G. Hyden and M. Bratton (eds.), *Governance and Politics in Africa*. Boulder: Lynne Rienner.

Zuccarelli, François, 1988, *La Vie Politique Sénégalaise, 1940–1988*. Paris: CHEAM.

Chapter 5

The Rise to Power of an Opposition Party: The MNSD in Niger Republic

Jibrin Ibrahim and Abdoulaye Niandou Souley

INTRODUCTION

With the embrace by virtually all the countries on the continent of one version or the other of political pluralism, it would seem that Africa has embarked on a bold, even if not yet fully irreversible transition towards a more democratic order. Numerous authoritarian regimes have been effectively challenged by a cross-section of the peoples whom they previously ruled without much effective opposition or open dissent and, in many countries, democratic forces have been able to bring their concerns to the forefront of public discussions. Some of Africa's most entrenched authoritarian regimes have been replaced by their erstwhile democratic opponents and the question that is now posed in several countries is that of the routinisation of democratic culture which includes not only the existence of independent and effective opposition parties but also the possibilities of a constitutionally-based change of power between ruling and opposition parties.

It is certainly a mark of the progress that has been recorded in Africa in recent times that almost no country on the continent today, not even any of those that are still dominated by the military, challenges the principle of plural democracy as a desirable political model. That apparent consensus is, however, in danger of masking a new problem, namely, that of a growing array of political actors who pretend to be committed to playing the new democratic game while, in reality, subverting it by refusing to adhere to the basic rules of participation and fair competition. Indeed, a new political practice appears to be emerging whereby the forces of authoritarianism which had earlier been destabilised by the democratic upheavals that led to the National Conferences of 1989–1992 are re-organising and "modernising" their strategies. They have now donned a "democratic" toga in order to be able to enact their authoritarian project. Clearly, so soon after the onset of the African political transition, we are compelled to pay greater attention to the tensions between *form* and *essence* in the practices of the leading political actors. For, as the transition progresses, the hope which many had that the second democratic wave in Africa which began in the late 1980s can be quickly consolidated is in danger of being dimmed by a re-invented and re-invigorated authoritarianism that threatens to undermine and even reverse the democratic gains/aspirations of the people. Niger is a good example of this new trend towards the reversal of democratic gains by the resurgent forces of repression and authoritarianism.

The democratic revolution that occurred in Niger in the early 1990s had a lot of initial promise. The National Conference that was convened was, on almost all counts, as successful as it was open and popular. The army which, as in many other West African states, had been the lightning rod of authoritarianism in Niger agreed, without resistance, to return to the barracks. The former single ruling party, the military-backed *Mouvement National pour la Société de Développement* (MNSD), having lost the elections that were convened after the National Conference, graciously accepted its fate and handed over power to the victors. More than this, in opposition, it embarked on what many saw at the time as a credible attempt to transform itself into a thriving political opposition, although it had no prior background in democratic struggles and was the party of local notables and senior bureaucrats.

The MNSD also had the dubious honour of being the ruling party that emerged out of prolonged military rule. Indeed, so pervasive was the military-guaranteed dominance which it enjoyed that, between 1992/1993 and 1996, the essence of national democratic politics in Niger was effectively reduced to a concerted effort at sidelining the MNSD from the corridors of power in spite of the fact that it always emerged as the single biggest party in all of the competitive elections that were held in the country. After the 1993 elections, an alliance was forged which prevented the MNSD from coming back to power, prompting one observer to note that "the multiparty democracy game has functioned well, but the MNSD, the number one Nigerien party by number of votes obtained has lost all" (Decoudras, 1994:50). However, in February 1995, the Nigerien President was obliged to name an MNSD militant as Prime Minister after an alliance led by the party won the fresh round of legislative elections that were held earlier that year. This chapter is about the hope for democracy that the MNSD represented as a once-authoritarian party that was able to adapt itself to the challenges of democratic politics, and about how that hope was shattered by an increasingly poisoned political climate and the military *coup d'état* of January 1996.

THE NEO-TRADITIONAL CORPORATIST STATE AND
THE RISE OF THE MNSD

The Republic of Niger developed as a neo-traditional corporatist state built
on a mode of governance that linked civilian technocrats in a close alliance
with the military officers who ran the state apparatus on the advice of donor
bureaucrats and an embryonic entrepreneurial bourgeoisie (Robinson,
1991:4). This mode of governance was perfected during the long rule of the
former President, Seyni Kountché, who toppled the first post-independence
government of the country headed by Hamani Diori. If Diori's rule was as
high-handed as it was corrupt, Kountché's regime turned out, by any stretch
of the imagination, to be one of the most austere and repressive ever witnessed on the African continent. Kountché attempted to herd all Nigeriens
into a unified community by military fiat. In so doing, he drew upon elements of re-invented tradition by resuscitating the Association of Traditional
Chiefs which had originally been invented during the French colonial
period. He also established the Islamic Association of Niger to serve as the
official, pro-establishment religious interlocutor of the people. A national
youth movement, inspired by the traditional youth associations known as
the *samariya*, was also established. Corporatism in Niger took a clearer
organisational form in 1983 when these different organisations were formalised by Kountché and his supporters into a single structure that was
named the *Société de Développement*. The new structure was organised at five
levels—village, local, sub-regional, regional and national. At the national
level, the *Conseil National de Développement* (CND) or National Council for
Development was presented as embodying the nation and its developmental
goals.

The CND was designed as a body that would eventually be transformed
into a "non-partisan" ruling party which, purportedly, would reflect the
aspirations of "*tous les Nigeriens*". The occasion for the CND's re-naming and
transformation into the sole and ruling party came with the inauguration of
Niger's Second Republic on 6 October, 1989, following the promulgation of a
new constitution which, officially, had been massively approved by 99.3 per
cent of eligible Nigeriens in a referendum that was held a month earlier. The
process of returning Niger to so-called democratic one-party rule was a long
and elaborate one which began in August 1983, when President Seyni
Kountché announced a programme of "gradual" movement towards constitutional rule and grassroots democracy. The first stage in the process consisted primarily of the drawing up of a National Charter that was to define
the operational principles of the future constitution and the instrument for
democratisation, namely, the CND. The main objective of the CND was to
dynamise and integrate state-sponsored neighbourhood, village and ward

associations into organs of democracy and development.[1] The first draft of the Charter was circulated in April 1986 and adopted by the Council of Ministers in May 1987 after a national debate. It had no provisions for the transfer of power to elected representatives but it proposed the establishment of the rule of law in the country (Raynal, 1990:379–381).This was the situation until the death of Seyni Kountché in November 1987.

The demise of Kountché and his replacement as Head of State by Ali Saibou, another senior military officer, accelerated the pace of political change in Niger. On assuming power, Saibou had declared that he would pursue the process of democratisation started by his predecessor more vigorously but would not accept the introduction of multipartyism to the country so as to preserve national stability and integration. As part of his own "democratisation" scheme, President Saibou transformed the CND into a single party which he named the *Mouvement National Pour le Développement de la Société* (MNSD)/the National Movement for the Development of Society. The Constitution that was adopted and the elections that were held in 1989 were aimed at the institutionalisation of this idea of single party democracy in the country (Maidoka, 1991). The directing principle of the Second Republic was to "restore democracy while maintaining order" (Raynal, 1990:382). Apart from these institutional changes, President Saibou also considerably mellowed the authoritarian, literally suffocating grip of the state on the society that had been put in place by Kountché (Adji, 1991:329). Furthermore, he initiated a policy of *decrispation* by making the regime less austere, more open, and more approachable. On 10 December, 1989, Ali Saibou was elected President of the Republic with 99.6 per cent of the vote; 93 legislators were elected into the National Assembly with 99.52 per cent of the vote, all in an apparently very orderly and successful manner (Niandou, 1990:249). But appearances turned out to be deceptive in this instance as Niger was soon gripped by widespread discontent which, more than the charade enacted by Kountché and Saibou, reflected the true and deeply held feelings of Nigeriens.

THE MARCH TO THE SOVEREIGN NATIONAL CONFERENCE

On 8 February, 1990, two months after the election of Saibou to the presidency, university students started a boycott of lectures over the adoption and implementation of International Monetary Fund (IMF)-inspired structural adjustment policy measures that saw the state attempting to substantially reduce funding for the educational sector. On 9 February, 1990, in furtherance of their protest action, the students decided to organise a peace-

---

[1] *Samariyya* is a Hausa term which refers to neighbourhood/community youth self-help groups which were the basic unit for the construction of Kountché's version of participatory grassroots democracy.

ful march to the centre of Niamey, the capital. As they got to the Kennedy bridge on the outskirts of the capital, soldiers attacked them violently and at least three unarmed students were confirmed killed (Niandou, 1990:268). The brutality of the soldiers' action, together with the cold-bloodedness of the massacre on that fateful day, served to usher Niger towards a major turning point in its history. It came as a great shock to the generality of the people that a government that claimed to be democratising society could go so far as to massacre unarmed students without provocation.

Immediately after the massacre, the central labour organisation, the *Union des Syndicats des Travailleurs du Niger* (USTN), was shocked out of 30 years of lethargy and collaboration with successive Nigerien governments. It withdrew from the governing council of the ruling MNSD party and began to openly agitate against the MNSD state. It played a major role in organis-ing a massive demonstration the following Friday, 16 February, 1990, after prayers at the mosque. That demonstration turned out to be the biggest protest march the country had seen since its independence. Soulay Adji (1991:333) argues convincingly that the massacre on what has come to be known as Black Friday signalled the re-birth of civil society in Niger. The culture of fear and silence that had been so characteristic of Francophone African political culture was decisively reversed in Niger and suddenly, as if inspired, the people wanted to define their own democracy rather than operate the one proposed by the state: the end of the old corporatist order had arrived.

In the face of popular agitation and resistance, the edifice of repression that had been built by successive Nigerien regimes unravelled. Four months after Black Friday, *Haske*, the first independent newspaper since independ-ence, was launched. Right from its first edition, it started a debate on the necessity for multipartyism and a National Conference in Niger. The trade unions, freshly emboldened, moved from merely calling for the respect of the constitution to demanding nothing less than its abrogation. A general strike was organised in support of a National Conference and multiparty democracy, with an estimated 100,000 people marching on the streets of Niamey to support the demands. These developments clearly marked the beginning of the end of an era; the days of the ruling authoritarian oligarchy were apparently numbered. The people had imposed a linkage between democratisation and popular multiparty participation which was hard to ignore or side-step. It is to Ali Saibou's credit that he accepted the people's verdict and agreed that a National Conference be convened.

The National Conference in Niger was declared open by President Saibou and it sat from 29 July to 3 November 1991. It attracted the participa-tion of over 1,200 delegates representing trade unions, students' unions, political parties, chambers of commerce, voluntary associations, and the civil service. As was the case in Benin Republic, the National Conference ruled from the very beginning that its decisions were sovereign and would override all pre-existing institutional powers and actions: the people had formally invested all sovereignty in themselves, at least for the duration of the Conference. As part of this process, delegates to the Conference decided to dissolve the government and ask the Directors-General of ministries to report directly to them. In effect, by their actions, the delegates turned President Ali Saibou into a ceremonial Head of State. They also removed the Chief of Army from office.

What was perhaps most striking about the National Conference was the spirit of liberty which it fostered all over Niger. The security forces were withdrawn from the streets and confidence, as well as an unaccustomed self-assuredness, seemed to return to the people. The National Conference experience served to reverse the marginality of the population while galvanising the popular will and the determination of the citizenry to participate in the politics of the country without being threatened and/or manipulated from above. It was, indeed, a major cathartic moment that helped to release the spirit of liberty lurking in Nigeriens.

Viewed from the angle of the Nigerien experience, Pearl Robinson (1994:576) is substantially right when she argues that the notion of a Sovereign National Conference such as has been recently witnessed in Africa was conceived as an instrument for regime change that is grounded in Rousseau's ideas about popular sovereignty and the right of the people to renegotiate the social contract. The point of departure of the politics of the Conference was the rejection of the MNSD authoritarian corporatist state that the country's rulers had tried to build. The Conference was, in fact, structured in such a manner as to disempower the corporatist oligarchy:

> Representational formulae, deliberative procedures and voting rules were crafted to ensure that Power (henceforth, the term used for government or the political class) could always be defeated by majority vote (Robinson, 1994:603).

The use of the National Conference to overthrow existing power structures had been successfully tried in other countries in the West African sub-region (Niandou, 1992). By the end of its deliberations, the National Conference in Niger had successfully swept aside the neo-traditional corporatist power structure that had long dominated the country. In its place, transitional institutions were established and empowered to manage the affairs of the country for fifteen months, after which fully democratic elections would take place. The transitional institutions included the office of the President of the Republic, which was allowed to have protocol functions only, having been stripped of executive and legislative powers by the National Conference; a *Haut Conseil de la République* (HCR)/High Council of State that had legislative as well as supervisory powers over the executive; and, finally, the Prime Minister and his ministers, who had executive powers. General Ali Saibou remained as President of the Republic, Professor André Salifou, the President of the Presidium of the National Conference, was elected President of the HCR, while Tcheffou Amadou was elected Prime Minister. All these elections were conducted at the National Conference which also decided that none of the three transition officers could contest the scheduled presidential elections that were to mark the end of the transitional period.

The inauguration of the transitional institutions was considered to be the final phase of the National Conference and their main function was to lead the country to democratic rule. The National Conference prepared a legal framework (the *Acte Fondamental*), and a programme (the *Cahiers des Charges*) which were to guide the transitional institutions in their task. The HCR adopted the new constitution on 30 September, 1992 and Nigeriens accepted it in a referendum which took place on 26 December, 1992. The *Acte Fondamental* did not spell out the functions and prerogatives of the transitional institutions very clearly, resulting in many conflicts of interpretation and clashes of personality during the transitional period. This weakness notwithstanding, the institutions were able, on the whole, to overcome the difficulties that arose on different occasions and lead Niger towards the adoption of its new constitution.

Successful legislative and presidential elections were held in 1993. The expansion of the local political space and the dynamics of democratisation that occurred in Niger also opened up the possibilities for the "ethnicisation" of the political process as different sections of the elite struggled for the control of political power. The principle of multiparty politics which had been accepted on 15 November, 1990 gave a new dynamism to politics in Niger. The establishment of parties opened the floodgates to free and effective mobilisation of support on a variety of grounds, including ethnic considerations. Thirty political parties participated in the National Conference. Most of them were formed in great haste, with little or no strategic thinking. As such, many of the parties did not represent any real political force and were soon to fade away. Some of them, however, had deep roots in Niger's political history, perhaps none more so than the MNSD on which we are focusing in this chapter.

THE MNSD AND ITS MAIN RIVALS

The MNSD was, from its origins, a party of notables and virtually all the top military, bureaucratic and business people in the country were registered members of the party before the National Conference was convened. Indeed, Ali Saibou in his capacity as Head of State was also the president of the party. Saibou however withdrew from the party leadership in 1991 and a congress was convened to elect a new leader. Two "military notables", who were leading power brokers under President Seyni Kountché, namely, retired colonels Adamou Djermakoye and Mamadou Tandja contested at the March 1991 leadership congress. Djermakoye is a scion of the Zarma ruling oligarchy in Niger and had been in the corridors of power since the days of Seyni Kountche. In fact, he was a major contender in the succession struggle after the death of Kountché. Tandja was also a part of the top politico-military leadership of the country and had been a prefect in Maradi and Tahaoua, interior minister in Kountché's cabinet, and ambassador to Nigeria. However, unlike most of the rest of the top leadership, he was not Zarma. He is of mixed Kanuri and Fulani parentage from Diffa, in the southeast of the country.

The leadership contest was won by Tandja, mainly because the non-Zarma party cadres teamed up to support him. Bala dan Sani, the very wealthy Hausa businessman and baron of the most densely populated region—Maradi—threatened to take Maradi out of the MNSD if Djermakoye was elected leader. The election of Tandja as party leader clearly saved the MNSD from being reduced to a Zarma ethnic party. He had a wide network of supporters, especially among the business community and being neither Hausa nor Zarma assured him even wider support. He is generally considered to be the most "de-tribalised" frontline politician in the country. On top of this, he also had very close connections with the military leadership in Nigeria, Niger's major economic partner. Indeed, he was to be the beneficiary of the open support of the regime of General Ibrahim Babangida which was in power in Nigeria at the time of the Nigerien transition.

The MNSD was a party that assumed that it was destined to win the scheduled elections that were to mark the end of the Nigerien transition. This is because it had within it, almost all the people of wealth and influence in the country. Its self-assured campaign slogan was *nassara*, meaning victory. Its main campaign platform was the necessity for state authority, which it claimed had been seriously compromised by the Tuareg rebellion and the "excessively libertarian atmosphere" introduced by the National Conference, to be re-established. It felt justified in pressing its case in part because the party's presidential campaign train had been attacked by armed Tuareg rebels at Abala (Filingue District) on 9 January, 1993; in the ensuing battle, Tandja led the successful army defence and counter-attack.

The MNSD was easily the most national of Niger's political parties. It not only won the most seats in the elections (29 out of 83) but also had the widest national spread, with at least two seats in all districts. Its candidate won the first round of the presidential elections, an outcome which compelled his main rival from the CDS to form the alliance with other parties that enabled him to win the second round of the elections. The MNSD itself was later to form an alliance with other parties in the next round of early elections that were held in 1995. That alliance won a majority of the seats in the January 1995 parliamentary elections, enabling the MNSD to establish the cohabitation government that ruled the country until the *coup d'état* of January 1996. The capacity of the MNSD to transform itself from an authoritarian sole party to an effective player in the democratic game was seen by many within and outside Niger as being truly remarkable.

The major rival of the MNSD was the *Convention Democratique et Sociale* (CDS-Rahama). The CDS was strongly associated with the interests of the Hausa bureaucratic elite and some elements of the Hausa commercial class that felt excluded from political power. Its origins have been traced to a regionalist-cultural association, the so-called *Association Mutuelle pour la Culture et les Arts* (AMACA), which was established in 1982 in Zinder, the centre of Hausa resistance to Zarma hegemony. AMACA was formed as the Hausa political response to the *Energie de l'Ouest*, a secret organisation, established in 1976 as a think tank for the preservation of Zarma political hegemony in the country. AMACA metamorphisised into the CDS in 1990 with the clear intention of relying on the Hausa majority for its electoral success. Yet, although the party was built to have a strong Hausa nationalist orientation, many of its top leadership are not "ethnically" Hausa. Mahamane Ousmane, for example, who was a leading figure in the party and who became the first post-transition president of Niger, considers himself to be Kanuri. Similarly, the First Vice President of the party, Sanusi Jackou, is of Tuareg origin. It should be noted, however, that Hausa identity has however never been a narrow "ethnic" issue and as such, these leaders are as Hausa as anyone else. The party was led by Mahamane Ousmane, who was also the President of Niger immediately prior to the *coup d'état* of January 1996. The party won 22 seats in the 1993 legislative elections, 14 of them in the Hausa strongholds of Maradi and Zinder.

The third party was the *Parti Nigerien pour la Democratie et le Socialisme* (PNDS-Tarayya). The PNDS presented itself as a socialist party formed by a broad cross-section of the Nigerien left. Most of its cadres had been active in clandestine Marxist revolutionary groups and in the students' movement, USN, as well as the teachers' union, SNEN. Many of the party's militants such as the party leader, Mahamadou Issoufou, had, however, risen to the top hierarchy of the civil service and public corporations and had become "embourgeoisified", at least in their material conditions of existence. The PNDS was widely acknowledged as the most ideologically committed and non-ethnic party in Niger. However, in the 1993 elections, the party got 5 out of its 13 seats in Tahoua, the region of origin of its leader, with the rest of the seats coming from all the other districts of Niger, except Niamey, the capital. It was a major surprise that PNDS-Tarayya was unable to get any seats in the intellectual and political centre of the country. This is partly because it did not have any major financial backers with the consequence that its campaign was rather low key.

The next most important party was the *Alliance Nigerienne pour la Democratie et le Progrès* (ANDP-Zaman Lahiya). The ANDP was the personal property of its leader, Moumouni Adamou Djermakoye who created it after he lost control of the MNSD to Mamadou Tandja. In setting up the party, his main objective seemed to be to take the Zarma vote away from the MNSD. Immediately after the MNSD Congress, he had formed the *Club des Amis de M.A. Djermakoye* (CAMAD)/ the Club of Djermokoye's Friends to facilitate his effort at establishing a party network. He had been Niger's ambassador to the United States and was conversant with modern campaign tactics which he used to good effect when CAMAD was transformed into the ANDP. His party was considered a great personal success because he stood against the huge MNSD party machine and won 11 seats, most of them in the Zarma area. With that performance, he got his final revenge against the MNSD which he felt had denied him the leadership position, and the presidency of Niger, by, in turn, creating a separate political platform that denied the party the extra Zarma votes that would have assured it of complete victory at the elections.

THE MNSD AS A PARLIAMENTARY OPPOSITION PARTY

The 1993 parliamentary elections resulted in the emergence of the MNSD, which won 29 of the legislative seats, as the single largest party in the country. Although it did not have an absolute majority in parliament, its share of the vote suggested that it was well on the way to capturing the presidential elections that were to follow the parliamentary ones. But this was not to be because immediately after the results of the parliamentary elections were known, an anti- MNSD coalition, known as the Alliance of the Forces of Change (AFC), was formed by the CDS, PNDS, ANDP, PPN/RDA, PSDN, UDPS, UDP, PUND and the PR. The AFC parties which, together, were able to aggregate 50 seats to the MNSD group's 33 seats were thus able to outflank their rivals and guarantee themselves the take-over of power.

The second and decisive round of the presidential elections took place on 27 March, 1993. A day later, the loser and leader of the MNSD, Mamadou Tandja, visited his rival, Mahamane Ousmane, to congratulate him on winning the elections and to promise him a vigorous but loyal opposition in the parliament of the country's Third Republic. The next morning the 120 foreign observers who had monitored the elections declared them free and fair, although a few problems had been observed in the Agadez region where the Tuareg uprising was strong. The results of the elections were confirmed by the electoral commission, the *Commission Nationale de Contrôle et de Supervision des Elections* (COSUPEL), less than 48 hours after the close of polling. There were no complaints about rigging or electoral fraud. It was a very smooth and genuinely successful operation.

The legislative elections were conducted on the principle of proportional representation which was, however, applied at the level of the eight departments of the country rather than on the basis of a national list. There were 618 candidates representing the 12 political parties that contested for the 83 parliamentary seats on offer; nine of the parties were able to obtain seats. The second party in the elections, the CDS, started off with the handicap of being widely considered as the party of the Hausa. It was, however, able to partially transcend the ethnic label by embarking on a campaign strategy of presenting itself as the party for change and the new breed.[1] The CDS leader and presidential candidate, Mahamane Ousmane, became the candidate of the AFC for the 27 March, 1993 final round of the presidential elections. Thanks to the Alliance, he won the elections with 54 per cent of the votes cast, leaving his rival, Mamadou Tandja with an impressive 46 per cent of the votes.

Table 1. *Party-Based Distribution of Parliamentary Seats in the February 1993 Legislative Elections*

Parliamentary Majority (The AFC Group)		Parliamentary Opposition (The MNSD and its allies)	
CDS	22	MNSD	29
PNDS	13	UDFP	2
ANDP	11	UPDP	2
RDA	2		
PSDN	1		
UDPS	1		
UDP	0		
PUND	0		
PRL	0		
Total	50		33

The members of the Alliance group had reached an accord that after the first round of the presidential elections for which each of them was free to field a candidate, all the parties would rally behind the Alliance candidate with the highest votes for the second and decisive round of polling. The Alliance was clearly formed to block the inheritors of the single party regime from winning power although that party had the highest number of votes in the elections. Indeed, the high scores of the MNSD represented a source of embarrassment for the students and trade unions as well as political parties that had been allied in the *Comité de Coordination des Luttes Démocratiques* (COCD)/Co-ordination Committee for Democratic Struggles, otherwise known as the "democratic forces", who fought for multipartyism as a strategy for regime change. The electoral results, in favouring the MNSD as they did, offered a partial "re-legitimation" of the old power structure. The AFC was a heterogeneous and to some extent contradictory alliance because it

---

[1] The idea of change (*canji* in Hausa) is an overflow from northern Nigeria where the People's Redemption Party campaign for social redemption during the second Nigerian Republic (1973–1983) became a powerful mobilisation platform for the politician who defined themselves as the progressives.

had within it, parties that declared themselves socialist, social democratic, pro- and anti-structural adjustment, federalist and centralist. The two "Tuareg" parties—UDPS Amanah and PUND Salama—were, for example, openly federalist while the others were centralist. The Alliance was, therefore, politically fragile from the outset; once it got into power, it was to be further weakened by internal perceptions and worries about monopoly and exclusion in the distribution of posts.

Following its electoral victory, the AFC set up a ruling triumvirate with Ousmane of the CDS as President, Issoufou of the PNDS as Prime Minister and Djermakoye of the ANDP as President of the National Assembly. The success of the AFC at the polls denied the MNSD, the single biggest party in the country, and its leader, Mamadou Tandja, the single most popular presidential candidate, access to the presidency. Tandja showed remarkable maturity by accepting the verdict, although many of his supporters felt he should have contested it because Article 138 of the electoral code prohibited the prior distribution of posts to enhance electoral chances. The formation of the AFC after the first round of the elections was based on a pact allocating the presidency, the prime minister's post and the presidency of the national assembly to the leaders of the CDS, PNDS and ANDP respectively and it could have been legally contested but Tandja chose not to. It did not take long however for the AFC to run into stormy waters, for the ruling coalition was only able to maintain its cohesion for about one year.

The MNSD and its allies were faithful to their promise of pursuing a very active opposition to the regime. Given the enormity of the challenge facing the country, it was never going to be easy for the AFC, or any other party for that matter, to rule Niger. The country's long drawn-out economic crisis was serious and worsening; indeed, the government had, for some time, been unable to pay salaries and student bursaries regularly and the social scene quite often became very agitated with the unions calling for frequent strike actions. From 18 to 22 May 1993, serious student demonstrations against the ruling coalition occurred in which party offices were destroyed. 27 students were arrested and taken to court for disrupting the public peace and destroying property (*Haske*, 9 June, 1993). Furthermore, students' demonstrations occurred in Agades on 10 January, 1994 and in Niamey on 10 March, 1994; many students were wounded in clashes with the security forces. Irked by the growing social agitation sweeping across the country, the AFC government became very intolerant of opposition. The MNSD was not intimidated by this development and, indeed, in April 1994, the parliamentary opposition embarked on a campaign of civil disobedience, an activity sanctioned by Article 6 of the 1992 Constitution.[1]

---

[1] This constitutional provision sanctioning mass civil disobedience against unjust government was one of the outcomes of the determination of the National Conference to promote notions of popular sovereignty.

On 16 April, 1994, the MNSD and the other opposition parties organised a massive demonstration against the policies of the government, the marginalisation of their cadres in the public service, and the creeping monopoly of the state apparatus by the AFC. 91 people, including Mamadou Tandja, the MNSD leader and André Salifou, leader of the UPPD, were detained and a process to charge them with assault, battery and the disruption of public order was set in motion. The AFC majority also teamed up in the National Assembly to lift the parliamentary immunity of 33 opposition deputies. It was a travesty of democracy and Tandja captured the mood of many people when he said that:

> We consider that the proper procedures were once again violated here, because one part of the National Assembly cannot be at one and the same time judge and prosecutor. The deputies of the opposition did not have the opportunity to defend themselves (*West Africa*, 16 May, 1994).

It was clear that the AFC was very jittery at the effectiveness of the opposition and tried, unsuccessfully, to use state power to repress it. The collapse of the AFC when it came was, however, more linked to its inability to maintain its internal cohesion.

THE 1993–1994 CONSTITUTIONAL AND POLITICAL CRISES

The December 1992 Constitution that established the institutions of the Nigerien Third Republic was very similar to the constitution of the French Fifth Republic. The Third Republic was based on a multiparty system with the provision that political parties must have a national, secular and republican orientation. The President was to be elected to serve a term of five years and he/she could only be re-elected once. The legislature was elected on a proportional basis and was also to serve for five years. As is the case with the French version, the constitution was semi-presidential. This meant that the President needed parliamentary support to govern through his/her Prime Minister and when he/she lost such support, the option available was either the dissolution of the National Assembly and the conduct of new elections that might or might not produce a new majority for the President, or cohabitation, which would mean the President calling upon the opposition to constitute the government. It is a system that has been difficult to operate even in France as was witnessed in relation to the two cohabitations that occurred during François Mitterand's fourteen-year rule, and as has been brought out by the current experience that is going on under Jacques Chirac's presidency.

The central constitutional idea that the President *presides* and the Prime Minister *governs*, is, to say the least, an ambiguous one, especially where cohabitation is involved. Constitutionally, the President has powers to appoint the Prime Minister and the government. He is also the chief of the army and has powers to direct the country's foreign policy. At the same time, the constitution defines the Prime Minister as the Head of the Government which he has powers to direct, conduct and coordinate. The Prime Minister is responsible for the execution of laws and he can delegate his powers to his ministers. However, he is legally obliged to call upon the President to preside over the meetings of the executive council over an agenda which he draws up. The government, under the leadership of the Prime Minister, determines and conducts national policy. The Prime Minister is also charged with the administration of the armed forces, although the President has responsibility for defence policy. The Prime Minister is responsible to the National Assembly for the conduct of government business.

The major strength of the constitutional provisions of the Nigerien Third Republic was that they were consciously fabricated to allow for a genuine division of powers between the key institutions of state, namely, the presidency, the government and the legislature, with the judiciary playing a significant arbitration role. The electoral code with its proportional system of representation fostered and entrenched this goal by allowing many parties to get a share of the seats in the National Assembly. There were even eight special seats reserved for ethnic minorities whose population was too small to allow them to win seats even in a proportional electoral system. The major weakness of the constitution, however, was the rather blurred line that separated the powers of the various institutions, especially those of the presidency and the government. In addition, there was a contradiction between the spirit of the constitution, which assumed the necessity of a parliamentary majority to govern, and the letter of the electoral code which favoured the presence of small parties in the National Assembly. With 19 parties recognised, it was unlikely that any party would have got a sufficient majority to allow it to govern alone.

The first sign of a crack within the AFC government came in September 1993 when the ANDP published a communiqué in which it complained that, in spite of its role in clinching the victory of the alliance, its cadres were being excluded from state prebends. The party specifically mentioned that it had been denied its quota of directorships of government departments and parastatals that had been promised to it. It noted that the CDS and PNDS had monopolised most of the posts. This was to set the tone for much of the political crisis that developed subsequently, a crisis which the press christened the prebendal *wasoso*.[1] The final crack that led to the demise of the AFC government was the conflict between the President and his Prime Minister. On 21 September, 1994, Mahamadou Ousmane published a decree reorganising the Presidency. In essence, the decree transferred many services from the Prime Minister's Office to the Presidency, including the Cabi-

---

[1] This is a Hausa term which suggests a greedy rush to grab everything within reach.

net Office, sections of the police and security forces, the Secretariat of the Council of Ministers, the Protocol Unit, and the State Inspectorate Division. The decree clearly undermined the semi-presidential nature of the regime and was meant to cripple the powers of the Prime Minister.

Mahamadou Issoufou refused to accept the scaling down of his powers and eventually resigned from the post of Prime Minister on 28 September, 1994. He argued that he decided to resign because he no longer enjoyed the support that would enable him to pursue the collective programme of the AFC which the National Assembly had accepted. In responding to the resignation, the President requested the PNDS to present another candidate for the Prime Minister's office but the party refused, opting instead to side with its leader. On 30 September, 1994, the PNDS decided to withdraw its participation in the AFC; by that act, the AFC lost its majority as it was left with only 37 of the 83 seats in parliament.

The PNDS argued that it had left the AFC because of creeping regionalism, ethno-centricism and corruption. However, since the PNDS boss was once, in his capacity as Prime Minister, the effective leader of government, his attempt to dissociate himself and his party from the vices of the ruling elite did not sound very credible. As Souley Adji has argued in his *Rose Story* series in the *Alternative* (12 October, 1994), it is the story of a beautiful bride and her divorce based on an enduring principle—*"faisons l'amour des prébendes, pas la guerre des principes"*/"lets promote the love of prebends, not a war over principles". It is precisely because of this love of prebends that we can begin to understand the ease with which the PNDS was able to switch its alliance from the AFC to the MNSD, a party which it had devoted all of its energies to combating. Only two PNDS leaders, Adji Kirgam and Mazou Ibrahim, publicly disagreed with the decision of their party to ally with the MNSD and they were promptly expelled for anti-party activities, an action that might have forced other potential dissidents to shut up and keep their peace.

Apparently, President Ousmane's own calculation in provoking the split with Issoufou was that he would be able to reconstitute another parliamentary majority, this time with the MNSD or one of its factions. In a sense, the MNSD led the President up the garden path because its leadership had consistently maintained that although it could not rule out future cooperation with the President, this would only happen on the condition that he broke his alliance with the PNDS. When, after the PNDS left and Ousmane contacted the MNSD to join him in forming a new alliance, his offer was flatly refused and, instead, the MNSD opted to team up with the PNDS. It was a most bizarre turn of events and an equally surprising alliance because the whole "progressive" history of the PNDS, from the days of its leaders and militants in student radicalism to the formation of the party, had been built on a vigorous critique of and struggles against the MNSD oligarchy. An alliance with that party was, therefore, the last thing that anybody had expected or thought possible. But then, as the saying goes, there are no permanent friends and permanent enemies in politics; Ousmane and his party, in coming face to face with this bitter fact, found that in the new alignment of forces, they had been left in the lurch.

Following the withdrawal of the PNDS from government and the inability of the President to get factions of either the PNDS or the MNSD to ally with him and constitute a new government, he appointed a close confident, his former campaign manager and the treasurer of his party who had also been finance minister, Souley Abdulaye, to head a new CDS-dominated government. The establishment of this government was clearly at odds with the spirit of the Nigerien constitution which assumed that governments needed a working parliamentary majority to rule; the notion of a minority government was out of the question. On 16 October, 1994, the parliament with the combined strength of the MNSD and the PNDS passed a vote of no confidence in Abdulaye, thereby bringing down his 11-day government. Cornered on all fronts, the President decided to play his last card by using his constitutional prerogative to dissolve the National Assembly and call for new, early elections.

The election campaigns started on 9 December, 1994 against a background of high social tension in the country. Salary arrears for the public sector had been accumulating for up to five months and workers were literally hungry and angry. The unions were bitterly opposed to a new labour legislation enforcing a "no work, no pay policy" and requiring longer notice before unions could embark on industrial action. A general strike which was called for every Wednesday had been in force since the beginning of November 1994 and was aimed at protesting against the social policies of the government. There were also intense debates over the material organisation of the elections and suspicion was widespread that plans were afoot to rig them, a situation that enhanced mutual checks and balances among the parties over electoral procedures and which clearly helped to discourage the propensities towards rigging that might have existed. The elections, like the others before it, turned out to have been free and fair. The President and what was left of his AFC alliance lost to the MNSD-dominated opposition.

Table 2. *Distribution of Seats Following the January 1995 Parliamentary Elections*

New parliamentary majority (The MNSD and its allies)		New parliamentary opposition (The AFC Group)	
MNSD	29	CDS	24
PNDS	12	ANDP	9
UPDP	1	PUND	3
PPN/RDA	1	PSDN	2
		UDPS	2
Total	43		40

After the elections, the President had no option but to reluctantly accept the principle of cohabitation. He asked the new majority to submit the names and curriculum vitae of three people from whom he would choose a new Prime Minister. The victorious group had, however, agreed among themselves on the person they wanted to see appointed as Prime Minister so they gave him only one name, that of Hama Amadou of the MNSD. Astonishingly, Ousmane refused to appoint Amadou and decided, instead, to appoint Ahmadou Cisse also of the MNSD. His decision in this regard was announced on 7 February, 1995. Although he was a member of the opposition MNSD party, Cisse also shocked observers by agreeing to serve without the approval of his party. Cisse had been a World Bank staff member in Washington since 1982 and had illusions that his country needed a "good" technocrat like himself who could stand above partisan politics and serve the vital economic interests of Niger, such as concluding an accord with the IMF and getting the economy to benefit from the devaluation of the CFA Franc (see his interview in *Le Sahel,* 9 February, 1995). The day after he accepted the post of Prime Minister, he was expelled from the MNSD and not a single member of the new majority agreed to cooperate with him. He finally got the message, packed his bags, and went back to Washington. The President also got the message and agreed to appoint the candidate of the new majority as the cohabitation Prime Minister. Hama Amadou of the MNSD and candidate of the new majority, was appointed Prime Minister on 21 January, 1995 to head the fourth government of the Third Republic.

EXPLAINING THE SUCCESS OF MNSD—NASSARA

As was noted in the first section of this chapter, the success of the MNSD was against the many odds that it faced. Since the onset of the wind of democratic change that blew over Niger and culminated in the organisation of the National Conference, considerable effort and resources had been committed to the marginalisation of the MNSD by an assortment of groups that considered themselves to be the "democratic forces" in the country. The party was, however, able to sustain its struggle for political relevance and power and, more than that, was able eventually to win elections. What accounts for this remarkable political turnaround and electoral success?

According to Hama Amadou, General Secretary of the MNSD and Prime Minister following the 1995 elections, the parties in the AFC coalition lacked political experience and were amateurish in the implementation of their programmes with the consequence that they were unable to effectively tackle the catastrophic economic situation in the country.[1] It is doubtful that the MNSD itself, even if it had had a free hand in governing, could have

---

[1] Interview with Hama Amadou by Niandou Souley in November 1995.

been more successful in resolving the serious economic crises which had been ravaging Niger since the early 1980s. Indeed, it is noteworthy that the economic crisis began when the MNSD and its cadres were in power before popular disaffection swept them out of office and paved the way for multi-party politics. Nonetheless, the fact that the parties in the AFC had obtained power partly because they had promised sweeping economic and political change, and then failed signally to deliver on their promises, weakened their political support considerably and created the basis for their defeat in the 1995 elections. Their lack of experience was certainly a factor in their own over-estimation of what could be realistically achieved in the circumstances under which they had to govern.

The second factor that explains the success of the MNSD as an opposition party was the in-built fragility of the AFC coalition in power. It was an heterogeneous group, almost an unnatural alliance by parties that had no ideological similarities, shared history of struggle, and common values. The only thing that united them was their determination to keep the MNSD out of power in the 1993 elections. After they won power, they made very little effort to evolve common platforms that could solidify the power-sharing arrangements that they had worked out. Against this background, it was easy for any minor conflict among the parties to provoke a breakdown in the alliance and this is precisely what happened following the withdrawal of the PNDS from the governing coalition on 28 September, 1994 (Niandou, 1996).

Thirdly, the MNSD was very successful in playing its role as an opposition party. Despite its defeat in the 1993 elections, the party succeeded in maintaining its cohesion in the face of sustained efforts by its rivals to desta-bilise its national and local structures. The party was also able to concentrate on its principal objective of preparing for the next elections while simulta-neously sustaining its role as the major opposition party in the country, a sincere player in the democratic game, and a viable alternative government. This credibility which it gained as a government-in-waiting further helped to sustain the cohesion of the party and the morale of its members. The early signs of the fragility of the AFC coalition served as a further source of encouragement in this regard.

Fourthly, there was growing disappointment among Nigeriens with the AFC government because of the numerous promises that it failed to keep. With the introduction of multiparty politics that followed the popular explo-sion of demands for democratic reform, the various Nigerien political parties focused their campaign on the notion of *changement* (change), thereby raising a lot of popular enthusiasm and expectations. When the AFC got power however, its representatives in government simply continued the traditional practices linked to the exercise of power in the country, including the arro-gant authoritarianism and corrupt practices of public figures. The impres-sion was soon created that the new regime was not composed of sincere democrats, but of people who were using democracy as a springboard for achieving their own selfish ambitions. Not surprisingly, the people soon coined the street-level expression *"changer le changement"*, which quickly gained in currency across the country. For the ordinary Nigerien, the implication of the expression was that if the AFC really represented the change that the people had been craving for and had been promised to expect, then they did not want it; the so-called change must be changed.

The success of the MNSD poses the issue of the historical reverses which the "democratic forces" that came to power in the early 1990s in Africa have been suffering. Have the forces of democratisation already exhausted themselves and are the "authoritarian forces" staging, or poised to stage a comeback? Are democratic processes under threat? Matthew Kérekou in Benin was able to stage a comeback through the same competitive electoral framework that earlier on swept him from power while Kenneth Kaunda in Zambia and Denis Sassou Nguesso in Congo are also attempting to achieve the same feat. The early experience of Niger following the 1995 elections was, initially at leat, re-assuring in this regard. For, the return of the MNSD to power was not based on the tapping of its old authoritarian history and methods, but on its ability to effectively adapt to the new democratic game. Even as the MNSD was re-gaining in credibility, the repeated attempts by the AFC coalition to control the mass media and the various violations of the law which it committed[1] seriously eroded its democratic credentials. The AFC's loss in this regard became the MNSD's gain and the leaders of the latter lost no opportunity to polish their democratic image. The success of the MNSD and the logic of cohabitation that was imposed therefore had a democratic character.

COHABITATION AND INTENSIFICATION OF POLITICAL CRISES

The coming to power of Hama Amadou of the MNSD was the first case of cohabitation in Francophone Africa and was, therefore, in itself destined to be an interesting experiment. As it turned out, the period of cohabitation was marked by only a few months of peaceful coexistence between the two party blocs in the corridors of power. A major crisis erupted when the Prime Minister started removing AFC loyalists and appointees from the government and replacing them with sympathisers and supporters of the MNSD coalition. The President responded by deciding, with effect from 6 April, 1995, to boycott the meetings of the Council of Ministers, which he had the constitutional obligation of presiding over. He also decided to stop meeting with or receiving the Prime Minister.

Then in July 1995, high drama was enacted in Niamey when the Prime Minister announced the summary dismissal of the management of para-

---

[1] Most of the rulings of the Supreme Court between April 1993 and December 1995 indicate that the AFC and the President were on the wrong side of the law.

statals, the affected officials being appointees of the AFC alliance. The Prime Minister went one step further to employ state security forces to physically eject the dismissed officials from office and install his own appointees.[1] The President took this as a direct affront and swiftly asked the Prime Minister to remove the new appointees and the security officials protecting them from the parastatals as his pre-condition for allowing the Council of Ministers to meet. The President's request was flatly rejected by the Prime Minister who insisted that he had no intention of taking any such action before the convening of the meeting of the Council of Ministers. Instead, the Prime Minister demanded that the President had to take immediate disciplinary action against the chief of the presidential guards whom he alleged had attempted to assassinate him. The country was headed for a political and administrative stalemate.

Against the background of the developing impasse, the Prime Minister decided unilaterally to take over a number of presidential prerogatives, in particular, those pertaining to the convening and chairing of meetings of the Council of Ministers. Two meetings of the Council were called under those circumstances, with the Prime Minister presiding. As could be expected, the President declared the decisions taken at the meetings to be both illegal and null and void. The Prime Minister then pushed provocation further by inviting the President to a ministerial meeting which he had convened; Ousmane, of course, did not attend. Next, the Prime Minister decided to start signing decrees, an action which the Supreme Court immediately declared to be illegal. By early August 1995, it was clear that both sides were not willing to negotiate or compromise and above all, they were not willing to stick by the institutional rules and regulations they had sworn to protect when they took their oaths of office. The contention between them went to the Supreme Court which ruled on 6 September, 1995 that the President should call and preside over the meeting of the Council of Ministers, with the agenda of the meeting fixed in consultation with the Prime Minister. If both these elected officials could not agree, then the Council itself could fix the agenda.

As the crisis deepened, the President made it clear that he was intent, once again, on dissolving the National Assembly and calling fresh elections. It appeared that he had only been waiting for the constitutionally-defined minimum period of 12 months before dissolving parliament.[2] To counter the dissolution threat, the Prime Minister announced that even if parliament

---

[1] This move initiated a struggle between the two in trying to use the armed and security forces to fight their political battles, thereby gradually re-legitimating political roles for the military, a role that had previously been eroded during the National Conference.

[2] The French National Assembly had been dissolved only four times in the history of the Fifth Republic, that is, since 1958 while President Ousmane was threatening to dissolve it twice in three years.

was dissolved, he was going to insist on staying in office until the new elections were held. On 26 January, 1996, Mahamadou Issoufou, a former Prime Minister and incumbent President of the National Assembly, lodged a formal request with the Supreme Court for the removal from office of the President on the grounds of an alleged incapacity to govern. Clearly, the experiment in cohabitation was in deep trouble, and largely because it had not been allowed to function. The protagonists in Niger's young democratic experiment had blocked the operations of political institutions and the political process and this was the pretext which the then Colonel Ibrahim Baré Mainasara used to justify the military *coup d'état* which he led on 27 January, 1996. The coup brought to an abrupt end, the increasingly turbulent experience of the Nigerien Third Republic.

THE *COUP D'ETAT* AND THE FRAGILITY OF NIGER'S DEMOCRACY

One of the signs of mature democracies is that they provide a possibility for opposition parties to get to power through the electoral process and, if necessary, rule in cohabitation with others either in the executive or in parliament. The MNSD opposition party in Niger was able to get back to power through the ballot but did not really have much of a chance to govern before the bullet ended its return to office. It was clear right from the 1993 elections that ushered in its Third Republic that democratic culture was yet to be routinised in Niger. The political class did not seem to be (sufficiently) committed to playing by the rules of the game and, in failing to so do, created an excuse for the military to intervene and overthrow the entire democratic experiment. Their politics of brinkmanship and the determination which they shared to eliminate, even annihilate one another from the constitutional-political process created a situation in which their collective interest was put at risk.

The *coup* leaders, not surprisingly, presented themselves to an exasperated Nigerien populace as the saviours of democracy who had reluctantly intervened in their country's political affairs only to correct the institutional ills of the Third Republic. They made an immediate promise to return the country to democratic rule by December 1996. Behind that discourse however was a more banal issue of an ambitious appetite for political power among senior military commanders (Niandou, 1996:1). The international community objected strongly to the intervention by the military and intense pressure was put on them to go back to the barracks immediately and allow democratic institutions the chance of sorting out the problems that had emerged in the political system. The pressure was maintained until Mainasara agreed to shorten the date for the return to elected government by five months from December to July 1996.

The *coup* appeared to be generally welcomed in many circles in **Niger**; support rallies were even organised/orchestrated to tap the depth of popular anger which most people felt at the petty quarrels of the political parties (Niandou, 1996:9; Mahamadou, 1996:9). This notwithstanding, the claim by two French researchers based in Niger, Gregoire and Olivier de Sardan (1996:117–121) that the *coup* was welcomed by the great majority of the people as a necessity to save the country and/or democracy would still seem to be overstated, if not outrightly mischievous. That was exactly the kind of message which the Mainasara junta was pushing out to the world and even if people were increasingly fatigued by the growing costs of the impasse that followed the 1995 elections, it is still incumbent on the researcher to make a more detached and sober assessment that is able to separate initial sentiments and propaganda from the implications of actions such as the *coup d'état* for democratic consolidation. That is why Patrick Quantin (1996:114) is right when he points out that Gregoire and Olivier de Sardan appeared to be more interested in promoting authoritarianism than in advancing political analysis.[1]

It ought also to be underlined that in the immediate aftermath of the *coup*, it was not easy at all for people to express their opposition to the military intervention. After the *coup*, the army and security services started arresting journalists and politicians who were critical of military rule in general and Mainasara in particular. Many were taken to distant military camps near the Mali border to be beaten and warned to desist from their opposition to or criticism of the new junta. Many other critics were detained in Niamey prison cells (Niandou, 1996:11). On taking over power, the junta replaced all prefects (governors of the regions) with military officers. Mayors and sous-prefects (district governors) were also changed. These actions were clearly designed to strengthen the grip of the military and narrow the scope for oppositional activity.

That the *coup d'état* represented a major setback for Niger is not in doubt but even before it occurred, most political observers in the country were of the view that some drastic institutional changes were necessary if the entire democratic experiment was to survive. Four days after coming to power, the junta called a National Forum which proposed that the way forward for the country was to change the constitution to a fully-fledged presidential type in which the President's powers would not be subject to easy contestation. The Forum also proposed a change in the electoral code from proportional representation to a first-past-the-post system so that it would be easier for one party to emerge with a clear majority in the national assembly.

The major protagonists of the Third Republic—ex-President Mahamane Ousmane, ex-Prime Minister Hama Amadou and ex-National Assembly

---

[1] They also published a letter in *Le Monde* of 8 February, 1996, justifying the *coup* in Niger.

President Mahamadou Issoufou—appeared on television in early February to add some drama to the push for the alteration of the electoral and constitutional bases of the Nigerien transition by reading a joint declaration before the Acting President of the Supreme Court stating that:

> The military *coup* was due essentially to difficulties arising from the application of the fundamental laws of the Republic, in particular, the Constitution of 26 December, 1992 (*Le Démocrate*, 12 February, 1996).

The three men then called for a new electoral code and constitutional amendments which could be put to the people for approval through a referendum. Their action might have been under duress as they were still under house arrest but it nonetheless went a long way in legitimating military intervention. It was after this televised statement that the military organised a National Forum for Democratic Renewal—*Forum National de Renouveau Démocratique*—which turned out to be an effort at a "counter-National Conference" and which blamed the civilians for their incapacity to govern. In so doing, the participants in the Forum attempted to wipe out the criticisms that had been made against army rule during the National Conference (Niandou, 1996:14).

The electoral and constitutional propositions favoured by the new military junta were rushed through committees and put before a constitutional referendum which was held on 12 May, 1996. The new Constitution was approved by 90 per cent of the electorate with a participation level of 35 per cent. Presidential elections were then scheduled for 7 July, 1996 and Colonel Ibrahim Baré Mainasara promoted himself to the rank of general and announced his intention to contest for the presidency as an independent candidate despite an earlier promise to relinquish power. Precisely because of his ambitions to run for office under rules which he set, General Mainasara engaged in a series of manoeuvres ultimately aimed at creating advantages for himself. Indeed, while candidate General Mainasara was openly campaigning in office and setting up local support committees for himself, political activities remained banned in the country and his rivals continued to be held in detention until 23 May, 1996 when they were released. Mainasara had, earlier on in April changed the electoral code so that he would not be obliged to resign first from the army in order to contest for elected office.

A few weeks before the elections, Mainasara also, by decree, changed the composition of the Constitutional Chamber of the Supreme Court, thereby undermining the independence and integrity of the only organ that had the powers to validate candidacies and results. Furthermore, while his major rivals were still under house arrest, he established a High Court of Justice with jurisdiction to try former office holders for crimes which they allegedly committed while in office. Although the Court did not sit, its existence served as a permanent threat against his rivals if they tried to upstage him in any way whatsoever. There was no clearer sign of the General's lack of commitment to fair play than his decision to ignore the repeated pleas of the Independent National Electoral Commission (CENI) either for the resources it needed to do its job or the postponement of the polls. Indeed, on three occasions, INEC had asked for the elections to be postponed because voters lists and election materials were not ready but was ignored by the government. Not surprisingly, on election day, voters registers and cards were not available in a lot of voting booths.

Meanwhile, the closeness of Mainasara to the old Kountché oligarchy became a genuine source of fear that the country was being returned to the old structure of authoritarian rule that had characterised post-independence political life in Niger until the popular revolt of the early 1990s. Unlike most African countries, Niger never had a period of liberal democratic rule during the transition from colonialism (Fuglestad, 1983). The country had, until the National Conference and the inauguration of the Third Republic, only experienced a succession of extremely harsh and authoritarian regimes, from Hamani Diori (1958–1974) to Seyni Kountché (1974–1987) and Ali Saibou (1987–1990). The National Conference, as we have argued, represented a serious attempt to reverse the course of the country's political history from one of repression to freedom, authoritarianism to liberal democracy. The *coup* amounted to an attempt to return the country to the old authoritarian order and to negate the spirit of liberty that had been released with such vigour by the National Conference (Ibrahim, 1996). The excuse that the constitutional crisis of the Third Republic had made democratic rule impossible was central to the legitimation of the *coup*. That done, the ground was then prepared for a farcical transition to "democratic" rule at the helm of which was none other than General Mainasara who transformed himself into an elected president through a process he could never lose.

That the presidential election which resulted in the inauguration of Niger's Fourth Republic was farcical is now too well-established to require an elaborate discussion. But a few pointers are still in order. On 6 July, 1997, the government announced that the impending presidential election would be spread over two days—7 and 8 July—instead of being held on 7 July only. On the evening of the first day of voting, the regime announced it had abolished the Independent National Electoral Commission (CENI), the body which was organising the elections, because, according to the officials of the government, the Commission had leaked results from the polling to the press indicating Mainasara might not win the elections. That night, a new organisation, the National Electoral Commission (CNE), was established to take over the conduct of the elections. The army was called in to collect ballot boxes and take them to town halls where the votes were counted in secret by the new CNE, without candidate representatives and independent observers. Analysis by the American National Democratic Institute (1996:3) revealed that on the first day of voting, General Mainasara had 29 per cent of the votes cast on a voter turnout of 61.6 per cent; by the second day, Mainasara's fortunes went up dramatically with his share of the votes jumping to 72 per cent on a 92 per cent turnout.

On 9 July, 1997, the day after the polls closed, the CNE declared Mainasara the outright winner of the presidential election in the first round with 52.2 per cent of the votes. The three candidates who had contested against Mainasara were arrested on the first day of voting (7 July) and were only released on 22 July, 1996, after the Supreme Court had confirmed the results the junta wanted. Mainasara called a press conference on that day to say that he hoped "the politicians have learnt their lesson" (Reuters, 22 July, 1996). The two private radio stations that were in existence in the country were also closed down for criticising what was going on in the country. Many journalists and politicians were arrested during the two days when General Mainasara turned himself into an elected president. On 9 July, 1996, the government issued a directive banning demonstrations and public meetings. On 10 July, 1996, anti-riot police tear-gassed hundreds of demonstrators who had assembled in front of the headquarters of the former ruling party, CDS, to protest against the electoral *coup* which Mainasara had executed. The central labour organisation, the USTN, called a general strike for 11 July, 1996 but it was only partially successful, probably due to the high level of intimidation and the show of force that was displayed. The tide of democratisation had been temporarily reversed.

The six major political parties in the country, including the MNSD and the CDS, had come together in June 1996 to establish a Republican Pact to checkmate General Mainasara's attempt to discredit the whole political class and remain in power. It was a good lesson that they seemed to have learnt, namely that, the civilian political class had a collective duty and self-interest in making democracy work so as to prevent the usurpation of power by the military and/or anti-democratic elements. The civilian politicians may have been very slow in grasping this fact but considering the joint actions which they set in motion to resist General Mainasara, it was clear that it was not a lesson learnt too late. The fact that Mainasara had to rig the elections as blatantly as he did in order to remain in power represented something of a moral victory for democracy and such moral victories are important in the long-term. Democracy in Niger is indeed fragile but the construction of sustainable democracy is a also a long- term process, attended by many ups and downs. The Nigerien people may yet win their struggle for a stable and open political system.

BIBLIOGRAPHY

Adji, Soulay, 1991, *Logiques socio-communautaires et loyautés politiques en Afrique: Essai d'analyse de la construction de l'État au Niger*. Ph D Thesis, Bordeaux II.

Adji, Souley, 1996, "Democratisation, PAS et Production de la Violence Populaire au Niger", paper for Conference on *Transitions in Africa: Violence and the Politics of Participation*, June 1996, Niamey.

Alou, T. Mahaman, 1994, "De Quelle Manière les Institutions Politiques et Administratives se Sont-Elles Adaptées aux Nouvelles Règles du Jeu Démocratique et à la Notion de Citoyenté". Mimeo. Niamey.

Charlick, R et al. (eds.), 1994, *Improving Democratic Governance for Sustainable Development: An Analysis of Change and Continuity in Niger*. USAID Report. Washington D. C.

Charlick, R., 1996, "Unions in Niger's Recent Political Transitions," Paper for conference on *Transitions in Africa: Violence and the Politics of Participation*, June 1996, Niamey.

Decoudras, P.M., 1994, "Niger: Démocratisation Réussie, Avenir en Suspens", *L'Afrique Politique*. 1994. Bordeaux.

Diop, M.C. and Diouf, M., 1990, *Statutory Political Successions: Mechanisms of Power Transfer in Africa*. Dakar: CODESRIA Working Paper, No 1.

Fuglestad, F., 1983, *A History of Niger: 1850–1960*. Cambridge: Cambridge University Press.

Gervais, Myriam, 1995, "Structural Adjustment in Niger: Implementation, Effects and Determining Political Factors", *Review of African Political Economy*, No. 63.

Gregoire, E. & J.P. Olivier de Sardan, 1996, "Niger: Le Pire a Eté Evité, mais Demain?", *Politique Africaine*, No. 61.

Ibrahim, Jibrin, 1994, "Political Exclusion, Democratisation and Dynamics of Ethnicity in Niger", *Africa Today*, Vol. 41, No. 3.

Ibrahim, Jibrin, 1996, "The Weakness of 'Strong States': The Case of Niger Republic", in A. O. Olukoshi and L. Laakso (eds.), *Challenges to the Nation-State in Africa*. Uppsala: Nordiska Afrikainstitutet.

Illiassou, A. and M.T. Alou, 1994, "Processus Electoral et Democratisation au Niger", *Politique Africaine*, No. 53.

Mahamadou, Laoel Kader, 1996, "Le Processus de Démocratisation au Niger: D'une Transition à l'Autre", paper for conference on *Transitions in Africa: Violence and the Politics of Participation*, June 1996, Niamey.

Maidoka, Abubacar, 1996, "Le Coup d'État Militaire du 27 Janvier, 1996 au Niger: Une Tentative d'Explication", paper for conference on *Transitions in Africa: Violence and the Politics of Participation*, June 1996, Niamey.

National Démocratic Institute, 1996, *The July 7 and 8 Presidential Election in Niger*. Washington D.C.

Niandou, Souley, A., 1990, "Le Niger après Seyni Kountché", *Année Africaine 1989*, Bordeaux: Pedone.

Niandou, Souley, A., 1992, *Crises des Autoritarisms Militaires et Renouveau Politique en Afrique de l'Ouest: Étude Comparative—Benin, Mali, Niger, Togo*. Ph.D. Thesis, Bordeaux.

Niandou, Souley, A., 1995, "La Démocratisation en Afrique, une Reconversion Porteuse d'Incertitudes: Le Cas du Niger", communication presenté à la *Huitième Assemblée Generale et Colloque du CODESRIA*, juillet 1995, Dakar.

Niandou, Souley, A. 1996, "De l'Instabilité du Modèle Compétitif à la Conquête Violente du Pouvoir: Le Cas du Niger", paper for conference on *Transitions in Africa: Violence and the Politics of Participation*, June 1996, Niamey.

Quantin, Patrick, 1996, "Niger: Retour sur l'Analyse d'un Coup d'État", *Politique Africaine*, No. 62.

Raynal, J.J., 1993, *Les Institutions Politiques du Niger*. Saint Maur: Sepia.

Robinson, Pearl, 1991, "Niger: Anatomy of a Neo-traditional Corporatist State", *Comparative Politics*, Vol. 24, No. 1.

Robinson, Pearl, 1994, "The National Conference Phenomenon in Francophone Africa", *Comparative Studies in Society and History*, Vol. 36, No. 3.

Chapter 6

The Dilemmas of Directed Democracy: Neutralising Ugandan Opposition Politics under the NRM

John Ssenkumba

> Governments must be kept awakened to the needs of the people. Only an opposition can do that. Without an opposition, there is no life (Daniel Arap Moi, 1964).
>
> Premature introduction of multiparties will lead to civil unrest and its disastrous consequences (Daniel Arap Moi, 1991).
> *Africa Demos*, Vol. 2, No. 1, November 1991.

INTRODUCTION

In modern times, the quality of a country's political process, and ultimately of its system and structure of governance, can best be judged by the level of organisation, autonomy, and diversity of its political forces. Although a society can be administered efficiently, and even fairly, by one like-minded group operating with complete power, this can only be for a very short time because without vigorous and effective accounting and the opportunity for members of the political community to freely and systematically challenge those in power, even the most efficient political system will corrupt itself and slide into decay. This is why the advocates of libertarian democracy, such as John Stuart Mill, contend that central to the conduct of rational politics is the existence of opportunities and structures for the expression of dissenting points of view. The very essence of democracy lies in the right of individuals and groups to differ, publicly canvass their opposing views, and choose either to cooperate with or oppose those in authority within a legally-/constitutionally-established framework. Since it is unreasonable to expect a complete uniformity of ideas and actions among all people and at all times, society must learn to accept diversity and work for mutual tolerance in a genuine search for an enduring basis for the unity and stability of the polity. So, in order to be able to choose and, hopefully, do so wisely, experiment with alternatives, explore the advantages and disadvantages of the different alternatives that are available, and to know what they want and how to go about getting it, the citizens of any country need an opposition. Within this perspective, the state is conceived as a bond of associations, each with a life of its own, where the only real security for social well-being is the free exercise of people's minds. Given the diverse notions of opposition that exist in the literature, it is in this broad sense of the existence of independent vehicles for the articulation of alternative policies and views in competition with those of the incumbents in power that we use the term in this chapter.

To many Ugandans, the widespread conception, mainly held by outsiders, that their country is an oasis of stability, economic progress, and democracy is a frustrating mirage. For those without privileged protection from the unilateral exercise of governmental authority, however benign or enlightened this authority may appear to be, this image of Uganda as an arena of boundless political openings and relentless economic progress is grossly deceptive. With this in mind, we begin our discussion of the experience of the Ugandan opposition with two inter-related questions. The first relates to whether there is any justification for the suggestion that multiparty politics is an automatic panacea for the problems of political and economic development confronting Africa? Secondly, what are the salient issues in the transition to a multiparty political framework? In addressing these questions, we take the view that the central issue in the transition from monolithic to plural systems centres on whether or not the political organisations that underpin the process are capable of providing a strong and credible challenge to the ruling establishment. This is because democracy can only thrive if the opposition is viable and is able, effectively, to compete with the incumbent. In other words, the state of the opposition in any political system sheds light on the extent to which political pluralism can become a viable vehicle for the realisation of democracy and the promotion of national development. Flowing from this, we shall attempt in this chapter to outline the major features of the Ugandan opposition as it has evolved since the rise to power of Yoweri Museveni and his National Resistance Movement (NRM). Our approach is rooted in an analysis of the relationship between the NRM and its main political adversaries, including the stakes involved, the strategies adopted by the different actors, and the implications of all this for the broad project of democratisation in contemporary Uganda.

UNDERSTANDING POLITICAL PLURALISM

The political and intellectual backdrop to the pluralist debate can be traced to the limitations that inhere in political arrangements dominated by a single, monolithic political organisation. Experience has demonstrated that such an arrangement not only stifles individual initiative but also tends to deny basic human rights as well as limit the freedom of the press and of association. In order to overcome the problems associated with political monopoly, pluralism as a concept and a framework for practice was developed in the hope that it would reduce abuses in the political system. Political pluralism is now considered as being at the heart of democracy. However, we must hasten to add, the concept of democracy can, and often does, conceal the exercise of power by a small, oligarchic group of persons who try to maintain themselves in office even as they appear to respect the democratic framework (Beckman, 1990). Democracy should not, therefore, merely be seen as only entailing the right to vote in a government or simply as the establishment of formal legal provisions in state constitutions. In order to ensure that democracy is not captured by a minority group of vested interests, we need to adopt a broader view of the notion which encompasses the range of concerns that are essential for ensuring that the citizenry enjoy the capacity to control their destinies and, in so doing, check the abuses that are often committed by dominant/vested interests (Nyong'o, 1987).

In the advanced capitalist states, the main vehicles for demanding change and participation in the governance process have, for a long time, been interest groups some of which eventually aggregated into political parties which, in turn, contested for political power. With time, political parties became important not only in the definition of pluralism but also as one of the major instruments available to citizens in their bid to promote democratic governance in their societies (Huntington, 1968). The literature is replete with different interpretations of the democratic aspirations of the citizenry but in the context of this essay, we associate three key issues with the concept of democracy. The first has to do with the extent to which the incessant demand by a people for the right to secure a central place in the governance process is recognised and accommodated. The second centres on the existence of a transparent context for the organisation of such demands, that is, the availability of the multiplicity and plurality of organisations and issues that form the basis for democratic practice. The third issue concerns the realisation that political parties, though very important, are not the only, and, in fact, may not even be the major vehicles for democracy in the face of the growing importance of other non-party organisations, including associations of civil society.

Bearing in mind that it is not entirely free of problems, a plural arrangement, which in most countries is nowadays seen as entailing multipartyism, is assumed to enhance free expression and the potential for the different segments of society to control their destiny. It also has in-built mechanisms for providing checks on the exercise of responsibility by the institutions and individuals entrusted with it by society. An essential function of parties in pluralist democracies is interest representation. Elections provide individuals and social groups with an opportunity to select political representatives who share their views at any given point in time. The pluralist electoral process necessarily produces winners and losers, the role of the former being to govern and the latter to voice political dissent. Within the framework of political pluralism, there is virtue both in dissent and in political stability and the two virtues have to be maintained for the benefit of the opposition and governing parties. All too frequently though, opposition parties crave for a definition of rights and not obligations while ruling parties insist on the obligations of opposition parties and not their rights. The challenge which this poses for constitutional arrangements centres on how the rights of the opposition can be reconciled with the needs of the ruling group to maintain an effective and functioning government.

Placing the African experience in a historical perspective, we are inevitably compelled to re-visit the colonial legacy on the continent. Colonialism was, first and foremost, an authoritarian and totalitarian system whose main legacy consisted of a politico-legislative culture that entailed a ruthless clamping down on individual initiative, freedom and liberty (Mamdani, 1996). Secondly, the colonial political order was, for a long time, a non-competitive one which, additionally, was opposed to the evolution of free/ autonomous labour and cooperative unions as well as individual and civic associations. The harshness of colonial rule, and its exclusion of the colonised from decisions that affected their daily lives led, inevitably, to development of resistance among the colonised. Faced with mounting nationalist pressure for independence, the colonial reform effort was, ironically, built on a programme of transfer of political power through multiparty competitive elections supported by a constitutional framework that provided for a host of freedoms. With independence, the parties to which the departing colonialists handed over power quickly reverted to the very system of unaccountable and unrepresentative governance which they had fought against; in many countries, the first decade of independence saw the re-institution of various forms of monopolistic politics.

Various scholars, among them Tordoff (1984), have pin-pointed the major tendencies that characterised post-independence politics in Africa. First was the trend towards single-party rule that derived, directly or indirectly, from the centralising traditions of colonial rule. Second was the deep ideological basis of party politics which was aimed at giving the followers a new sense of direction and purpose. Third was the gradual personalisation of power by the party leaders who became heads of state and who strived to exercise almost unlimited executive powers in the same way as the colonial governors-general whom they replaced. Last was the subordination of the party to the state and the subsuming under the state bureaucracy of various party elements whose role was reduced to a public relations function of explaining and/or justifying the decisions and actions of the state.

For the purposes of our present discussion, the most relevant aspect of the tendencies associated with early post-colonial politics in Africa was the process of clamping down on the opposition and the attempt to dominate free and autonomous organisations in civil society such as trade unions, the interest groups of various professionals, and other such associations. Parallel to this was the rapid erosion of the popular and broad-based support which political institutions had gained in the struggle for independence (Drake, 1964). Under such conditions, the development of the democratic potentials of African countries was faced with enormous constraints. For, as political monopoly was consolidated, all the general channels through which democratic expression could be made were increasingly suppressed. In consequence, major deficits in popular participation by the citizenry in the affairs of their countries, and in the accountability of the rulers to those over whom they ruled, developed.

It is against the background of the adverse consequences of political monopoly that the current pre-occupation with political pluralism is premised in the hope that it will provide a conducive environment for the emergence of more transparent political processes, a multiplicity of individual and group initiatives, individual freedom, and the accountability of rulers to the citizenry (Sklar, 1987). But as the experience of many countries, for example Moi's Kenya and Mobutu's Zaire, demonstrates, formal political pluralism does not necessarily deliver more accountable, representative and participatory government. In order to transcend the limitations of the plural system, society has to promote grassroot organisations that are built around particular concerns such as regional development and class, ethnic and gender solidarity. The formation of issue-specific non-governmental organisations as a means of ensuring more meaningful popular participating in the governance process is, therefore, worthy of attention. Clearly, the creation of a multiparty framework is not, necessarily, the final leg in the march to democracy, even though it may be necessary for arriving at such a system of rule (Young, 1993).

There is also need to underline another point which serves to distinguish the experiences of advanced capitalist countries with a fairly long history of institutionalised political pluralism from those of African countries that are products of a brutalising colonial experience and which are currently making a fresh attempt at multiparty politics. This point relates to the intrinsic connection between structure and function that is clearly discernible in larger, more developed majoritarian systems but which is not as clear-cut in developing countries (Chazan, 1993). What this means is that although similar political structures might exist in advanced and developing political systems, personality often preponderates over structure in the latter and, consequently, function devolves more from personal loyalty and patronage, than from the roles that structure should perform. Under such conditions, the opportunities and strategies available to the opposition often do not reflect or resemble those that are available in the older democracies.

POPULAR PROSPECTS FOR DEMOCRATISATION IN AFRICA

Before we enter into our discussion of opposition politics in Uganda, it is necessary to address some of the issues relevant to this essay that have featured in the democracy discourse in Africa. The starting point in this regard is the basic African social structure, which, it has been argued in some quarters, does not embody the social forces that are necessary for/compatible with democratic forms of rule. One perspective, focusing on social classes, suggests that the low level of capitalist development that is the lot of virtually all African countries, and the associated absence of strong social classes, including especially the problems posed by a weak but avaricious bourgeoisie which is based in the state and is internally divided by considerable social pluralism, preclude the initiation/consolidation of democratic forms of governance. Popular-democratic demands are, in this context, seen by some as being obstructive of the process of domestic capital accumulation and the speedy rise of a bourgeoisie. The insinuation is that democratic forms are only possible/sustainable in the distant future when the successful expansion of capitalism can ensure that free competition within the economic domain is able to sustain, nourish, and reinforce free competition and contestation in a politically plural society. But we by now all know the very poor correlation that exists between capitalist development and democracy: the presence of the one does not necessarily guarantee the existence of the other since, historically, they are two separate projects. Conversely, it can be argued, in a further critique of this perspective, that the very absence of a strong bourgeoisie may itself constitute a basis for a democratic possibility in the political arena. Much as popular forces are poorly organised, their economic powers of veto and the withdrawal of their political loyalty could create serious crises of governance whose resolution might compel the ruling elite to obtain a stability and predictability pact from the people built on the acceptance and institution of democratic forms of rule.

Another perspective which has been developed to suggest that Africa's democratic prospects are limited centres on ethnicity. There are various angles that have emerged to give credence to this perspective but, in general, it is stated that ethnic pluralism tends to become highly politicised under democratic forms, thereby exacerbating elite and societal divisions which, in turn, preclude the establishment of the minimum political unity and effective state system that are integral to the democratic process. This perspective is partly captured by the second quotation at the beginning of this chapter, where Daniel Arap Moi, president of Kenya, very opportunistically, warned of the disastrous consequences which "premature" democratisation in a multi-ethnic society would allegedly produce. Moi in fact proceeded to organise a number of ethnic clashes in the Kenyan Rift Valley to prove his point and ward off donor pressures on him to accept multiparty reforms. Yet, historically, effective state systems have been built in Africa on the basis of ethnic pluralism and a framework of governance that allows a free interplay of plural identities with democratic forms. Such systems have been more successful than those that rest on attempts to go round ethnic pluralism by denying the reality of its existence, thereby making ethnicity more volatile and less amenable to democratic rules and procedures.

It has been further argued that the divisions among Africa's economic, political and military elites constitute the prime factor which has led them to promote "democratisation"—not for the purpose of facilitating popular participation, but rather as a means of resolving their differences and, in so doing, strengthening their influence and channelling political action in the broad directions that are compatible with their general interests. It is, of course, hard to deny the fact that elite-supported reforms have created an opportunity for restricted "democracy" to emerge in many countries but it is equally important to underline the important role which pressures from below played in the onset of the political reform process. As to whether the elite-driven effort at democratisation will endure and evolve in a more participatory direction, this will, to a large extent, depend on the strength of civil society and the effectiveness of the political parties that have been established to meaningfully stamp their influence on the political terrain. If the unions, professional associations and grassroot movements are capable of expanding the limits of the newly created political space, and if they are able to evolve a capacity to build and sustain a broad pro-democracy coalition, then it is likely that African countries will succeed in maintaining the delicate balance between pressures from below and threats from above in their uneven, unsteady path towards a more democratic order.

IDEAL CRITERIA FOR EVALUATING OPPOSITION PARTIES

Clearly, in our view, neither the fact of multi-ethnicity nor the low level of accumulation need automatically be sources of blockage towards democratic reform. With these points in mind, we propose that the main yardsticks for evaluating the opposition parties that are now a part of the political landscape in many African countries should, in an ideal situation, include: the extent to which they pursue their organisational goals through the electoral process; the extensiveness and inclusiveness of their organisational structure and political constituency; the extent to which they employ established political avenues for achieving their goals; and, their record of internal organisational stability. In practical terms, this implies several things. First, the opposition must be based on entities that have a demonstrable internal stability and coherent organisation. Second, it has to have organisational extensiveness and inclusiveness to attract a substantial and diverse membership. Furthermore, it should have a well-focused set of objectives to serve as a rallying point not only for the leadership, but also the membership. Finally, it must have adequate resources to handle its organisational affairs, and must command respect, approval and a general appeal from a broad cross-section of the population.

The opposition party, if it functions well, should serve to provide a check-and-balance mechanism against the government, rather than collaborate with the incumbent to corrupt political society or destroy the basis for the accountability of the governors to those over whom they rule. For this purpose, it not only has to have credibility before the electorate, it also has to be organised autonomously of the ruling party. This way, it will be able to present coherent challenges to the government on all the issues on which it may choose to focus its attention. Implicit in this is a certain notion of reasonable permanence in that the opposition party ought to exist as a continuous entity or an enduring structure, rather than forming and disbanding in an *ad hoc* fashion. Its representativeness is derived in part from the fact that it is at the forefront of a group of dedicated followers throughout the country with whom it is organically connected and whose aspirations it attempts to develop into a coherent programme. It is also an alternative to the government, waiting as it were in the wings to take over power in case the government falls or is defeated in an election. The opposition party can also be seen as a participant in the governmental process since through its activities, it helps the government, directly or indirectly, to shape its programmes and policies (Kiggundu, 1987).

As a political structure with the main function of providing checks and balances in the broad political process, the opposition does several things. It participates in deliberations in parliament. It opposes objectionable policies by voice and vote. It compels the government by all acceptable (legal and constitutional) methods to modify its policies. It also attempts to create public sentiment against the government and public sympathy for itself as a precondition for winning the next election. Above all, and this is the essence of its very existence, it proposes alternative programmes. In doing all of these, three courses of action are open to the opposition. The first consists of concerted action aimed at winning amendments to legislation emanating from the government. The second has to do with the exposure of the weakness or injustice of governmental policies, thereby eliciting modifications or cancellations by the incumbent. Thirdly, through its rhetoric and criticisms, the opposition aims to create an anti-government mood amongst the electorate. The opposition can achieve its objectives, and pursue them more assiduously and effectively if there are salient factors such as ideology, race/class, religion or ethnicity around which significant segments of the electorate can converge (Kasfir, 1976).

In a society like Uganda, that does not have a fully developed culture of loyal opposition, the ideals which we have discussed above face several constraints. In general, the Ugandan opposition, as elsewhere in Africa, has a weak resource base (most opposition parties are financed from outside) and the main opposition leaders have very little experience in the conduct of party work and in managing organisational problems. This deficit of experience adversely affects the stability of the opposition groups, their capacity to attract a large following, and develop a set of well-focused objectives. Because of this reality, the political organisations that have evolved to play the role of the opposition cannot be judged solely on the basis of the ideal criteria we described above; we also need to factor in a discussion of the ways in which they grapple with the problems they confront in their attempt to create an environment conducive to their operations and development. This implies that the capacity of the opposition to transform the adverse legacy of political monopoly without degenerating into anarchy or destroying society has to be an important element in a discussion of its performance. It must also display a resolve to deal with internal crises without destroying the party organisation. This is how it can present itself as a determined force potentially capable of creating space for itself in the political system.

THE NRM GOVERNMENT AND ITS POLITICS

The National Resistance Movement (NRM) government came to power in 1986 following a five-year guerrilla war. During its first years in office, it presented itself as a movement committed to following a "scientific" model of political and economic development loosely derived from the classes in political economy and socialism taught in the 1970s at the University of Dar-es-Salaam where many of its leaders were educated. The NRM came to power with a self-conceived superiority of thought which it sought to superimpose upon the largely incompetent and decadent civil service and other state structures which it inherited. Soon after seizing power, the NRM suspended the existing political parties in the country on the argument that they rested on narrow and exclusivist religious and ethnic foundations which prevented the possibility of the creation of a harmonious multi-ethnic political order; the parties then exploited the divisions which they helped to create or reinforce to the point where they completely poisoned Uganda's political climate and brought the nation-state to the brink on several occasions. They were accused of not having clearly defined secular ideological positions or platforms, and, therefore, could not help but continue to appeal to divisive parochial loyalties which brought out the worst in Ugandans. The NRM also accused the parties of being dominated by self-serving urban elites with little or no anchorage among the rural majority. But in spite of the decision to formally suspend them, the parties did not wither away as the NRM radicals had initially hoped for. Uganda has, therefore, in reality operated more or less as a three-party system with the NRM increasingly taking on most of the characteristics of the other parties, namely, the Democratic Party (DP) and the Uganda People's Congress (UPC).

The DP and the UPC were, before the rise of the NRM, the two dominant conventional parties in post-independence Uganda. In suspending, rather than outrightly banning them, the NRM was able to claim that Uganda was neither a one-party state nor a no-party state. The decision to suspend the DP and UPC however, had the ironic effect of endowing them with more credibility in the eyes of sections of the populace than they probably would have had had they been left to operate openly.

Under the NRM political dispensation, party members are allowed to speak freely and run for office, but only on their own individual/personal merit and not on the platform of their parties. The realisation that, given Uganda's recent bloody political history, there would be no popular agitation for the return of political parties played a key role in NRM's decision to insist on maintaining the suspension of the parties whilst simultaneously extending the "interim" period of its rule. During this period, the NRM also devoted resources to amplifying its initial tentative critique of political parties into a fully-fledged theory of an alternative path to democracy. While thus formally restricting the freedom of assembly and political organisation along political party lines, it managed to uphold a degree of freedom of political participation that, in some respects, is highly unusual in Africa. Central to this approach, and serving as an alternative to party-based political competition, was the institution by the NRM of non-party elections, built on individual candidacies, into Resistance Councils and Committees (RCs). It also organised itself as a movement for unity and change in Uganda and invited prominent political figures of all stripes to participate in a broad-based government under the leadership of Yoweri Museveni.

The NRM's political philosophy rests on the position that Uganda's political culture is not particularly conducive to a Western-style democratic system built around political parties and periodic elections contested by candidates sponsored by the parties. Yoweri Museveni and several of his associates have constantly emphasised the point that in a "backward" country like Uganda (declared to be pre-industrial by the president on several occasions), where communications are poorly developed and the majority of the people are illiterate, living in a state of poverty and are mostly to be found in the rural areas, it is neither possible nor meaningful to attempt to organise people on the basis of the kinds of interest group aggregation that exists in the Western world. This being the case, Museveni and his colleagues insist that it is not appropriate to develop Uganda's political system on the basis of Western-type political parties. What is needed, according to the NRM, is a social movement that is able to champion the task of mobilising the people to be part and parcel of decision-making at the various levels where their livelihood is affected. The task of educating the populace generally and politically, of promoting national integration, and building a national civic identity/culture are important goals which such a movement should spearhead.

In our view, the dichotomy between undemocratic and democratic political culture, implied in the NRM's conception, is too simplistic to say the least. The currently predominant form of distinction between democratic and anti-democratic political cultures is contained in the concept of "civic culture" or "civic community" (Chazan, 1993). From this perspective, "civicness" is a quantifiable and unilinear variable, which one can use to predict any given community's ability to sustain democratic institutions. Civic communities are those in which there is a generalised trust and willingness to participate in voluntary civic associations. Their opposite is communities in which there is a generalised distrust and an orientation towards personalised relations of patronage. Much as these are important elements of political culture, laying them out in the form of a unidimensional continuum makes it impossible to theorise an internally coherent transition from a noncivic to a civic culture. While it may seem unrealistic to expect an immediate and widespread transition to Western-style democracy in Africa in the near term, the current Ugandan experiment has created an illusory optimism that Africans are contriving alternative models of democratic political participation more suited to their own institutional and cultural circumstances. The possibility is ignored that what may be going on is, in fact, an attempt at re-inventing the monopolisation of power.

BETWEEN MULTIPARTYISM AND A NO-PARTY SYSTEM: THE UGANDAN DEBATE

The central issue in the on-going debate in Uganda about the organisation of politics is focused on the nature of pluralism and the role of political parties in the democratisation process (Mamdani, 1994). The political parties, particularly the partisans of the DP and UPC, argue that democracy is not possible without political pluralism, and that pluralism means freedom of political activity. The NRM insists that political parties have, in Uganda's historical experience, undermined rather than furthered or defended democracy, and that multipartyism is not the only, or, for Uganda, the best form of democracy. Cadres of the NRM also deplore the fact that political parties in Uganda have, over time, become corrupt state parties: small coteries of professional politicians whose primary interest is to secure positions and privileges for themselves at the expense of society at large. The parties have also been accused of organising support not on the basis of "principled" discussion of issues and policies, but through an "opportunistic" manipulation of divisive issues like religion and ethnicity. It has been repeatedly emphasised that election times for parties are not a time to educate and unite the people along "national" lines, but another opportunity to divide them along "sectarian" lines. Their support base is not a membership that can hold the leadership accountable, but more of a bandwagon of followers that has little control or influence over the leadership. Besides, there is little that is democratic about the internal organisation of these parties. For the NRM, parties are, therefore, more of an obstacle to democratisation than a vehicle for its furtherance.

There are many in Uganda who will easily agree with the NRM's critique of party-based politics in the light of the post-colonial history of the country. Between 1962 and 1986, the country experimented with a variety of political arrangements ranging from multipartyism to a single party system and a no-party approach. None of the systems however proved to be an effective barrier against the erosion of rights and the spread of state violence. As if to confirm this, one of the harshest experiences of state repression unfolded in the context of a multiparty arrangement under the second Obote administration in the first half of the 1980s. Opposition parties were so preoccupied with seeking and protecting their own private positions and privileges that they could not be counted on to defend the population effectively against state terror. Unlike in those African countries which had only a very limited experience of multiparty arrangements, the people of Uganda have, from their experience, little, if any, reason to succumb to the illusion that political parties, by and of themselves, can be an effective institutional vehicle for safeguarding democratic rights. This is, however, not to say that every Ugandan accepts the NRM's no-party agenda hook, line and sinker. It is, rather, to say that experience has taught Ugandans to approach multipartyism less with unbridled euphoria and more with realism.

Lacking any element of self-criticism, the NRM critique of parties generally and Ugandan political parties in particular is, on closer scrutiny, nothing but self-serving. If political parties turned into breeding grounds for the individuals who go into politics as the quickest road to position and privilege, it is also clear that the NRM, after over ten years in power, has trod exactly the same path as the parties that have been the target of its attack. Just like the parties, the NRM does not have a credible and tested internal mechanism for holding its leaders accountable. The parties are funded by a few wealthy individuals and institutions just like the NRM is essentially a state-funded body. What might be considered as the party question, namely the problem of holding political organisations accountable, concerns the NRM as much, if not more, than the parties that have historically dominated political life in Uganda until Museveni's rise to power. Viewed more dispassionately, it can be convincingly argued that much of the generalised attack on political parties as enemies of peace and democracy which the NRM developed and popularised really only applies to the period of anarchy that prevailed in the early 1980s when the UPC was at the helm of affairs in the country. The NRM's hostility towards the UPC was, however, to be cleverly generalised to encompass political parties in general and the very principle of a political system based on party competition in particular. Thus it was that Uganda's problems since independence came to be blamed primarily on political parties, and politics took on a pejorative meaning connoting conflicts between sectional, divisive interests.

In the NRM critique, parties are said to violate the principles of legitimate authority and democracy. Party-based regimes are too deeply partisan to uphold standards of fairness. They respond repressively to criticism, thus negating freedom of speech and rendering open communication between the rulers and the ruled impossible. Elections are not conceived as opportunities for opening up a dialogue with the electorate but as a bazaar where votes are freely bought and voters are intimidated. Of graver concern, parties have been blamed for being inimical to peace and order since they allegedly disrupt even the most fundamental of solidarities, pitting brother against brother and neighbour against neighbour. Parties are also accused of promoting a winner-take-all attitude towards political competition, disenfranchising the losers and thus creating permanent resentments and antagonisms. They are alleged to promote an ambition for power which is so excessive and so unregulated as to undermine the possibility of broader unities and compromise. The destructive ambition inherent in parties is held responsible for infecting the very internal structure of the parties themselves, making them not only outwardly disordering, but inwardly disorderly as well.

The general theme running through much of the NRM critique is that political parties are destructive of the principle of structural hierarchy on which the democratic virtues in the political system are anchored (Diamond, 1993). Parties do not compete for limited power within a regulated hierarchy which encompasses the social totality. Instead, they form totalities of their own, competing to capture the power structure and exclude all others from access to it. And as partial totalities and totalities of exclusion, they lack the necessary flexible articulation with society for an inclusive hierarchical framework (Schatzberg,1993). For example, they interpret free speech not as communication from within the structure but as a threat from without. Since a party's authority has no transcendent anchorage or status, it remains mired in partisanship and cannot treat its subjects as equals in judging their conflicts. And sustained NRM propaganda against parties and party politics has deeply reinforced this conception.

Yoweri Museveni himself has relentlessly criticised multiparty democracy and has publicly indicated that he favours a no-party democracy. He asserts that multiparty democracy would not be problematic if the parties would polarise themselves along lines of principle and/or on policy issues. Most of the time however, they polarise themselves along sectarian lines—either on religious lines where, for example, the UPC was for Protestants and the DP was for Catholics, or on a "tribal" basis as was the case of Nigeria in the 1960s. Museveni and the NRM state that their fear of multipartyism is not in the parties themselves, but in the effect that they will have on the unity of the people and stability of the country given their tendency to form and organise on the basis of ethnicity and religion. The NRM does not think there is, as yet, a social basis for party politics in Uganda. Although it accepts that democracy is a cherished ideal, the NRM has continued to insist that its form is as important as its essence. A form of democracy without parties is favoured not because it is the most democratic, but because it is safer in the Ugandan circumstances. Not only does it prevent negative forms of mobilisation and polarisation from going too far, it also affords the population the three basics of democracy, i.e. representation, accountability and regular, peaceful changes of leadership. It is a democracy without sectarian divisions. As a strategy for maintaining harmony for long enough to promote social transformation, which will then permit the establishment of a healthy system of party competition, the no-party approach is less confrontational in the short run. According to the NRM, it is only opportunists who fear to be judged on the basis of their own merit and who prefer to hide behind parochial issues and groups, such as "tribe" and/or religion, who can expect to lose out in its no-party experiment. For the NRM, therefore, many of its critics fear its approach to organising Ugandan political life because it completely undermines their base.

THE NRM AND THE OPPOSITION: THE DYNAMICS

It is important to note at this stage that even among literate/educated Ugandans and in middle class circles, the level of "democratic" awareness and actual political participation by the general public in the affairs of the country is low. From our careful reading of the attitude of the individual to the state, even the averagely informed urban Ugandan views the present NRM state not as a structure of democratic negotiation which is ultimately empowered and controlled by himself or herself, but as a "sacrosanct" outside entity which nurtures and protects but which should not be challenged, and which is essentially a continuity, rather than a break with previous experiences, colonial and post-colonial. This persistent conception of the state as beyond civil control and criticism has a profound political effect. In the southern and central regions of the country, partial satisfaction with some aspects of the performance of NRM, particularly the guaranteeing of relative security which had long eluded this area, must be an important, if not the crucial factor explaining the lack of opposition to Museveni's political project and the absence of an effective autonomous democratic movement.

In order to properly contextualise the state-opposition dynamic, we have to begin by reiterating that there is no agreement among the major political stakeholders about the essential character of the established political system in the country. This is as true for the prevailing constitutional order as for the economic system that sustains and reinforces it. The important implication here is that there is no agreement among the contenders in the Ugandan political terrain to attain their political goals through the existing political framework. The practice that has been evolved by the parties with respect to the NRM's political programmes and policies in general, and, more particularly its system of local government as embodied in the Resistance Councils has developed in two phases. The first phase was one of open hostility and opposition but when this did not yield the expected result, the parties entered a second phase that saw them joining the Councils in order to fight them from within. Furthermore, even this strategy of fighting from within NRM structures was two-pronged: from within the RCs themselves and from within the NRM broad-based government into which the leaders of the main parties were incorporated.

Because the NRM and its main political adversaries, namely, the UPC and the DP, hold rival definitions of democracy, this has created opposing ideas about how democratic structures should be organised. On the one hand, the older parties say they believe in, although they may not always have been successful in practising, a conventional version of multiparty representative democracy based on institutional guarantees. The NRM, on the other hand, drawing on the support base it built for itself during its guerrilla war, has striven to modify the conventional ideas on representative democracy championed by its opponents by emphasising features of popular democracy based on mass participation and politicised popular organisations (Kasfir, 1990). But what the NRM has gained by incorporating other groups, it seems to have lost in the distinctiveness of its own political identity as it sought to widen its political base by accommodating other social forces in the government and the army whose views differed from its own. In weakening the NRM's originally distinct political programme, this process also led Museveni and his advisers to desperately contrive schemes for outwitting the political parties.

Let us illustrate the latter point a little. In preparing the country for presidential and parliamentary elections that had been scheduled for May 1996, the NRM took steps to ensure that its power would not be substantively challenged by the outcome of the polls. It utilised the advantage of incumbency to lay down certain guarantees in the statutory framework for the elections that would maintain the balance of forces in its favour. For example, although the statutory framework broadened the political space by providing for the representation of previously unrepresented interests/groups like the youth, women, workers and the disabled who are now to be formally represented in the legislature, the groups that were targeted under this programme are basically among those who form the support base of the NRM. That is why the question of the autonomy of social movements and their participation in the political process has become a problematic one in Uganda, with the political opponents of the NRM, arguing, with some justification, that the groups for which the NRM has made special dispensations are drawn from the sections of society that are beholden to it. This way, the NRM guaranteed itself a working parliamentary majority even before the elections were held.

Whilst selectively opening up the political space to groups and interests drawn from its support base, the NRM has simultaneously sought to narrow the space for its known and potential opponents by prohibiting the official participation of the organised interests represented by the political parties. In the absence of the participation of other organised social forces in the elections, the predictable result was the atomisation of the citizenry, so much so that the outcome of the political processes was shifted to depend on factors external to it. With the NRM freely spreading its gospel that parties are responsible for all the misery in the country and that, consequently, Ugandans should hate them, it becomes hard to verify the extent to which the populace shares this outlook as long as the parties remain muzzled by the government. Even as formal party-based competition is prohibited, the NRM has lost no opportunity to use the factor of incumbency and public resources to its own political advantage.

In view of all of the foregoing, it is easy to understand why the most contentious issue in contemporary Uganda remains whether competitive party-based politics or "popular participation" co-terminous with RC organisation ought to serve as the framework for the quest for democratisation (Ddungu, 1989; Kasfir, 1990). If popular participation is to be the key to democracy, then revitalising the RC system and organisation to raise the consciousness of the people about their real problems is fundamental. But if presenting alternative frameworks of policy to voters is central to democracy, then allowing parties to organise and campaign openly is critical. In this regard, the problem is, essentially, about the fate of the NRM itself, and the choice between the two alternatives, we need to appreciate, is as much about democratic principle as it is about power and how to keep or gain it.

But there are further difficulties which are posed by a political set up which categorically excludes the participation of organised forces in society or any systematic, open discussion of issues. The absence of open campaigning before elections, for example, makes it virtually impossible to discuss policies. Discussion focuses on the personal qualities of the candidates, their moral character, honesty and willingness to mix with ordinary people and not on the relevant policy issues that are demanded by the developmental and political challenges confronting the country. The opportunity to frame policies is, therefore, monopolised by the NRM and its top leadership. This re-affirms the position which we argued earlier, namely that when the legal framework excludes organised activity, then the outcome depends significantly on factors outside the formal political process.

Consequently, in spite of the much applauded improvements in the level of political participation in Uganda under the NRM, political choices are still limited by strict government controls on opposition politics at the national and local levels. Most social organisations like trade unions, the cooperative movement and business associations which have long been controlled by the government have, during the NRM years, become even more closely integrated into the state machinery. How has all this been possible? The secret of NRM's success is its skilful combination of carrots and sticks. Partial concessions have been combined with repression, conditioning access to material gains on political subordination. Furthermore, the state has not, in all cases, waited to be pressured into reforms; its capacity for pre-emptive measures has been demonstrated time and again. While it bargains and occasionally makes concessions, this approach is operated in the shadow of its undoubted and unmistakable capacity for fierce repression in case negotiations break down.

It is important to emphasise this point because in Uganda, the empowerment of the military has been accompanied by the militarisation of society. Leaders of the NRA and its political wing, the NRM conceive of the army as a political force which will transform Ugandan politics by demonstrating the virtues of discipline and unity, thus exposing the deficiencies of the main traditional parties. This is another way of saying that they intend the military to remain at the centre of national politics.

So, in addition to the mismatch between an inept opposition and a cagey incumbent willing to do almost anything to stay in power, the support of the military and the security forces, has been, and is likely to remain, the single most important domestic factor against any meaningful democratisation in Uganda. In the Ugandan society, with its strong centrifugal tendencies, military officers have tended to look at multiparty politics more as a threat to the integrity of the state than an opportunity to effect fundamental change in state-society relations. The dangerous flaw in this thinking, of course, is its equation of the survival of the government in power with the survival of the state. Consequently, crucial to the NRM's overall power strategy is the army. Whatever new political construction is undertaken, the army will play a pivotal role in determining the direction of the country. And, as things stand, there is very little that the various groups within the opposition coalition can do about the army's role in the national political process.

Feeling the playing field not to be level and all of the odds loaded against them, there has also emerged a dramatic trend centring on defections to the NRM by high profile/staunch supporters of the other main political groups, especially those of the UPC. Some of the defectors from the UPC have included former government ministers and party executives. This development has furthered weakened the party and presented the entire political opposition with a serious crisis. Leading members of the parties appear, in the public perception at least, always to desert them for "greener pastures" at critical moments. Viewed historically, it would seem that such occurrences, instead of enhancing unity or democracy, often lead to a steady growth of authoritarian tendencies. In Uganda, carpet-crossing from the opposition to the ruling party began in 1964. The then leader of the opposition in parliament, Basil Bataringaya of the DP, crossed over to the UPC with five other members of parliament. The UPC's Obote appointed the defectors to ministerial positions, with the chief defector becoming Internal Affairs Minister. Soon after, Kabaka Yekka (KY) MPs, whose party was in coalition with UPC, crossed *en masse* to the UPC. They were soon to be followed by the remaining DP MPs. By 1969, Uganda had become a *de facto* one party state, a situation which Obote merely rubber stamped by banning opposition parties in 1969. The ruling party became strong and dangerous. It would pass draconian laws without a dissenting voice. The Deportation Ordinance and the Preventive Detention Act were two such laws. In such a context, political life was reduced to petty conflicts among the president's confidants over the distribution of favours. The principle became either you bootlick or sink into political oblivion.

Going by recent developments, the NRM appears to be slowly treading the same path as the UPC. Even after serving a ten-year term, the NRM is not keen on opening any new avenues of formal power-sharing with any other force both at the local government level and in the national political arena. The failure (refusal?) of NRM to transform itself into a fully fledged political organisation has made it attractive to many politicians whose primary concern is with the material benefits that they can obtain for themselves, not the building of a popular local support base. Some of the party members who have crossed over to the NRM cited the alliance between the two main political parties, the DP and UPC, to form a joint front with other political formations as the ostensible reason for their action. Yet, given the fact that one common threat which the political opponents of the NRM face is the NRM's determination to destroy them, it should not be surprising that one of their responses is to try to forge a common front that can guarantee their survival. Indeed, in justification of its indiscriminate attacks on them, the NRM has always publicly asserted that it sees no differences between DP and UPC in terms of principles, ideas, manifestos, class, etc. Although a principled change of mind is understandable and excusable, there is little doubt that for the great majority of people who have defected from the DP and UPC to the NRM, their stomach has dictated their minds and erased their principles. The conscious failure of the NRM to mould or allow the evolution of a potential successor or alternative to itself implies, in practice, that it is not contemplating or foreseeing any loosening of its grip on power.

As indicated above, one issue of prime concern to the opposition parties is the absence of a level playing field. The parties have openly expressed their worry over the way in which the NRM has used its control over the state apparatus to advance its own cause while suppressing the parties' voices. Using its virtual monopoly over the means of communication (especially the print and electronic media), the NRM has succeeded in spreading its messages far and wide, repeatedly and without challenges from its opponents. The ubiquitous political education and military science courses which the NRM introduced nation-wide are a chief avenue through which it has undertaken its campaigns of discrediting the opposition, particularly the parties. The opposition, with no means of amplifying its message and image, is left with only its weak and, in some cases, limited attempts at developing a response. Thus, although the opposition may have quality, it finds it extremely difficult to convert this into quantity; its message may have some truth, but there is no audience with which it can share it.

The NRM's decision to ban political party activities has meant that the parties are not allowed to hold open political meetings. For any open public function, permission must be sought in writing from the police, at whose discretion it can be pre-judged that an intended meeting will most likely culminate in a breach of peace and law and order, and consequently that a permit cannot be granted. The most serious attempt to challenge the structural obstacles to opposition activity occurred when a splinter faction of the DP stubbornly insisted that its meeting in the city square must proceed, a challenge to which the government responded by deploying a massive police presence, in addition to a helicopter gunship which hovered over the intended venue for several hours. The same thing happened when other groups like the federalists and monarchists attempted to hold public meetings to press their claims. In addition, opposition politicians and other activists have had to opt for careers outside of the governmental system in the knowledge that they were likely to be penalised by thwarted promotion opportunities, if not outright dismissal, if they pursued their activities from their positions in the public sector.

On the basis of the foregoing, we can argue that even as the NRM has taken measures which would appear to be aimed at opening up the national political space, it has not taken steps to dismantle the authoritarian elements that underly the very constitution of the Ugandan state. There is, consequently, as yet no noticeable transition in the state-opposition dynamics, from emphasis on protest (confrontational opposition) towards efforts to build concrete social and political alternatives (positive policy alternatives). In the absence of viable pluralist structures, opposition to the NRM is bound to acquire extremist and militant tendencies.

Nothing best underscores the ambiguity that characterises the NRM's political reform project than the three nation-wide elections held in 1989, 1992, and 1994. These elections could not be considered fully democratic because they did not provide an opportunity for the emergence of and participation by political forces capable, potentially, of replacing the ruling NRM government. But the elections should not, however, be dismissed out of hand as an exercise aimed at dressing up a dictatorship, because, after the rules were set, the government did not interfere with the voting. Several ministers who were important members of the NRM lost in these elections just as well-known members against whom the NRM fought a violent war were not prevented from occupying the lower level and parliamentary seats that they won in the elections. But even as it insisted that elections were to be held on a non-party, non-sectarian basis, Yoweri Museveni surprised Ugandans when he declared after the 1995 constituent assembly elections that the NRM had emerged victorious. The question which arose was: victorious against whom? That was one rare, unguarded moment when the president confirmed the persistent assertion by his opponents that the NRM was but a contending political force in Uganda's democratisation process. The work of the constituent assembly itself was to reflect a polarisation which took clearly discernible party political lines.

In a bid to check the apparent free ride of the NRM, the opposition parties have been striving to devise fresh strategies for getting themselves into the centre-stage of national politics. One of the most interesting recent efforts occurred in the NRM-dominated Constituent Assembly where an attempt was made to forge a National Caucus for Democracy (NCD) to coordinate the activities of those multipartyists and federalists who felt that they were losing out on every point that concerned them during the debates on the constitution. After the Constituent Assembly had finished its work and endorsed the continuation of the movement system for another five years, with the associated continuation of the suspension of political parties until new laws are made to govern their operations, this caucus tried to adopt the form of a movement since this is what the constitution allows for, and it is not enshrined in the constitution that the only movement that is allowed is the NRM.

Were the NCD to succeed in its objectives of being accepted as a movement, it would have the potential of producing a profound reconfiguration of the county's politics and this would present the NRM with awkward challenges. The coalition, particularly if it was joined by more political formations, could take on the form of a broad-based movement, leaving the NRM to look more or less like the only party. And if it pressed its argument that as a movement it is entitled to be active politically, the NRM would have problems banning its activities. This explains why the NRM spared no effort to undermine it at birth. In criticism of the NCD idea, supporters of the NRM pointed out that it underlined the validity of their argument that there are no differences between the political parties but that they are all merely factions of the political elite fighting over the control of power.

Beyond the systematic campaigns by the NRM to obstruct and discredit them, the opposition parties have also been faced with a host of other problems, among them the lack of funds, internal fragmentation, a low degree of grassroots organisation, and the reality that the ruling NRM's powers of co-optation and the appeal it enjoys as the organ for peace and unity cuts across political boundaries. A key tactic which the NRM uses in order to perpetuate its position of dominance is the appointment of additional members to elected bodies (in the National Resistance Council (NRC) and the Constituent Assembly, for example), which ensures that the opposition can never have a majority. The NRM also cajoles or subtly coerces key opposition members to cross over to its fold. Another strategy is that of postponement of the implementation of unpopular decisions like cost sharing in government hospitals, the levying of license fees on television, the introduction of Value Added Tax, until after elections. A related and even more general strategy is the securing of public support in exchange for such facilities as the state has to offer like schools, clinics, boreholes and road infrastructure. A situation has developed where the president himself is like the chairman of some kind of allocation committee, distributing vehicles to religious and traditional leaders, doling out milling machines and heifers to women's groups, ordering the construction of bitumenised roads to communities, and offering the extension of electricity to areas he visits. Coming before elections, this is nothing but a campaign strategy which is unavailable to the opposition. The Constituent Assembly has ended up retroactively legitimising the ten-year rule of NRM by providing for Uganda to be governed under a movement system for five more years after the promulgation of Uganda's new constitution. Councils were manipulated to publicise resolutions by the various levels of the Resistance Committees endorsing the sole candidate of the incumbent president in the presidential elections that were held in 1996.

CONCLUDING REMARKS: WHITHER THE UGANDAN DEMOCRATISATION PROJECT?

The passage of time has resulted in the considerable scaling down of some of the exaggerated hopes and fears expressed at the beginning of the (re)birth of multiparty politics in Africa in the late 1980s and early 1990s. It has now become clear, for example, that in many countries, the creation of parties has not directly involved many citizens from outside the existing political elite, and particularly those in the rural areas. The resurgence of dominant parties and the absence of alternative leaders are again threatening to become a permanent feature of the African political landscape. Some of the most powerful "new breed" politicians are simply old breed politicians who chose the right moment to break with the past and engage in the rhetoric of "good governance" and "respect for human rights" which are the new catchwords/catch phrases of which the international donor community is particularly enamoured. As if the popular agitation for change that was witnessed during the late 1980s and early 1990s count for little, politicians still generally regard the state as a cow to be milked in their own interests whilst the rest of the populace watch in resignation.

As we noted earlier, the very idea of an opposition only becomes meaningful if it offers an alternative to what exists and effectively plays the role of a watchdog with a view to safeguarding society's interests. For a variety of reasons which we have attempted to capture in this essay, the Ugandan opposition is far removed from this position. At the least, the prevailing conditions do not allow the opposition to play such a role effectively. As Uganda prepared for another round of elections in mid-1996, a variety of political groups mushroomed, some in a disguised form, to participate in the contest. At least ten such new groups emerged in the six months from November 1995 to April 1996. There was a distinct danger that the groups would become so many that Uganda could have ended up having as many political opinions as there are opposition groups. We must observe that the opposition will only become viable if the groups are able to overcome some of their petty differences and pool their efforts and resources in order to offer a critical and credible policy perspective on the central concerns of Ugandans at the present time. There is considerable popular doubt that the emerging political organisations may fail to capture and represent the real political opinion around which they attempt to organise and rally support from the population in order to capture power. This is all the more so as they have tended to concentrate on the weaknesses of the NRM and have left society in doubt as to whether they would not commit the same mistakes or worse if they took over the helm.

Uganda's recent experience would seem to suggest that democratisation has been adversely affected by the unfairness of the fundamental rules and the systematic exclusion of opposition forces from public goods or the spoils of office. The three common mechanisms for ensuring the durability of incumbents in power have all been fully invoked by NRM and these include: the discrediting of the opposition, the conjuring up and managing of popular support, and the manipulation of the military (to at least maintain a "benevolent neutrality"). The NRM strategy has remained simple: keep rewarding indispensable supporters, even if all other institutions are falling apart and encourage the crippling proliferation of opposition parties. So regardless of who wins future elections, the lesson is clear: if the rules are unfair, the winners not generous and magnanimous in victory, and the losers inadequately represented and prevented from venting their views freely, incentives to continue playing the democratic game according to the set rules will diminish. That is one of the main dangers confronting the quest for democratisation in Uganda.

It took a lot of struggle, and some would say it was a long time in coming but NRM now feels compelled to accept, at least in theory, the necessity for further democratisation in Uganda. The debate will and should continue about the most appropriate political forms that will be required for building a stable democratic polity in the country based on the aspirations for change shared by wide sectors of civil society. The guided forms of democracy which the NRM has been seeking to promote may represent an advancement over some of the worst days of authoritarianism witnessed in Uganda's recent history. There is, however, no doubt that they would by and by exhaust themselves. For guided democracy is, by definition, and in practice, limited democracy. Limited democracy always contains the seed for its own replacement by (hopefully) more thorough-going processes of political reform. The role of the opposition, both in political and civil societies will be central to the prospects for moving Uganda beyond guided democracy.

By way of conclusion, we must stress that the current fashionable model of democracy (pluralism), is a very specific, and far from universal, form of political culture, which needs to be carefully and critically studied before it can be expected to be applied, and which operates in the context of alternative and contrasting views of participation, legitimation and constitutional procedure. In order to appreciate the substantial national variations within this process, national level analyses must be fully rooted in on-going research into how people structure their political life and strive to interpret politics within their particular framework of expectations and concerns.

As for the democratisation movement which has developed in Africa since the second half of the 1980s, there has emerged a tempting tendency to portray it as a return to the model of national democracy that allegedly was there at the dawn of national independence but that had merely been eroded in the subsequent years. Our own view of these developments is that the current democratisation movement is only the latest phase in the on-going struggles for the transformation of Africa, in the course of which various conceptions of political power, and constitutional and philosophical alternatives, are being tested, accommodated or discarded. The contradictory outcomes of this process need to be taken into account, particularly by those who believe that the quest for a new, modern democratic model can and should transcend its North Atlantic origins and become the cornerstone of a new and better world.

REFERENCES

Beckman, B., 1990, "Whose Democracy? Bourgeois versus Popular Democracy in Africa". Mimeo. Department of Political Science, University of Stockholm.

Bwengye, F.A.W., 1985, *The Agony of Uganda: From Idi Amin to Obote*. London: Regency Press.

Chazan, N., 1993, "Between Liberalism and Statism: African Political Cultures and Democracy", in Larry Diamond (ed.), *Political Culture and Democracy in Developing Countries*. Boulder: Lynne Rienner.

Ddungu, E., 1989, *The Crisis of Democracy in Africa: The Case of Resistance Councils in Uganda*. M.A. Dissertation. University of Dar-es-Salaam.

Ddungu, E. and A. Wabwire, 1991, *The Electoral Mechanisms and the Democratic Process: The 1989 RC-NRC Elections*. Working Paper No. 9. Kampala: Centre for Basic Research.

Diamond, L. (ed.), 1993, *Political Culture and Democracy in Developing Countries*, Boulder, Co.: Lynne Rienner Publishers.

Drake, St. Clair, 1964, "Democracy on Trial in Africa", *The Annals of the American Academy of Political and Social Sciences*. Philadelphia.

Gendzier, I.L., 1985, *Managing Political Change: Social Scientists and the Third World*. Boulder, Co. and London: Westview Press.

Huntington, S.P., 1968, *Political Order in Changing Societies*. New Haven: Yale University Press.

Kasfir, N., 1976, *The Shrinking Political Arena: Participation and Ethnicity in African Politics, with a Case Study of Uganda*. Berkley: University of California Press.

Kasfir, N., 1990, "The Uganda Elections of 1989: Power, Populism and Democratisation", Mimeo.

Kiggundu, P., 1987, *The Right to Vote and Participate in Government: With Special Reference to Uganda*. LLM Dissertation. Cardiff University.

Lobel, J., 1988, "The Meaning of Democracy: Representative and Participatory Democracy in the New Nicaraguan Constitution", *University of Pittsburgh Law Review* , Vol. 49, No. 3.

Mamdani, M., 1987, "Contradictory Class Perspectives on the Question of Democracy: The Case of Uganda", in P. A. Nyong'o (ed.), *Popular Struggles for Democracy in Africa*. London: Zed Books.

Mamdani, M., 1996, *Citizen and Subject: Contemporary Africa and the Legacy of Late Colonialism*. Princeton: Princeton University Press.

Nyong'o, P.A. (ed.), 1987, *Popular Struggles for Democracy in Africa*. London: Zed Books.

Nyong'o, P.A., T. Mkandawire and S. Gutto, 1988, "Political Instability and Development", *Africa Development*, Vol. XIII, Nos. 3 and 4.

Schatzberg, M.G., 1993, "Power, Legitimacy and Democratisation in Africa", *Africa*, Vol. 63, No. 4.

Sklar, R.L., 1987, "Developmental Democracy", *Comparative Studies in Society and History* , Vol. 29, No. 4.

Tidemand, P., 1995, *The Resistance Councils in Uganda: A Study of Rural Politics and Popular Democracy in Africa*. Ph.D. Thesis, Roskilde University, Denmark.

Tordoff, W., 1984, *Government and Politics in Africa*. London: Macmillan.

Young, T. , 1993, "Elections and Electoral Politics in Africa", *Africa*, Vol. 63, No. 3.

Chapter 7

From Peoples' Politics to State Politics: Aspects of National Liberation in South Africa

Michael Neocosmos

Al die mamas en die papas, die boeties en die sussies, die oumas en die oupas, die hondjies en die katjies—almaal is saam in die struggle (popular slogan/song from Cape Town, 1985). (All the mothers and the fathers, the brothers and the sisters, the grandpas and the grandmas, the dogs and the cats—all are together in the struggle).

Generally... I can say that the community is the main source of power, because the state has really lost the control over the people. He (sic) has no power over the people in terms of controlling them. This is why the people have formed these area committees, so that they can try to control themselves. What has been preached in the past about the Freedom Charter, even now we are trying to do that practically. (An activist from the Eastern Cape, Isizwe, Vol. 1, No. 2, March 1986).

There is a remarkably strong corporatist current flowing in South Africa. The major actors—labour, capital and the state—are so caught up in it that they are hardly aware of the fact that they have become part of the current (Maree, 1993:24)

South Africa's tradition of a strong and vibrant civil society needs to be re-asserted. We must not replace apartheid statism, and top-down rule, with a new form of statism (Sam Shilowa—General Secretary of COSATU—1995:27).

INTRODUCTION

In early May 1994, less than a week after the first government of a liberated South Africa had been elected, the new foreign minister, Alfred Nzo, gave his first speech in his new capacity to a meeting of the Organisation of African Unity. In the speech, he, *inter alia,* made the point that South Africa had finally won the struggle for political freedom, and that it now had to address the battle for the development of its oppressed majority. In uttering those words, the minister was truly conveying a widely shared sense of South Africa's final arrival into the community of free African post-colonial

states. Since Nkrumah, practically every African leader had reiterated the
same basic message at independence. It was this message, and the aspiration
which it embodied which formed the basis for post-colonial "development-
alism" and the nation-state project in Africa, namely, the end of popular
politics and the beginning of state mobilisation for bureaucratic "development", with its attendant emphasis on "nation building" and "Africanisation" (now known in South Africa as "affirmative action"). While "nation-
building" in Africa was reduced to state building and the systematic sup-
pression of regional and ethnic grievances under an obsessive concern to
retain colonially inherited boundaries, "Africanisation" was the way in
which the creation of a "national" petty-bourgeoisie could be undertaken by
providing access to jobs in the expanding "public" sector.

These jobs were ostensibly to be reserved for all citizens, but often ended
up being provided simply to members of the state-controlling ethnic group/
coalition, thus undermining any "national" pretensions that a newly forming class might have. In addition, access to state jobs meant, for this petty-
bourgeoisie, access to state resources which could then be utilised for private
appropriation rather than accumulation. Hence, economic appropriation by
the new ruling groups largely went hand in hand with the reproduction of
"ethnic" or regional divisions as these increasingly constituted the main
routes to such appropriation. This process of state formation was related,
therefore, to the well-known absence of a clear separation between politics
and economics in Africa—between political power and accumulation—
which itself provided the conditions for authoritarianism and statism. It has
now clearly been recognised, largely as a result of the crisis of legitimacy
which has become more apparent in the SAP and post-SAP periods, that this
state project in Africa has reached a point of profound crisis from which
some even argue, the state seems incapable of extricating itself (Nzongola-
Ntalaja, 1993; Wamba-dia-Wamba, 1993, 1994; Olukoshi and Laakso, 1996).

Despite the currency of this debate, there is evidence that a consensus on
some fundamental points is emerging, namely, that this crisis is the result of
the entrenched authoritarianism, more simply the overall *statism*, of the
African state since independence, that to a great extent this statism was built
on the coercive practices taken over from the colonial period, and that the re-
emergence of ethnicity as a central issue in Africa is intimately related to the
failure of statism. At the same time, it is also reasonably apparent that
statism prevailed relatively independently of whether state politics were
based on a no-party, one-party or multiparty system, as, in the words of
Wamba-dia-Wamba (1993:103), the African state was, "in the "decolonization process", grafted onto a colonial, essentially undemocratic (variant of
apartheid) state". But statism was not an inevitable outcome of independence. Rather, its features, it is argued, have their origins in what Mamdani
(1990) has called the "defeat of popular movements" in the period of transition from colony to independent state.

The more or less protracted struggles for independence in Africa had involved large numbers of people (overwhelmingly but not exclusively from the most oppressed and exploited strata) in a process of struggle over a more or less long period of time. These processes had been ones in which a whole variety of organisations (parties, trade unions, women's organisations, youth organisations, peasant cooperatives, small business organisations and so on) expressed the aspirations of the majority of the hitherto oppressed population. Although they were not always clearly distinguishable (nor did they always wish to distinguish themselves) from a broader "national movement" during the anti-colonial struggle, these organisations were rarely simply appendages of the political party which was eventually to achieve state power. They, arguably, always had a significantly independent existence and often an independent support base as well as distinct, if not always explicitly articulated, demands. Neither were popular movements simply stages or steps on the road to the realisation of a nationalist ethos. The popular movements of which such varied organisations were the complex expression, had often distinct forms of organisation and demands which were not always simply reducible to the common denominator of political independence. They often involved (explicitly or implicitly) demands for social transformation, popular forms of democracy and equality, which went beyond the slogans of the political party which was to emerge victorious at independence (Kriger, 1992; Mamdani, 1990; Gibbon, 1994).

In Africa, it has generally been the case that as the independence process proceeded, these popular and politicised "civil society" organisations were gradually replaced by state organisations in a number of ways—incorporation, co-optation, disbanding (voluntary or enforced), the bribing of leaders, and the general destruction of their autonomous basis of existence. In brief, these organisations of civil society were usually eliminated or transformed and substituted with state (and/or party) institutions as part of a gradually developing nation-state project. Although these defeats were in no way inevitable, it is this general process which arguably lay at the inception of the statism which has been dominant in Africa since independence. The consolidation of this form of state power was largely secured in the run up to independence, as the colonial state and its chosen successors collaborated in structuring the new state (Mamdani, 1990; Gibbon,1994).

Part of this process was one whereby such popular organisations which had, during the struggle for independence, entered the realm of political society (by addressing explicitly political questions, through interpellating their supporters as citizens) were gradually restricted to the realm of civil society (where they were to address the narrower concerns of "interest groups" defined by the division of labour) before finally losing their independence altogether. The gradual restriction of popular organisations from a role in political society to one in civil society, is, arguably, part of the general trend of demobilisation experienced by popular organisations in the period immediately preceding and following independence/liberation (Gibbon, 1993). More precisely, this process amounted to the exclusion of popular organisations from the plane of territorial politics where "national" issues were addressed exclusively by the colonial state and its chosen interlocutors, usually in the form of the incoming nationalist party, itself already organised along state lines (e.g. with various departments corresponding to ministries, foreign representatives, etc.) (Gibbon, 1994).

It is the argument here that the transition to liberation in South Africa (the equivalent of independence in other countries) can only be understood in this African historical context. Indeed, it may be suggested that despite many important differences, the process of transition in South Africa exhibits fundamental elements which parallel the history briefly outlined above. While it was thought by many, including the present author, that the popular movements which had developed during the 1980s in that country were strong enough to provide a counterweight to statist tendencies, the 1990s have witnessed a systematic (and astonishingly rapid) process of political demobilisation in the country. This has reached an extreme situation where the urban population, which had been massively involved in political activity in the 1980s as all aspects of life were politicised, was in 1995 showing signs of extreme apathy towards the local elections (*Mail and Guardian*, 27 October, 1995).

During the 1980s, South Africa had the unique experience of having a mass popular movement which was inaugurated in 1976, and which differentiated it sharply from the experience of the rest of Africa in the 1960s. This largely urban movement differed from the African norm not simply because of its spatial uniqueness, but, much more importantly, in its involvement of large numbers of ordinary people in a mosaic of political organisations of an enormous variety engaged in independent and coherent nation-wide political activity. It was an experience which transformed people's lives and often resulted in the setting up of democratic popular political structures autonomous of (and directed against) the state (Marx, 1992; Murray, 1987; Lodge et al., 1991). This process was arguably typified by practices (and not just slogans) of "People's Power" particularly associated with the United Democratic Front (UDF), along with the establishment of what has been called "Social Movement Unionism", i.e. the involvement of trade unions in mass national politics (Webster, 1987). Along with these went practices and debates on the nature of "non-racialism" and the future character of a non-racial, and not just a "multi-racial", state. While such practices were undoubtedly contradictory and should not be idealised, they differed starkly from the present context (which has its origins in the early 1990s) in which "nation-building", "affirmative action" and elite-based "reconciliation" all organised and led by the state, are more typical of a now "official" practice and discourse of "liberation".

The popular experience of liberation politics in the South Africa of the 1980s was a far cry from that of the largely elitist guerrilla army in the bush, more often trampling on water rather than swimming like a fish in it, or, for that matter, from the equally elitist, teacher-dominated organisation having independence thrust upon it by a departing colonial power, which was so typical of the experience of other African countries. And yet, interestingly, the period 1990-94 was, in South Africa, largely also characterised by a process of popular demobilisation as an elitist deal was struck behind closed doors by an outgoing National Party and an incoming ANC in their interests (the story of which is told, with some accuracy, in Sparks, 1995) and, arguably, in those of a "new" South African bourgeoisie, while in the townships, whatever popular structures that remained were largely destroyed through systematic, state-inspired violence. The objective of this essay is to trace the main features of this process of transformation of the politics of liberation from a situation where dominant popular politics (with all their attendant contradictions) were substituted by state politics, i.e. a process whereby the centre of gravity of "national politics" was moved from the people to the state.

The argument will follow a structure whereby some of the main political and ideological features of the South African popular struggles of the 1980s and their alteration into different forms of politics in the 1990s will be outlined. This will be followed by a brief assessment of the competing interpretations of this period in the literature, and an outline of a theoretical perspective which encompasses recent debates on the African experience. Implicitly underlying our argument in this chapter is the view that the weakening of the autonomous, popular organisations of the people represents a significant dilution of oppositional capacity to the ANC-led project of statism that is currently taking shape, a project which, if it is to be successful, requires the autonomous democratic prescriptions of the people as opposed to the impositions of the state elite.

KEY FEATURES OF THE STRUGGLE FOR LIBERATION IN THE 1980s AND 1990s

It is not intended in this section, to provide a history, however brief, of popular struggles in the South Africa of the 1980s as such histories can be found elsewhere (Marx, 1992; Lodge et al., 1991; Murray, 1987). Rather, after some brief comments on its origins, illustrations of the most characteristic aspects of popular politics in the 1980s in both township-based and trade union movements will be given and contrasted to the liberation politics of the 1990s. Throughout, the emphasis will be placed on urban movements, the dominant source of protest during the period.

Struggles in the Townships

The origins of the mass urban protests of the 1980s are usually traced to the student upsurge of 1976 in Soweto. It was these youth struggles which forged, in Mamdani's terms, "a new path of liberation" which was based on the lived experiences of ordinary people rather than on the failed sterility of the strategies of exiled movements cut off from the people on whose behalf they were supposed to be struggling (Mamdani, 1996:232). The so-called "decade of peace" after Sharpville was a testament to the overall weakness of these exiled organisations. The 1976 Soweto uprising, along with the series of mass strikes in Durban three years earlier, shattered this "phoney peace". In fact, in structural terms, it was effectively this period of extreme repression which was to provide, through exceptional economic growth, the seeds of the destruction of the apartheid state.

During the 1960s, South Africa's GNP grew at 6 per cent per annum and South Africa was at the time, along with Japan, the country with the highest growth rate in the world (Baskin, 1991:17). This had a number of important consequences, including a dramatic increase in the number of Africans working in manufacturing (from 308,332 in 1960 to 780,914 in 1980) denoting not only an increase in the industrial working class but also a rise in the number of skilled African workers. At the same time, the South African economy became more dependent on consumption by Blacks for its internal market (Marx, 1992:193). Another effect was an increase in the number of Black South Africans entering the education system to acquire the skills necessary for this increased industrialisation. Between 1965 and 1975, the number of Black students in secondary schools increased nearly fivefold, while between 1980 and 1984, their enrolment doubled from 577,000 to over a million; the number of graduates tripled during the same period (Lodge et al., 1991:30–31).

By 1982 however, not only were the effects of the world economic crisis being felt in South Africa, but a fall in the price of gold which lasted until 1985, along with a balance of payments deficit created by the importation of capital equipment for this mini-import substitution industrialisation process, led to "an unprecedented level of foreign indebtedness" (Lodge et al., 1991). As a result of IMF loan conditionalities, the government scrapped whatever subsidies to consumers were in place and increased sales tax which shifted the fiscal burden to the poor. By 1985, the inflation rate was just below a record 17 per cent. All this led to a steep increase in the unemployment rate, beginning in 1982 and accelerating thereafter:

> By 1985, African unemployment represented about 25 per cent of the economi-
> cally active population. Two-thirds of all unemployed Africans by the mid-
> 1980s were under the age of thirty, and unemployment was often long-term
> especially for school leavers (Lodge et al., 1991).

A prolonged drought increased the price of food and also the level of rural-urban migration, while cutbacks in state expenditure affected the townships in particular, so that the local authorities administering them had accumulated a deficit of R32 million by 1982–1983. From 1981, township residents were subjected to rent hikes which increased in frequency after municipal elections in 1983. At the same time, reviled township councillors were given more powers in 1982 through the Black Local Authorities Act which increased their control over the allocation of housing, trading licences, business sites, student bursaries and the collection of rents (Lodge et al., 1991). They were obviously seen as benefiting from "the system", as the apartheid state structures came to be known among activists. The state attempted to manage the growing discontent by legal reforms which were designed to regulate union activity and restrict it to the workplace (primarily through the Industrial Relations Act of 1979) and to co-opt Indian and Coloured South Africans into a tricameral parliament while power rested firmly with Whites (the new constitution was inaugurated in 1984). It was these structural changes which formed the background to the mass upsurge of the second half of the 1980s.

The Birth, Growth and Dissolution of the United Democratic Front

The most important and truly original organisational expression of popular resistance in South Africa in the 1980s was the United Democratic Front (UDF) which was formed in 1983 initially/ostensibly to mobilise opposition to the state's constitutional proposals and other legislation (known collectively as the Koornhof Bills), including the Black Local Authorities Act. The UDF brought together under its umbrella, a coalition of civic associations, student organisations and youth congresses, women's groups, trade unions, church societies, sports clubs and a multitude of organisations which retained, and often increased their ability to organise independently as a result of their affiliation to the UDF. At its peak, the UDF claimed it had around seven hundred affiliates grouped in ten regional areas and amounting to a total of over two million people (Lodge et al., 1991:34). With the upsurge of township unrest beginning in earnest in 1984, it was the young people of the townships who provided the main impetus behind the struggle, while the leadership passed over to the trade unions in 1988. In one important respect at least, the UDF managed to build on the experience of township-based organisations such as the "civic associations", in that it successfully combined local and national grievances. In the words of one civic activist and intellectual:

> From the late 1970s, civic associations not only opposed community councils, they challenged the very laws upon which such bodies were founded. For example, in 1979 the Port Elizabeth Black Civic Organisation (PEBCO), (now the P.E. People's Civic Organisation), called for a single municipality for the city of Port Elizabeth and rejected the community councils (in charge of African town-

ships) and the white municipalities (in charge of white local affairs). PEBCO's aims included a commitment to fight discriminatory legislation, to seek participation in all decision-making processes, to fight for African freehold rights and to resist attempts to deprive Africans of their citizenship. Thus it can be seen that from their inception, civic associations tackled both local problems and issues with national political implications. In due course, local demands assumed a national dimension (Botha, 1992:63).

It is not possible to undertake a detailed history of the UDF here due to considerations of space; fortunately this can be found elsewhere (e.g. Swilling, 1988; Lodge et al., 1991:23–141; Marx, 1992). Nevertheless, it is important to point out some of the phases which this organisation went through, as they provide an accurate reflection of the changes in urban-based forms of struggle and popular involvement during the period of the UDF's existence until 1990 when it was disbanded. The analysis which we undertake here largely follows those of Swilling, 1988, and Lodge et al., 1991.

The first phase of the UDF followed its activity to oppose elections to the tricameral parliament and the Koornhof bills. But soon after August 1984, opposition political activity shifted to struggles initiated by local communities and became concerned with basic issues affecting township life. This inaugurated its second phase. The mass upsurge started in earnest in September 1984 and took the form of bus and rent boycotts, housing movements, squatter revolts, labour strikes, school protests and community stayaways. This change in the focus of protest was not the result of any strategy by the leadership of the UDF or of a change in policy. It seems ultimately to have been forced on the leadership from below (Swilling, 1988:101). Indeed, by mid-1985, it was becoming clear that the UDF leadership was unable to exert effective control over developments despite its popularity. In Lodge's words:

> The momentum for action came from the bottom levels of the organisation and from its youngest members. It was children who built the roadblocks, children who led the crowds to the administrative buildings, children who delegated spokespersons, and children who in 1984 told the older folk that things would be different, that people would not run away as they had in 1960 (Lodge et al., 1991:76).

According to Swilling, local organisations:

> ... exploited the contradiction between the state's attempts to improve urban living conditions and the fiscal bankruptcy and political illegitimacy of local government. They managed to ride a wave of anger and protest that transformed political relations in the communities so rapidly that the UDF's local, regional and national leaders found themselves unable to build organisational structures to keep pace with these levels of mobilisation and politicisation (Swilling, 1988:101–102).

He also stresses that mass actions mobilised unprecedented numbers of people. These succeeded in mobilising:

... all sectors of the township population including both youth and older residents; they involved coordinated action between trade unions and political organisations; they were called in support of demands that challenged the coercive urban and education policies of the apartheid state; and they gave rise to ungovernable areas as state authority collapsed in many townships in the wake of the resignation of mayors and councillors who had been "elected" onto the new Black Local Authorities (Swilling, 1988:102).

The third phase of UDF activity was inaugurated by the declaration of the first state of emergency in 1985 (and lasted until 1986) as the apartheid state attempted to control this mass upsurge and reassert control over "ungovernable areas". Interestingly, both popular rebellion and political organisation grew during this period which saw the setting up of "street committees" in particular. These took over the functions of local government, especially in ungovernable areas. One local activist in the Port Elizabeth area stated:

We said [to our people]: In the streets where you live you must decide what issues affect your lives and bring up issues you want your organisation to take up. We are not in a position to remove debris, remove buckets, clean the streets and so on. But the organisation must deal with these matters through street committees (Lodge et al., 1991:82).

The ANC view as expressed by their spokesman, Tom Sebina, was that street committees "grow out of the need of the people to defend themselves against State repression...and in response to ANC calls to make the country ungovernable and apartheid unworkable [so as to forge them into] contingents that will be part of the process towards a total people's war". Contrary to this view which saw street committees as tactical adjuncts to the development of a militaristic process and as simply "oppositional" to the apartheid state, local activists spelt out a different assessment:

The people in Lusaka can say what they like...we know that the purpose is to enable people to take their lives in their hands. Local government has collapsed. The state's version of local government was corrupt and inefficient in any case, but local government is necessary for people to channel their grievances. The street committees fill the vacuum. They give people an avenue to express views and come up with solutions (Mathiane, 1986:13).

These popular state structures were proliferating in the urban townships. Marx (1992:167) notes that by 1987, 43 per cent of the inhabitants of Soweto, for example, were reporting the existence of street and area committees in their neighbourhoods. In many townships, rudimentary services began to be provided by civic and youth congresses, while crime also began to be checked and punished through "people's courts". These developed in some areas originally to regulate disputes between neighbours (as in Atteridgeville in Pretoria) and also as attempts to control the proliferation of brutal kangaroo courts (e.g. in Uitenhage and Port Elizabeth). In Alexandra, outside Johannesburg, five members of the Alexandra Action Committee were nominated in February 1986 to sit in judgement over cases of assault and theft, while street committees were empowered to settle quarrels. In Mamelodi, one of Pretoria's townships, a number of "informal" systems of justice operated in the 1970s and 1980s and there were long-term struggles over the setting up of popularly accountable courts, which were also highly influenced by traditional African custom (e.g. the importance of elders etc.).[1] Lodge et al. concludes that:

> Of all the manifestations of people's power...the efforts of local groups to administer civil and criminal justice were the most challenging to the state's moral authority. More than any other feature of the insurrectionary movement, people's justice testified to the movement's ideological complexity and to the extent to which it was shaped from below by popular culture (Lodge et al., 1991:135).

In addition to popular control of townships and popular justice, there was a complementary development of institutions geared towards the provision of "people's education". These included, in particular, attempts to bring local schools under community control through the establishment of Parent-Teacher-Student Associations (PTSAs) and even attempts to develop a new curriculum in response to "Bantu Education", the central plank of the apartheid state in this sphere. The struggle for people's education was seen as intimately linked to establishing "People's Power". In the words of Zwelakhe Sisulu:

> The struggle for People's Education is no longer a struggle of the students alone. It has become a struggle of the whole community with the involvement of all sections of the community. This is not something which has happened in the school sphere alone; it reflects a new level of development in the struggle as a whole ... The struggle for people's education can only finally be won when we have won the struggle for people's power ... We are no longer demanding the same education as Whites, since this is education for domination. People's education means education at the service of the people as a whole, education that liberates, education that puts the people in command of their lives. We are not prepared to accept any "alternative" to Bantu Education which is imposed on the people from above. This includes American or other imperialist alternatives designed to safeguard their selfish interests in the country ... To be acceptable, every initiative must come from the people themselves, must be accountable to the people and must advance the broad mass of students, not just a select few (Sisulu, 1986:106, 110).

Or again:

> I want to emphasise here that these advances were only possible because of the development of democratic organs, or committees, of people's power. Our people set up bodies which were controlled by, and accountable to, the masses of the people in each area. In such areas, the distinction between the people and their organisations disappeared. All the people, young and old, participated in committees from street level upwards (Sisulu, 1986:104).

---

[1] For greater detail see Lodge et al., 1991: 135–139; Seekings, 1989; and also UDF, 1986: 35–41.

However, at the same time as street committees were taking up local "grassroots" issues, they also functioned as vehicles for the direct challenge to apartheid state power by the people. A detailed assessment from 1986 made this point forcefully.

> The street/area committees—the structures of an embryonic People's Power—are not only restricted to playing this kind of [local—MN] role, but also have a far more directly or narrowly political dimension to them. At the same time as they are taking up the grassroots issues described above, they also form the units in and through which major political issues and strategies (e.g. the consumer boycott) are discussed and organised. Thus the street committee system is beginning to form not only the avenue through which people can begin to take greater and more democratic control of the immediate conditions of their existence, but they are also emerging as the form through which direct political action against the state and the ruling bloc can be decided on and implemented (White, 1986:92).

Not surprisingly under such conditions, the apartheid state did not hesitate to intensify its repression. The fourth phase of the UDF lasted between 1986 and 1988 and was characterised by the massive repression of the second state of emergency which now covered the whole country. In the first six months of the emergency, around 25,000 people were arrested and isolated, the ability of the press (especially the vibrant "alternative press") to report objectively was systematically curtailed and the townships were placed under direct military rule while the state introduced a militarised bureaucracy (the National Security Management System) to run local government and to "win hearts and minds" (known as WHAM) following the classic counter-insurgency pattern which the Americans had perfected in Vietnam. In brief, this state offensive succeeded in undermining popular organisations considerably, and probably eliminating popular leadership altogether. This was not because the UDF ceased its activities; on the contrary, rent, bus and consumer boycotts continued unabated at least until 1987 (Lodge et al., 1991:87–100). Rather, it was the popular aspect of the struggle which was fatally wounded as it depended for its democratic operation on consultative processes, relative freedom of movement etc., and there was no army under popular control capable of defending popular gains and structures against military onslaught from the apartheid state.[1]

By 1986, a contradiction had emerged between those who wished to retain the broad *front* structure of the UDF with diverse affiliated organisations, and those who argued for a move to a more centralised *party* structure; in practice it seems that the latter position was becoming dominant (de Villiers, 1986; UDF, 1987:18–22). From late 1986 onwards, UDF campaigns were more and more initiated "from above", by the "national leadership" operating exclusively at the territorial level. At the same time, more and

---

[1] The activities of MK, the ANC's armed wing, were never successfully integrated into the popular struggle, suggesting a failure by the exile movement to adapt organisationally to the changed internal conditions. See Barrell, 1990.

more coercive measures were being applied on township residents in order to get them to adhere to various boycotts (a fact which shows the weakening of popular control); "the struggle" was acquiring more of a militaristic character, and vigilante activities acquired more and more support from businessmen affected by youth directed boycotts.[1]

As a result, when resistance resurfaced in the final phase of the UDF, from 1988 to 1990, it became characterised by completely different practices from earlier periods. While the movement (now in alliance with COSATU and calling itself the Mass Democratic Movement that became closely linked to the mainstream churches) was able to organise mass campaigns (e.g. the "defiance campaigns" of 1989) against segregated facilities such as hospitals etc., these became more and more reminiscent of the American Black Civil Rights Movement of the 1960s. These campaigns were now all organised on a territorial plane so that:

> ... in contrast to the mid-1980s, when the insurrectionary movement was being pulled onto unchartered courses by cadres of youth in the streets of the townships, the popular protest in the late 1980s was choreographed and coordinated and seemed much more under the command of its leaders (Lodge et al., 1991:114).

Under such circumstances, it would be relatively easy for leaders to disband the UDF in the wake of the unbanning of the ANC, as it was felt that the latter could now take over the organisation of popular political protest.

Understanding the Popular-Democratic Nature of the UDF

Before moving to a brief assessment of the 1990s, it is pertinent to make some general points regarding the ideology and practice of the mass movement in the way it developed in the mid-1980s. What stands out from that experience is the attempt to develop genuinely popular forms of democracy in both ideology and practice. In particular, the general characterisation of the mass struggle as national and democratic combined both territorial as well as popular democratic aspects of the process. In fact, the two were regularly combined in attempts by leading activists to theorise the process of struggle. As Murphy Morobe, the "Acting Publicity Secretary" of the UDF, stated in 1987:

> We in the United Democratic Front are engaged in a national democratic struggle. We say we are engaged in a *national* struggle for two reasons. Firstly, we are involved in political struggle on a national, as opposed to a regional or local level. The national struggle involves all sectors of our people—workers (whether in the factories, unemployed, migrants or rural poor), youths, students, women and democratic-minded professionals. We also refer to our struggle as national in the sense of seeking to create a new nation out of the historical divisions of apartheid. We also explain the *democratic* aspect of our

---

[1] For a detailed study of vigilantes in South Africa during this period, see Haysom, 1986.

struggle in two ways...Firstly, we say that a democratic South Africa is one of the aims or goals of our struggle. This can be summed up in the principal slogan of the Freedom Charter: "The People Shall Govern". In the second place, democracy is the means by which we conduct our struggle ... The creation of democratic *means* is for us as important as having democratic *goals* as our objective...When we say that the people shall govern, we mean at all levels and in all spheres, and we demand that there be a real, effective control on a daily basis...The key to a democratic system lies in being able to say that the people in our country can not only vote for a representative of their choice, but also feel that they have some direct control over where and how they live, eat, sleep, work, how they get to work, how they and their children are educated, what the content of that education is; and that these things are not *done for them by the government of the day*, but [by] the people themselves ... The rudimentary organs of *people's power* that have begun to emerge in South Africa (street committees, defence committees, shop-steward structures, student representative councils, parent/teacher/student associations) represent in many ways the beginnings of the kind of democracy that we are striving for ... Without the fullest organisational democracy, we will never be able to achieve conscious, active and unified participation of the majority of the people, and in particular the working class, in our struggle (Morobe, 1987:81–83, emphasis added).

I have cited this passage at length because it clearly sums up the systematisation of popular experiences and demands which some leaders were able to make so eloquently. Clearly, this statement has more the character of an ideal to be struggled for than a simple description of reality; nevertheless it indicates the centrality of popular democracy within the ideology and practice of the movement. It is important to note first (I shall have occasion to return to this below) that the main slogan of the Freedom Charter ("The People Shall Govern") is given a specific interpretation by the UDF, namely, to mean a popular form of democracy and not simply an electoral multiparty system, or, for that matter, a one-party system (as its vagueness could also imply). In fact, the former is explicitly rejected as the exclusive form of representation, and as too limited a form of democracy. Thus an evidently vague and indeed "populist" slogan could, in the circumstances of the time, be given an unambiguous popular-democratic content. It would be a fundamental error to confuse the content of such democracy with its own slogans and its self-presentation as many who at the time dismissed the UDF as a "populist" organisation in fact did. In practice the social movement was giving rise to a form of mass democracy and a form of state unique in South Africa (and probably also in Africa as a whole); these forms of democracy and state have, arguably, gone largely unrecognised by most intellectuals, by the party of state nationalism, the ANC, and even by many of the movement's own leaders.

Two features of this democracy worth noting include a detailed system of controlling leaders to make them accountable to the rank and file membership, and a different way of demarcating "the people" from "the oppressors". Attempts at instituting internal democracy within organisations were strongly followed, although they obviously had various degrees of success. The important point, however, was that such a struggle for democracy *existed* within organisations. The various dimensions of this democracy were, according to Morobe:

> 1) *Elected Leadership*. Leadership of our organisations must be elected (at all levels), and elections must be held at periodic intervals...Elected leadership must also be recallable before the end of their (sic) term of office if there is indiscipline or misconduct.
> 2) *Collective Leadership*. We try and practice collective leadership at all levels. There must be continuous, ongoing consultation ...
> 3) *Mandates and Accountability*. Our leaders and delegates are not free-floating individuals. They always have to operate within the delegated mandates of their positions and delegated duties ...
> 4) *Reporting*. Reporting back to organisations, areas, units, etc. is an important dimension of democracy...We feel very strongly that information is a form of power, and that if it is not shared, it undermines the democratic process. We therefore take care to ensure that language translations occur if necessary ...
> 5) *Criticism and Self-Criticism*. We do not believe that any of our members are beyond criticism; neither are organisations and strategies beyond reproach ... (Morobe, 1987:84–85).

However, by (February) 1989, it had become clear that some individuals were beyond criticism, for, when an attempt was made by the UDF (and COSATU) to publicly censure Winnie Mandela (by a committee including Murphy Morobe, among others), it was blocked by the ANC in Lusaka.[1] In fact, the danger posed to popular democracy by the lack of control by the popular movement over a number of "charismatic" leaders who felt they had the authority to speak and act without being mandated, was one of which many were aware. Thus, *Isizwe*, the main journal of the UDF made a rather prophetic statement in 1985:

> One thing that we must be careful about...is that our organisations do not become too closely associated with individuals, that we do not allow the development of personality cults. We need to understand why we regard people as leaders and to articulate these reasons. Where people do not measure up to these standards they must be brought to heel—no matter how "charismatic" they may be. No person is a leader in a democratic struggle such as ours simply because he or she makes good speeches...*No individual may make proposals on the people's behalf—unless mandated by them*...We need to say these things because there are some people and interests who are trying to project individuals as substitutes for political movements (United Democratic Front, 1985:17, emphasis added).

The practices of "mandates and report backs" which had been adopted largely as a result of trade union influence were taken particularly seriously in the mid-1980s, although there is evidence that they started to decline at the end of the decade.[2] By 1991, the position had changed substantially so

---

[1] See the *Race Relations Survey, 1988/89*, p. 639. As a result, Morobe was "purged" from leadership positions and he paid the price for taking popular democracy seriously, while a famous graffito in Johannesburg at the time read: "Free Nelson, Lock up Winnie".

[2] It is interesting to note here the distance between these popular methods of holding leaders accountable and those conveyed in the utterances of returning exiles such

that *Mayibuye*, the journal of the ANC, now pompously proclaimed:

> Accountability is the basis of democratic organisation. Accountability means that leadership must discuss decisions with the membership. Decisions must be explained so that members understand why they are made (*Mayibuye*, Dec. 1991, p. 36).

We are a far cry here from "People's Power".

The manner in which the popular movement demarcated its members ("the people") from the oppressive state, is also worthy of note. This largely surrounded the notion of "non-racialism" as a way of characterising the ideology of the movement as well as the nature of the state which was being fought for. Originally inherited from a Black Consciousness discourse which used the term to refer to all oppressed racial groups in South Africa under the characterisation "Black", "non-racialism" was adapted by the UDF to include Whites who supported the struggle. This struggle was visualised as uniting into a national opposition, the disparate groups which the apartheid state divided, hence the main slogan of the UDF: "UDF Unites, Apartheid Divides!". One important aspect of non-racialism was the fact that rather than distinguishing "the people" or "the oppressors" on racial grounds, it did so by demarcating on political grounds: popular-democrats from anti-democrats. The former were those who supported change "from below", the latter those who proposed some form of "tinkering from above" and who had by this period, lost the confidence of the majority. Democrats were all those who opposed "minority rule" and supported "majority rule" through popular democracy. In the words of a UDF discussion document from 1986:

> The essential *dividing line* that we should promote is between supporters of *minority rule and majority rule*. The common ground between the Botha (sic), the PFP (Popular Federal Party, the main White, big business-backed liberal opposition at the time—MN) leadership and big business is that they all seek solutions within the framework of adapting minority rule. Although they differ fundamentally on who to involve in negotiation and how much adaptation is necessary, these elements all agree that the system must be changed from the top down, with the solutions being decided over the heads of the people. All those who accept the right of the people to determine the process of change are allies of the people and part of the NDS (National Democratic Struggle—MN) (UDF Cape Town Area Committee, 1986:10).

This meant that the way the popular struggle was to be conducted should also be "non-racial". Terror Lekota, a senior UDF figure put it this way:

---

as "leadership codes". See, for example, an interview with Joe Slovo in *New Era*, Vol. 5, No. 1, March 1990, pp. 35–40. The Chinese wall between popular practices and the isolated exiles is clearly exposed here. There is also evidence that at the first ANC national consultative conference inside the country, there was "tension between the patrician style of the previously jailed and exiled leaders of the 1950s and the activists who [had] developed constituencies during the 1980s.; the former were accused of ignoring the principles of mandate and accountability which had developed inside the country" (Friedman, 1992, p.85).

> In political struggle ... the means must always be the same as the ends ... How can one expect a racialistic movement to imbue our society with a non-racial character on the dawn of our freedom day? A political movement cannot bequeath to society a characteristic it does not itself possess. To expect it to do so is like asking a heathen to convert a person to Christianity. The principles of that religion are unknown to the heathen let alone the practice (cited Marx,1992:124).

Such a position was possible precisely because the social movement was not an elite movement and because White "progressives" (to use the jargon of the time) provided invaluable work both in the trade unions as well as in the UDF, thus becoming known and appreciated by the people of the townships. It served to divide a minority of White democrats from White racists (while forcing the uncommitted to commit themselves), in the same way as affiliation to popular organisations divided Blacks between collaborators with the state (so-called "sell-outs") and the majority of the oppressed.[1] This attempt to create the unity of a "new nation" can be contrasted with the attempts, in the 1990s, to do so "from above" via "reconciliation", "nation-building", the Reconstruction and Development Programme or indeed "affirmative action".

The Retreat of Civics and the Rise of Statist Nationalism

Let us now turn our attention to a brief examination of the period after the unbanning of the ANC and other proscribed organisations in the lead up to the national elections of April 1994. In doing so, my intention is simply to make the point that the politics of liberation has been conducted in a markedly different way which I would describe as "state centred" rather than "people centred". I do not wish here to attempt a detailed explanation for such a change as not only are considerations of space prohibitive, but this is intended to be the subject of future research. Two examples will help to illustrate these changes. The first is the altered role of "civics" and some of the views surrounding this changed role. The second is the changed role of mass mobilisation at least up to the end of 1992, after which it largely ceased to exist altogether.

It is very instructive to note the path taken by civic organisations. Perhaps the most important step that was taken was the setting up of the South African National Civic Organisation (SANCO) in 1992. As its name indicates, SANCO was set up explicitly as an organisation designed to operate at a territorial level while its member-organisations transformed themselves from being autonomous affiliates of an umbrella organisation (such as

---

[1] A similar process was debated at length in relation to the 'Indian community' and the formation of the Transvaal Indian Congress, but interestingly enough not in relation to 'Coloureds', although the UDF's non-racialism was criticised as phoney by various coloured organisations such as the Unity Movement and the Cape Action League for example.

the UDF) into the *branches* of a national body. In the words of one critical activist: "it requires that local civics surrender their autonomy and local accountability" (Jacobs, 1992:24). The preamble to SANCO's constitution defines it as a body that will "act as a non-partisan democratic watchdog of the community on local government and community development". While not all civics joined SANCO, the overwhelming majority have. Thus the leadership of the "civic movement" no longer sees it as a *political* mass movement or a form of state ("People's Power") but as a *"watchdog"*, i.e. an "interest group" reflecting the aspirations of a narrow constituency defined by the division of labour (urban communities).

The first point to make in this context is that civics, as indeed all other popular organisations, systematically surrendered the plane of territorial politics to the ANC at its unbanning. This surrender was expressed ideologically through the acceptance of all in the "National Liberation Movement" of the organisational "leadership" (i.e. dominance) of the ANC in the "National Democratic Revolution". In other words, it was overwhelmingly agreed by all "mass formations" that now that the ANC was unbanned, it alone was to concern itself with "national politics". All existing organisations which had taken a political role were now to drop such a role in favour of the ANC.[1] While the trade unions and civics relegated themselves to their sectional interests, the UDF was dissolved, and the South African Youth Congress and the Federation of South African Women disbanded and reconstituted themselves as the ANC Youth and Women's Leagues respectively. As a result, the youth have disappeared entirely from the political scene as an independent organised force, while women's organisations are now clearly elite controlled (e.g. the so-called "National Women's Coalition" made up of leading figures from the main political parties).

Insofar as the civics were concerned, the key question that was posed can be summarised as follows: should they retain organisational independence or should they be collapsed into ANC branches? In order to retain organisational independence, it was held, they were required to exit from politics. In other words, having conceded the monopoly of politics to the ANC, civics were forced (or forced themselves) into a position that if they were to retain independence, they should withdraw from politics altogether. There was never any question of them retaining a political role distinct from the ANC (i.e. popular politics). After a short debate in which some (a minority in the ANC/SACP, represented by Nzimande and Sikhosana) argued that the political role of the civics should be maintained as they were the future bases

---

[1] As far as I am aware, the idea was never mooted that the returning ANC could disband and become integrated into existing popular organisations, or form a structure responsible to such organisations. The main reason for this is basically that the dominant formations in the 1980s all recognised the 'leadership' of the ANC and its dominant figures over the struggle for liberation, as did the apartheid state, the world powers and the United Nations. The ANC was both organised as a state in exile and treated as such in the international arena. See note 1 on page 231.

of a people's state and thus should become ANC branches/state structures (i.e. "soviets" of some form), the majority view prevailed that civics should not be collapsed into ANC branches, but should continue to represent residents irrespective of party-political affiliation.[1] At the same time, the ANC was adamantly maintaining that it alone should be seen as the "leading organisation" ("vanguard") of the "broad liberation movement" and that all other organisations within this movement should recognise the primacy of the ANC insofar as political questions were concerned (Lanegran, 1995:114). There is also evidence to suggest that the ANC feared losing popular support to the civics if no clear division of labour between them was agreed (Lodge, 1992:61–62).

The compromise eventually worked out and which became the dominant viewpoint, was one in which the ANC would have the sole monopoly of politics while civics would restrict themselves to an independent (party-political) role. This compromise was made substantially easier by the fact that the majority of leaders in the civic movement were ANC supporters anyway. It is this dominant perspective, with all its contradictions, which is expressed by a civic leader as follows:

> The basic role of the civics is not changed in my view. This role is building people's power and it is something that must play itself out in civil society ... Although the civics, within the UDF, were dominated mainly by the concerns of civil society, the front's overall role was largely political. *Pulling the civic movement clear of the political net is not easy*—and overlaps of personnel make that very clear (cited in Collinge, 1991:8, emphasis added).

The question does not seem to have been asked as to how "People's Power", a supremely *political* project, could be secured by civics if they were to be "pulled clear of the political net". At the same time, it was clearly appreciated that the dangers of civics becoming bureaucratised or turning into the "conveyor belts (sic) of the ruling party" (Collinge, 1991) could easily lead to *étatism*. In addition to arguing in favour of a distancing from the leading party, this dominant position also resolved that they should distance themselves from the local state and "not attempt to take over local government"(Collinge, 1991). This was justified in terms of the same arguments but is probably more accurately explained by the fact that the nature of local government was the subject of negotiations at the territorial level along with the nature of the central state. In fact, the comment by the civic leader cited above accurately expressed a real political contradiction between popular politics which civics had incarnated, and the emerging dominance of state politics which required the "depoliticisation" of civics if these were to remain independent of the ANC (as they rightly insisted on being). It is noteworthy that the same debates did not surface as forcefully with respect

---

[1] See for example Nzimande and Sikhosana (1991, 1992a, 1992b, 1992c); Mayekiso (1992a, 1992b) as well as the pieces by Swilling (1990, 1991); Botha (1992); Friedman (1991) and Fine (1993).

to the youth and women's movements. These were organisationally much weaker than the civics and allowed themselves to be "swallowed up" by the ANC.

Currently, a new contradiction has arisen between the "civil society role" and the "state role" of civics. This contradiction which is a product of state-centred politics is as yet unresolved, as while civics are said to be "watchdogs" for the community on the one hand, their work is also being pushed more and more towards that of "development" on the other.[1] While the idea behind their "development role" is to replace top-down planning with "community participation", the focus has been on "development through negotiation" as opposed to mass popular struggles for self-help (see *WIP*, 92, Sept./Oct. 1993; Pieterse and Simone, 1994). At the same time report-backs and other measures to ensure accountability have fallen into disuse, while donor funds for "training" and other ostensibly technical programmes have "depoliticised" the role of civics even further and have bolstered the spurious view of these organisations as politically neutral. This supposed neutrality in fact leaves them open to becoming state organisations through another route, whether as development institutions at the bottom of the ladder and/or as adjuncts of the state, incorporated into a corporatist structure.[2]

The events which unfolded following the unbanning of the ANC are also expressed more or less clearly by activists organising in some rural areas in a manner which is of wider significance:

> During the days of the UDF, it was easy for people to understand the struggle. Activity such as stay-aways, barricading etc. involved people on the ground and made sense to them. When it came to [territorial—MN] politics, people lost interest ... When we started, our struggle involved activity, but during the period of the unbanning, people had to go deeper into politics and they lost interest. They no longer wanted to participate ... After the unbanning, there was a lot of confusion amongst the civic organisations because the programme of the ANC and UDF was not the same ... The UDF had encouraged grassroots activity. Even football clubs had a voice in the UDF. The ANC structure and understanding was different as civic structures were not high on the ANC agenda and the civic momentum during the UDF period could not be taken forward. The disappearance of the UDF crippled civic organisations because the ANC was now looking strictly to political issues and not looking to civic related issues and this weakened them (Eastern Transvaal activist cited in Levin and Solomon, 1994:256).

---

[1] One civic leader stated: "We must learn how to run organisations better and, I hope, to run local government. But civics must always remain independent, and act like unions for the communities". A footnote to this remark adds that the author "is currently in India studying local government administration"! (See Mdluli, 1991: 12).

[2] As in the Local Government Negotiating Forum where only organisations which mobilise on a nationwide/territorial basis such as SANCO, the state and political parties are allowed to operate. See Ngcobo, 1993, pp. 4–5.

The consequences of this process were rather predictable. As the link between local and territorial politics which the UDF had successfully managed to enable was broken, erstwhile organisations of "People's Power" collapsed. A report in the ANC aligned *New Nation* newspaper, which reflected the dominant view among state-nationalists of the role of "popular organisations" in the post-apartheid period, proclaimed soon after the April 1994 territorial elections:

> Except for some of the more centrally located urban settlements, civic organisations are either poorly organised or completely non-existent. And even when they do exist, few have been able to revive street and block committees, which would serve as the ideal forums through which [the government could] consult communities about their [development] needs (*New Nation*, June 3, 1994).

The transformation of popular politics from 1990 was not only expressed in the debates surrounding the role of civics, it was also obvious in the changed role of "mass mobilisation". It became more and more obvious that such mobilisation was now initiated and directed solely "from above" by leading members of the ANC hierarchy, and seen as a measure to "put pressure" on the negotiating partner, the National Party and the state. It was no longer part of a process of "empowerment". So that when the ANC declared 1991 "The Year of Mass Action for the Transfer of Power to the People", such action was designed to force the government to meet territorial demands such as "the immediate release of political prisoners...and the unconditional return of exiles, the dismantling of bantustans, an end to violence against the people, the immediate repeal of all repressive legislation, the establishment of an interim government and Constituent Assembly".[1]

In fact, one of the main differences between the "left radicals" and the more "moderate nationalists" within the ANC, seems to have been the role which such mobilisation was to play in the transition process. This is brought out clearly in a frank review by Jeremy Cronin, one of the main theorists of the South African Communist Party (SACP). He distinguishes between three different "strategic outlooks" characterising liberation politics: "the boat, the tap and the Leipzig way". The first position was one where democratisation was seen as resulting from a negotiated pact between elites which deliver their constituencies. Mass action was perceived as "rocking the boat". The second position was one where "mass action" was to be turned on and off like a tap. He comments, quite correctly, that "struggle in strategy 2 is not about the self-empowerment of the working masses. Instead, struggle is rather more narrowly seen as empowering the negotiators so that they can bestow upon the people their liberation" (Cronin, 1992:42–43). It is hinted, although never openly stated, that this was the dominant position within the ANC which was associated with Mandela himself.

---

[1] Mayibuye, February 1991, July 1991 and February 1992 for example.

The third "strategic outlook" according to Cronin was "the Leipzig way" or the position according to which "the people transfer power to themselves in a revolutionary moment" of insurrection as in Eastern Europe in 1989. He argues also quite correctly that such a perception is also in essence elitist apart from being impracticable in the South African case so that it ultimately reduced itself to the "tap" position. The author frankly acknowledged that "all three have a tendency to fall into one or another version of statism" (Cronin, 1992:53). These words proved prophetic as an attempt to "turn on the tap" on 7 September, 1992 outside the Ciskei as part of the bid to remove Gqozo, the local bantustan leader, from office through the mobilisation of "mass action", resulted in twenty-eight deaths and over two hundred injured in what became known as the "Bisho massacre". More long-term effects were the end of "mass action" as a tactic, as the ANC dropped it like a hot potato, and the final demise of the "left statists" as a meaningful force within the ANC.[1] This not only showed that "mass action" had by that time little popular content other than providing canon fodder for the state's bullets, but it also allowed the right-wing in the ANC to present the choice facing the political movement as being between peaceful transition which was equated with negotiations on the one hand, and the escalation of violence including mass action, on the other.[2] This comes across very clearly in the ANC document *Negotiations: A Strategic Perspective* (ANC, 1992) which provided, following on from Slovo's theorisation of the famous "Sunset Clauses", the rationale for entering into a government of "national unity" with the National Party.[3]

It must be recalled that state and Inkatha violence was being systematically unleashed on township residents during the period leading to the elections, and that the ANC was powerless to stop it. Even though the formation of "self-defence units" (SDUs) was originally encouraged by the ANC, these were ordered to disband in 1994 as a *quid pro quo* in the disarming of Inkatha and all "private armies". The following highly informative newspaper

---

[1] The Bisho action had been the brainchild of Ronnie Kassrils who had also led the demonstration. He was one of the leading figures of 'radical' or 'left statism' within the ANC and has a military and intelligence background. For his views on the role of 'mass mobilisation' see *Work in Progress* No. 72, January/February 1991. He is now deputy minister of defence.

[2] See Molamu and Fako (1993) for a discussion of some aspects of the violence leading up to the elections. It is important to get some perspective on 'violence' in South Africa, especially as this is not only an emotive issue, but one which is clearly central to state propaganda. The following figures give some idea of the scale of violence during the 1980s and 1990s: during the highest period of popular mobilisation against apartheid between September 1984 and December 1988 the total number of fatalities from political violence were reported as 2,450. The corresponding figure was reported as 3,400 for 1990 alone, 2,580 for 1991, 3,446 for 1992 and 4,398 for 1993 during the period of state and Inkatha induced violence on the people (Southall, 1994: 633, No.2).

[3] On the 'Sunset Clauses' see Slovo (1992), and the special issue of the *African Communist*, No. 131, 4th quarter 1992, "Negotiations: The strategic debate".

reports which showed that not everyone concurred with the disbanding of SDUs appeared in 1994, immediately after the territorial elections:

> While self-protection is an inalienable right to any person, this has to be done within the existing laws of the country. We also accept that the SDUs came about under special circumstances—the time when police were refusing to apprehend known "vigilantes" ... The SANCO (South African National Civics Organisation) activist said the time had come for the weapons of both the SDUs and other private armies (sic!) including the right-wing groups, to be handed to the authorities of the democratic government for safe-keeping (*New Nation, No 4 May 13, 1994*). Gunmen armed with AK47 rifles executed 12 residents in Thokoza on the East Rand on Friday night just three days after South Africa's first democratically elected State President, Nelson Mandela was inaugurated. The massacre is the first since the elections (*New Nation*, May 15, 1994). Although the SDUs have been at the centre of controversy, residents described their role as vital—especially at the height of unrest in the township. South African National Defence Force spokesperson Colonel Chris du Toit said initial inquiries indicated [that] "since the ANC ordered (sic!) the units to cease operating there has been evidence of in-fighting" (*New Nation*, May 20, 1994).

Trade Union Struggles

Interestingly, the trajectory of the modern trade union movement in South Africa was not all that different from that of other popular organisations. The main difference lay in the fact that trade unions were able to organise a constituency which was capable of effectively challenging the system beyond the structure of apartheid local government. The challenge to South African business interests represented by a relatively powerful and disciplined trade union movement was instrumental in pressurising big business in particular to push towards a negotiated transition to democracy. Trade unions were much less successful in organising workers in small businesses, women, rural labour, and the unemployed, while eventually they even lost support among migrant workers as they concentrated most of their work on the fully urbanised. Their broad historical trajectory was also one of "politicisation from below" followed by a process of depoliticisation which itself only acted as a prelude to a deeper process of "repoliticisation from above"—of entering political society in the 1980s and then exiting from it only in order to re-enter politics on the side of the post-apartheid state in the 1990s.

As is well known, the history of the modern South African trade union movement largely originates in 1973 when 100,000 workers went on strike in the Durban area. These largely spontaneous mass strikes revitalised trade union activity which had been dormant during the "decade of peace" that followed the banning of the ANC/SACP (and the PAC) along with SACTU (South African Congress of Trade Unions), which was, largely, the organ of the "Congress Alliance". The unions which developed as a result of the Durban strikes saw it as crucially important to maintain their independence from nationalist organisations in order to avoid the same fate as SACTU.

Rather, they concentrated on developing strong shop-floor structures and a system of worker representation based around shop-stewards. Apart from being intrinsically democratic, it was argued that such a system would enable a small union organisation to better withstand state repression (Webster, 1987; Lambert and Webster, 1988).

This fiercely independent stance became the dominant position in FOSATU (Federation of South African Trade Unions) which was launched in 1979, and actually came to be adhered to rigidly like an article of faith (until the formation of COSATU in November 1985), theorised by the intellectual high priests of the "White Left" who had been instrumental in servicing the development of the new unions. Basically, the view was that "working class politics" should grow out of shop-floor struggles. Unions should not identify with any nationalist political organisation as union members belonged to different organisations, and also because it would mean accepting the dominance of a petty-bourgeoisie who supposedly dominated the township-based organisations, which, in any case, were said not to be as democratic as trade unions.[1]

With the increasing development of popular struggles in the townships (which, after all, was where most of the trade unionists lived), the question which was to occupy the centre of the intellectual stage on the Left in South Africa came to the fore, namely, the relationship, if any, between trade union struggles and township struggles, or workers' organisations and national politics. This single question has given rise to a large volume of debate covering not only the above issues, but also ranging more broadly to include the question of class alliances, the road to socialism, the nature of the Freedom Charter, the question of "unity in the struggle", "liberation vs. transformation" and so on.

Briefly, it is known as the debate between the "workerists" and "populists" and was conducted far beyond the confines of popular organisations, where it was transformed beyond its original spheres of concern on the relationship between civil society and politics, into an often acrimonious academic debate in which arguments merely served to further entrench already rigidly held positions. Shortage of space precludes a detailed assessment of this debate here although it is proposed to study it in detail as part of future work. What is crucial for our immediate purposes in this chapter is to offer a very brief account of the changes in the trade union movement which paralleled this debate. In this regard, it is important to note that the pressure for unions to become more involved in township nationalist politics came overwhelmingly from the workers themselves as they experienced oppression not only in the workplace but also in their

---

[1] For an elaborated argument see the speech by Joe Foster, FOSATU general secretary reprinted in *ROAPE*, No 24. May–August 1982.

homes where they faced the same problems and coercion as all other residents.

The main organisations which voiced the pressures for workers to become involved in township politics were the Local Shop-Steward Councils (known simply as "locals") which brought together shop stewards from a given urban area and which originated in the East Rand (Germiston, Wadeville, Katlehong). According to Webster (1987:183).

> Founded as a way of involving shop-stewards in the organisation of unorganised factories, these councils spread rapidly during the 1981–82 strike waves ... At the centre of this social movement in the East Rand hostels was the migrant worker.

Although the locals were originally founded as a way of spreading union organisation to other factories and to fight against scabbing, since they were organised in urban townships, they were bound to become involved in township issues as well. Among the questions that initially commanded their attention were, *inter alia*, questions of housing, unemployment benefits, adequate pensions and maternity rights (Webster, 1988.; Swilling 1984:118). In the words of Jeremy Baskin who conducted a study on a Shop-Steward Council in 1982:

> The shop-stewards' council is characterised by its militancy, mutual support ... and strong grassroots organisation ... All this is made possible by strong *local* organisation. Workers in the area share many problems. They use the same buses and trains, they live in the same areas and they know other workers in neighbouring factories. The common conditions which workers face at local level become a major spur to militancy, once organisation gets started...The fact that workers began presenting common demands generally strengthened their position in the area ... Workers are encouraged to see beyond their own union to the struggles of workers as a whole (Baskin, 1982:47–48).

In addition, the locals became the bedrock for democratic control over unions as more power lay in the hands of shop-stewards and these structures were not bureaucratic. One shop-steward explained:

> We talk of unity ... what kind of unity and how far we should go as a local. What sort of help, what sort of things we should do, and the disciplinary procedures. Because if we are to be united, we have to have disciplinary procedures and some clear objectives ... As workers, then we are involved in political issues, so we have to be clear on how to react to such things ... Problems like rent have come up ... we have to do some things outside the factory (Baskin, 1982:52).

As a result of these developments, the "FOSATU line" came more and more into conflict with that of its own shop-stewards, especially after the formation of the UDF, the accompanying intensification of community struggles, and the increasingly irresistible pressure from below for joint community-trade union action. What had been a very correct tactic in the early 1980s, had become, by the middle of the decade, a sterile dogma, as the objective situation had fundamentally changed. One shop-steward from the Metal and Allied Workers Union (MAWU) argued:

> The situation of the worker in South Africa is that they are oppressed and exploited. The struggle goes beyond the factory gates. Workers must address themselves to the problems of rents, shacks, electricity tariffs, schools, recreation, etc. In FOSATU and MAWU, workers have been openly discouraged from taking up these issues and political organisations have been openly criticised. We recognise that the trade unions are not political organisations. But for them (MAWU) to say no politics in trade unions is nothing else but to keep their politics of reformism inside the trade unions (cit. Swilling, 1984:119).

It was this pressure from below which ultimately led to the formalisation of what Webster has called "social movement unionism", finally expressed in the formation of a new giant union federation, the Congress of South African Trade Unions (COSATU) in 1985. Unlike its predecessor, COSATU encouraged the politicisation of trade union activity and collaboration between unions and the UDF, even adopting the Freedom Charter as a guiding principle. COSATU, therefore, became involved in building "worker control" (the equivalent of democratic "People's Power" in the factories and unions) and insisted on contributing to the "working-class leadership" of the "national democratic struggle" (although what precisely was meant by such leadership was not always clarified). Thus, Jay Naidoo, the general secretary of COSATU, was to declare that:

> Non-political unionism is not only undesirable but impossible in South Africa. Therefore, we believe that though COSATU is not a political party, COSATU has a responsibility to voice the political interests and aspirations of organised workers and also more broadly the working class. To do this, we have to look at how *we build workers [power]* and how do we locate workers as the leading force in our struggle for national liberations (sic) ... The key element in the building of the labour movement was, and still remains, the democratic principles of worker control ... In real terms, it means that the members of the trade union must have absolute control over all decision-making in the organisation ... COSATU has high regard for those communities and organisations that are building strong grassroots organisation in the form of area and street committees. We encourage this and see it as COSATU's policy for members and local structures of COSATU to play an active role in building such structures (Jay Naidoo, 1986:3,4,8).

In this way, COSATU entered political society and its national campaigns made a conscious attempt to address issues which were pertinent to the interests of the poor and unorganised in general, and not only/solely those of the organised workers. The most famous campaign which COSATU undertook in this regard was the "Living Wage Campaign". A survey on the state of the unions published in 1985 noted that in a sample of twenty-three of the largest industrial unions, there were 12,462 shop stewards, with 1,443 shop-steward councils in place (Collins, 1994:35). Not surprisingly then, COSATU placed much emphasis on the role of "locals" which were seen as the foundation of the organisation:

> In particular, the role of the shop steward councils was crucial. They assisted in organisational work and developed ordinary worker leadership. The locals confronted the political issues of the day and developed resistance in practice (Collins, 1994:36).

However, by 1987, a number of weaknesses were revealed by an assessment of the locals conducted by national office bearers. The assessment noted that "local structures were weak and the COSATU regions were not functioning" (Collins, 1994). Moreover, COSATU was unsuccessful in organising the poorer sections of the population. An attempt to organise the unemployed failed, migrant workers were increasingly ignored as the fully urbanised workers came to dominate trade unions more and more (Mamdani, 1994:Ch. 6), while rural labour was left unorganised, a fact which cost the National Union of Mineworkers dearly during its 1987 strike (as scabs could be recruited from rural areas). It is not clear whether an attempt was made to explain and correct these weaknesses.

At the same time, for the overwhelming majority of leaders and commentators, the entry by trade unions into political society was explicitly or, more often, implicitly, taken to be a temporary situation. In the words of the sociologist Eddie Webster:

> Where, as in South Africa, the majority does not have a meaningful voice within the political system, unions will inevitably begin to play a central role within the political system (Webster, 1988:176).

There was of course nothing inevitable about that. If the FOSATU line had remained dominant, the entry of trade unions into political society would have been limited. But the unstated assumption always seemed to have been that as soon as political parties with support among the oppressed majority were able to operate openly, unions would then "withdraw" to their "natural domain" in civil society, ascribed to them by the division of labour.

This is, indeed, what happened but it happened in a complex and contested way. COSATU actually attempted but failed to get a place at the negotiating table, where only political parties and state agencies (e.g. bantustan governments) were represented. The National Party government absolutely refused to countenance the issue of union participation in the negotiations and the ANC did not pursue it with much vigour anyway; neither probably did COSATU as it was agreed that its interests would be represented by the ANC and SACP delegations to the talks[1] (and eventually, a number of COSATU figures joined state structures ostensibly in order to represent "workers' interests" in the state). In actual fact then, the unions in general and COSATU in particular did not so much desert the realm of politics as that of popular politics. In the context of this shift, COSATU has, during the 1990s, geared its main efforts towards having an input in all

---

[1] The issue was the subject of a brief debate in *Work in Progress*, No 80, January/February 1982, p. 10.

aspects of policy as they affect workers, and this process has extended more and more into a dominant corporatist trend.[1]

In one recent assessment of COSATU's role in the 1990s, this rather astonishing remark appears: "the opening up of political space after 1990 has meant that the unions are now in a position to directly extend their influence beyond industry to the national economy" (Collins, 1994:36). This statement is astonishing because it has been regularly stated in different ways since 1990[2] (often precisely as an argument in favour of corporatism) and because COSATU's role had never been restricted to "industry" alone. The remark systematically brushes aside the political role of COSATU in the 1980s and is indicative of the political amnesia suffered by many leading trade unionists in the 1990s (in this case, of a person ostensibly opposed to corporatism). Yet another major writer on trade unions (this time a major advocate of corporatism) openly remarks:

> *the trend is towards corporatism*—whether it is expressed through a social contract, reconstruction accord or socio-economic pact. While there remain different expectations of the scope, form and duration of such an arrangement, these are basically differences of emphasis. The end point is the same, and the NEF (National Economic Forum), NMC (National Manpower Commission) and NTB (National Training Board) are first steps in this direction...for its proponents, bargained corporatism is nevertheless the best available option or, more pessimistically, the least worst alternative. For the union movement in South Africa, the corporatist path is, in effect, unavoidable (Baskin, 1993:2, 7; cited Shaw, 1994:247).

Like the supposed inevitability of trade unions entering the political arena in the 1980s, there was nothing inevitable about corporatism in the 1990s. It was the result of a political choice by the COSATU leadership as it decided to vacate the political space, surrender it to the ANC and then attempt to "influence" the policies of the ANC.[3] This concentration on policy was undertaken in such a way that it emphasised the technical aspects of policy detached from explicit politics (let alone popular politics). Policy now became an issue for "experts" (who are overwhelmingly White given South African conditions), and "consultation" with "interested parties" became one for "workshops", so that policy has been depoliticised, reduced to tech-

---

[1] For some of the more useful discussions of corporatism in South Africa see Schreiner (1994), Bird and Schreiner (1992) and Maree (1993). For a more propagandistic approach see Baskin (1993) along with debates in the *South African Labour Bulletin* during 1992 and 1993.

[2] See for example the columns of the *South African Labour Bulletin* since 1991, a journal which accurately reflects and debates dominant developments in South African trade unions.

[3] A nationwide survey of the opinions of COSATU shop stewards in 1991, showed that an overwhelming majority of 80 per cent favoured the involvement of trade unions in politics while "the idea of 'workers' control' ... is deeply entrenched in the labour movement". At the same time, the overwhelming majority ANC (94 per cent) expressed support for the main liberation organisation, the ANC as opposed to any "socialist" party. See Pityana and Orkin (1992: 24, 56–58).

nical questions and removed from scrutiny by democratic structures. As one unionist put it: "policy has become "received wisdom" and the result is that the structures are simply "transmission belts" for discussion from above" (Collins, 1994:38). Or again:

> Local agendas are dominated by the very many issues that come from "head office" which require mandates for national policy or national action ... the local has become a function of the national, the passive recipients (sic) of national directives (Marie, 1992:22–23).

At the same time, union representatives often go to "negotiating forums":

> without clear mandates either from the federation (COSATU—MN) or their unions ... Where report-backs are given at the local level, they are often presented as top-down reports with little room for debate. They are often not discussed at all, in favour of dealing with more local issues (Collins, 1994:38).

A survey of trade unionists conducted by the *South African Labour Bulletin* in 1992 (see Keet, 1992 and also Pityana and Orkin, 1992) found a general trend of the weakening of worker control with one national leader remarking that "workers are losing and losing workers control and it is in danger of becoming just a slogan" (Keet, 1992:29). This was manifested *inter alia* in the fact that few shop stewards now turn up to (shop steward council) local meetings (100 out of 500 possible members in Durban, 100 out of 1000 in Johannesburg). "COSATU office bearers are less subject to the direct workers' control that shop stewards can exercise within their own affiliates" (Collins, 1994:35.); "bureaucratic tendencies have become evident both at COSATU and affiliate level. These tendencies are not restricted to officials, but extend to worker leaders as well" (Collins, 1994:39).[1] The reviewer concludes:

> To abandon worker control is to abandon union democracy, and to accept that ... formal democracy empty of any ongoing, direct control by members is the best that the trade union movement can do, given the conditions in South Africa in the 1990s ... Workers' control of unions was seen as a means to worker control of production and society as a whole. It is a significant irony that in the 1990s, the unions are struggling to return to worker control of their own organisations, with control of production and society an ever receding possibility (Collins, 1994:40).

It would, indeed, be tempting to causally link the dominance of corporatism among trade unions in South Africa with the weakening of control from below but there is, as yet, little to suggest that the former is a function of the latter. It could, in fact, be the case that they are both effects of much broader tendencies which, as we have seen, have involved other organisations of

---

[1] At the same time, recent data show a decline i union membership of about 6 per cent between 1993 and 1995 while total employment has remained constant. Manufacturing unions were the hardest hit, with a decline in membership of 15 per cent between 1991 and 1995. Se Baskin, 1969:8–11.

civil society—such as the civics—as well. In any case, it is not *a priori* impossible that some form of social contract between the state and various organisations of civil society, including trade unions and civics, is compatible with popular politics and genuine popular participation. In fact it is arguably the case that in the absence of such a combination, reversal to other forms of statism is practically inevitable. Corporatism however implies the *"étatisation"* of popular organs of civil society, their "politicisation from above" which in no way requires, of necessity, a surrendering of organisational independence; it only requires the absence of *political* independence. Organisational independence is fully compatible with incorporation within state structures and, after all, this is typical of classical social democracy, where social democratic parties have "their" trade unions in the same way as communist parties had "theirs". Rather than being about the *democratisation of the state from below* as in the 1980s, the dominant trend in South Africa which is in the process of becoming entrenched, is about the *étatisation of civil society from above*. It is not difficult to agree with Sam Shilowa, the general secretary of COSATU (in one of the quotations heading this essay), that a new form of statism is beginning to dominate in post-apartheid South Africa.

I have, so far, attempted to show that between the 1980s and the 1990s there has been an important process of political change in South Africa, involving the major popular organisations of civil society (civics and trade unions in particular) and their relations to the state. This shift in the "mode of politics" has involved a process where a form of *popular politics*, with all its contradictions, has been replaced by "top down" politics, bureaucratic tendencies and, in brief, the greater centrality of *state politics* in the operation of hitherto popular organisations which have either been, or are in the process of being, radically transformed. I have restricted myself to outlining some aspects of this change without attempting to discuss at length any explanations for it. Nevertheless, no explanation, however limited, is possible without some theoretical perspective. We must now turn to the task of briefly elaborating such a perspective.

CIVIL SOCIETY AND POLITICAL SOCIETY

In the 1990s, the process of democratisation in South Africa has been overwhelmingly state-directed not only because political parties and state agencies have taken the initiative and provided the fora in which decisions on such democratisation processes are made, but also largely because of the weakness of a culture of popular democracy and the absence of popular institutions through which that culture could be expressed. At the same time, many of the official documents emanating from the ANC (such as the *Reconstruction and Development Programme*—RDP) pay lip service to the "South African tradition of a strong and independent civil society" and often uncritically assume that such civil society, in particular what are now called CBOs (community-based organisations—the term basically refers to civics), can provide the vehicle for popular direction of the democratisation process. More sober assessments, however, as we have seen, paint a different picture of a moribund popular movement, so that Sam Shilowa, the general secretary of COSATU recently had to emphasise that: "'the mass-driven character' of the RDP is at this stage a total myth" (Shilowa, 1995:36).

Central to the new process of transformation in the 1990s is what the ANC, drawing from American jargon, calls an "affirmative action programme" which, in the main, corresponds to what, in post-independence Africa, was known as "Africanisation", namely, the appointment of personnel in the civil service particularly and the public sector more generally, from the ranks of the hitherto excluded/colonised population. In Africa, this policy, arguably, had three major effects. First, it created a middle class and especially one which was tied to the state and mainly consisting of those who were appointed as colonial officials left their posts (the lower levels of the civil service were, by and large, Africanised anyway). Second, it transformed a demand for democratisation (i.e. *inter alia* the opening up of job opportunities to as many people as possible and the democratisation of access to resources and, thereby, the democratisation of state structures) into a replacement of "white faces by black faces" in the state apparatuses; in other words, democratisation was reduced to the formation of a middle class "from above". Third, it created important new divisions (or at least intensified old ones) over access to resources as it was only *some* Africans who were given access to jobs (e.g. "Kikuyuisation" was a more accurate description of this process in Kenya under Kenyatta). This last point became extremely dangerous as only some nationalities (or political parties), through their exclusive access to state resources, monopolised possibilities of accumulation, with the petty-bourgeoisies of other nationalities (and parties) left out. In sum, in post-colonial Africa, democratisation was reduced to "Africanisation", popular democracy "from below" was replaced by state nationalism "from above" (Mamdani, 1990).

In South Africa, "affirmative action" has been exhibiting some similarities to as well as some differences from the pattern above. On the one hand, it is difficult to refer to "Africanisation" in South Africa as everyone (including White South Africans) is African; on the other hand, the term "African" tends to be restricted to the apartheid category (in relation to "European", "Indian" or "Coloured") so that such a term would privilege only one section of the (hitherto oppressed) population. So much for terminology. Turning to more fundamental aspects, affirmative action is described as:

> a type of "positive discrimination" as a measure to correct imbalances created by centuries and generations of ... oppression. It cannot be a permanent feature of society or an organisation, but rather an interim measure and a means towards full equality and an end to discrimination (*Mayibuye*, Sept. 1991, p. 32).

The above definition is, in a sense, contradictory since if affirmative action is supposed to correct "centuries and generations of oppression", it can hardly be temporary (unless its temporary nature is measured in decades, if not longer) and if it is to be temporary, it can hardly hope to correct such "imbalances". This is, in a sense, revealing as the contradiction is only reconcilable if we are talking of the creation of a middle class. In this case, racial "imbalances" can be overcome pretty rapidly as Blacks can be appointed to jobs without regard for issues of popular-democratic participation. In actual fact, this is precisely what has been happening. The state bureaucracy rather than contracting as the ANC had always argued in the 1980s, is expanding as the ANC acceded to a demand to keep apartheid civil servants in their jobs (including in the ex-bantustans) and is attempting to by-pass their lack of cooperation by creating new appointments.

In addition, in South Africa, businesses in the private sector are cooperating in recruiting Blacks for managerial positions. Whatever the extent of progress on this score, the point really remains that the process is one where a middle class is being created among "Black Africans" primarily (the lower ranks of the civil service, especially in the ex-bantustans as well as the overwhelming majority of employees in all sectors are Black anyway). In neither of these cases is it a question of democratising appointments or indeed state structures themselves. The popular struggle for democracy has been replaced by a scramble for state posts.[1] This has been but an effect of the ANC's obsessive concern with "attaining state power" as a pre-condition for democratisation, as opposed to the reverse position—the democratisation of politics and social relations as a prelude to the establishment of a democratic state—which was gradually being developed by the popular movements.

The last aspect of this question worth mentioning is that such a procedure is creating contradictions between "racial groups", most obviously expressed as White (and, indeed, Coloured in the Western Cape) resentment against allegedly "unqualified" Blacks taking over highly paid jobs amidst fears for their own job security/prospects. This was a factor in the Western Cape voting for the National Party at the general elections in April 1994, for example. At the same time, the top echelons of the civil service remain largely under the control of appointees of the apartheid regime (as the ANC guaranteed that all civil servants would retain their jobs). This way, the top echelon of the civil service is able to retard (and perhaps even sabotage) government policy. This leads to frustrations and resentment by impatient

---

[1] At this point it is perhaps important to mention the fact that although 'affirmative action' seems to be the main ANC plank for the 'democratisation' of society, the organisation seems less than happy to apply the same procedure to equalisation between genders. While there have been numerous resolutions supporting 'affirmative action' for women within the ANC, the organisation rejected a quota system for women members at its 1991 national conference (see *Mayibuye*, August 1991). Women in the ANC weakened themselves through dissolving FEDSAW and by undermining the existence of a popular independent women's organisation.

politicians who can also use this as an excuse for the lack of progress in "delivering" promises to the majority.

While this is happening, the state is directing a process of "reconciliation" between the races which, arguably, has little "public support". The choice of language is deliberate as, in a state-directed endeavour like "affirmative action" or "reconciliation", it is no longer possible to speak of popular democracy but only of "public support" where the people are reduced to passive spectators. While during the period of the UDF, as we have seen, the construction of a "new nation" was attempted on the basis of combining South Africans of all races under the banner of popular democracy and opposing them to anti-democrats, now the issue is the construction of a nation by the state itself and thereby the reproduction and even possible deepening of racial divisions. This is especially obvious in conditions where the majority have yet to see any benefits from liberation or the RDP (despite its exclusive accent on top down "delivery"), and where official "reconciliation" appears to mollify extreme right-wing racists and to permit the "perpetrators of apartheid" to escape retribution.[1] In this manner, popular "anti-racism" has been replaced by state directed "reconciliation". As a result, nationalism has now acquired a new meaning. A media report commented recently:

> the mood of non-racialism ... is fading. The views of the proponents of Black Consciousness are increasingly being heard again and people are listening to them. It is giving rise to the development of an Africanist ideology ... (*Southern Africa Report*, 8 September, 1995).

In brief, these examples point to a process similar to that of the "statisation" of nationalist politics that was earlier noted with reference to both popular civic organisations and trade unions. Insofar as a dialogue is taking place regarding the nature of democracy, it is increasingly dominated by technical-legal questions regarding the constitution, a bill of rights, regional versus central powers, individual freedoms, "truth commission" and so on, with the result that ordinary people are largely by-passed by debates (although they are asked in the press to participate by writing to the constituent assembly with their suggestions!), and "consultation" is supposed to take place through "workshops". Indeed "workshops" have proliferated in all spheres of political activity and have been justified ostensibly as a way of "consulting" and involving all "interested parties" in the debating and even formulation of policy. This has largely amounted to an extensive form of corporatism where "experts" together with the leaders of various community organisations and trade unions have gradually become part of a complex state structure. In the sphere of "liberation politics", "workshop politics" has gradually come to replace "mass politics". Having no real legal, let alone constitutional, authority, "workshops" have no powers other than

---

[1] See for example the *Mail and Guardian*, Vol. 12 No. 7 1996, pp. 4, 12, 28.

"consultative" ones. They are more often than not representative of no one other than themselves, as participants have not usually been mandated by any political body or organisation. Not only are workshops largely unrepresentative, but popular representatives when they exist are rarely mandated, so, as a result, their resolutions and recommendations can be ignored as and when necessary.

De facto, therefore, the "dialogue on democracy" is not being conducted between the ANC and the people organised under distinct, independent and clearly defined politicised organisations. Rather, it is being conducted between the ANC and the representatives of White capital and the White fraction of the bourgeoisie overwhelmingly represented by the National Party, (along with right-wing Afrikaners and the Inkatha Freedom Party insofar as "regionalism" or "traditional leaders" are concerned), above the heads of the majority of the population[1]. The role of multipartyism and universal suffrage in this process requires some elaboration, as both have been uncritically celebrated as major achievements by the media and in supposedly more academic writing (e.g. Friedman and Atkinson, 1994).

It is perhaps important to recall first of all that multipartyism was established in the immediate post-independence period in Africa as the departing British colonial power in particular imposed a "Westminster system" of government on the newly independent states. Political parties, however, generally mobilised ethnic and regional interests, as the African petty-bourgeoisie had not by then been able to constitute itself as a unity and was fundamentally divided along such lines. Multipartyism was quickly scrapped as the nation-state project could not countenance ethnic resistance and purported threats to territorial unity. Multipartyism imposed "from above", therefore, quickly proved to be a failure. In recent years, African authoritarian statism has generally survived the (re-)introduction of multipartyism under the pressure of "political conditionalities" imposed by the West as a requisite for continued financial and political support in the "New World Order".

There have been some similarities between the South African and wider African experiences as neither the incoming ANC nor the outgoing NP government had ever been committed to multipartyism and universal suffrage. Indeed, the ANC only started mentioning its adherence to multiparty democracy in the 1980s as the dialogue was initiated between it and the apartheid regime. Although the Freedom Charter made a commitment to "government by the people", this could easily have been interpreted as a

---

[1] In the same way as the economic debate is being conducted between World Bank economic liberalism and social democratic statism, the latter being the weaker partner. This can be seen in the various drafts which the RDP parliamentary paper has gone through and in which the market has been taking a more and more prominent position. See Adelzadeh and Padayashee (1994) who measure the distance between the original statist ANC version of the RDP and the current "free market" version adopted as government policy.

project for a one-party system where the party is said to represent "the people" (as had been done on numerous occasions in Africa and elsewhere), although it could also have been operationalised in the popular democratic variant represented by the UDF in the 1980s. As to the National Party, it was, after all, the main architect of the refinement of the colonial disenfranchisement of the majority known as "apartheid". Neither the ANC nor the NP, therefore, had a history of commitment to multipartyism and universal franchise. Their commitment to both these features of the state in South Africa was the result of a number of factors both external and internal to the country.

The external factor was clearly the changed international conjuncture and the end of the Cold War which generated pressure from the Western powers for democratisation in Africa (as well as in the Third World and in the ex-Soviet Union more generally). Internally there were arguably two major factors. The first was the obvious fact that both the National Party and the ANC, together with White capital and the emergent Black petty-bourgeoisie, realised that they had to compromise over control of the state and that neither could win an outright victory over the other. A power-sharing arrangement through universal suffrage had to be worked out and, in fact, they went so far as to agree to share the "governance" of the country through the establishment of a "Government of National Unity" until the next territorial elections in 1999.

The second factor was the pressure "from below" which could not have countenanced a "one-party state" as in the rest of Africa, as popular organisations (especially the trade unions, but also the civics) were quite jealous of their independence and, as we have seen, argued strongly against statisation whose dangers they were aware of. Multipartyism and universal suffrage were, therefore, in South Africa, the result of an internal compromise between class forces and not the result of an external imposition. This is why it is seen as having a more secure basis in the country than it had in the rest of Africa, although the two main parties are still representative of racial groups and there is no indication yet of a change in this regard. At the same time, the evident cynicism of the major parties vis-a-vis the first territorial elections of April 1994, whereby honest voting was apparently less important than the clinching of a deal in which all main parties were "given something" and were thus "satisfied", bodes ill for the future as it shows contempt for the "popular will" (Southall, 1994).

Through the formation of a "government of national unity", all radical opposition has largely been delegitimised, and insofar as such opposition is being expressed from the Left, it is emanating from marginalised groups influenced by the "Trotskyist tradition" in Cape Town which restricts itself to denouncing the "politics of class compromise" and the dominance of the petty-bourgeois nationalists, and calling for the formation of a "workers' party". There is little in these statements concerning democracy of the popular or any other variety, and they largely consist in re-stressing the vulgar fundamentals of some kind of millenarian "Marxism" divorced from popular experience.[1] This perspective is still overwhelmingly statist (as can be seen in any of the political writings of Neville Alexander for example). At the same time, the Left within the "Congress Alliance" is hamstrung by its support of the state (and particularly of statism) to such an extent that even though the need for independent popular organisations is often reiterated, there is a complete failure to understand how this could be accomplished other than by initiatives "from above". Any genuine popular initiative would, of course, have to start by re-politicising "civil society" and would thus come into (some sort of) conflict with the ANC dominated state, something which would be too much of a risk for the territorial leadership. Thus, calls for greater democracy from these quarters remain, unfortunately (and predictably), rather empty.[2]

There is, as yet, as far as I am aware, no serious analytical study of the transition period in South Africa. There are, however, some important studies which attempt to assess the period of the 1980s. Most prominent among these are Marx (1992), Murray (1987) and Lodge (1991).[3] Marx's book provides a wealth of detail but concentrates exclusively on a discussion of the changing ideology of the anti-apartheid movements through the words of their leading personnel. Because of this, it restricts itself to the territorial level and absolutely fails to recognise not only the differences between local and territorial ideologies and struggles, but also possible contradictions between the leaders of such movements and the led. This *modus operandi* is particularly unacceptable in the case of South Africa, as much of the ideological struggle in the 1980s surrounded precisely the issue of internal democracy and the accountability of leaders to the rank and file.

Moreover, it is not particularly useful to concentrate, as Marx does, on a discussion of the ideology of the leadership if, as we have argued, it was in fact the rank and file who were the main motive force behind the opposition

---

[1] This ideological perspective has been accurately described as follows:
It posits that under conditions of capitalist accumulation, which inevitably reduces the masses to ever-deepening misery, independent organizations, primed with a socialist consciousness and under working-class leadership, will rise up against their unbearable conditions and effect a transition to a society in which "there will be no apartheid, no oppression, and no exploitation (Lodge et al., 1991:213).

[2] For example: "We need also to rebuild and reawaken the web of relatively independent mass democratic formations and struggles that characterised the 1980s" (Cronin,1992: 52).

[3] The three works provide general histories of resistance in the 1980s and therefore attempt some kind of account of the features and ideology of the social movement. Other authors restrict themselves to description or to analysing specific episodes overwhelmingly as organisational histories of the UDF in specific areas. This is particularly the case with Seekings for example (1988, 1992a, 1992b, 1992c, 1993). See also Chaskalson, Jochelson and Seekings (1987), Carter (1991, 1992), Hughes (1987), Naidoo (1992) and especially Jochelson (1990), Sapire (1992), Bundy (1985) and Sitas (1992) whose discussions are more illuminating.

to the apartheid state for a considerable period of time. Marx is thus forced into accepting the leadership view at face value such as the apparent "pragmatic" conception of the all-inclusive ideology of nationalism contained in the "Freedom Charter". The point was that ordinary people, mobilised as they were in their own organisations, were actually giving the populist slogans of the "Freedom Charter" a popular content most obviously apparent in "People's Power" which was anything but "all inclusive" and "populist", but which had an evident bias towards the working people. Marx's own perspective ultimately leads him to adopt a linear conception of ideological change in South Africa, whereby the opposition's ideology is seen as following the chronological and somewhat teleological path of the organising principles of "race" (Black Consciousness), "nation" (UDF) and "class" (COSATU).

Murray (1987) is more critical of the "populism" of the UDF than Marx, preferring the supposedly more "working class" orientation of the "National Forum" (a small association of Cape Town-based Trotskyist and Black Consciousness groups with little popular support). This is determined by the former's adherence to a supposedly "multi-racial radical populism" dominated by the "petty-bourgeoisie", rather than the more frank anti-capitalism of the "National Forum" which understands that the "working-class struggle against capitalist exploitation and the national struggle have become one struggle under the general control and direction of the black working class" (Murray, 1987:230). Again, there is little attempt to understand the complexities of ideology here. Not only is this simply the slogan of an intellectual leadership with weak relations to the working people, but there is no attempt to investigate the possible relations or contradictions between the two, or even the possible inventiveness of popular struggle. In fact, there is little attempt to listen to popular perspectives which may not fit within the parameters of the author's rigid dogma.

In many ways, the account of Lodge et al. is the most sophisticated of the three main analyses of the 1980s, as the authors are sensitive to the complexities of ideological formation and identity, and indeed recognise the importance of popular initiatives in the construction of struggles from below. Thus:

> Notwithstanding the ANC's popularity and the universal authority of the Freedom Charter, the UDF was an intellectually intricate organisation, perhaps more so than even its leaders were aware. In its public rhetoric and printed polemics, different political persuasions were evident. And if ideology is taken to mean more than the self-conscious expression of doctrine and principle, and if the term is understood to embrace an organisation's repertoire of activities, then the picture becomes quite elaborate. For, just as the UDF's rhetoric animated its huge army of supporters, the organisation became infused with their ideas and beliefs. These drew on folk morality and local interpretations of tradition as much as on externally derived conceptions of capitalism or socialist democracy. People's power was the crystallisation of the rich and volatile mixture of ingredients within the UDF (Lodge et al., 1991:140).

And yet, despite this excellent assessment, Lodge insists on demarcating the ideology of the UDF along three strands: "nationalist", "national democratic", and "socialist" which, at the time, were clearly "vertical" divisions (Lodge et al., 1991:129–134). They were "vertical" because they corresponded to divisions around which leaders would attempt to gather support and interpellate audiences. Thus, whether or not one agrees with Lodge that these currents were the dominant ones, the fact remains that it could be argued that a far more important division in the movement, especially with some historical hindsight, was that between those who attempted to stress popular democracy and control, consultation in decision-making, independence from political parties and leadership accountability, and those who were on the side of authoritarianism, statism and, later, the exclusive adherence to multiparty democracy. In other words, it could be argued that a more important ideological division which cut across those identified by Lodge, was a "horizontal" one between popular democracy and statism ("state democracy" or authoritarianism). In the absence of an attempt to at least examine this distinction—to detach popular-democratic nationalism (or socialism) from state (petty-bourgeois) nationalism—it seems to me difficult to do justice to the popular movement in South Africa in the 1980s, or to adequately explain the transition from the popular politics of this period to the state politics of the 1990s.

African scholars have recently begun to reassess this kind of question from the perspective of the recent crisis of the African state, which is, in large part, a crisis of legitimacy. Earlier conceptions of the "betrayal" of "the revolution" by a petty bourgeoisie have been rightly rejected as explanations which not only rely on conspiracy theories but often idealise class subjects (the working class and/or petty bourgeoisie) and endow them with innate powers to make history on their own independently of social relations and struggle.[1] Like most such analyses, these conceptions end up ignoring issues of democracy, along with struggles between different forms of democracy and nationalism, conceding such notions in argument and in political practice to the dominance of the hated "petty-bourgeoisie". They, therefore, have little to offer as an alternative to nationalist statism; indeed, what they offer is more statism, albeit one tainted with a different ideological brush.

Central to this new work has been the writings on popular movements and especially the theorisation developed by Mamdani (1990) and Mamdani and Wamba-dia-Wamba (1995). The former in particular analyses the development of state nationalism in the Africa of the 1960s, along with the defeat of the popular movements which had been a major component of the struggle for a new democratic and independent state. He makes two crucial distinctions: first between "popular democracy" or "national democracy" on the one hand, and "state nationalism" (the "nation-state") on the other; and

---

[1] Perhaps the best-known example of this kind of argument is Astrow, 1983.

second, between the "national" as an equivalent of "democratic" on the one
hand, and "national" as the opposite of "local" (i.e. as the equivalent of
"nationwide" or "territorial" on the other). Through these distinctions, he is
able to argue that popular demands and organisations, although often
"local", were also usually more democratic than "territorial" demands and
organisations which reduced all such demands to the single one of
"independence". Anti-colonialism was not necessarily the same as anti-
imperialism; for this perspective the latter implies democracy, the former
does not necessarily do so. In addition, for Mamdani, state nationalism was
legitimised by the nationalist historian who:

> tried to play down whatever features may detract from the national character of
> a social movement so as to emphasise its nationalist credentials, to remove the
> notes which could not easily be harmonised within a single national chorus,
> s/he also ended up obscuring local issues so as to cast in bold the one single
> national demand: self-government or independence! To use a somewhat
> modern metaphor, what was really a "rainbow coalition" was painted in a
> single grey! (Mamdani, 1990:54).

Mamdani argues that the social movements which together made up the
nationalist movement in the 1940s were gradually defeated by a reform
strategy initiated by the colonial state and continued after independence.
This reform had two consequences. First, it led to a splitting of the anti-
colonial forces as concessions were made to bourgeois aspirants within the
broad front. Secondly, it enabled the legalisation of "the most important
political organisations (trade unions, cooperatives, friendly societies) [in
order] to bring them under the scrutiny of the state and [thus] undermine
their autonomy and any element of popular accountability they may have
developed" (Mamdani, 1990:49). He also draws a distinction between the
"social movement" and the "political movement", the latter transforming
itself into the state at independence.

Gibbon (1993) develops this perspective in his work on civil society and
"developmentalist" states. He argues that a democratisation process which
functions in the interests of the working people must, fundamentally,
always involve not a "deepening" or "strengthening" of civil society but
rather two mutually reinforcing aspects: on the one hand, the *politicisation*
(not statisation) of civil society, and, on the other hand, the *democratisation* of
the state. The former implies the entering of civil society organisations into
the political sphere whereby their members are addressed as citizens and
not simply as members of a(n) ("interest") group with particular interests
determined by the division of labour. The latter suggests the transformation
of the state so that it reflects the "sovereignty of popular institutions". This
argument is elaborated in his work on late colonial Tanganyika (Gibbon,
1994) where he distinguishes a realm of "territorial politics" ("national politics" without the popular democratic content). He shows that local movements were often raising issues and democratic questions which went far

beyond what TANU was prepared to countenance and that TANU and the colonial state actually combined to suppress and otherwise undermine the autonomy of such movements (similar points are made by Kriger (1992) in her work on the liberation war in Zimbabwe). The determining factor in the defeat of popular movements, he argues, was TANU's monopolisation of territorial politics.

It is interesting to reflect on the South African case in the light of this perspective. Evidently, it is clear that the multiple popular organisations which formed the basis of the opposition in the urban areas entered political society systematically in the 1980s, and very much as a result of pressure from below. Through the "umbrella" of the UDF, they also occupied the terrain of territorial politics which was at the time not distinct from democratic politics. An important characteristic of this movement was the communication between the national leadership and the rank and file, especially while the former were reasonably accountable. Nevertheless, in this connection, a number of different and opposite trends and practices—democratic and authoritarian, consultative and coercive, analytical and celebratory, accountability of the leadership and independence of dominant (often charismatic) figures—were all evident simultaneously within the movement.

At the same time, there was no distinction between the "political movement" and the "social movement" as the latter put itself squarely within the ideological ambit of the "Congress Tradition". Clearly, while the ANC was physically removed from the people and the struggle, divisions between the two were not evident.[1] Distinctions between the two movements probably started developing in an obvious way as the "internal leadership" would regularly visit the capitals of the frontline states for "consultations" with the ANC.[2] At this stage, the latter shared the territorial space with the internal organisations and the South African state. As time went by however, the ANC and the apartheid state started to monopolise this political space and the internal leaders began to deal with the regime as part of ANC delega-

---

[1] Ideological differences did pertain however and not solely at the level of practice as I have tried to show. Perhaps the most obvious conscious ideological difference concerned the fact that while the UDF and COSATU referred to the "leadership of the working class" of the "national democratic revolution", the exiled organisations (ANC and SACP) referred rather to "the leadership of the liberation movement" in organisational terms and bestowed it on the ANC. This ideological contradiction was never satisfactorily resolved although such a resolution was attempted by Slovo who insisted that the ANC had a "working-class bias". See *Work in Progress* nos. 50–51, 1987, p. 14, for example.

[2] This process sometimes took extreme forms as when a Cape Town civic association (WECUSA) actually went to the ANC in Lusaka to "get a mandate" to organise squatter areas. It was given the "mandate". (See Pieterse and Simone, 1994:23. The terminology is theirs.) The cynicism of both parties to this deal is quite amazing, and it seems that this episode was in no way unique. Clearly under such conditions it should not be surprising how the ANC managed to effectively monopolize the territorial political space.

tions. This process took off after 1990, although the journalist Allister Sparks shows quite clearly that the ANC and the apartheid state had been engaged in secret talks long before that (Sparks, 1995).

In general, the politicised popular movement of the 1980s was not incorporated into state politics against its will. What seems to have been the case is that popular control over this movement was severely weakened by the second state of emergency. By the time the organisations were emerging from this extreme repression in the late 1980s, they had much more of a character of being led "from above". It was, therefore, easier for them to disband altogether, to transform themselves into adjuncts of the ANC (a procedure which severely weakened the women's movement and killed off the youth movement altogether—"the young lions were tamed", to use the jargon)[1] or to retreat from politics into "interest groups". The voluntary nature of the ceding of the territorial political space to the party of state nationalism—the ANC—in South Africa is, therefore, interesting to note. It is this distancing from politics which then makes it possible for these organisations, civics and especially trade unions, to re-enter politics within the realm of the state as corporatism becomes more entrenched, and politics is reduced to *state* politics.

CONCLUSION

I have, in this chapter, argued, following recent writings by African intellectuals on popular movements, that it is impossible to provide an adequate explanation of the transition period in South Africa, and to do justice to the experience of the social movements in that country without distinguishing popular-democratic nationalism from state nationalism. The former, I have suggested, was the dominant trend in the liberation politics of the 1980s, while the latter is in the process of consolidating itself in the 1990s. In the 1980s, the dominant trend of popular nationalism corresponded to the *politicisation of civil society and the democratisation of the state from below*, while in the 1990s, we are witnessing the *statisation of civil society or its politicisation from above*. Central to the distinction between the two political and ideological forces of popular and state nationalism were different conceptions of the relationship between leaders and led. While the former stressed popular

---

[1] The following front page report appeared in the *Sunday Times* 3 December, 1995:
In [an] action to rid the organisation of "ill-disciplined elements", Mr Mandela is said to have taken drastic action against the ANC's militant Youth League. Mr Mandela is believed to have issued instructions to the ANC's treasury to stop all cheques destined for the league, effectively scuttling its congress planned for next month. This follows a statement by the league's leader, Lulu Johnson, criticising Mr Mandela's call for the Springbok to be retained as the rugby emblem, and other statements critical of the government.

democracy and control, accountability and direct mandating of leaders, the latter stressed the independence of leadership, top-down prescriptions and statist arguments of various kinds. The latter conception of politics in fact reduced politics to state politics so that, in the words of Wamba-dia-Wamba, in his discussion of post-colonial Africa: "political consciousness and state consciousness tended to be identical [so that—MN] the state tended, then, to be internalised by those fighting or resisting it. This facilitated the emergence of "territorial nationalism" as the foundation of post-colonial politics" (Wamba-dia-Wamba, 1994:250). South Africa has been no exception to this general African trend. The best the state-nationalist position has been able to produce has been a negotiated compromise between different statist forces expressed in multipartyism and various other features of state-controlled democracy, which defeated the experiment of emancipative politics begun under "People's Power". None of the popular experiments of democracy seem to have found their way, so far, into the constitution of the country, and seem unlikely to do so.

I have stressed the importance, therefore, of distinguishing between horizontal divisions between democratic and authoritarian tendencies and ideologies within the nationalist movement, rather than the usual vertical divisions between socialists, nationalists or whatever. This distinction might also help to make sense of what often seem to be the contradictory positions espoused by activists, such as those pointed out in the survey of shop-stewards in 1991 which discovered, as we have seen, that a massive majority supported the ANC and "workers' control" (including socialisation of the means of production and state control over industry). This combination seemed *a priori* contradictory as it suggested support for nationalism (the ANC *never* claimed to be socialist) and some form of "socialism" simultaneously; it seemed to suggest a combination of "nationalist" and "socialist" "consciousness" which are often considered as mutually exclusive (or at least distinct). In addition, it cannot be argued that such a combination implied support for an SACP position which argued for short-term support for the ANC, and long-term support for socialism (even though the "length of the term" was never elucidated); it seems rather that shop-stewards supported "workers' control" as an immediate concern (in any case only a minority mentioned their support for the SACP).

What seems contradictory, if we remain at the level of vertical ideological distinctions, becomes somewhat clarified if we move towards considering horizontal distinctions. There is nothing particularly contradictory in holding that "liberation" ("The People Shall Govern") is equivalent to "People's Power" or "workers' control". After all, this was the actual experience of a large number of people in both townships and unions in the 1980s, and it was the dominant view of activists within civics and trade unions during the same period. Liberation was equated for many with national popular democracy (while this popular democracy was referred to as "socialism" by some, and in the unions could more accurately be referred to as "syndicalism"), and there is nothing contradictory in doing so; in actual fact, the rigid opposition between "nationalism" and "socialism" has arguably been the overwhelming concern of South African intellectuals. Such an ideological distinction (especially but not exclusively) in Africa has generally contrasted two marginally different forms of statism in which, what Wamba-dia-Wamba (1993; 1994) has called an "emancipative mode of politics", has been precluded. In other words, whether the post-colonial state in Africa called itself "nationalist" or "socialist", was of marginal significance to the majority of the people who were, in either case, equally the subjects of intense oppression. The arguments of South African intellectuals, as I shall show at length in future work, were no exception to this general statist trend.

The kinds of politics which were developing within the mass movement in South Africa stressed (although obviously not exclusively) a distinction between popular and state politics, thus providing some of the fundamental elements of a genuinely emancipatory politics. Thus both "nationalist" and "socialist" oppositional discourses comprised statist as well as popular/ emancipatory political trends. The latter form of politics can be understood as conforming in all essentials to democratic politics as formulated by Wamba-dia-Wamba:

> Democracy is society instituting itself against its own past traditions [of politics—MN] for better ones. It is a break with the submissive consciousness or culture sustaining past traditions. This means that emancipatory politics emerging in civil society (grass-roots based), should be the originating site of the political prescriptions on the state leading to real state reforms consistent with the rising social demands.

> ... This [emancipatory—MN] consciousness emerges and develops through the active participation in the development and treatment of matters political. When this participation is stopped, the consciousness is replaced by the internalisation of the state perspective and the ensuing self-censorship. The party in its present form, cannot enhance this development; nor can a multipartyism which reduces politics to a matter of numbers (Wamba-dia-Wamba, 1995:16; 1994:259–260).

It was precisely such a break with submissive consciousness that the South African working people were attempting to institute in the urban townships during the 1980s, and precisely its replacement by self-censorship which seems to have permeated popular consciousness in the 1990s. In the experience of many ordinary people, national liberation in the 1980s came to be equated with such a popular democratic project of emancipation as, in the words of Murphy Morobe:

> the key to a democratic system lies in being able to say that the people in our country can not only vote for a representative of their choice, but also feel that they have some direct control over where and how they live, eat, sleep and work, how they get to work, how they and their children are educated, what the content of that education is; and that these things are not done for them by

the government of the day, but [by] the people themselves. In other words, we are talking about ... mass participation rather than passive docility and ignorance, a momentum where ordinary people feel that they can do the job themselves, rather than waiting for their local MP to intercede on their behalf (Morobe, 1987:84).

How can the defeat of this popular project for emancipatory politics and its replacement by state politics then be explained? Clearly, many factors were responsible and a full history can only be the outcome of future research. Yet four main factors seem to be thrown up by the above discussion. State inspired violence was a first crucial factor. This was successful in weakening popular structures, not only because of the lack of a developed underground (including military) with structures subjected to the popular movement, but also because of often bureaucratic practices within the movement itself. Although such authoritarian practices had been contested, especially under the "People's Power" process, they were never successfully supplanted by popular democratic practices and control. Second, such undemocratic practices became more prevalent and dominant as popular structures disintegrated, while the ANC and its leadership who were to negotiate "liberation", were completely unaccountable to any popular structures within the country. Third, popular organisations in both townships and trade unions vacated the realm of popular politics in the 1990s (although there were signs that this had been vacated *de facto* by 1988-89) and withdrew to a supposed "apolitical" civil society where they became "interest groups" with concerns limited by the division of labour. Fourth, the monopoly of territorial politics was thus acquired by the unaccountable party of state nationalism, initially as it became the only legitimate interlocutor of the moribund apartheid state and international forces, then as state structures were left untransformed and untouched by popular culture, and finally as popular forces, accepting its organisational "leadership", ceded the plane of territorial politics to it.

The outcome of the process was a negotiated series of compromises between the outgoing political forces representing overwhelmingly White capital, and the incoming new Black petty-bourgeoisie eager to appropriate and accumulate and/or to fill state positions with minimal control from below. Because the struggle over the content and form of the new state has, in the 1990s, only very marginally involved democratic popular forces and has largely been conducted over their heads, the prospects of statism dominating in South Africa, albeit within a multiparty context, are overwhelming.

BIBLIOGRAPHY

Adelzadeh, A. and V. Padayashee, 1994, "The RDP White Paper: Reconstruction of a Development Vision", *Transformation*, No. 25.

African National Congress, 1992, "Negotiations: A Strategic Perspective", *The African Communist*, special issue, No. 131, 4th Quarter.

Astrow, B., 1983, *Zimbabwe, A Revolution that Lost its Way?* London: Zed Press.

Atkinson, D. (ed.), 1992, "The State and Civil Society", *Theoria*, special issue, No. 79, May.

Barrell, H., 1990, *MK, the ANC's Armed Struggle*. London: Penguin.

Baskin, J., 1982, "Growth of a New Worker Organ: The Germiston Shop Stewards' Council", *South African Labour Bulletin*, Vol. 7, No. 6, April.

Baskin, J., 1991, *Striking Back: A History of COSATU*. Johannesburg: Ravan Press.

Baskin, J., 1993, *Corporatism: Some Obstacles Facing the South African Labour Movement*. Research Report No. 30, April. Johannesburg: Centre for Policy Studies.

Baskin, J., 1996, "Unions at the Crossroads: Can They Make the Transition?", *South African Labour Bulletin*, Vol. 20, No. 1, February.

Bird, A. and G. Shreiner, 1992, "COSATU at the Crossroads: Towards Tripartite Corporatism or Democratic Socialism", *South African Labour Bulletin*, Vol. 16, No. 6.

Botha, T., 1992, "Civic Associations as Autonomous Organs of Grassroots' Participation", in Atkinson, D. (ed.), 1992.

Bundy, C., 1987, "Street Sociology and Pavement Politics: Aspects of Youth and Student Resistance in Cape Town, 1985", *Journal of Southern African Studies*, Vol. 13, No. 3, April.

Carter, C., 1991, "'We are the Progressives: Alexandra Youth Congress Activists and the Freedom Charter, 1983–1985", *Journal of Southern African Studies*, Vol. 17, No. 2, June.

Carter, C., 1992, "Community and Conflict: The Alexandra Rebellion of 1986", *Journal of Southern African Studies*, Vol. 18, No. 1.

Chaskalson, M., K. Jochelson and J. Seekings, 1987, "Rent Boycotts, the State and the Transformation of the Urban Political Economy in South Africa", *Review of African Political Economy*, No. 40, December.

Cobbett, W. and R. Cohen (eds.), 1988, *Popular Struggles in South Africa Today*. London: James Currey.

Collinge, J.A., 1991, "Civics: Local Government from below", *Work in Progress*, No. 74, May.

Collins, D., 1994, "Worker Control", *South African Labour Bulletin*, Vol. 18, No. 3, July.

Cronin, J., 1992, "The Boat, the Tap and the Leipzig Way", *The African Communist*, 3rd Quarter.

de Villiers, R., 1986, "UDF: Front or Political Party", *Work in Progress*, No. 40.

Fine, B., 1993, "Civil Society Theory and the Politics of Transition in South Africa", *Review of African Political Economy*, No. 56.

Foster, J., 1982, "The Workers' Struggle: Where Does FOSATU Stand?", *Review of African Political Economy*, No. 24, May–August.

Friedman, S., 1991, "An Unlikely Utopia: State and Civil Society in South Africa", *Politikon*, Vol. 19, No. 1, December.

Friedman, S., 1992, "Bonaparte at the Barricades: The colonisation of Civil Society", in Atkinson, D. (ed.), 1992.

Friedman, S. and D. Atkinson (eds.), 1994, *The Small Miracle: South Africa's Negotiated Settlement*. Johannesburg: Ravan Press.

Gibbon, P., 1993, "'Civil Society' and Political Change, with Special Reference to Developmentalist States" Mimeo. Nordiska Afrikainstitutet.

Gibbon, P., 1994, "Some Reflections on State, Civil Society and the Division of Labour in Late Colonial Tanganyika (Some Notes on the Origins of the One-Party State)", paper presented at the conference on *Dimensions of Economic and Political Reform in Contemporary Africa*, Kampala, April.

Haysom, N., 1986, *Mabangalala: The Rise of Right Wing Vigilantes in South Africa*. London: CIIR.

Hughes, H., 1987, "Violence in Inanda, August 1985", *Journal of Southern African Studies*, Vol. 13, No 3, April.

Jacobs, B., 1992, "Heading for Disaster", *Work in Progress*, No. 86, December.

Jochelson, K., 1990, "Reform, Repression and Resistance in South Africa: A Case Study of Alexandra Township, 1979–1989", *Journal of Southern African Studies*, Vol. 16, No. 1.

Kasrils, R. and Khuswayo, M., 1991, "Mass Struggle is the Key", *Work in Progress*, No. 72, January/February.

Keet, D., 1992, "Shop Stewards and Worker Control", *South African Labour Bulletin*, Vol. 16, No 5, May/June.

Kriger, N., 1992, *Zimbabwe's Guerrilla War: Peasant Voices*. Cambridge: Cambridge University Press.

Lambert, R. and E. Webster, 1988, "The Re-emergence of Political Unionism in Contemporary South Africa", in W. Cobbett. and R. Cohen (eds.), 1988.

Lanegran, K., 1995, "South Africa's Civic Association Movement: ANC's Ally or Society's Watchdog? Shifting Social Movement-Political Party Relations", *African Studies Review*, Vol. 38, No. 2, September.

Levin, R. and I. Solomon, 1994, "National Liberation and Village Level Organisation and Resistance: A Central Lowveld Case Study", in R. Levin and D. Weiner (eds.), *Community Perspectives on Land and Agrarian Reform in South Africa*. Project Report for MacArthur Foundation.

Lodge, T., 1992, "The African National Congress in the 1990s", in G. Moss and I. Obery (eds.), *South African Review 6*. Johannesburg: Ravan Press.

Lodge, T. et al., 1991, *All Here and Now: Black Politics in South Africa in the 1980s*. Cape Town: Ford Foundation/David Phillip.

Mamdani, M., 1990, "State and Civil Society in Contemporary Africa: Reconceptualising the Birth of State Nationalism and the Defeat of Popular Movements", *Africa Development*, Vol. 15, No. 3/4.

Mamdani, M., 1994, "Non-Racial Apartheid: The Making of Citizen and Subject in Contemporary Africa". Mimeo.

Mamdani, M. and E. Wamba-dia-Wamba (eds.), 1995, *African Studies in Social Movements and* Democracy. Dakar: CODESRIA.

Mamdani, M., 1996, *Citizen and Subject: Contemporary Africa and the Legacy of Late Colonialism*. Princeton: Princeton University Press.

Maree, J., 1993, "Trade Unions and Corporatism in South Africa", *Transformation*, No. 21.

Marie, B., 1992, "COSATU Faces Crisis: "Quick Fix" Methods and Organisational Contradictions", *South African Labour Bulletin*, Vol. 16, No. 5, May/June.

Marx, A.W., 1992, *Lessons of Struggle: South African Internal Opposition 1960–1990*. Cape Town/Oxford: Oxford University Press.

Mathiane, N., 1986, "The Strange Feeling of Taking Control", *Frontline*, Vol. 6, No. 7.

Matiwana, M. and S. Walters, 1989, *The Struggle for Democracy: A Study of Community Organisations in Greater Cape Town from the 1960s to 1988*. University of Western Cape, Centre for Adult and Continuing Education.

Mayekiso, M., 1992a, "Working Class Civil Society: Why We Need It and How We Get It", *The African Communist*, 2nd Quarter.

Mayekiso, M., 1992b, "Hands off the Civics and Civil Society! A Response to Blade Nzimande", *Work in Progress*, No. 21, April.

Mdluli, D., 1991, "Uniting Civics across the Eastern Transvaal", *Work in Progress*, No 74, May.

Molamu, L. and T. Fako, 1993, "Violence in the Political Culture of Contemporary South Africa: Lessons for SADC", paper presented to the SADRA workshop on *SADC After Ten Years*, NUL, Roma, October.

Morobe, M., 1987, "Towards a People's Democracy: The UDF View", *Review of African Political Economy*, No 40, December.

Murray, M.J., 1987, *South Africa: Time of Agony, Time of Destiny, the Upsurge of Popular Protest*. London: Verso.

Naidoo, J., 1986, "Building People's Power: A Working Class Perspective", speech held at Grassroots Conference, 5th April.

Naidoo, K., 1992, "The Politics of Youth Resistance in the 1980s: The Dilemmas of a Differentiated Durban", *Journal of Southern African Studies*, Vol. 18, No. 1.

Ngcobo, E., 1993, "Local Government Negotiating Forum off to a False Start", *Work in Progress Reconstruct Supplement*, No. 93, November.

Nzimande, B. and M. Sikhosana, 1991, "Civics Are Part of the National Democratic Revolution", *Mayibuye*, Vol. 2, No. 5, June.

Nzimande, B. and M. Sikhosana, 1992a, "Civil Society and Democracy", *The African Communist*, First Quarter.

Nzimande, B. and M. Sikhosana, 1992b, "Civil Society and Democracy: A Rejoinder", *The African Communist*, Third Quarter.

Nzimande, B. and M. Sikhosana, 1992c, "'Civil Society' Does Not Equal Democracy", *Work in Progress*, No. 84, September.

Nzongola-Ntalaja, G., 1993, "Nation Building and State Building in Africa", *SAPES Occasional Paper*, No. 3 , Harare.

Olukoshi, A.O. and L. Laakso (eds.), 1996, *Challenges to the Nation-State in Africa*, Uppsala: Nordiska Afrikainstitutet in cooperation with Institute of Development Studies, University of Helsinki.

Pieterse, E.A. and A.M. Simone, 1994, *Governance and Development: A Critical Analysis of Community-Based Organisations in the Western Cape*, FCR;

Pityana, S.M. and M. Orkin, 1992, *Beyond the Factory Floor: A Survey of COSATU Shop-Stewards*. Johannesburg: Ravan Press.

Sapire, H., 1992, "Politics and Protest in Shack Settlements of the Pretoria-Witwatersrand-Vereeneging Region, South Africa, 1980–1990", *Journal of Southern African Studies*, Vol. 18, No. 3, September.

Schreiner, G., 1994, "Beyond Corporatism: Towards New Forms of Public Policy Formulation in South Africa", *Transformation*, No. 23.

Seekings, J., 1988, "The Origins of Political Mobilisation in PWV Townships, 1980–84", in Cobbett, W. and R. Cohen (eds.), 1988.

Seekings, J., 1989, "People's Courts and Popular Politics", in G. Moss and I. Obery (eds.), *South African Review 5*. Johannesburg: Ravan Press.

Seekings, J., 1992a, "'Trailing behind the Masses': The United Democratic Front and Township Politics in the Pretoria-Witwatersrand-Vaal Region, 1983–84", *Journal of Southern African Studies*, Vol. 18, No. 1 March.

Seekings, J., 1992b, "From Quiescence to 'People's Power': Township Politics in Kagiso, 1985–1986", *Social Dynamics*, Vol. 18, No. 1.

Seekings, J., 1992c, "The United Democratic Front and the Changing Politics of Opposition in Natal, 1983–85", paper presented at the Ethnicity Conference, University of Natal, Pietermaritzburg, September.

Seekings, J., 1993, *Heroes or Villains: Youth Politics in the 1980s*. Johannesburg: Ravan Press.

Shaw, T., 1994, "South Africa: The Corporatist/Regionalist Conjuncture", *Third World Quarterly*, Vol. 15, No. 2.

Shilowa, S., 1995, "Challenges of the Transition Period: A COSATU Perspective", *The African Communist*, Nos. 139/140, 1st Quarter.

Sisulu, Z., 1986, "People's Education for People's Power", *Transformation*, No. 1.

Sitas, A., 1992, "The Making of the "Comrades" Movement in Natal, 1985–1991", *Journal of Southern African Studies*, Vol. 18, No. 3, September.

Slovo, J., 1992, "Negotiations: What Room for Compromise?", *The African Communist*, No. 130, 3rd Quarter.

Race Relations Survey, 1988/89, 1989. Johannesburg: South African Institute of Race Relations.

Southall. R., 1994, "The South African Elections of 1994: The Remaking of a Dominant-Party State", *Journal of Modern African Studies*, Vol. 32, No. 4, December.

Sparks, A., 1995, *Tomorrow is Another Country: The Inside Story of South Africa's Negotiated Revolution*. Sandton: Struik.

Swilling, M., 1984, "Workers Divided: A Critical Assessment of the Split in MAWU on the East Rand", *South African Labour Bulletin*, Vol. 10, No. 1, August/ September.

Swilling, M., 1988, "The United Democratic Front and Township Revolt", in W. Cobbett and R. Cohen, R. (eds.), 1988.

Swilling, M., 1990, "Political Transition, Development and the Role of Civil Society", *Africa Insight*, Vol. 20, No. 3.

Swilling, M., 1991, "Socialism, Democracy and Civil Society: The Case for Associational Socialism", *Work in Progress*, No. 76, August. Also published in Atkinson, D. (ed.), 1992.

United Democratic Front, 1985, 1986, 1987, *Isizwe*, Vol. 1, No. 1; Vol. 1 No. 2; Vol. 2, No. 1;

United Democratic Front, Cape Town Area Committee, 1986, "Broadening the Base". Discussion Document.

Wamba-dia-Wamba, E., 1993, "Democracy, Multipartyism and Emancipative Politics in Africa: The Case of Zaire", *Africa Development*, Vol. 18, No. 4.

Wamba-dia-Wamba, E., 1994, "Africa in Search of a New Mode of Politics", in H. Himmelstrand (ed.), *African Perspectives on Development*. London: James Currey.

Wamba-dia-Wamba, E., 1995, "The State of All Rwandese: Political Prescriptions and Disasters", paper presented at the Arusha conference on the Great Lakes Region, September 4–7.

Webster, E., 1987, "The Rise of Social Movement Unionism: The Two Faces of the Black Trade Union Movement in South Africa", in P. Frankel et al., *State, Resistance and Change in South Africa*. Johannesburg: Southern Book Publishers.

White, R., 1986, "A Tide has Risen. A Breach has Occurred: Towards an Assessment of the Strategic Value of the Consumer Boycotts", *South African Labour Bulletin*, Vol. 11, No. 5, April–May.

Newspapers and Periodicals

Frontline	*South African Labour Bulletin*
Mayibuye	*Sunday Times*
New Era	*Weekly Mail/Mail and Guardian*
New Nation	*Work in Progress*

Chapter 8

Political Opposition and Democratic Transitions in Nigeria, 1985–1996

Osita Agbu

INTRODUCTION

The festering political crisis in Nigeria which broke out with the annulment of the 12 June, 1993 presidential elections that marked the end of the protracted transition programme pursued by the military government of General Ibrahim Babangida has re-focused attention on the potentials for the survival of Africa's most populous country as a stable, united and democratic system. Central to the crisis facing Nigeria is the military which, as of 1996, had ruled the country for nearly 27 out of 36 years of independence. So prolonged has the experience of military rule been in Nigeria that many of the people of the country are increasingly concerned that elected civilian administration now appears to be the political aberration, not the seizure of power by soldiers. In the years since it attained its independence in 1960, Nigeria has only known two episodes of fully elected government—1960 to 1966 and 1979 to 1983. Military rule has, of course, always occurred with the support of one section or the other of the civilian political elite, although, formally at least, the country has never been run as a military-civilian diarchy. However, the fact that successive military governments have relied on civilian technocrats and politicians for the administration of the country has, of late, generated a growing level of concern as the costs to Nigeria of authoritarianism in general and military rule in particular amount to the detriment of the welfare of the citizenry, the democratic rights of the populace, and the unity of the nation-state. By the time the 1993 presidential elections were annulled, many Nigerians had concluded that the military had become the single greatest threat to the progress, stability, and unity of the country. This conclusion was to serve as a factor galvanising opposition to continued military rule.

This chapter is concerned to assess the political opposition to the transition to civil rule programme which was implemented by the military government of General Ibrahim Babangida which was in power from 1985 to

1993. In doing this, we shall also be focusing on the organisation of the opposition in the period after 1993 when General Babangida's administration was replaced first by an interim government and then by another military junta headed, this time, by General Sani Abacha. The transition programme which the Babangida regime developed was probably the most elaborate in Nigeria's history but as its implementation progressed, it soon became clear that it was aimed at perpetuating the corrupt and increasingly personalised rule of General Babangida and his clique. This realisation, facilitated as much by the increasingly ridiculous and bizarre sets of shifting rules that governed the transition as by the repeated postponement of the terminal date for the disengagement of the military from power and the campaigns waged by the government for General Babangida's continued stay in office, fuelled the development and activism of opposition to the transition and the military. As the military government repeatedly shuffled the political cards, the opposition, mostly made up of civil society activists, stepped up its campaign against what it referred to as the "hidden agenda" which the Babangida regime had of perpetuating military rule and thwarting the democratic aspirations of the people. The transition programme was abruptly terminated with the annulment of the 1993 presidential elections, an action which ushered the country into a fresh round of crises from which it is yet to recover. Indeed, the annulment of the elections merely opened a new, ever more bitter chapter in the struggle between the military and its opponents as we shall attempt to document in this chapter.

Several basic questions come to mind in any attempt to study oppositional politics in Africa: Who are the main players in the opposition? Who and what do they represent? What is their programme and how do they attempt to mobilise support? What are their tactics and strategies for opposing the ruling power bloc and how useful are these? What is their capacity for responding to shifts in the political environment? Do they have any international linkages and, if so, how do these feed into their local campaigns? As a totality, are the actions of the different strands of the opposition sufficiently coherent as to make a dent in the power of the ruling power bloc? In the specific Nigerian context, following the abrupt termination of the Babangida transition programme, how did the opposition group that opposed his rule respond to the rise to power of yet another military officer, General Sani Abacha? These and other related questions will, to varying degrees, be addressed in this chapter in the context of a review of the Nigerian experience. This is by no means an easy task considering the fragmentary nature of the evidence that is available on the Nigerian crisis. What we attempt to do here, therefore, is to offer a general overview of the responses of the opponents of military rule to the annulment of the democratic aspirations of Nigerians by the Babangida regime and the attempts by the Abacha regime to treat that annulment as a *fait accompli* that can be swept under the carpet by another round of military rule, backed up by yet another political transition programme.

The importance of the organised opposition in any political transition process cannot be overemphasised. Indeed, for many commentators, the coherence and vigour of the opposition is seen as being central to the entire political process, for, the opposition is the *altera pars* of government and power (Ionescu and Isabel de Madariaga, 1968). The first major work to attempt to systematically explore the concept and practice of opposition was that of Robert Dahl which was published in 1966 under the title *Political Oppositions in Western Societies* (see also Barker, 1971). In this work, Dahl set out to develop an understanding of the modern democratic process by examining the opposition. However, it is important to underline the fact that, in practice, the concept and practice of opposition has many different meanings and usages depending on the particular context we are dealing with. For example, in a context that is marked by institutionalised political pluralism, the expression of opposition would be different from that in another system which is characterised by political monopoly. It is, therefore, important to understand the meaning attached to the concept in the Nigerian context. In the Nigerian case, which is the focus of our attention in this chapter, the notion and practice of opposition have been defined by the context of prolonged military autocracy which does not brook open dissent. Indeed, during the Babangida years, the official perception of the opposition was that it was made up of "extremists"; the Abacha junta, for its part, came to see and treat the opposition as consisting of "subversive elements". The relationship between the government and the opposition is mainly seen in highly antagonistic, zero-sum terms with the former using all the resources in its arsenal, including violence, to attempt to suppress the latter. In this regard, the case of the minorities' rights groups, such as the Movement for the Survival of the Ogoni People (MOSOP), serves as a prime example .

THE ONSET OF NIGERIA'S ON-GOING POLITICAL CRISIS

The military government of General Ibrahim Babangida assumed power in August 1985 after a palace *coup d'état* in which the Muhammadu Buhari/Tunde Idiagbon military junta (1983–1985) was overthrown. On assuming the leadership of Nigeria, General Babangida announced the intention of his government to undertake a programme of political transition aimed at returning the country to an elected civilian administration. The first concrete steps in this direction were taken in 1986 with the launching of a political debate on the type of political system that would be most suitable for establishing an enduring basis for the civilian-led Third Republic that was to be the objective of the transition programme. A Constituent Assembly was subsequently inaugurated to prepare a new constitution while an artificially-constructed two-party system was designed and imposed on the people by the government after the dissolution of 17 political organisations that had sought, unsuccessfully, to win recognition from the government. The launching of the two political parties was also followed by the disqualification of 23 presidential aspirants (Olukoshi and Agbu, 1995).

Concern about the Babangida regime's transition programme began to grow with the increasingly desperate attempts made by the government to manipulate the process in a direction which suggested that the military were intent on foisting a pre-determined outcome on the people. Nowhere was this manipulation more glaring than in the area of the formation and registration of political parties. The rules which were outlined by the government for the registration of parties were remarkable as much for the discretionary and arbitrary elements that were built into them as for the sheer impossibility of any political group fulfilling them. In the end, for all the efforts which the aspirant politicians made, the Babangida regime refused to recognise any of the political associations which they established. Instead, the government decided to create two parties whose constitutions and manifestos it also wrote and whose operations it funded. Furthermore, the national, state and local offices of the two political parties were built for them by the government and their interim administrative officers were appointees of the military. In addition, the two parties were given their names by the regime: the Social Democratic Party (SDP) and the National Republican Convention (NRC). The SDP was, according to the government, to be "a little to the left" while the NRC was "a little to the right". Under this dispensation, the government made it clear that there was no place for "extremists", an omnibus term for human rights activists and pro-democracy elements who were not prepared to accept the military's political fiat and the strait-jacket which the NRC and the SDP amounted to.

On the whole, the Babangida government spent over four billion Naira on the transition programme, with 2.5 billion out of this accounted for by the activities of the National Electoral Commission (NEC) between 1987 and 1991 (Olagunju et al., 1993). By the time the presidential election was held in 1993, General Babangida had not only postponed the terminal date for the transition to civilian rule three times, but had also repeatedly banned and unbanned many politicians with every round of postponement of the terminal date until the criteria for participation and non-participation in the electoral process became completely blurred (Olukoshi and Agbu, 1995). The national executive committees of the two recognised political parties were also dissolved once by the government. Candidates selected by the parties to run for office were, in some cases, disallowed from contesting elections on "security" grounds, those grounds not being transparent or subject to appeal. The air of political uncertainty in the country was not assuaged by the fact that between 1987 and 1992, several elections were held to fill positions at the local government and state levels and to the National Assembly. In 1987, non-party local government elections were conducted by the regime to be followed in 1991 by another round of local elections, this time on a party basis. State governors, members of the state houses of assembly, the federal house of representatives and the Senate were also elected in 1991 and 1992.

The reckless decision taken by General Babangida and the members of his inner circle to annul the June 12 1993 presidential elections was the culmination of the attempt by the regime to manipulate the entire transition process with the aim of keeping Babangida and the military in power. Those elections, generally declared free and fair by local as well as international observers in spite of the best efforts of the government and *agents provocateurs* whom it sponsored to derail them, were set to be won by Moshood Abiola who had earlier emerged as the presidential candidate of the SDP. The cancellation of the elections threw the country into complete disarray from which it is yet to recover. The Abacha regime which took over from the interim government that Babangida had hurriedly assembled as he made a forced exit, did not help matters by its high-handedness towards the opposition. The regime was to arrest Moshood Abiola over his decision to force a recognition of his electoral victory by declaring himself president in 1994. Nigerians showed their anger at the annulment of the 1993 presidential elections through violent protests, demonstrations, civil disobedience and strikes which resulted in the loss of lives and the arrest of many people. The crackdown on the opponents of the continuation of military rule that was the result of the annulment was intensified by the Abacha junta. Today under Abacha, a large number of Nigerians considered to be security risks are being detained by the government without trial. These include politicians, human rights activists, journalists, labour leaders and students. Many other opponents of the regime have either had to flee into exile or go underground within Nigeria. A couple have been murdered in their homes or on the streets of Lagos under circumstances that suggested that they had been targeted for their oppositional activities.

THE 12 JUNE, 1993 CRISIS AND OPPOSITION TO MILITARY RULE

The initial protests which greeted the annulment of the 12 June, 1993 presidential elections were spearheaded by a civil rights organisation known as the Campaign for Democracy (CD). Its calls for mass protests, boycotts and civil disobedience received wide support from the generality of the people in the main urban areas, especially in the southwest of Nigeria, Abiola's home region. Indeed, for close to two months in 1993, the southwest of Nigeria which includes Lagos, the country's economic nervecentre, was in a state of semi-paralysis as protests raged against the actions of the military in cancelling the election results. Street protests and civil disobedience were backed up with strike action by some categories of workers. The government responded to the protests by violently repressing the opposition which it faced and unleashing a massive campaign of subversion and misinformation targeted at its critics. Under siege, the Babangida regime spared no effort to whip up ethnic, regional, and religious sentiments in order to becloud the fundamental injustice and irresponsibility of its action. Unfortunately for the opposition, the propaganda machinery of the regime was a formidable one which succeeded eventually in weakening national agitation for the restoration of Abiola's mandate. Increasingly, the struggle over the 12 June, 1993 elections was reduced to a north-south regional conflict tinged with religious interpretations and narrow ethnic considerations. What started as a national movement against military rule in general and General Babangida's regime in particular was robbed of its momentum and reduced, primarily by the government, to a series of overlapping, narrow and sectionalist conflicts.

In addition to the CD and its affiliates like the Civil Liberties Organisation (CLO) and the Constitutional Rights Project (CRP), other organisations that were active in the resistance to General Babangida's ploy for keeping himself in power after 12 June 1993 were the Nigerian Bar Association (NBA), a host of other associations of professionals, the National Association of Nigerian Students (NANS), and the Nigeria Labour Congress (NLC). These organisations, in the face of the divisive propaganda of Babangida aimed primarily at preventing the consolidation of a national anti-military campaign, attempted to ensure, first and foremost, that General Babangida's rule was terminated immediately and secondly that the struggle against the military was carried out as a *national*, as opposed to sectional effort. As if it was not sufficient to have to contend with the spirited campaign of deception, misinformation, and division which the Babangida clique had resorted to as a survival strategy, these organisations also had to deal with the fact that the majority of the members of the political elite as represented by those who were active in the NRC and the SDP were more intent on seeking opportunities for access to power and resources and less on the struggle for the enthronement of democracy in the country. Apart from a small section of the political "class" which was later to become central in the opposition to the military, the bulk of Nigerian politicians appeared to be pre-occupied with taking advantage of the crisis which the annulment unleashed in order to feather their own personal nests even if this meant the continuation of military dictatorship. With opportunism so rife in political society, the military were able not only to divide the politicians but also eventually weaken civil society-based opposition.

It was a mark of the success of the opposition's campaign of civil disobedience and strikes that after he announced the annulment of the 12 June 1993 elections, General Babangida was forced to relinquish the presidency on 26 August, 1993. An unelected Interim National Government (ING), headed by Ernest Shonekan, was thereafter imposed on the country by the military after negotiations with officials of the NRC and SDP that excluded Abiola's (direct) participation. The ING was immediately faced with a crisis of legitimacy as much for the fact that it was not the outcome which Nigerians had voted for as for the fact that it was very clear that its head, Ernest Shonekan, was little more than a clueless puppet of a section of the military that continued to wield real effective power behind the scenes. For much of the period of its existence, the ING was dogged by controversy; the position of its head was also extremely shaky. Shonekan was named head of government but it was never clear if this meant that he was also head of state; the instrument appointing him was also silent on whether or not he was commander-in-chief of the armed forces. Meanwhile, the presence in the ING of General Sani Abacha, a central player in the Babangida junta, loomed large over the government. In his capacity as defence minister, he appeared to be the person who wielded real power in the ING, an interpretation which was confirmed when he ignominiously shoved Shonekan aside in a palace *coup* on 17 November, 1993 (Olukoshi and Agbu, 1995). Following the *coup* of 17 November, 1993, it became clear that the decision to establish the ING was a strategy designed to pre-empt the military and allow the forces of authoritarianism to re-organise themselves and re-group under the leadership of General Abacha.

Upon seizing power, one of General Abacha's first acts was the dissolution of the National Assembly (comprising the Senate and the House of Representatives), the state houses of assembly, and local government councils. The thirty elected civilian state governors were also dismissed and replaced by senior military and police officers. In addition, the National Electoral Commission (NEC) headed by Humphrey Nwosu, was dissolved. The two-party political party arrangement evolved under Babangida's transition was dismantled and both the NRC and SDP were proscribed. A ban was placed on all political activities. In short, Nigeria was returned to full scale military rule with none other than General Abacha, one of Babangida's right hand men, at the helm. The fury which this development generated within opposition circles was not diminished by the attempt by General Abacha to distance himself and the clique of military officers around him from the decision to annul the 1993 elections. General Abacha and his supporters had argued, disingeniously, that the annulment of Abiola's victory and the collective choice of all the 14 million Nigerians who voted on 12 June, 1993, was a "judicial" decision which had nothing to do with the military (*Vanguard*, 19 April, 1995). Yet, in the many contradictory explanations he gave for his action, General Babangida had gone on record to say that the annulment was necessitated by the unwillingness of the military establishment to accept an Abiola victory. He claimed that the high command had told him that Abiola would not be acceptable as the commander-in-chief of the armed forces (*Times*, 18 July 1995). The Abacha regime, therefore, was born on the basis of a lie; much of the political energy of the government was to be devoted to covering up that lie.

If the assumption of power by General Abacha was greeted by pro-democracy forces in civil society with a great deal of disquiet, influential sections of the political elite, including leading figures in the disbanded NRC and SDP, appeared to have little or no difficulty joining the first government which Abacha set up in November 1993. That government comprised leading members of the so-called political class, including, astonishingly, Abiola's running mate, Baba Gana Kingibe. But if Nigeria's new military rulers expected that the co-optation of influential members of political society would take the wind out of the sails of the civil society-based opposition to the return of the military to power on the back of the highly unjust annulment of Abiola's victory and a cynical disregard for the right of Nigerians to choose their leaders, they were grossly mistaken. The assortment of civil liberties, human rights, minority rights, and professionals' associations in the country stepped up their campaign against military rule in general and General Abacha and his civilian collaborators in particular. This was so in spite of the fact that the government had committed itself to convening a constitutional conference which the regime said would have "full constituent powers". This proposal was rejected by the civil society activists who demanded nothing short of a Sovereign National Conference (SNC) to be convened by a national unity government headed by Abiola (*Newswatch*, 10 July, 1995). The gap between the junta and the opposition could not have been wider and the government decided that it would have to take drastic measures to suppress challenges to its rule.

The increasingly defiant attitude which the government took in relation to its critics, coupled with its determination to crush all agitations for the upholding of the results of the 12 June, 1993 presidential elections and its refusal to announce a date for its disengagement from power, set it on a collision course with the opposition consisting of civil society pro-democracy activists, labour unions, and a small section of political society that demanded the restoration of all the elected structures of government that had been dissolved by Abacha on 17 November, 1993 when he seized power. As the first anniversary of the 12 June, 1993 elections drew near, opposition to General Abacha's rule rose to a new crescendo just as popular pressure mounted on Moshood Abiola to assert his mandate by declaring himself president. Workers in the highly influential oil sector declared a strike which brought the country to a state of near paralysis for almost three months; market women, students, and several associations of professionals also took strike action in order to back up the demand that the military should immediately leave the political stage and hand back power to those who had been elected by the citizenry. Abiola himself felt emboldened by the sheer expression of popular enthusiasm for him to take on a military establishment which had not only cheated him and the generality of Nigerian voters by the annulment of the 1993 elections but also rubbed salt into the wound by seizing power from the ING barely a few days after he had won a court case he instituted challenging the legality of the interim arrangement hurriedly cobbled together by Babangida and headed by the hapless Shonekan. As political events assumed a frenzied dimension in June 1994, some of the leaders of the disbanded National Assembly attempted to reconvene the national legislature while, for his part, Abiola declared himself president and then went into hiding, only to re-emerge after a couple of weeks. He was promptly arrested by the government which had earlier declared him wanted and charged him with treasonable felony (*Newswatch*, 4 September, 1995:10).

The arrest and detention, without trial, of Abiola was followed swiftly by a wave of highly repressive actions that quickly marked out the Abacha junta as probably the most repressive and cruel in Nigeria's entire post-colonial history. Many people were arrested and detained without trial under the preventive security Decree No. 2 of 1994. Some of the most influential newspapers in the country were also proscribed by the government and several journalists detained. Among the newspapers and magazines that were proscribed were the *Guardian, Punch and Concord;* they remained shut for well over a year (*Daily Times*, 1 October, 1995). Furthermore, organised interest groups were targeted for attack, with the government dissolving the executive committees of the NLC and some of its most influential affiliates, including NUPENG and PENGASSAN, respectively representing junior and senior staff employees in the petroleum sector. Other associations were infiltrated and weakened both by the use of the carrot and the stick. Like the Babangida regime before it, the Abacha regime also resorted to fanning the embers of ethnic, regional, and religious suspicion and hatred as a means of dividing the opposition and localising its actions. It was assisted in this by scores of politicians who, out for personal gain, became cheerleaders for Abacha. Thus it was that the opposition to the regime became increasingly, although never exclusively, centred around Lagos and the geographical south west, enabling the junta to claim that its opponents were mainly the Yoruba kith and kin of Abiola. Many of the opposition activists themselves unwittingly swallowed this political line by increasingly resorting to ethnic interpretations of the socio-political base of the regime and of its harsh actions against pro-democracy activism in the country.

At the same time as state violence was being unleashed on the opponents of the Abacha junta, the regime took desperate measures to outline an alternative political programme that it expected would further divide the political "class" and enable the regime to control the pace of political developments in the country rather than merely responding to the initiatives of the opposition. Thus, amidst widespread calls for its boycott, the regime stepped up plans for the constitutional conference which it promised to convene by hastily arranging the "election" of two-thirds of the delegates while nominating the remaining one third. The turnout of voters for the "elections" was pitifully low, with some delegates returned on a majority which indicated widespread voter apathy across the country generally and in the south west in particular. Of the total of 365 delegates to the conference, 272 were purportedly elected. The total number of Nigerians who bothered to vote was a mere 300,000 out of about 25 million registered and eligible voters. 93 other delegates were nominated by the government (*Newswatch*, 10 July, 1995:11). Compared with about 14 million Nigerians who voted in the annulled presidential elections in 1993, the turnout of voters for this election represented nothing less than an embarrassment on which the government nevertheless put a bold face as its propagandists proclaimed victory. To prevent the opposition from using the low turnout to scuttle the arrangements for the constitutional conference, more arrests were effected and the environment of terror which the regime tried to create was stepped up.

The constitutional conference was inaugurated on 18 January 1994 but if there was any hope that the conference would enjoy the "full constituent powers" which Abacha had promised in his maiden speech after seizing power, it was soon dashed. The regime, apart from nominating one third of the conference delegates and using the security services to ensure that only those who would toe its general anti-Abiola, anti-June 12 line were "elected", also proceeded to nominate the chair and deputy chair of the conference. Furthermore, the delegates were explicitly barred from discussing or negotiating any issues pertaining to the unity and territorial integrity of the country, a clear attempt to prevent any open debate on the contentious issue of the basis for national-territorial administration in Nigeria. The government was also emphatic that the Provisional Ruling Council (PRC), the highest ranking military body in the country, reserved the right to veto any decisions reached by the conference delegates which it did not like. But in spite of the government's best efforts, the constitutional conference was faced with serious problems of legitimacy, deriving in part from the wider legitimacy deficit from which the Abacha regime itself was suffering. Moreover, the non-resolution of the June 12 crisis was a fact which haunted the conference for the entire period over which it lasted. Matters were not helped in this regard by the fact that Abiola remained in detention without trial. In fact, his incarceration and the attempts at humiliating him underlined the necessity for a detailed re-appraisal of the circumstances that led to the criminal annulment of the election and for confidence-building measures to ensure the possibility of holding future elections in the country with credibility.

For all the crisis of legitimacy that haunted the conference and the spirited efforts made by the government to control its work and channel the debates among the delegates on the direction it wanted, the forum was to witness occasional flashes of vigorous discussion on some of the most controversial questions in the Nigerian political system. The issues that generated the most heat were connected to the "National Question", including the contentious matters of political succession, power sharing, federal character, and revenue allocation. Also vigorously debated for a short period was the issue of the terminal date for the Abacha government to hand over power to elected politicians. Shortly after its inauguration, the conference, under the influence of Shehu Musa Yaradua, a former chief of staff under the Obasanjo military regime and frontline civilian player in the aborted transitional programme of General Babangida, sent shock waves through the highest echelons of the government when it fixed 1 January 1996 as the terminal date for the Abacha regime to leave office (*Newswatch*, 8 May, 1995:10). The Abacha junta had clearly not anticipated this and, all official protestations to the contrary notwithstanding, was, in fact, preparing itself for a prolonged stay in power.

All the resources and forces at the disposal of the government were immediately mustered to effect a reversal of the decision of the conference delegates to recommend that the military should disengage from the political scene by 1 January, 1996. Pro-military delegates, *agents provocateurs*, and an array of sycophants were mobilised to protest the decision of the conference; monetary and non-monetary inducements were freely deployed at the same time as strategies were developed for disorganising the Yaradua group at the conference, strategies which culminated in the arrest of Yaradua himself on allegations that he was plotting the overthrow of the junta. It was, therefore, not surprising when in May, 1995, the conference reversed its earlier decision asking the Abacha regime to terminate its rule in January 1996. In the new resolution, the delegates decided that it was now up to the government to fix a date for the termination of military rule whenever that was deemed appropriate in accordance with the "national interest" (*Vanguard*, 26 April, 1995). This resolution was made in spite of the fact that the government had itself stated, shortly after Abacha and his clique seized power, that it was up to the conference to determine the length of its tenure. The arrest of Yaradua and the passing of the new resolution were the clearest indication that the attempt to forge an opposition within the conference to the Abacha regime had been defeated and that whatever else was debated by the delegates, it would have to be on terms that were broadly acceptable to the government and on issues with which it felt comfortable.

As to the issues that centre around the "National Question", there was a clear split between the delegates from the geographical north and south of the country amidst a growing restlessness displayed by the representatives from the minority areas, especially the oil delta. Most of the "southern" delegates, including the minorities, put forward a resolution calling for the introduction of a "rotational presidency" in the country. According to the delegates, the annulment of Abiola's victory had sharply posed the question of the overwhelming domination of political power at the federal centre by military officers and civilian politicians from the geographical north of the country, including the northern minorities. They quoted statistics (see table 1) to show that seven out of the ten heads of state which the country had had since 1960 were from the north and the middle belt of the country. The three who came from the south mainly achieved that office by default and served only very brief terms—Ironsi for less than six months following the failure of the coup attempt that was launched in January 19966 and in which Balewa, the independence prime minister was killed; Obasanjo for three years after he succeeded Muhammed who was assassinated in office; and Shonekan for about 82 days after Babangida was forced to "step aside" from power. Abiola, had his victory been upheld, would have been the first politician from the south of the country to be freely and popularly elected to the presidency of the country.

Table 1. *Geo-ethnic Origins of Nigerian Leaders, 1960–1995*

Period	Head of state	Geo-ethnic origin	Type of government	How the government was ended
1960–66	Balewa	Hausa-Fulani	Civilian	Attempted Coup/Assassination
1966	Ironsi	Igbo	Military	Coup/Assassination
1966–75	Gowon	Middle-Belt	Military	Coup
1975–76	Muhammed	Hausa-Fulani	Military	Attempted Coup/Assassination
1976–79	Obasanjo	Yoruba	Military	Elections
1979–83	Shagari	Hausa-Fulani	Civilian	Coup
1983–85	Buhari	Hausa-Fulani	Military	Coup
1985–93	Babangida	Middle-Belt	Military	Forced exit
1993	Shonekan	Yoruba	Civilian (ING)	Coup
1993–	Abacha	Kanuri/Fulani	Military	-

Source: Culled and updated from Stephen Wright, *Nigeria: The Dilemmas ahead (A Political Risk Analysis)*, The Economist Intelligence Unit, Special Report Number 1072, November 1986, p. 7.

According to the southern delegates to the constitutional conference, the introduction of a rotational presidency would enhance power sharing, increase the sense of belonging of all Nigerians, and promote political stability. After a great deal of acrimony which, on occasions, threatened to undermine the conference completely, the resolution on the rotation of the presidency between the geographical north and south was carried. This resolution was later to be modified by the military regime. The country was divided into six geo-political zones for the purpose of implementing the resolution instead of the simple north-south arrangement agreed at the conference; power-sharing at the highest levels of the executive was also recommended with a presidency that was to include the president, the vice-president, a prime minister and a deputy prime minister. It was also recommended that a federal character commission be established to ensure that all appointments into the federal civil service, the judiciary, and political offices adequately reflected the delicate multi-ethnic character of the country. We shall return to a discussion of the resolution of the conference on the rotation of the presidency later.

POST-JUNE 12 DEVELOPMENTS AND THE EMERGENCE OF PSEUDO–POLITICAL ASSOCIATIONS

With the conclusion of the National Constitutional Conference (NCC) and the submission of a draft constitution to the government on 27 June, 1995, a new chapter began in Nigeria's chequered political history. On receiving the draft constitution, General Abacha stated that the completion of the conference marked the end of the first phase of his government's political transition programme (*Daily Times*, 28 June, 1995:7). He also stated that over a three-month period, the PRC would deliberate on the draft before approving it. In the meantime however, a 39-member committee was set up to co-ordinate a national debate on the draft in order to collate "additional" views from different sections of the country. This decision contradicted Decree No. 3 of 1994 which set up the constitutional conference and barred anyone, except the PRC, from discussing the provisions of the draft constitution (*Daily Times*, 25 August, 1995:1). In setting up the committee to collate additional views, General Abacha and his inner circle appeared to be signalling that there were certain aspects of the draft constitution which they were not happy with; the country was awash with speculation that the notion of a constitutionally-guaranteed rotational presidency in particular was a target for removal and politicians from the south immediately began a campaign in the press for its retention, together with other provisions in the draft constitution. As of the time this chapter was being written in May 1996, Nigerians had still not seen the constitution in its final version and nobody, except the members of the Abacha inner circle, seemed to have been privy to the final contents of the document, including whatever amendments the government may have effected.

Following the submission of the draft constitution in June 1995, the government announced a partial lifting of the ban on political activities, with a warning to politicians that they were expected to exhibit "maturity", "tolerance" and "orderliness". However, political rallies and campaigns remained banned pending the production of a detailed transition programme by the regime. With the partial lifting of the ban on their activities, politicians began to organise in the open for the transition to the Fourth Republic. A plethora of political and pseudo-political groupings were established preparatory to their transformation into political parties. The new associations joined several pre-existing ones that were created, mostly along regional lines, following the annulment of the 1993 presidential elections. The national political terrain was, therefore, littered with a host of associations, ranging from those that were virulently anti-Abacha and actively supportive of Abiola and his June 12 1993 mandate to those that were completely pro-military and anti-June 12 and others that were opposed to the revisiting of 12 June, 1993 elections without being supportive of a prolongation of General Abacha's stay in power. Most of those who were involved in the political manoeuvrings that followed the partial lifting of the ban on politics included people who took a frontline role in the politics of the aborted Third Republic.

There were also associations that were set up to canvass minority interests in the north and south. Particularly active were the organisations set up to advance the interests of the minority ethnic groups from the delta area, the main oil-producing region of the country. Perhaps the best known of these southern minority groups is the Movement for the Survival of the Ogoni People (MOSOP) which, even after the execution in November 1995 of its leader and several activists, remained an active player in the delta. Other associations were simply intent on building a regional/ethnic/religious base in readiness for the elections that would usher in the transition to the Fourth Republic. The tenor of transitional politics generally consisted of the severe, sometimes violent attacks on the pro-June 12 opponents of the military by the government and a determined effort to sideline all other players who appeared to be intent on following their own independent path. The manner in which the regime intervened in the political process suggested to some observers that another hidden agenda was probably being executed, this time with a view to perpetuating General Abacha's rule as an "elected" president. Also singled out for systematic repression were journalists and civil liberties/human rights activists that were implacably opposed to military rule and who, against all the odds, consistently pointed to the extremely poor record of the Abacha junta on all fronts. Even as the pro-June 12 and human rights/civil liberties groups were being attacked, the regime made efforts to bolster associations that were supportive of Abacha and the military; those groups that were simply interested in making a bid for power whenever the military were ready to leave the political stage were barely tolerated. Among the latter, several of the groupings had been active during the constitutional conference where their members caucused preparatory to establishing formal political organisations.

As of May 1996, over seventy groupings comprising the supporters and opponents of the Abacha junta were in existence in the country. Those opposed to the regime operated despite the fact that the regime described them as illegal and arrested many of their front-line members, even as others were forced into exile. Prominent among the groupings that were active, whether legally or not, were the National Democratic Coalition (NADECO), *Egbe Afenifere*, later renamed the Peoples Consultative Forum (PCF), the National Unity Club (NUC), the Eastern Mandate Union (EMU), New Dimension, the Middle Belt Forum, Imeri Unity Group (IUG), Peoples Democratic Movement (PDM), All Nigeria Congress (ANC) and the Social Democratic Union (SDU). As we noted earlier, these associations fell into different categories; in Table 2, we present a categorisation of 25 out of the over 70 associations focusing on their regional base, their ideological outlook, their attitude the June 12 question, and, where appropriate, the religious sentiments that some of them tried to appeal to. In general, the ideologically conservative, anti-June 12 groups constituted the bulwark of support for the military government while the pro-June 12, self-professed progressives tended to be anti-military and at the receiving end of state intolerance.

Foremost among the political associations that were opposed to military rule in general and General Abacha's continued stay in power in particular were NADECO, associations of exiled activists, including Soyinka's NALICON and Edward Okparaji's National Democratic Awareness Committee (NDAC), and the human rights/civil liberties groups such as the CD, CLO, CDHR and the CRP. In response to intensifying local and international criticism of its records on human rights and civil liberties, criticism which reached a new crescendo following the murder of Ken Saro-Wiwa and eight other Ogoni activists on 10 November, 1995, the regime established a National Commission on Human Rights (NCHR) (*This Day*, 11 August, 1995:1). The establishment of the NCHR did not, however, stop the regime from its campaign of repression against the opposition; nor did it imply the generalised review of the cases of all persons who were being held in detention without trial or who had been jailed on a variety of charges which many Nigerians saw as pretexts for eliminating some of the most fearless critics of General Abacha. Thus, even as it responded to local and international opposition by setting up the NCHR, opposition elements continued to face arbitrary arrest and detention. The rampant abuse of procedure and due process remained rife, with the regime using "security" as an omnibus framework for justifying the denial of the basic rights of its opponents.

Table 2. *Political Associations Active in Nigeria as of 1995*

Association	Support base/ composition	Ideological outlook	Objective
ANC	Broad-based	Conservative	Anti-June 12
APP	South-West	Progressive	Pro-June 12
EMU	East	"	"
EPM	Mid-West	"	"
ESF	East	"	"
IUG	South-West	"	"
LA	North	Conservative	Anti-June 12
MBF	Middle-Belt	Progressive	Pro-June 12
MPF	Mid-West	"	"
NADECO	Broad-based	"	"
NDYM	Pro-Government	Conservative	Anti-June 12
ND	South-West	Progressive	Pro-June 12
NGDA	Pro-Government	Conservative	Anti-June 12
NF	North	"	"
NCEF	North	Religious	Pro-June 12
NPDA	Minorities	Progressive	"
NPWA	Minorities	"	"
NUC	Broad-based	"	Anti-June 12
OGANIRU	East	"	Pro-June 12
PAEO	Pro-Government	Conservative	Anti-June 12
PCF	South-West	Progressive	Pro-June 12
PPA	Middle-Belt	"	"
PDA	North	Conservative	Anti-June 12
SDH	South	Progressive	Pro-June 12
SGN	North	Conservative	Anti-June 12

* See Glossary on page 263 for the full meanings of the abbreviations.

Among the many victims of the arbitrariness of the government were Anthony Enahoro, elder statesman and NADECO leader, who was detained for 121 days, released on 16 December, 1994, and, soon after, forced into exile after repeated threats to his life; Generals Olusegun Obasanjo, former head of state, and Shehu Yaradua, his deputy, and, respectively, leaders of the National Unity Council of Nigeria (NUON) and the Peoples Democratic Movement (PDM), for alleged involvement in a plot to overthrow the Abacha government, Frank Kokori and Wariebi Agamene, leaders of Nigerian oil workers; pro-democracy activists such as Sylvester Odion-Akhaine, Shehu Sanni, and Chima Ubani, minority rights activists, including Ken Saro-Wiwa who was later executed after a most farcical trial before a kangaroo tribunal made up of the government's henchmen; and journalists Chris Anyanwu and Ben Charles Obi, among others (*Newswatch*, 3 July, 1995:10). In addition many newspapers and magazines such as those in the *Punch*, *Guardian* and *Concord*; groups were proscribed. Abiola, winner of the 12 June 1993 elections remained in detention. It was clear then that the government had become more repressive as public criticisms oftentimes mistaken for, and taken as opposition, mounted. The government saw its relation with the opposition as a zero-sum game in which it felt justified in crushing its critics as an insurance for its own survival.

NADECO, the leading opposition group in the country was started as a loose coalition of distinct organisations that had their own autonomous structures and leadership. These organisations include *Egbe Afenifere* or the PCF, the Movement for National Reformation (MNR), CD, fragments of the Middle-Belt Forum, the EMU and some Eastern based groups (*Champion*, 5 February, 1995:11). The organisation was the brainchild of 49 prominent Nigerians, among them former military and civilian governors, leading politicians, business executives, intellectuals and human rights activists. Prominent among them were Anthony Enahoro, Michael Ajasin, Bolaji Akinyemi, Bola Tinubu, Odigie Oyegun, Christian Onoh, Chukwuemeka Ezeife, Arthur Nwankwo, Abraham Adesanya, Bola Ige, Cornelius Adebayo, and Ndubuisi Kanu, a retired admiral. Most of them were members of the proscribed Council for Unity and Understanding (CUU) founded in 1990 as popular unease grew about Babangida's transition programme. As repression against the organisation mounted, several of its key leaders were forced into exile where they constituted the NADECO Abroad that was in the forefront of the international campaign against the Abacha regime. NADECO Abroad came to be led by Anthony Enahoro while those who remained in the country were led by Michael Ajasin.

In articulating its opposition to the Abacha junta, NADECO built its campaigning strategy on efforts at ensuring that the regime was denied local acceptance and international legitimacy. Central to this was its insistence that the resolution of the crisis created by the annulment of the 12 June, 1993 crisis must be the starting point for efforts at restoring political normalcy to

Nigeria. For the leaders of NADECO, the first requirement in this regard was the immediate and unconditional release from detention of Moshood Abiola, the vacation of office by Abacha and his military colleagues, and the installation of Abiola at the head of a government of national unity which would be charged with supervising a fresh transition programme. As part of this process, NADECO also insisted that the military junta should release all political detainees, de-proscribe all media houses that had been shut down, desist from using state security agents from harassing the citizenry, including opponents of the government, and institute an open probe of the decision to annul the 1993 elections (*Newswatch*, 15 May, 1995:11). NADECO also supported the call for the convening of a Sovereign National Conference (SNC) and, as part of this, campaigned, with some success, for the boycott of the elections for delegates to the constitutional conference that was convened by the regime.

In anticipation of the complete lifting of the ban on party formation and political activities, many of the political associations that were active in the country, including some that were in opposition to the military, began to enter into discussions with a view to forming alliances and merging. For instance, over twelve discussion sessions were held as of the end of September 1995 between *Afenifere* and the NUC on a possible merger (*Guardian*, 1 October, 1995). Similar discussions were held between NUON and EMU with a view to promoting southern solidarity and unity in the run up to the Fourth Republic, the expectation being such an outcome would considerably strengthen the southern voice in the national political process. Talks were also held between the PCF and the ANC, PDM and New Dimension, as well as between the "progressives" (SDU, UDU, NUC) and the National Awoist Movement (NAM). Of all these groupings, however, it was principally NADECO, the NUC, ANC, PCF and to a lesser extent EMU, PDM, the Middle-Belt Forum, the PPA and the NPDA that seemed to have any serious potential or political weight. In any case, for those of them that expected to participate in the transitional process according to the rules set by the Abacha junta, it was clear as of the time this chapter was being written that many would not stand a good chance of being registered by the government, for even a hint of a desire for an independent voice in the political system was routinely treated with suspicion by the regime.

We noted earlier that apart from a section of political society, opposition to the Abacha regime was also rife among a variety of organisations active in civil society. Interestingly, religious associations such as the Christian Association of Nigeria (CAN), the Catholic Bishops' Conference of Nigeria (CBCN) and the Council of Ulema added their voices to the criticisms of the extreme high-handedness of the Abacha junta; they too came to be seen by the regime as part of the broad opposition coalition. At the international level, criticism of the government was co-ordinated by NADECO Abroad, NALICON, and an assortment of groups formed by Nigerians resident in

Europe and North America. Non-Nigerian organisations like Trans Africa (Nyiam, 1994), Transparency International, the Commonwealth and the European Union added to the discomfort of the military junta through their campaigns against its human rights and governance record. Several of these organisations were to actively campaign for the imposition of sanctions on the government in a bid to pressure it to release political detainees, be more respectful of the rights of Nigerians, and turn the administration of the country over to elected politicians. Although the regime pointedly refused to bow to the demands of the opposition, it also did not find the imposition of its will free-sailing. This is why much of the period since General Abacha seized power has been marked by sustained tension and unease in the country. The question which many increasingly asked was whether the transition programme which the government introduced would, on its own, be sufficient to bring the country out of the prolonged stalemate which it was faced with.

THE OPPOSITION AND THE TRANSITION TO THE FOURTH REPUBLIC

The period after the submission of the draft constitution witnessed leading members of the Abacha regime congratulating themselves on successfully "defeating" the 12 June movement and consigning it to the dustbin of history. They also pointed to the production of the document as evidence of the complete "marginalisation" and "irrelevance" of the opposition led by NADECO. But beyond the confines of the government and its propaganda machinery, many observers were less certain about the "death" of the 12 June movement and/or the "marginalisation" of the opposition for all the intense repression visited on those who were agitating against the military. It was clear that the intensifying economic and social crises in the country together with the environment of political uncertainty, institutional decay, and systematic terror continued to provide useful ammunition for the opposition. Moreover, the handling of such touchy issues as the rotational presidency, revenue allocation, the minorities question, especially in the oil delta, and the federal character principle were widely seen as acid tests which, if the military junta failed to pass them, could easily bolster opposition to the government.

The regime itself seemed to understand the fact that the volatile situation in the country was a potential source of ammunition to the opposition when it announced that it had, with slight amendments, decided to uphold some of the key recommendations of the constitutional conference. Thus, the principle of rotational presidency was approved but on the understanding that it would be for an experimental period of 30 years. In addition, instead of political power rotating just between the north and south as recommended by the constitutional conference, the military government decided that it should rotate between six distinct political zones in the country, namely,

North East, North West, Middle-Belt, South-West, East Central and the Southern Minorities. The rotational arrangement was to be applicable also to the posts of Vice President, Prime Minister, Deputy Prime Minister, Senate President and Speaker of the House of Representatives, in addition to that of the President. On the agitations of the minority nationalities for a redress in the revenue allocation formula, a 13 per cent derivation principle for natural resources was accepted by the government, a significant increase over the previous figure of 5 per cent. The government also accepted that more powers should be devolved to the states and local governments from the federal centre, especially in respect of health, education, agriculture, transportation and housing. In addition to the rotational power structure, the government also endorsed the multiparty system for Nigeria's next democracy. In this wise, a transition implementation committee was set up and a new national electoral commission, known as the National Electoral Commission of Nigeria (NECON), created. Abacha also announced that the transition period would last a total of 36 months, terminating October 1, 1998.

This latter decision was in defiance of the demands of the opposition and the international community, as represented by the Commonwealth, for example, that the military should speedily disengage from government. This fact, together with the continued detention of Abiola, the symbol of the democratic aspirations of Nigerians, the jailing of Obasanjo, Yaradua, Beko Ransome-Kuti, and scores of other people provided the opposition with strong grounds for continuing its attacks on the regime. As part of this, pirate radio broadcasts within the country on the so-called freedom frequency that operated, sporadically, on the FM band were commenced as were more regular broadcasts from abroad by Radio Democrat International, later renamed Radio Kiudirat in memory of Kudirat Abiola, the senior wife of the detained Moshood Abiola, who was brutally murdered by armed assailants in Lagos on account of her relentless campaign for the release of her husband and the recognition of his popular mandate. The broadcasts were part of an effort by the opposition to break the monopoly over the air waves of the government and pro-government private broadcasters who had been licensed by the junta. Furthermore, the opposition abroad made threats about constituting a government in exile with Abiola as its symbolic head. Mysterious bomb explosions also occurred in the country, especially in Lagos and environs, and targeted specifically at the military. Predictably, the government blamed NADECO for the explosions, proceeded to arrest several of its leaders that were still in the country while declaring those who were abroad wanted together with the Nobel laureate and leader of NALICON, Wole Soyinka (*The News*, 1995:17; *Daily Times*, 5 July, 1995:1).

CONCLUDING REMARKS

The opposition to military rule, though weakened by sustained repression, unleashed on an unprecedented scale with venom and determination, has courageously engaged the military rulers in a running battle for democracy. The press, human rights groups, political groupings and courageous individuals have, through their individual and collective actions, tried to convey the message to the government that military rule is an aberration which is not acceptable to the generality of Nigerians, not least those who voted in the 12 June 1993 elections that were so cynically and unilaterally annulled by the Babangida junta in which General Abacha was a frontline player. Although the opposition to the regime was not successful in bringing the government to heel or securing the implementation of Abiola's mandate, it was at least able to ensure that General Abacha did not have an easy ride. Indeed, the international reprimand and isolation which the regime suffered, together with the severe denting of its legitimacy and credentials, were concrete results of the tenacity of the opposition in the face of the odds against it. Apart from the reign of terror which opponents of the regime suffered, the cause of those sections of political and civil society that challenged military rule was made more difficult by the many civilian politicians who, in return for state patronage, were willing to collaborate with the ruling junta.

The rampant opportunism displayed by many civilian politicians was facilitated by the environment of sharp economic and social decline in the country as well as the permeation of society of the culture of bribery and "settlement", targeted at actual and potential critics, that Babangida elevated into a directive principle of Nigerian state policy. The decay of institutions that has been a less remarked component of the Nigerian crisis also did not make the task of opposition easier. Still, so potent is the experience of 12 June, 1993 that it is inconceivable that the country could ever go very far politically without seriously revisiting the circumstances that led to the annulment of the free choice exercised by Nigerians. The entire Abacha transition has been built on a pretence that June 12 counts for nothing; the continuing crises of the Nigerian state, economy, and society make it clear that the ghost of that event will haunt the country for a long time to come until it is squarely addressed. A key plank of the strategy of the opposition is to keep this issue alive even as Nigeria marches, unsteadily, uncertainly towards the Fourth Republic which the military have promised to inaugurate in October 1998. As this chapter was being written, one key concern in the country centred on whether or not that march itself would be derailed by what increasingly looked like a determined but undeclared desire by General Abacha to succeed himself.

GLOSSARY OF ABBREVIATIONS IN TABLE 2

ANC	All Nigeria Congress
APP	Association of Patriotic Professionals
EMU	Eastern Mandate Union
EPM	Edo People's Movement
ESF	Eastern Solidarity Front
IUG	Imeri Unity Group
LA	Liberal Alliance
MBF	Middle-Belt Forum
MPF	Mid-West Progressive Forum
NADECO	National Democratic Alliance
NDYM	Nigerian Democratic Youth Movement
ND	New Dimension
NGDA	New Generation Democratic Alliance
NF	Northern Front
NCEF	Northern Christian Elders Forum
NPDA	National Patriotic Democratic Association or the 4th Force
NPWA	Nigerian Peoples Welfare Association
NUC	National Unity Council
PAEO	Pan-African Elite Organisation
PCF	Peoples Consultative Forum (Afenifere)
PPA	Patriotic Peoples Association
PDA	Peoples Democratic Alliance
SGN	Solidarity Group of Nigeria

BIBLIOGRAPHY

Barker, Rodney (ed.), 1971, *Studies in Opposition*. Macmillan: St. Martin's Press.

Dahl, Robert, 1966, "Conflict and Opposition", in R. Dahl (ed.),*Political Oppositions in Western Democracies*. New Haven: Yale University Press.

Herz, F. Martin (ed.), 1995, *Contacts with the Opposition*. Georgetown University, Institute for the Study of Diplomacy.

Ibrahim , Jibrin, 1995, "Democratic Transition in Africa: The Challenge of a New Agenda—Concluding Remarks", in Eshetu Chole and Jibrin Ibrahim (eds.), *Democratisation Processes in Africa*. Dakar: CODESRIA.

Ionescu, Ghita and Isabel de Madariaga, 1968, *Oppositions: Past and Present of a Political Institution*. London: C.A. Watts and Co. Ltd.

Ihonvbere, J. and E. Ekekwe, 1988, "The Irrelevant State: Structural Adjustment and the Subversion of Democratic Possibilities in the Third Republic", in S.G. Tyoden (ed.), *Democratic Mobilisation in Nigeria: Problems and Prospects*. Proceedings of the 15th Annual Conference of the Nigerian Political Science Association (NPSA).

Keesings Record of World Events, 1993, "Nigerian-Military Takeover". Vol. 39, No.11.

Mustapha A. R., 1968, "The National Question and Radical Politics in Nigeria", *Review of African Economy*, No. 37, December.

Mustapha A. R., 1992, "Nigeria: The Challenge of Nationhood", *Nigerian Forum*. September/December.

Nnoli, Okwudiba, 1980, *Ethnic Politics in Nigeria*. Enugu: Fourth Dimension Publishers.

Nwolise, O.B.C., 1990, "The Military as an Obstacle to Democracy in Nigeria", in S.G. Tyoden (ed.), *Constitutionalism and National Development in Nigeria*. Proceedings of the 17th Annual Conference of the NPSA, Jos.

Nyiam, Tony, 1994, "Towards Democratic Management of Nigeria's National Security: To Regain Power from the Cabal", paper delivered during the NAS Conference on the Prevailing Political Crisis in Nigeria at the Commonwealth Institute, London, October.

Ojiako, James, 1981, *Nigeria: Yesterday, Today, And...?*. Onitsha: Africana Educational Publishers (Nig.) Ltd.

Olagunju, Tunji et al., 1993, *Transition to Democracy in Nigeria (1985–1993)*. Ibadan: Safari Books Ltd.

Olukoshi, Adebayo and Osita Agbu, 1995, "The Deepening Crisis of Nigerian Federalism and the Future of the Nation-State", in Olukoshi, A and L. Laakso, (eds.), 1996, *Challenges to the Nation-State in Africa*. Uppsala: Nordiska Afrikainstitutet in cooperation with the Institute of Development Studies, University of Helsinki.

Onoge O. (ed.), 1993 *Nigeria: The Way Forward*. Ibadan: Spectrum.

Otite, Onigu, 1990, *Ethnic Pluralism and Ethnicity in Nigeria*. Ibadan: Spectrum Books.

Newspapers and periodicals

Vanguard
Times
Newswatch
Daily Times
This Day
Champion
The News

NOTES ON CONTRIBUTORS

Osita Agbu—Dr Agbu is a research fellow at the Nigerian Institute of International Affairs, Lagos, Nigeria.

Aminata Diaw—Dr Diaw is a lecturer in Philosophy at the Cheikh Anta Diop University, Dakar, Senegal.

Mamadou Diouf—Dr Diouf is the programme officer responsible for the research section of the Council for the Development of Social Science Research in Africa (CODESRIA), Dakar, Senegal.

Solveig Hauser—Ms Hauser is the assistant on the Nordic Africa Institute's Programme on *The Political and Social Context of Structural Adjustment in Sub-Saharan Africa.*

Jibrin Ibrahim—Until recently, Dr Ibrahim was a reader in Political Science at Ahmadu Bello University, Zaria; he is currently a research fellow at the Centre for Research and Documentation in Kano.

Karuti Kanyinga—Mr Kanyinga is a research fellow at the Institute for Development Studies, University of Nairobi. He is currently based in Denmark where he is completing his doctoral studies at Roskilde University.

Michael Neocosmos—Dr Neocosmos is currently an associate professor in the Department of Sociology, University of Botswana, Gaborone.

Tandeka Nkiwane—Ms Nkiwane is a lecturer in the Department of Political and Administrative Studies, University of Zimbabwe. She is currently undertaking her doctoral studies at the School of Advanced International Studies, Johns Hopkins University.

Adebayo Olukoshi—Dr Olukoshi is a senior researcher and the co-ordinator of the Nordic Africa Institute's research programme on *The Political and Social Context of Structural Adjustment in Sub-Saharan Africa.*

Abdoulaye Niandou Souley—Dr Niandou Souley is a lecturer in the Faculty of Economics and Law at the University of Niamey, Niger.

John Ssenkumba—Mr Ssenkumba is a research fellow at the Centre for Basic Research in Kampala, Uganda.

Kajsa Övergaard—Ms Övergaard is currently the assistant to the director of the Nordic Africa Institute. She was previously the assistant to the programme on *The Political and Social Context of Structural Adjustment in Sub-Saharan Africa.*

Appendix 1

DIRECTORY OF PARTIES AND ELECTIONS IN CONTEMPORARY AFRICA

Compiled by Solveig Hauser

Introductiory note on sources

In compiling this directory, several sources of information were consulted. Among them are: Michael Bratton and Nicholas Van de Walle, et al., 1996, *Political Regimes and Regime Transitions in Africa: A Comparative Handbook*, MSU Working Paper No. 14, Department of Political Science, Michigan State University; Willie Breytenbach, 1996, *Democratisation in Sub-Saharan Africa: Transitions, Elections and Prospects for Consolidation*, Pretoria: Africa Institute of South Africa, Working Paper No. 58; John Wiseman, 1996, *The New Struggle for Democracy in Africa*, Aldershot: Avebury; Africa Research Bulletin, Political, Social and Cultural Studies Series, 1989-1997, Oxford: Blackwell Publishers Limited; Africa Today, London: Africa Books Limited, 1996; Wilfred Derksen, 1997, *Presidential and Parliamentary Elections around the World* (Political websites: http://www.geocities.com/~derksen; and The Economist Intelligence Unit, Country Reports and Country Profiles, 1989-1997. Data contained in some of these sources were used, in some cases, to compile this directory. In other cases, the sources were simply consulted for the purpose of cross-checking information already collected. Needless to say, the information offered by the different sources was often conflictung and attempting to overcome this problem has not been easy. We have, nevertheless, strived to ensure that the information contained in this directory is as accurate as possible by, in several cases, contacting researchers in the countries where some of the greatest inconsistencies in the figures reported elsewhere were noticed. We hope readers will find the directory useful.

Country and Date of Independence	Date of Election	Type of Election	Presidential Candidates/Main Parties/Party Leaders and Election Outcome in terms of percentage share of votes received and number of legislative seats won	Comments
Angola Nov. 11, 1975	Sept.1992	Presidential	José Eduardo dos Santos (MPLA-PT) (Movimento Popular de Libertação de Angola-Partido de Trabalho/Popular Movement for the Liberation of Angola-Labour Party) 49.67% Jonas Savimbi (UNITA) (Unio Nacional para a Independência Total de Angola/National Union for the Total Independence of Angola) 40.1% Antonio Alberto Neto (Partido Democrático Angola / Democratic Party of Angola) 2.13% Holden Roberto (FNLA) (Frente Nacional para a Libertação de Angola/National Front for the Liberation of Angola) 2.1% Others 6%	The elections were generally considered by local and international observers to have been relatively free and fair. Unita refused to accept the UN-certified results and went back to war.
	Sept. 1992	Legislative	MPLA (José Eduardo dos Santos) 129/220 UNITA (Jonas Savimbi) 70 Others 21	
Benin Aug. 1, 1960	June 1989	Legislative	PRPB (Parti de la révolution populaire du Bénin/Benin People's Revolutionary Party) (Ahmed Mathieu Kérékou) 206/206	Benin was still under one-party rule when these elections were held.

| Feb. 1991 | Legislative | Alliance 1:
UTR (Union pour le triomphe du renouveau démocratique/Union for the Victory of Democratic Renewal) 12/64 (Consists of three political parties: (UDFP) Union démocratique des forces du progrès/Democratic Union of Progressive Forces (Analin Timothée); (MDPS) Mouvement pour la démocratie et les progrès social/Movement for Democracy and Social Progress (Marcelin Degbé); and (ULD) Union pour la liberté et le développement/Union for Liberty and Development (Francisco Marius)
All of the parties in this alliance declared their support for Soglo.

Alliance 2:
PNDD (Parti national pour la démocratie et le développement/National Party for Democracy and Development) (Hubert Maga); PRD (Parti du renouveau démocratique/Party for Democratic Renewal) (Adrien Houngbédji) 9

Alliance 3:
PSD (Parti pour la social démocratie) (Bruno Amoussou); UNSP (Union nationale pour la solidarité et le progrès) (Eustache Sarré) 8

Other
RND (Rassemblement National pour la démocratie/National rally for democracy) (Joseph Kéké) 7
NCC (Notre cause commune/Our Common Cause) (Albert Tévoedjré) 7
MNDD-MSUP-UDRN (Mouvement nationale pour la démocratie et le développement (Bertin Borna) 6
UDS (Union pour la démocratie et le solidarité nationale/Union for Democracy and National Solidarity) (Amadou N'Diaye Mama) 5
RDL-Vivoten (Rassemblement des démocrates liberaux pour la reconstruction nationale-Vivoten/Rally of Liberal Democrats for National Reconstruction) (Adjovi Severin) 4
ASD-BSD (Alliance pour la social-démocratie/Alliance for Social Democracy) (Robert Dossou) 3
ADP-UDRS (Alliance pour la démocratie et le progrès/Alliance for Democracy and Progress) (Adekpedjou S Akindes) 2
UNDP (Union nationale pour la démocratie et le progrès/National Union for Democracy and Progress) (Emile Derlin Zinsou) 1 | In 1992, a partial army mutiny collapsed when it turned out that the bulk of army remained loyal to the new government. |

March 1991	Presidential	Nicéphore Soglo (UTR) 36.16% Ahmed Mathieu Kérékou (PRPB) 27.38% Albert Tévoédjré (NCC) 14.24% Second round results: Nicéphore Soglo 67.6% Ahmed Mathieu Kérékou 32.2%	A peaceful handover of power from Kérékou to Soglo was effected after the latter won the second round of voting. Kérékou had ruled Benin for a long time as the "marxist"leader of the military-backed PRPB.
March /May 1995	Legislative	PRB (Parti de la renaissance du Bénin/Party for the Rebirth of Benin) (Nicéphore Soglo) 21/83 PRD (Parti du renouveau démocratique/Democratic Renewal Party) (Adrien Houngbedji) 18 FARD (Front d'action pour le rénouveau et le développement/Action Front for Renewal and Development) (Salif Aka) 14 PSD (Bruno Amoussou) 8 IPD (Impulsion au progrès et la démocratie/Impulse for Progress and Democracy) 2 NCC (Albert Tevoedjre) 4 RDL (Rassemblement des démocrates libéraux/Rally of Liberal Democrats) (Sévérin Adjovi) 4 NG (Nouvelle génération/New Generation) 1 AC (Alliance caméléon/Chameleon Alliance) 1 ADP (Adekpedjou S Akindes) 3 ASD (Robert Dossou) 1 MNDD (Mouvement nationale pour la démocratie et le développement/National Movement for Democray and Development) (Bertin Borna) 1 UDSN (Union pour la démocratie et la solidarité nationale/ Union for Democracy and National Solidarity) 1 PCB (Parti communiste du Bénin/Communist Party of Benin) (Magloire Yansunnu) 1 RAP (Rassemblement africain pour le progrès et la solidarité/African Rally for Progress and Solidarity) (Hubert Maga) 1 RDP (Rassemblement pour la démocratie et le progrès/Rally for Democracy and Progress) 1 UNDP (Emile Derlin Zinou) 1	

		Results	Notes
	March 1996	Presidential	Nicéphore Soglo (PRB) 37.1% Mathieu Kérékou (UFP) (Union des forces du progrès/Union of Progressive Forces) 34.1% Adrien Houngbedji (PRD) 18.7% Bruno Amoussou (PSD) 7.4% Pascal Fantodji 1.0% Lionel Agbo 0.9% Lenadre Djagoue 0.8% Second round results: Mathieu Kérékou 52.5% Nicephore Soglo 47.5%	This marked the first time, since the spread of multipartyism in Africa, that a former one-party president who was defeated in a free election was later returned to power in another free election. Kérékou had a lead of slightly less than 100,000 votes over Soglo. For a while, Soglo refused to recognize his defeat but eventually he conceded.
Botswana Sept. 30, 1966	Oct. 1989	Legislative	BDP (Botswana Democratic Party) (Ketumile Masire) 31/34 (plus four nominated seats) BNF (Botswana National Front) (Kenneth Koma) 3 BPP (Botswana People's Party) (Knight Maripe) 5% of the votes cast Others 5% of the votes cast	Botswana has always been a formal multi-party liberal-democracy governed by the BDP since its independence. The president is elected for a five year term by the parliament.
	Oct.1994	Legislative	BDP (Ketumile Masire) 27/40 (plus four nominated seats) BNF (Kenneth Koma) 13 BPP (Knight Maripe) 5% Others 4%	
Burkina Faso Aug. 5, 1960	Dec. 1991	Presidential	Blaise Compaoré 86.9% (ODP-MT) (Organisation pour la démocratie populaire-Mouvement du travail/Organization for People's Democracy-Labour Movement)	21.65% of the registered voters voted for Compaoré, leader of the military regime that had been in power since 1987 when Thomas Sankara was overthrown and assassinated. The opposition boycotted the elections and there was a high voter abstention rate.

May 1992	Legislative	ODP-MT (Blaise Compaoré) 78/107 CNPP-PSD (Convention nationale des patriotes progressistes-Parti Social-Democrate/National Convention of Progressive Patriots-Social-Democratic Party) (Pierre Tapsoba) 13 UDV/RDA (Rassemblement démocratique africain/African Democratic Rally) (Gérard Kango Ouedraogo and Joseph Ouedraogo) 5 ADF (Alliance pour la démocratie et la féderation/Alliance for Democracy and the Federation) (Herman Yameogo) 4 PAI (Parti africain pour l'indépendence/African Party for Independence) 2 MDP (Mouvement des démocrates progressistes/Movement of Progressive Democrats) 1 MDS (Mouvement pour la démocratie sociale/Movement for Social Democracy) 1 PSB (Parti socialiste burkinabé/Burkinabe Socialist Party) 1 USD (Union des sociaux-democrats/Union of Social-Democrats) 1 USDI (Union des sociaux-democrats indépendants/Union of Independent Social Democrats) 1	The majority of the seats were won by parties associated with the reconstituted FP (Front Populaire/Popular Front) of Compaoré but other minority parties also made gains.
Burundi July 1, 1962			
June 1993	Presidential	Melchior Ndadaye (FRODEBU) (Front pour la démocratie au Burundi/Front for Democracy in Burundi) 65% Pierre Buyoya (UPRONA) (Union pour le progrès national/Union for National Progress) 33%	Ndadaye became the first Burundian President from the majority Hutu ethnic group. In October 1993, he was assassinated in a failed *coup* attempt by Tutsi soldiers. Cyprien Ntaryamira was installed as the new president. However, in April 1994 he was killed in a plane crash. In July 1996, a *coup d'état* was carried out by Pierre Buyoya.
June 1993	Legislative	FRODEBU (Melchior Ndadaye) 65/81 UPRONA (Pierre Buyoya) 16	

Cameroon Jan. 1, 1960	March 1992 Legislative	RDPC/CPDM (Rassemblement démocratique du peuple camerounais/Cameroon People's Democratic Movement) (Paul Biya) 88/180 UNDP (Union nationale pour la démocratie et le progrès/National Union for Democracy and Progress) (Bello Bouba Maigari) 68 UPC (Unions des populations du Cameroun/Union of Cameroonian Peoples) 18 MDDR (Mouvement pour la défense de la république/Movement for the Defence of the Republic) 6	The 1992 elections were boycotted by some opposition parties. The elections were not generally seen as free and fair.
	Oct. 1992 Presidential	Paul Biya (RDPC/CPDM) 40% John Fru Ndi (FSD) (Front social démocratique/Social Democratic Front) 36% Bello Bouba Maigari (UNDP) 19.2% Adamou Ndam Njoya (UDC) (Union démocratique du Cameroun/ Cameroon Democratic Union) 3.6% Jean-Jacques Ekindi (MP) (Mouvement progressif/Progressive Movement) 0.8% Emah Otu (RFP) (Rassemblement des forces patriotique/Regrouping of Patriotic Forces) 0.4%	Biya was the leader of the previous single-party regime.
	May 1997 Legislative	RDPC/CPDM (Paul Biya) 109/180 FSD (John Fru Ndi) 43 UNDP (Bello Bouba Maigari) 13 UDC (Adamou Ndam Njoya) 5 Others 3 Results cancelled: 7 constituencies	The outcome was contested by the opposition, backed up by the reports of international observers; for these reasons, the results for 7 seats were cancelled by the Supreme Court
Cape Verde July 5, 1975	Jan. 1991 Legislative	MPD (Movimento para Democracia/Movement for Democracy) (António Mascarenhas Monteiro) 56/79 PAICV (Partido Africano da Independencia de Cabo Verde/ African Party for the Independence of Cape Verde) (Aristides Pereira) 23	The opposition movement won the elections and a peaceful transfer of of power was effected. The voting in Cape Verde represented the first democratic multi-party elections held in sub-Saharan Africa by a former single-party regime.
	Feb. 1991 Presidential	António Mascarenhas Monteiro (MPD) 74% Aristides Pereira (PAICV) 26%	Pereira became the first African head of state in recent times to be voted out of office.

	Dec. 1995	Legislative	MPD (António Mascarenhas Monteiro) 50/72 PAICV (Aristides Pereira) 21 PCD (Partido da Convergência Democrática/Democratic Convergence Party) (Eurico Moteiro) 1	
	Feb. 1996	Presidential	António Mascarenhas Monteiro (MPD) 80%	The victorious candidate stood unopposed.
Central African Republic Aug. 13, 1960	Aug./Sept. 1993	Legislative	MLPC (Mouvement pour la libération du peuple centrafricain/Movement for the Liberation of the People of Central Africa) (Ange-Félix Patassé) 34/85 RDC (Rassemblement démocratique centrafricain/Central African Democratic Rally) (André Kolingba) 13 FPP (Front patriotique pour le progrès/Patriotic Front for Progress) 7 PLD (Parti libéral démocratique/Liberal Democratic Party) 7 ADP (Alliance pour la démocratie et le progrès/Alliance for Democracy and Progress) 6 MDD (Mouvement pour la démocratie et le développement/Movement for Democracy and Development) 6 CN (Convention nationale/National Convention) 3 PSD (Parti social démocratique/Social Democratic Party) 3 MESAM (Mouvement de la évolution sociale de Afrique noire/Movement for the Social Evolution of Black Africa) 1 PRCA (Parti républicain centrafricain/Central African Republican Party) 1 FC (Forum civique/Civic Forum) 1 MDREC (Mouvement pour la démocratie, rénaissance et évolution de Centrafrique/Movement for Democracy, Rebirth and Evolution of Central Africa) 1 Non-partisans/Independents 2	Opposition parties won the majority of seats in the parliamentary elections.

	Aug./Sept. 1993	Presidential	Ange-Félix Patassé (MLPC) 37.32% Abel Goumba (CFD) (Conseil des forces démocratiques / Council of Democratic Forces) 21.68% David Dacko (MDD) 20.11% André Kolingba (RDC) 10.10% Enoch Derant Lakoue (PSD) 2.39% Timothée Malendoma (FC) 2.3% François Bozize (RPRC) (Rassemblement populaire pour la réconstruction de la Centrafrique/Popular Rally for the Reconstruction of Central Africa) 1.5% Ruth Rolland (PRCA) 1% Second round results: Ange-Félix Patassé 52.5% Abel Goumba 45.6%	Kolingba was placed fourth in the first round and was, thus, eliminated from the contest. Initial attempts by Kolingba to suppress the results failed. (He had come to power in a military coup in 1981.) (Abel Goumba was a former prime minister from the Bokassa era.)
Chad Aug. 11, 1960	Dec. 1989	Presidential	Hissène Habré 99.4% (PPT) (Parti progressiste tchadien)	

Date	Type	Results	Notes
June/July 1996	Presidential	Idriss Déby 43.8% (MPS) (Mouvement patriotique du salue/ Patriotic Salvation Movement) (but campaigned under the ticket of the Republican Front made up of 12 political parties) Abdelkader Wadal Kamougué (URD) (Union républicaine démocratique/Union for Renewal and Democracy) 12.39 % Saleh Kebzaboh (UNDR) (Union nationale pour la démocratie et renouveau/National Union for Democracy and Renewal) 8.6% Jean Bawoyeu Alingue (UDR) (Union pour la démocratie et la république/Union for Democracy and the Republic) 8.31% Lol Mahamat Choua (RDP) (Rassemblement pour la démocratie et le progès/Rally for Democracy and Progress) 5.93% Adoum Moussa Seif (CNDS) (Convention nationale pour la démocratie et le socialisme/National Convention for Democracy and Socialism) 4.9% Second round results: Idriss Déby 69.09% Abdelkader Wadal Kamougue 30.91%	Déby is the former guerilla leader who seized power in a French-backed coup in 1990.
Jan. 1997	Legislative	MPS (Idriss Déby) 63 /125 URD (Abdelkader Wadal Kamougué) 29 UNDR (Saleh Kebzaboh) 15 UDR (Jean Bawoyeu Alingue) 4 RDP (Lol Mahamat Choua) 3 PLD (Parti libéral-démocrate) (Njoh Litumbe) 3 Other oppositionals 8	
Comoros July 6, 1975 / March 1990	Presidential	Said Mohamed Djohar (Parti Udzima) 55.3% Mohammed Taki (UNDC) (Union nationale pour la démocratie aux Comores/National Union for Democracy on the Comoros) 44.7%	In 1989, Ahmed Abdullah, leader of the single-party regime (Parti Udzima) was assassinated in a mercinary-backed coup. In 1990, the free formation of political parties was allowed.

Nov. 1992	Legislative	Candidates supporting President Djohar (RDR) (Rassemblement pour la démocratie et le renouveau/ National Rally for Democracy and Renewal) won a narrow majority 22/42 Opposition 20 (No official figures were available to us on the distribution of these seats among the parties that participated in the elections.)	Udzima and UNDC, which are both among the largest parties in the country, boycotted the elections and called for the annulment of the results. Several candidates withdrew from the elections as a gesture against the way the elections were being carried out in the capital. Several opposition politicians were sent to jail and a rebellion in the army occured during the election campaign. In 1990 and 1992, there were abortive coup attempts against the government. In 1993, a general strike was called because of delays in the holding legislative elections. A no-confidence vote against the government was passed in 1n May 1993.
Dec. 1993	Legislative	RDR (Mohamed Djohar) 22/42 Mzingara (–) 2 UDD (Union pour la démocratie et le développment/Union for Democracy and Development) (Ibrahim Halidi) 2 Uwezo (Mouzaoir Abdallah) 1 The Opposition Group: UNDC (Mohammed Taki) 4 Others 11	The opposition called for the annulment of the results and boycotted the second round of elections to back up its demands.
March 1996	Presidential	Mohamed Taki Abdoulkarim 21.3% (RND) (Rassemblement national pour la développement/National Rally for Development) Abbas Djoussouff 15.5% (FRN) (Forum pour le redressement national/Forum for National Renewal) Omar Tamou 13% (Parti Udzima) Others 49.8% Second round results: Mohamed Taki Abdoulkarim 64.3 % Abbas Djoussouff 35.7%	

	Dec. 1996	Legislative	RND (Rassemblement national pour la développement/National Rally for Development) (Mohamed Taki Abdoulkarim) 36/42 FNJ (Front national pour la justice/National Front for Justice) 3 Non-partisans 3	The opposition called for a boycott of the elections.
Congo Aug. 15, 1960	Aug. 1990	Presidential and legislative		Concrete information on the results was hard to come by. According to the various sources consulted, the elections were held. In December 1990, the PCT held a Fourth Extraordinary Congress, at which the party abandoned Marxism-Leninism as its ideology and agreed to the introduction of a multi-party system effective from January 1991. President Sassou Nguesso's term was extended.
	Aug. 1992	Presidential	Pascal Lissouba (UPADS) (Union panafricaine pour la démocratie sociale/Pan-African Union for Social Democracy) 35.9% Bernard Kolebas (MCDDI) (Mouvement congolais pour la démocratie et le développement/Congolese Movement for Democracy and Integral Development) 22.9% Denis Sassou-Nguesso (PCT) (Parti congolais du travail/Congolese Labour Party) 16.9% André Milongo (UDR) (Union pour la démocratie et la république/Union for Democracy and the Republic) 10.2% Jean-Pierre Thystere-Tchikaya (RDPS) (Rassemblement pour la démocratie et progrès social/Rally for Democracy and Social Progress) 5.9% Second round results: Pascal Lissouba 61.3% Bernard Kolebas 38.7%	

June 1992	Legislative	UPADS (Pascal Lissouba) 39/125 MCDDI (Bernard Kolebas) 29 PCT (Denis Sassou-Nguesso) 18 RDPS (Jean-Pierre Thystere-Tchikay) 9 RDD (Rassemblement pour la démocratie et le développe- ment/Rally for Democracy and Development) (Saturnin Okabe) 5 Union des démocrates sociales/Union of Social Democrats 3 Union pour le progres social et la démocratie/Union for Social Progress and Democracy 2 Others 11 Independents 6	On November 17, 1992, the president dissolved the National Assembly. His action was prompted by the passing of a no-confidence motion in the government by the parliament on October 31.

	May, June, Oct. 1993	Legislative	Coalition: Presidential Tendency UPADS (Pascal Lissouba) 47/125 RDD (Saturnin Okabe) 6 UFD (Union des forces démocratiques/Union for Congolese Democracy) (David Charles Ganao) 3 PCR (Parti congolais du renouvellement/Congolese Party of Renewal) 2 UDC (Union pour la démocratie congolaise/Union for Congolese Democracy) (Félix Makasso) 1 UDPS (Union pour le développement et progrès social/Union for Development and Social Progress) 1 Other pro-presidentials 1 Coalition: Opposition Front MCDDI (Bernard Kolebas) 28 PCT (Denis Sassou-Nguesso) 15 RDPS (Jean-Pierre Thystere-Tchikay) 10 URD (Union pour le renouveau démocratique/Union for Democratic Renewal) 2 Non-partisan 1 Groups not in either of the coalitions: UDR (André Milongo) 3 UPRN (Union patriotique pour le reconstruction national/Patriotic Union for National Reconstruction) 1 Other non-partisan 1	Armed clashes occurred between the army and the PCT's supporters following objections raised by the opposition to the electoral procedures adopted by the government.
Congo, Democratic Republic of (Former Zaire) June 30, 1960				The last general election in Zaire was held in September 1987. The country was ruled by Mobuto Seso Seko and MPR (Mouvement populaire de la révolution) until Mobuto was forced to stand down and flee into exile following the rebellion led by Laurent-Desiré Kabila (AFDL-Alliance des forces démocratiques pour la libération du Congo) in 1997.

Côte d'Ivoire Aug.7, 1960	Oct.1990	Presidential	Felix Houphouet-Boigny (PDCI) (Parti démocratique de la Côte d'Ivoire/Democratic Party of Côte d'Ivoire) 81.68% Laurent Gbagbo (FPI) (Front populaire ivorienne/Ivorian People's Front) 18.32%	The opposition claimed that electoral malpractice was widespread , but many observers considered the elections to have been relatively fair. In December 1993, the death of Houphouet-Boigny occurred. Henri Konana Bédié took over the reins of power.
	Nov. 1990	Legislative	PDCI (Henri Konana Bédié) 153/175 Independents 2 FPI (Laurent Gbagbo) 9 PIT (Parti ivorien des travailleurs/Ivorian Workers' Party) (Francis Wodié) 1 Ten deputies from other parties	Voter turn out stood at only 30 %
	Oct./Dec. 1995	Presidential	Henri Konana Bédié (PDCI) 95.2% Francis Wodié (PIT) 3.8%	The main opposition parties (FPI/RDR) decided to boycott the presidential elections because of the exclusion of Alassane Ouattara, the former prime minister, from the race. He was the only candidate who represented a real alternative and who, if he had been allowed to run, could have posed a serious threat to Bédié. In the event, Francis Wodié was the only opponent who remained in the race.
	Oct./Dec. 1995	Legislative	PDCI (Henri Konana Bédié) 148/175 RDR (Rassemblement des républicains/Rally of the Republicans) (Djény Kobina) 14 FPI (Laurent Gbagbo) 12 Vacant 1	
Djibouti June 27, 1977	Dec. 1992	Legislative	RPP (Rassemblement populaire pour le progrès/Popular Rally for Progress) (Hassan Gouled Aptidon) 65/65 PRD (Parti pour le renouveau démocratique/Democratic Renewal Party) (Mohamed Djame Elabe) 28%	The election was boycotted by most parties. RPP, the ruling party, was declared the winner of all the legislative seats.

	May 1993	Presidential	Hassan Gouled Aptidon (RPP) 60.8% Mohamed Djame Elabe (PRD) 22.0% Aden Robleh Awaleh (PND) (Parti national démocratique/ National Democratic Party) 12.2% Mohammed Moussa Ali (MUD) (Mouvement pour l'unité et la démocratie/Movement for Unity and Democracy) 3.0% Ahmad Ibrahim Abdi 2	The opposition accused the government of electoral fraud in both elections: armed opposition to government continues.
Equatorial Guinea Oct.12, 1968	Nov. 1993	Legislative	PDGE (Partido Democratico Guinea Ecuatorial/Democratic Party of Equatorial Guinea) (Teodoro Obiang Nguema) 68/80 CSDP (Convencón Social Democratica y Popular/Social Democratic and Popular Convention) 6 UDS (Unión Democratico y Social/Democratic and Social Union) 5 CLD (Convención Liberal Democrática/Liberal Democratic Convention) 1	The election was boycotted by most of the opposition.
	Feb. 1996	Presidential	Teodoro Obiang Nguema (PDGE) 97.85% Buenaventura Mezi M'asumu (PCSD) (Partido de la Convergencia Social Démocrata/Social Democratic Coalition) Secundino Oyono Angguong Adong (Social Democratic and Popular Convergence)	All opposition candidates, except one, boycotted the elections.
Eritrea May 24, 1993				No elections have been held since independence.

Ethiopia	June 1992	Regional		The EPRDF was one of the main opponents of Mengistu Haile Mariam's regime (the WPE/Worker's Party of Ethiopia). The elections were boycotted by some non-EPRDF movements (e.g. the OLF) which claimed that the exercise was marred by fraud. The elections were organized on the basis of *kebele,* the local government unit, and in the cities the urban districts called *woreda.* Local representatives were elected directly, and the new local councillors then elected the regional councillors.
	May, June 1995	Legislative	EPRDF (Ethiopian People's Revolutionary Democratic Front) (Meles Zenawi) 483/547 (Members of EPRDF: TPLF (Tigray People's Liberation Front); OPDO (Oromo Democratic People's Organization); ANDM (Amahar National Democratic Movement); DFSP (Democratic Front of Southern Peoples) Regional political groupings 46 Non-partisans 8 Unconfirmed 10	The elections were boycotted by most opposition groups

| Gabon Aug. 17, 1960 | Sept./Nov. 1990 | Legislative | PDG (Parti democratique gabonais/Gabonese Democratic Party) (Omar Bongo) 63/120
Morena-Bûcherons (Paul M'ba Abessolé) 20
PGP (Parti gabonais de progrès/Gabonese Progress Party) (Pierre Louise Agondjo-Okawé) 18
Morena-Orginel (Nöel Ngwa-Nguena) 7
APSG (Association pour le socialisme au Gabon/Associ-ation for Socialism in Gabon) 6
USG (Union socialiste gabonaise/Gabonese Socialist Union) 4
CRP (Cercle pour le renouveau et progrès/Circle for National Renewal and Progress) 1
UDD (Union pour la démocratie et le développement/Union for Democracy and Development) 1 | Irregularities were reported in the polling. The election of five deputies during the general elections that were held in September 1990 was declared invalid because the rules and conditions laid down in the electoral code were violated. |
| | March 1991 | Legislative | PDG (Omar Bongo) 66/120
PGP (Pierre Louise Agondjo-Okawé) 19
RNB (Rassemblement national des bûcherons) (Paul M'ba Abessolé) 17
Morena (Mouvement de redressement national/Movement for National Renewal) (Nöel Ngwa-Nguena) 7
APSG 6
USG 3
CRP 1
UDD 1 | Partial elections. |

	Dec. 1993	Presidential	Omar Bongo (PDG) 51.2% Paul M'ba Abessolé (RNB) 26.5% Pierre Louise Agondjo-Okawé (PGP) 4.8% Pierre Clavier Maganga-Moussavou (PSD) (Parti social-démocrate/Social-Democratic Party) 3.6% Jules Bourdès-Ogouliguerdé 3.4% Alexandre Sambat 2.6% Lidjob Divungi di Dingo 2.2% Léon Mboyebi (PSG) (Parti socialiste gabonais/Gabonese Socialist Party) 1.8% Jean-Pierre Lepandou (PGCI) (Parti gabonais du centre indépendant/Gabonese Party of the Independent Centre) 1.4%	
	Dec. 1996–Jan. 1997	Legislative	PDG (Omar Bongo) 76/120 CLR (Cercle des libéraux réformateurs/Convention of Liberal Reformers) (Jean-Boniface Assélé) 3 USG (Union pour le socialisme au Gabon/Union for Socialism in Gabon) 2 Opposition alliance: HCR (Haute conseil de la resistance/High Council of the Resistance) 20 seats: RNB (Paul M'ba Abessolé) 7 PGP (Pierre Louise Agondjo-Okawé) 6 Independents 7	111 members elected were in single-seat constituencies while the remaining 9 members were nominated by the president (another 12 seats were awarded to the PDG after a series of re-runs). (Final results announced on January 28, 1997 gave the PDG victory in 100 out of the 120 legislative seats available.)
Gambia Feb. 18, 1965	Sept. 1996	Presidential	Yahaya Jammeh (APRC) (Alliance for Patriotic Reorientation and Construction) 55.8% Ousanu Darbo (UDP) (United Democratic Party) 35.3% Hamat Bah NRP (National Reconciliation Party) 5.5% Sidia Jatta (PDOIS) (Popular Democratic Organisation for Independence and Socialism) 2.9%	
	Jan. 1997	Legislative	APRC 33/45 (Yahaya Jammeh) (plus four deputies appointed by the President) Opposition: UDP (Ousanu Darbo) 7 NRP (Hamat Bah) 2 PDOIS (Sidia Jatta) 1 Independents 2	

Ghana March 6, 1957	Nov. 1992	Presidential	Jerry Rawlings (NDC) (National Democratic Congress) 58.3 % Adu Boahen (NPP) (New Patriotic Party) 30.4% Hilla Limann (PNC) (People's National Convention) 6.7%	48.3% of the electorate took part in the elections.
	Dec. 1992	Legislative	Election alliance: the Progressive Alliance: NDC (Jerry Rawlings) 189/200 NCP (National Convention Party) 8 EGLE (Every Ghanaian Living Everywhere) 1 Independents 2	The main opposition parties boycotted the December 1992 legislative election, claiming electoral fraud.
	Dec. 1996	Presidential	Jerry Rawlings (NDC) 57.4% John Agyekum Kufuor (NPP/PCP) (New Patriotic Party / People's Convention Party) 39.6% Edward Mahama (PNC) 3%	
	Dec. 1996	Legislative	NDC (Jerry Rawlings) 132/200 NPP 60 PCP 5 PNC (Edward Mahama) 1 Vacant 2	
Guinea Oct.2, 1958	Dec. 1993	Presidential	Lansane Conté (PUP) (Parti de l'unité et du progrès/Party of Unity and Progress) 51.7% Alpha Condé (RPG) (Rassemblement du peuple guinéen/ Rally of the Guinean People) 19.6% Mahamadou Ba (UNR) (Union pour la nouvelle république/ Union for a New Republic) (Mahamadou Ba) 13.4% Siradiou Diallo (PRP) (Parti du renouveau et du progrès/ Party of Renewal and Progress) 11.9% Facinet Toure (UNPG) (Union national pour la prosperité de la Guinée/National Union for Prosperity of Guinea) 1.4%	

	June 1995	Legislative	PUP (Lansane Conté) 71/114 RPG (Alpha Condé) 19 PRP (Siradiou Diallo) 9 UNR 9 UNPG (Facinet Toure) 2 Parti Djama/Djama Party 1 PDG-RDA (Parti démocratique de Guinée-Rassembelment démocratique africain/Democratic Party of Guinea-African Democratic Rally) 1 PDG (Parti démocratique de Guinée-Ahmed Sejou Touré/Democratic Party of Guinea-Ahmed Sejou Touré) 1 UNP (Union national pour le progrès/National Union for Progress) 1	Disunity was rife in the opposition.
Guinea-Bissau Sept.10, 1974	July 1994	Legislative	PAIGC (Partido Africano da Independência de Guiné e Cabo Verde/African Independence Party of Guinea and Cape Verde) (João Bernardo Vieira) 62/100 RGB-MB (Partido sa Resistência da Guiné-Bissau-Movimento Ba-Fatá/Resistance Party of Guinea-Bissau-Bafatá Movement) (Domingos Fernandes Gomes) 19 PRS (Partido para a Renovação Social/Party for Social Renewal) (Kumba Yalá) 12 UM (União para a Mudança/Union for Change) 4 LIPE (Liga Guinense de Protecção Ecoloógico/Guinean Environmental Protection League) (Bubacar Djaló) 2 FLING (Frente da Libertação para a Independência Nacional da Guiné/Front for the Liberation and National Independence of Guinea) (François Kankoila Mendy) 1	

Aug.1994	Presidential	João Bernardo Vieira (PAIGC) 46.2% Kumba Yalá (PRS) 21.9% Domingos Fernandes Gomes (RGB-MB) 17.3% Carlos Domingos Gomes (PCD) (Partido da Convergência Democrática/Party of Democratic Convergence) 5.1% François Kankoila Mendy (FLING) 2.8% Bubacar Djaló (UM/LIPE) 2.8% Victor Saúde Maria (PUSD) (Partido Unido Social Democrata/United Social Democratic Party) 2.2% Antonieta Rosa Gomes (FCG/SD) (Fórum Cívico Guinese-Social Democracia/Guinean Civic Forum-Social Democratic) 1.8% Second round results: João Bernado Vieira 52% Kumba Yalá 48%	
Kenya Dec. 12 , 1963	Dec. 1992	Legislative	KANU (Kenya African National Union) (Daniel arap Moi) 100/200 FORD-Asili (Forum for the Restoration of Democracy) (Kenneth Matiba) 31 FORD-Kenya (Oginga Odinga) 31 DP (Democratic Party) (Mwai Kibaki) 23 PICK (Party of Indepedent Candidates) (Harun Mwau) 1 KSC (Kenya Social Congress) (George Anyona) 1 KNC (Kenya National Congress) (Chibule wa Tsuma) 1 Presidential nomination 12	In November 1991, donors decided to withhold aid worth $ 1 billion in order to pressure the ruling KANU government to implement political reforms. The following month, President Moi announced the end of the single-party state. However, as the 1992 elections approached, splits inthe opposition allowed Moi to win and retain the post of president. The elections were also marred by reported cases of irregularity. A breakdown of the election results shows that although Moi received 36 per cent of the votes cast nation-wide, the total combined vote for the opposition candidates who stood against him exceeded 60 per cent.

	Dec. 1992	Presidential	Daniel arap Moi (KANU) 36.4% Kenneth Matiba (FORD-Asili) 26.2% Mwai Kibaki (DP) 19.1% Oginga Odinga (FORD-Kenya) 17.6% Chibule wa Tsuma (KNC) 0.2% Harun Mwau (PICK) 0.1% Makaru Ng'ang'a (KENDA)	In April 1991, General Lekhanya was removed from power in a bloodless *coup* and replaced as head of the Military Council by Colonel Elias Phisoano Ramaema. The ban on political activity was lifted in May 1991 and a new constitution, largely modelled on the 1966 version, set the ground rules for elections.
Lesotho Oct.4, 1966	March 1993	Legislative	BCP (Basotholand Congress Party) (Ntsu Mokhehle) 65/65 BNP (Basotho National Party) 16% MFP (Marema (Tlou) Freedom Party) 1.44% Others 1.35%	Civil war between 1990 and 1996.
Liberia	Sept.1996	Presidential	Charles Taylor (NPP) (National Patriotic Party) 75.3% Ellen Johnson-Sirleaf (UP) (Unity Party) 9.6% Alhaji Kromah (ALCP) (All Liberia Coalition) George Boley	
	July 1997	Legislative	NPP (Charles Taylor) 49/64 UP (Ellen Johnson-Sirleaf) 7 ALCP (Alhaji Kromah) 3 Others 5	
Madagascar June 26, 1960	Nov. 1992- Feb. 1993	Legislative	Albert Zafy (Comité des forces vives/Living Forces) 45.16% Didier Ratsiraka (AREMA) (Avant-garde de la révolution malgache/Vanguard of the Malagasy Revolution) 29.22% Manandafy Rakotonirina 10.21% Evariste Marson (RPSD) (Rassemblement pour le socialisme et la démocracie/Rally for Socialism and Democracy) 4.60% Ruffine Tsiranana (Mrs) 3.51% Jacques Rabemananiara 2.87% Tovonanahary Rabetsitonta 2.19% Second round results: Albert Zafy 66.74% Didier Ratsiraka 33.26%	

| June 1993 | Legislative | Alliance:
Forces Vives Rasalama/Living Forces of Rasalama (Albert Zafy) 46/138
Fihaonana (Fihaonana/Confédération des sociétés pour le développement/Confederation of Civil Societies for Development) 8
AKFM-F (Antoky Kongresy Fahaleonvantenani Madaagaskar-Fanavaozana/Renewal Faction of the Congress Party for the Independence of Madagascar) (Rev. Andriamanjato) 5
Farimbona/Acting Together 2
UNDD (Union nationale pour dévelopment et démocracie/National Union for Development and Democracy) 2
CSDDM (Comité de souties à la démocratie et au développement de Madagascar/Committee for the Support of Democracy and Development in Madagascar) 2
Vatomizana/Measures and Weights 1
GRAD-Iloafo (Groupe d'action et réflexion pour le développement de Madagascar/Action and Reflection Group for the Development of Madagascar) 1

Others:
PMDM (Parti militant pour le développement du Madagascar/ Militant Party for Development of Madagascar) 15
Fanilo/Torch 13
Famima/Association of United Malagasies 11
RPSD 8
UNDD-R (Union nationale pour dévelopment et démocratie-Rasalama/National Union for Development and Democracy-Rasalama) 5
Fivoarana/Progress 2
Accord 1
Forces Vives Rasalama - Teachers 1
Other parties 10 | Didier Ratsiraka, the incumbent president who had been in power since 1975 at the head of a military "marxist" government and party (AREMA) was defeated. Albert Zafy, the main opposition leader, emerged victorious. 100 parties registered for the elections but only 26 managed to win seats in Parliament. |

	Nov. 1996/ Jan. 1997	Presidential	Didier Ratsiraka (AREMA) 36.61% Albert Zafy (Forces Vives Rasalama) 23.39% Herizo Razafimahaleo (Fanilo) 15% Norbert Lala Ratsirahonana 10% Richard Andriamanjato 4.9% Second round results: Didier Ratsiraka 50.72% Albert Zafy 49.28%	Didier Ratsiraka was returned to power.
Malawi June 6, 1964	May 1994	Presidential	Bakili Muluzi (UDF) (United Democratic Front) 47.3% Hastings Kamuzu Banda (MCP) (Malawi Congress Party) 33.6% Chakufwa Chihane (AFORD) (Alliance for Democracy) 18.6 Kampelo Kalua (MNDP) (Malawi National Democratic Party) 0.5	Banda, former "president-for-life" and leader of the MCP, was voted out of office.
	May 1994	Legislative	UDF (Bakili Muluzi) 85/177 MCP (Hastings Kamuzu Banda) 56 AFORD (Chakufwa Chihane) 36	

Mali Sept. 22, 1960	Feb./ March 1992	Legislative	ADEMA (Alliance pour la démocratie en Mali/Alliance for Democracy in Mali) (Alpha Oumar Konaré) 76/116 CNID (Congrès national pour la initiative démocratie/National Congress for Democratic Initiative) (Mountage Tall) 9 US-RDA (Union Soudanise-Rassemblement démocratique Africaine/Sudanese Union-African Democratic Rally) (Tieoule Mamadou Konate) 8 MPD (Mouvement populaire pour la développement et la république unie de l'Afrique l'Ouest/Popular Movement for Development and a United Republic of West Africa) 6 RDP (Rassemblement pour la démocratie et le progrès/Rally for Democracy and Development) 4 UPD (Union pour démocratie et développement/Union for Democracy and Labour) 4 RDT (Rassemblément pour la démocratie et le travail/Rally for Democracy and Development) 3 UFDP (Union des forces démocratiques pour le progrès/Union for Democracy and Progress) 3 PDP (Parti pour la démocratie et le progrès/Party for Democracy and Progress) 2 UMDD (Union malien pour démocratie et développement/Malian Union for Democracy and Development) 1	The elections came about after massive internal pressures for change. Demonstrations during 1990-91 resulted, in March 1991, in a military mutiny against the military regime of Maoussa Troaré and the ruling single- party, the UDPM (the Democratic Union of Malian People). After Traoré's overthrow, the way was opened for Mali to move towards a multi-party political system.
	April 1992	Presidential	Alpha Oumar Konaré (ADEMA) 45% Tieoule Mamadou Konate (US-RDA) 14.5% Mountage Tall (CNID) 11.4% Second round results: Alpha Oumar Konaré (ADEMA) 69% Tieoule Mamadou Konate (US-RDA) 31%	The voter turnout stood at 20%.

Mauritania Nov. 28, 1960	Jan. 1992	Presidential	Maaouiya Ould Sid' Achmed Taya (PRDS) (Parti républicain démocratique et sociale/Democratic and Social Republican Party) 62.65% Achmed Ould Daddah (RDUN) (Rassemblement pour la démocratie et l'unité nationale/Rally for Democracy and National Unity) 32.8% Mustapa Ould Mohammed Salech 2.9% Mohammed Mahmoud Ould Mah (UDPS) (Union démocratique sociale et populaire/Social and Popular Democratic Union) 1.4	Maaouiya Ould Sid' Achmed Taya came to power in a *coup d'état* in 1984. The UFD (Union des forces démocratique et social/Union of Democratic Forces) supported Daddah.
	March 1992	Legislative	PRDS (Maaouiya Ould Sid' Achmed Taya) 67/79 PMR (Parti mauritanien pour le renouveau/Mauritanian Renewal Party) (Moulaye al-Hassan Ould Jeyid) 1 (RDU) (Rassemblement pour la démocratie et l'unité) (Ahmed Ould Sidi Baba) 1 Independents 10	Only eight parties contested the elections - those which had supported the candidacy of the head of state in the presidential elections. Six other parties boycotted the legislative elections.
	Oct. 1996	Legislative	PRDS (Maaouiya Ould Sid' Achmed Taya) 70/79 RDU (Ahmed Ould Sidi Baba) 1 AC (Action pour changement/Action for Change) 1 Non-partisan 7	
Mauritius Dec. 3, 1968	Dec. 1995	Legislative	MMM (Mouvement militant mauricien/Mauritian Militant Movement) (Paul Bérenger) in coalition with PT (Parti Travaillist/Labour Party) (Navin Ramgoolam) 60/66 MSM (Mouvement socialiste mauricien/Mauritian Socialist Movement) (Sir Anerood Jugnauth) in coalition with RMM (Renouveau militant Mauricien/Mauritian Militant Renewal) (Dharmanand Fokeer and Paramhansa Nababsing) 0 OPR (Organisation du peuple Rodriguais/Rodrigues People's Organisation) (Louis Serge Clair) 2 MR (Mouvement Rodrigues/Rodrigues Movement) 2 PGD (Parti Gaetan Duval/Gaetan Duval Party) 1 H (Hizbullah/Party of God) 1 Two seats on the Island of Rodrigues were won by OPR and four allocated to "the best losers".	The President is elected by the parliament.

Mozambique June 25, 1975	Oct. 1994	Presidential	Joaquin Alberto Chissano (Frelimo) (Frente da libertaçao de Moçambique/Liberation Front of Mozambique) 53.3% Alfonso Dhlakama (Renamo) (Resistencia nacional Moçambicana/Mozambican National Resistance) 33.7% Wehia Ripua (Pademo) (Democratic Party of Mozambique) 2.9% Carlos Reib (Unamo) (National Union of Mozambique) 2.4% Maxiom Dias (MNM-PSDM) (National Movement of Mozambique/Social Democratic Party of Mozambique) 2.3%
	Oct. 1994	Legislative	Frelimo (Joaquin Alberto Chissano) 129/250 Renamo (Alfonso Dhlakama) 112 União Democrática/Democratic Union, consisting of: PALMO (Partido liberal e demcrático de Mozambique/ Liberal and Democratic Party of Mozambique) (Martins Bilal and Antonio Palange) PANADE (Partido nacional démocrático/National-Democratic Party) (José Massinga) PANAMO (Partido nacional de Moçambique/National Party of Mozambique) 9
Namibia March 21, 1990	Nov. 1989	Legislative	SWAPO (South West People's Organization) (Sam Nujoma) 41/72 DTA (Democratic Turnhall Alliance) (Mishake Muyongo) 21 UDF (United Democratic Front) (Justuce Garoëb) 4 ACN (Action Christian National) (Jan. de Wet) 3 NFF (Namibia National Front) (Vekuui Rukoro) 1 NPF (Namibia Patriotic Front) (Moses Katjiuongua) 1 the National Convention (Hans Diergaardt) 1
	Dec. 1994	Legislative	SWAPO (Sam Nujoma) 53/72 DTA (Mishake Muyongo) 15 UDF (Justuce Garoëb) 2 MAG (Monitor Action Group) 1 DCN (Democratic Alliance of Namibia) 1

	Dec. 1995	Presidential	Sam Nujoma (SWAPO) 76.3% Mishake Muyongo (DTA) 23.7%	Niger was still a single-party state at the time these elections were held.
Niger Aug. 3, 1960	Dec. 1989	Presidential and Legislative	Brigadier Ali Saibou (MNSD) 99.6% MNSD (Mouvement national pour la société de développement/National Movement for a Developing Society) 93/93	
	Feb. 1993	Legislative	MNSD (Tandja Mamadou) 29/83 AFC (Alliance des forces du changement): CDS (Convention démocratique et sociale/Social Democratic Convention) (Mahamane Ousmane) 22 PNDS (Parti nigérien pour la démocratie et le socialisme/National Party for Democracy and Socialism) (Mahamadou Issoufou) 13 ANDP (Alliance nigérienne pour la démocratie et le progrès/Niger Alliance for Democracy and Social Progress) (Moumouni Djermakoye Adamou) 11 PPN/RDA (Parti progressiste nigérien-Rassemblement démocratique Africain) (Dan Dicko Dan Koulodo) 2 PSDN (Parti social-démocrate nigérien/Nigerien Social Democratic Party) (Kalzelma Taya Oumar) 1 UDPS (Union pour la démocratie et le progrès social/Union for Democracy and Social Progress) (Akoli Djibo) 1 UDFP (Union democratique des forces progressistes/Democratic Union of Progressive Forces) (Djibo Bakary) 2 UPDP (Union des patriotes démocrates et progressistes/Union of Patriotic Democrats and Progressives) (André Salifou) 2	An alliance of opposition parties known as the AFC won the legislative elections.

Date	Type	Results	Comments
Feb./ March 1993	Presidential	Tandja Mamadou (MNSD) 34.22% Mahamane Ousmane (CDS) 26.59% Mahamadou Issoufou (PNDS) Mounouni Djermakoye (ANDP) Second round results: Mahamane Ousmane (CDS) 54.8% Tanja Mamadou (MNSD) 45.2%	The elections were generally adjudged to be free and fair. The elections came about after massive internal pressures for change organized by a variety of groups, including the major trade union federation, USTN, which called general strikes in 1990 and again in March 1992 after an army mutiny. Mahamane Ousmane, the leader of the main opposition alliance was elected president and, thus, became the first Hausa head of state.
Jan. 1995	Legislative	MNSD (Tandja Mamadou) 29/83 CDS (Mahamane Ousmane) 24 PNDS (Mahamadou Issoufou) 12 ANDP (Moumouni Adamou Djermakoye) 9 PPN/RDA (Dan Dicko Dan Koulodo) 1 UPDP (André Salifou) 1 PSDN (Kazelma Oumar Taya) 2 PUND (Parti pour l'unité nationale et le développement/ Nigerien Party for Unity and Democracy) (Akoli Dawel) 3 UDPS (Union pour la démocratie et progrès social/Union for Democracy and Social Progress) (Mohamed Abdullahi) 2	The few irregularities that were noted were not at a level as to jeopardise the final results.
July 1996	Presidential	Ibrahim Mainassara Bare 52.22% Mahamane Ousmane (CDS) 19.75% Mamadou Tandja (MNSD) 15.65% Mahamadou Issoufou (PNDS) 7.60% Adamou Moumouni Djermakoye (ANDP) 4.77%	Ibrahim Bare Mainassara (independent candidate and the leader of the *coup d'état* of January 1996). The elections were marred by profound irregularities.

Nov. 1996	Legislative	UNIRD (Union nationale des indépendants pour le renoveau démocratique/National Union of renoveau démocratique/National Union of Independents for Democratic Renewal) 56/83 ANDP (Moumouni Adamou Djermakoye) 8 UPDP (André Salifou) 4 Daradja 3 PMT (Parti des masses pour le travail/Party of the Masses of Labour) (Idi Ango Omar) 2 MDP (Movement for Democracy and Progress) (Mal Manga Boukar) 1 UDPS (Mohamed Abdullahi) 3 Other 3 Non-partisans 3 (Source: Derksen) UNIRD 59/83 (three seats in the by-election held on January 19, 1997) Daraja 3 PMT 3 UPDP 3 MDP 1 ANDP 8 UDPS 3 Independents 3 (Source: ARB No. 1, 1997) UNIRD 60/83 FRD (Front pour la démocratie et le progrès) 9 ANDP 9 UDPS 2 Independents 3 (Source: Abdoulaye Niandou Souley)	The Nigerien National Assembly was dissolved after the military *coup* that took place in January 1996. The opposition boycotted the legislative elections that were convened in November 1996. The turn-out for the elections was put at about 27% by the government (the opposition claimed that only 5% of eligible voters bothered to participate). Note the conflicting figures given by the various sources used on the number of seats won by the different parties.

Nigeria Oct.1, 1960	July 1992	Legislative	SDP (Social Democratic Party) (Moshood K. O. Abiola) 314/589 NRC (National Republican Convention) (Bashir O. Tofa) 276	In 1989, the ban which had been placed on political parties after the military *coup* of December 1983 was lifted but only two parties (the SDP and the NRC) were allowed.
	June 1993	Presidential	Moshood K. O. Abiola (SDP) Interim results showed that Abiola had won 52.28% of the votes, clearing beating Bashir Tofa of the NRC but the elections were cancelled.	General Babangida annulled the results, opportunistically alleging election fraud. The military then installed an interim government led by Chief Ernest Shonekan. That government was toppled in November 1993 by General Sanni Abacha and Nigeria was returned to full military rule.
Réunion (French colony)	March 1994	Legislative	PCR (Parti communiste réunionnais/Réunion Communist Party) (Paul Vergès) 12/47 PSR (Parti socialiste réunionnais/Socialist Party) (Jean Claude Fruteau S-G) 12 UDF (Union pour la démocratie française/Union for French Democracy) (Gilbert Gérard S-G) 11 RPR (Rassemblement pour la république/Rally for the Republic) (Alain Defaud) 5 Others 7	
Rwanda July 1, 1962	Dec. 1988	Presidential and Legislative	Juvénal Habyarimana MRND (Mouvement démocratique républicain/Republican Democratic Movement) 70/70	The present president, Pasteur Bizimungu, was appointed in 1994 after the civil war. The FPR/ Rwanda Patriotic Front is presently in power

Sao Tomé & Principe July 12, 1975	Jan. 1991	Legislative	PCD-GR (Partido de Convergencia Democrática-Grupa de Reflexão/Democratic Convergence Party-Reflection Group) (Leonel d'Alva) 33/55 MLSTP-PSD (Movimento de Libertaçao de São Tomé e Príncipe-Partido Social Democrata/Movement for the Liberation of Sao Tome and Principe) (Manuel Pinto da Costa) 21 Codo (Coligação Democrática de Oposição) (Albertino Neto) 1 FDC-PSU (Frente Democrata Cristã-Partido Social da Unidade) (Alfonso dos Santos) 2%	The ruling authorities were ousted by way of free elections.
	March 1991	Presidential	Miguel Trovoada 83%	Pinto da Costa did not contest; the two other contestants also withdrew
	Oct. 1994	Legislative	MLSTP-PSD (Manuel Pinto da Costa) 27/55 PCD-GR 14 ADI (Acção Democrática de Independente/Independent Democratic Action) (Miguel Trovoada) 14	The 1995 *coup d'état*, collapsed after a few days and the elected government was restored.
	July 1996	Presidential	Miguel Trovoada (ADI) 40.9% Manuel Pinto da Costa (MLSTP) 39.1% Alada Bandeira (PCD) 14.6% Second round results: Miguel Trovoada 52% Manuel Pinto da Costa 48%	

			Results	Notes
Senegal Aug. 20, 1960	Feb. 1993	Presidential	Abdou Diouf (PS) (Parti socialiste/Socialist Party) 58.4% Abdoulaye Wade (PDS) (Parti démocratique sénégalais/Senegalese Democratic Party) 32% Landing Savane (PADS) (Parti africain pour la démocratie et le socialisme/African Party for Democracy and Socialism) 2.9% Abdoulaye Bathily (LD-MPT) (Ligue démocratique-Mouvement pour le parti du travail/Democratic league) 2.4% Iba Der Thiam (CDP) (Convention des démocrates et patriots/Convention of Democrats and Patriots) 1.6% Madior Diouf (RND) (Rassemblement national démocratique/National Democratic Rally) 1% Mamadou Lô (SC) (Société civil/Civil Society) 0.9% Babacar Niang (PLP) (Parti pour la libération du peuple/People's Liberation Party) 0.8%	The opposition claimed electoral fraud.
	Feb. 1993	Legislative	PS (Abdou Diouf) 84/120 PDS (Abdoulaye Wade) 27 Alliance: Japoo-Liggueyal Senegal AJ/PADS (And-Jëf/Parti Africain pour la démocratie et le socialisme/African Party for Democracy and Socialism) (Landing Savane) CDP (Iba Der Thiam) 3 RND (Madior Diouf) 3 LD-MPT (Abdoulaye Bathily) 3 PIT (Parti l'indépendence et du travail/Party of Independence and Work) (Amath Dansokho) 2 UDS-R (Union démocratique sénégalaise-rénovation/Senegalese Democratic Union-Renewal) (Mamadou Puritain Fall) 1	The elections resulted in a considerably reduced majority for the PS, 84 deputies instead of 103.
Seychelles June 29, 1976	July 1993	Presidential	France Albert René (FPPS) (Front progressiste du peuple seychellois/Progressive Front of the Seychelles) 59.5% James Mancham (DP) (Democratic Party) 36.7% Philippe Boulé (OU) (Opposition unie/United Opposition) 3.8%	

	July 1993	Legislative	FPPS (France Albert René) 27/33 DP (James Mancham) 5 United Opposition: NAP (National Alliance Party) (Philippe Boulle) SNM (Seychelles National Movement) (Edmond Camille and Robert Frichot) PS (Parti Seychellois-Parti Seselwa/Seychelles Party) (Wavel Ramkalawan) 1	Military rule between 1992 and 1996. In 1997 there was a new military coup and the democratically elected government was overthrown.
Sierra Leone April 27, 1961	Feb. 1996	Legislative	SLPP (Sierra Leone People's Party) (Ahmad Tejan.Kabbah) 27/80 Four other parties allied to the SLPP won 24 seats: PDP (People's Democratic Party) (Thaimu Bangura) 12 APC (All People's Congress) (Edward Turay) 5 NUP (National Unity Party) (John Karimu) 4 DCP (Democratic Centre Party) (Abu Aiah Koroma) 3 UNPP (John Karefa-Smart) 17 Paramount Chiefs 12	
	March 1996	Presidential	Ahmad Tejan.Kabbah (SLPP) 35.8% John Karefa-Smart (UNPP) 22.6% Thaimu Bangura (PDP) 16.1% John Karimu (NUP) 9.3% Adu Aiah Koroma (DCP) 4.9% Abass Chernon Bundu (PPP) (People's Progress Party) 3.5% Amadu M.B Jalloh (NDA) (National Democratic Alliance) 2.3% Edward John Kargbo (PNC) (People's National Convention) 2.1% Desmond Luke (NUM) (National Unity Movement) 1.1% Second round results: Ahmad Tejan.Kabbah 59.49% John Karefa-Smart 40.51%	
Somalia July 1, 1960				No elections held in recent years.

South Africa	April 1994	Legislative	ANC (African National Congress) (Nelson Mandela) 252/400 NP (National Party) (Frederick Willem de Klerk) 82 IFP (Inkatha Freedom Party) (Mangosuthu Gatsha Buthelezi) 43 VF (Freedom Front) (Constand Viljoen) 9 DP (Democratic Party) (Tonny Leon and Mudene Smuts) 7 PAC (Pan African Congress of Azania) (Clarence Makwetu) 5 ACDP (African Christian Democratic Party) (Johann van der Westhuizen) 2	
Sudan Jan. 1, 1956	March 1996	Presidential	Omar Hassna el-Bashir 75.7% 40 other candidates 24.3%	All politcal parties were banned in 1989.
Swaziland Sept. 6, 1968	Sept./Oct. 1993	Legislative	Only non-partisans have been elected to the senate. The House of Assembly has 65 members, 55 of them "elected" from a list of candidates nominated by traditional local councils and the remaining 10 appointed by the government. The Senate has 30 non-partisan members, 10 members elected by parliament and the remaining 20 appointed.	
Tanzania Dec. 9, 1961 (United Rep. April 27, 1964)	Oct./Nov. 1990	Presidential and Legislative	CCM 169/169 Ali Hassan Mwinyi 95%	Mwinyi was the sole presidential candidate; CCM was still the only party in the country at the time these elections were held.
	Oct. 1995	Presidential	Benjamin Mkapa (CCM) (Chama Cha Mapinduzi) 61.8% Augustine Mrema (NCCR-Mageuzi) (National Convention for Construction and Reform) 27.8% Ibrahim Lipumba (CUF) (Civic United Front) 6.4% John Cheyo (UDP) (United Democratic Party) 4.0%	

	Date	Type	Results	Remarks
	Oct. 1995	Legislative	CCM (Benjamin Mkapa) 214/275 (excluding the Attorney General and the Zanzibar delegates) CUF (Ibrahim Lipumba) 28 NCCR-Maguezi (Augustine Mrema) 19 UDP (John Cheyo) 4 CHADEMA (Chama cha Democracia na Maendeleo) (Edwin Im Mtei) 4 Zanzibar: Salmin Amour (CCM) 50.2% Seif Sharif Hamad (CUF) 49.8% CCM 50.2% of votes CUF 49.8%	The CCM was easily the best organised and most broad-based political party in the country. Foreign observers noted major deficiencies in the running of elections. On November 2, 1995, ten opposition parties filed a law suit asking the High Court to cancel the elections. The victory of Salmin Amour on the Island of Zanzibar has been seriously questioned.
Togo April 27, 1960	Aug. 1993	Presidential	Gnassingbe Eyadema (RPT) (Rassemblement du peuple togolais/Rally of the Togolese People) 96.4% Jacques Amouzou Ife Adani (two relatively unknown individuals)	The election was boycotted by the opposition. Voter turn-out was put at 36.16 per cent. The use of state violence was widespread.
	Feb. 1994	Legislative	CAR (Comité d'action pour le renouveau/Action Committee for Renewal) (Yao Agboyibo) 36/81 RPT (Gnassingbe Eyadema) 35 UTD (Union togolaise pour la démocratie/Togolese Union for the Democracy) 7 UJD (Union pour justice et démocratie/Union for Justice and Democracy) 2 CDN (Coordination des forces nouvelles/Coordination of New Forces) 1	Parties opposed to President Eyadema emerged with a narrow majority in the legislature.
Uganda Oct. 9, 1962	Feb. 1989	Legislative	Officially, a no-party system is being operated.	The NRA came into power in 1986 and formed a broad based government. The election resulted in a much expanded NRC of 278 members, increased from 98, of whom 210 were elected.

	March 1994	Legislative	Officially, a no-party system is being operated.	Candidates were all nominally independents, but the leaders of DP, UPC and Conservative Party, and those campaigning for parties to be recognized later, were allowed to explain their views on radio and TV several weeks before the elections.
	May 1996	Presidential	Kaguta Yoweri Museveni (NRM) (National Resistance Movement) 74.2 % Paul Kawanga Ssemogerere (DP) (Democratic Party) 23.7% Mohammed Mayanja Kibirige 2.1	
Zambia Oct.27, 1964	Oct.1991	Legislative	MMD (Movement for Multi-Party Democracy) (Frederick Chiluba) 125/150 UNIP (United National Independence Party) (Kenneth Kaunda) 25	Peaceful transfer of power from Kaunda to Chiluba. More than half of the electorate did not vote.
	Oct.1991	Presidential	Chiluba 75.79% Kaunda 24.21%	
	Nov. 1996	Legislative	MMD (Frederick Chiluba) 127/150 NP (National Party) Humphrey Mulemba 5 AZ (Agenda for Zambia) (Akashambatwa Mbikusita Lewanika) 2 ZDC (Zambia Democratic Party) (Dean Mungomba) 2 NLP (National Lima Party) Non-partisans 11 Vacant 3	The election was boycotted by the main opposition party, UNIP. The National Assembly also includes 8 appointed members and the speaker.
	Nov. 1996	Presidential	Frederick Chiluba (MMD) 70.2% Dean Mungomba (ZDC) 12.1% Humphrey Mulemba (NP) 6% Akashambatwa Mbikusita Lewanika (AZ) 4.2% Chama Chakoboka (MDP) (Movement for Democratic Process) 3%	
Zimbabwe April 18, 1980	March 1990	Legislative	ZANU-PF (Zimbabwe African National Union-Patriotic Front) (Robert Mugabe) 116/119 ZUM (Zimbabwe Unity Movement) (Edgar Tekere) 2 ZANU-Sithole (Ndabaningi Sithole) 1	

March 1990	Presidential	Robert Mugabe (ZANU-PF) 78.3% Edgar Tekere (ZUM) 16% Spoilt papers 5.7%	
April 1995	Legislative	ZANU-PF (Robert Mugabe) 147/150 ZANU-Ndonga (Ndabaningi Sithole) 2 Independent Candidates (Margaret Dongo) 1 FPZ (Forum Party of Zimbabwe) (Enoch Dumbushena) 0 (6.3%)	Opposition leaders made several attempts to regroup under different banners to challenge the government but little headway was made. 20 seats are reserved for nominees of the president and 10 are taken by traditional leaders (making a total of 150 seats in all).
March 1996	Presidential	Robert Mugabe (ZANU-PF) 92% Abel Muzorewa (United Parties) 4.7% Ndabaningi Sithole (ZANU-Ndonga) 2.4%	Only 750 000 out of 4.9 million eligible Zimbabweans bothered to vote.

Appendix 2

SELECT BIBLIOGRAPHY ON POLITICAL LIBERALISATION AND MULTIPARTYISM IN CONTEMPORARY AFRICA

Compiled by Kajsa Övergaard

Adam, Hussein M., 1993, "Franz Fanon as a Democratic Theorist", *African Affairs: The Journal of the Royal African Society*, Vol. 92, No. 369.

Adedeji, Adebayo (foreword), 1990, "Coalition for Change", *Alternative Strategies for Africa*. London: Institute for African Alternatives.

"Africa Pressing for Pluralism—Channels for Democracy", 1993, *IDOC Internazionale*,Vol. 24, No. 2, special issue.

"African Charter for Popular Participation in Development and Transformation", 1990, *IFDA Dossier*, No. 79.

"African Governance in the 1990s: Objectives, Resources and Constraints", 1990, *Working Papers from the Second Annual Seminar of the African Governance Program*. Atlanta: The Carter Center of Emory University.

Ake, Claude, 1991, "Rethinking African Democracy", *Journal of Democracy*, Vol. 2, No. 1.

Ake, Claude, 1993, "The Unique Case of African Democracy", *International Affairs*, Vol. 69, No. 2.

Ake, Claude, 1996, *Democracy and Development in Africa*. Washington, D.C.: Brookings Institution.

Allen, Chris, "Surviving Democracy", 1992, *Review of African Political Economy*, No. 54.

Allison Jr., T. Graham and Robert P. Beschel, 1992, "Can the United States Promote Democracy?", *Political Science Quarterly*, Vol. 107, No. 1.

Amin, Samir, 1992, "About Democracy in Africa...", *COOPERAZIONE*, Vol. 17, No. 111.

Apter, David E. and Carl G. Rosberg (eds.), 1994, *Political Development and the New Realism in Sub-Saharan Africa*. Charlottesville and London: University Press of Virginia.

Ayittey, George B.N., 1991, *Indigenous African Institutions*. New York: Transnational Publishers.

Bakary Akin, Tessy D., 1992, "Pour une approche non-partisane de la démocratie en Afrique", *Afrique 2000:Revue Africaine de Politique Internationale*, No. 9.

Bangoura, Dominique, 1993, "Armées et défis démocratiques en Afrique", *Afrique 2000:Revue Africaine de Politique Internationale*, No. 2.

Bayart, Jean-Francois, 1991, "La problématique de la démocratie en Afrique noire: 'la Baule, et puis après?'", *Politique Africaine*, No. 43.

Bayart, Jean-Francois, 1993, *The State in Africa: The Politics of the Belly.* London: Longman.

Baynham, Simon, 1991, "Geopolitics, Glasnost and Africa's Second Liberation: Political and Security Implications for the Continent", *Africa Insight,* Vol. 21, No. 4.

Beachler, J., 1992, "Des institutions démocratiques pour l'Afrique", *Revue Juridique et Politique,* Vol. 46, No. 2.

Beckman, Björn, 1988, "When Does Democracy Make Sense? Problems of Theory and Practice in the Study of Democratisation in Africa and the Third World", *Paper to AKUT Conference on Democracy,* October. Uppsala.

Beckman, Björn, 1989, "Whose Democracy? Bourgeois versus Popular Democracy in Africa", *Review of African Political Eonomy,* 45/46.

Beckman, Björn, 1990, *Structural Adjustment and Democracy: Interest Group Resistance to Structural Adjustment and the Development of the Democracy Movement in Africa,* Research Proposal Submitted to SAREC. Stockholm: University of Stockholm, Deptartment of Political Science.

Beckman, Björn, 1993, "The Liberation of Civil Society: Neoliberal Ideology and Political Theory", *Review of African Political Economy,* No. 58.

Beetham, David, 1994, "Conditions for Democratic Consolidation", *Review of African Political Economy,* No. 60, June.

Belotteau, Jacques, 1991, "La marche vers le multipartisme", *Afrique Contemporaine,* Vol. 30, No. 58.

Beyeck, Abba A., 1990, "La démocratisation de la vie politique est le facteur décisif pour un développement de l'Afrique, *EADI General Conference.* Oslo: EADI/NUPI.

Bienen, H. S. and M. Gersovitz, 1985, "Economic Stabilisation, Conditionality and Political Stability", *International Organisation,* Vol. 39, No. 4, Autumn.

Bing, Adotey, 1991, "Salim A. Salim on the OAU and the African Agenda", *Review of African Political Economy,* No. 50.

Bourgi, Albert, 1991, *Le printemps de l'Afrique. Suivi d'un document du ministère français des affaires étrangères: scénarios de crise en Afrique.* Paris: Hachette.

Bourmaud, D. and P. J. Wuantin (eds.), 1991, "Chemins de la Démocratie", *Politique Africaine,* No. 43.

Bouvier, Paule, 1991, "L'Afrique politique face à son devenir", *Civilisations,* Vol. 40, No. 2.

Bratton, Michael, 1989, "Beyond the State: Civil Society and Associational Life in Africa (review article), *World Politics,* Vol. 41, No. 3.

Bratton, Michael and Nicolas van de Walle, 1992, "Popular Protest and Political Reform in Africa", *Comparative Politics,* Vol. 24, No. 4, July.

Bratton, Michael and Nicolas van de Walle, 1994, "Neopatrimonial Regimes and Political Transitions in Africa, *World Politics,* Vol. 46, July.

Bratton, Michael and Nicolas van de Walle, 1996, "Political Regimes and Regime Transitions in Africa: A Comparative Handbook", *MSU Working Papers on Political Reform in Africa,* Working Paper No. 14, Michigan State University.

Bruno, Koffi Ehul, 1993, *Le pouvoir de la brousse: ni démocratie ni développement en Afrique noire sans les paysans organisés.* Paris: L'Harmattan.

Buijtenhuijs, Rob and Elly Rijnierse, 1993, *Democratisation in Sub-Saharan Africa (1989-1992): An Overview of the Literature*. Leiden: Afrika-Studiecentrum.

Busia, Nana K. A., 1992, "The Right to Self-Determination, the State and the Quest for Democracy in Africa: An Exploratory Analysis", *Annual Conference, African Society of International and Comparative Law*, Vol. 4.

Campbell, B., 1989, "Structural Adjustment and Recession in Africa: Implications for Democratic Process and Participation", Paper to the 1989 African Studies Association Meeting. Atlanta.

Caron, B., A. Gboyega and E. Osaghae (eds.), 1992, *Democratic Transition in Africa*. Ibadan: Centre for Research, Documentation and University Exchange (CREDU).

Chabal, Patrick (ed.), 1986, *Political Domination in Africa: Reflections on the Limits of Power*. Cambridge: Cambridge University Press.

Chabal, Patrick, 1992, *Power in Africa: An Essay in Political Interpretaion*. New York: St Martin's Press.

Chabal, Patrick, 1994, "Democracy and Daily Life in Black Africa", *International Affairs*, Vol. 70, No. 1.

Chazan, N., R. Mortimer, J. Ravenhill and D. Rothchild, 1988, *Politics and Society in Contemporary Africa*. Boulder: Lynne Rienner.

Chazan, Naomi, 1992, "Africa's Democratic Challenge", *World Policy Journal*, Vol. 9, No. 2, Spring.

Chazan, Naomi, 1993, "Between Liberalism and Statism: African Political Cultures and Democracy", in Diamond, Larry (ed.) *Political Culture and Democracy in Developing Countries*. Boulder: Lynne Rienner.

Chege, Michael, 1991/92, "Remembering Africa", *Foreign Affairs*, Vol. 71, No. 1.

Cheru, Fantu, 1989, *The Silent Revolution in Africa: Debt, Development and Democracy*. London: Zed Books Ltd.

Chitala, Derrick, 1988, "Democracy, Militarism and Economic Intervention", *Africa and the World*, Vol. 1, No. 3.

Chomsky, N., J.J. Linz and S.M. Lipset (eds.), 1991, "Africa in a New World Order", *Review of African Political Economy*, No. 50, special issue.

Clapham, Christopher, 1993, "Democratisation in Africa: Obstacles and Prospects", *Third World Quarterly*, Vol. 14, No. 3.

Clark, John F., 1993, "Theoretical Disarray and the Study of Democratisation in Africa", *The Journal of Modern African Studies*, Vol. 31, No. 3.

Cliffe, Lionel and J. D. Seddon, 1991, "Africa in a New World Order", *Review of African Political Economy*, No. 50.

Cohen, Robin and Harry Goulbourne (eds.), 1991, *Democracy and Socialism in Africa*. Boulder: Westview Press.

Coparans, Jean, 1991, "No Shortcuts to Democracy: The Long March towards Modernity", *Review of African Political Economy*, No. 50.

Coquery-Vidrovitch, Catherine, 1992, "Histoire et historiographie du politique en Afrique: la nécessité d'une relecture critique (à propos de la démocratie)", *Politique Africaine*, No. 46.

Crenshaw, A., (ed.), 1993, *Terrorism in Africa*. Aldershot: Dartmouth.

Davidson, Basil, 1990, "The Crisis of the Nation-State in Africa", *Review of African Political Economy*, No. 49.

Davidson, Basil, 1992, *The Black Man's Burden: Africa and the Curse of the Nation State*. London: James Currey.

Decalo, Samuel, 1989, *Psychoses of Power: African Personal Dictatorships*. London: Westview Press.

Decalo, Samuel, 1990, *Coups and Army Rule in Africa: Motivation and Constraints*. New Haven: Yale University Press.

Decalo, Samuel, 1991, "Back to Square One: The Redemocratization of Africa", *Africa Insight*, Vol. 21, No. 3.

Decalo, Samuel, 1991, "Towards Understanding the Sources of Stable Civilian Rule in Africa: 1960–1990", *Journal of Contemporary African Studies*, Vol. 10, No. 1.

Decalo, Samuel, 1992, "The Process, Prospects and Constraints of Democratization in Africa", *African Affairs*, Vol. 91, No. 362, January.

Decalo, Samuel, 1992, "Democracy in Africa: Toward the Twenty-First Century", in Tatu Vanhanen (ed.), *Strategies of Democratization*. Washington: Crane Russak.

"Democracy, Civil Society and NGOs", 1992, *Review of African Political Economy* (special issue), No. 55.

"Démocratisation en Afrique: bibliographie commentée", *INADES*. Abidjan: INADES.

"Democratisation in Sub-Saharan Africa: The Search for Institutional Renewal", 1992, *ECDPM Occasional paper*. Maastricht: European Centre for Development Policy Management.

Deng, Lual, Markus Kostner and Crawford Young (eds.), 1991, *Democratization and Structural Adjustment in Africa in the 1990s*. Madison, Wisconsin: University of Wisconsin-Madison, African Studies Program.

Dennis, Austin, 1993, "Reflections on African Politics: Prospero, Ariel and Caliban", *International Affairs*, Vol. 69, No. 2.

Diamond, L., 1987, "Class Formation in the African State", *Journal of Modern African Studies*, Vol. 25, No. 4.

Diamond, Larry, Juan J. Linz, Seymour Martin Lipset (eds.), 1988, *Democracy in Developing Countries: Volume 2, Africa*. Boulder: Lynne Rienner.

Diamond, Larry (ed.), 1993, *Political Culture and Democracy in Developing Countries*. Boulder: Lynne Rienner.

Diouf, M. and M. C. Diop, 1989, "La revanche des élèves et étudiants sur l'état et la société civile 1978-1988", paper to AKUT Conference. Uppsala.

Diouf, Mamadou, 1990, "Africa in the 1980s: State and Social Sciences—Proceedings of the Sixth General Assembly of CODESRIA", *Africa Development*, Vol. 15, No. 3/4, special issue.

Doornbos, Martin, 1990, "The African State in Academic Debate: Retrospect and Prospect", *The Journal of Modern African Studies*, Vol. 28, No. 2.

"Dossier—Africa's New Democracies", 1993, *The Courier: Africa-Caribbean-European Community*, No. 138.

Dumont, René and Charlotte Paquet, 1991, *Démocratie pour l'Afrique: la longue marche de l'Afrique noire vers la liberteé*. Paris: Éditions du Seuil.

Eastern & Southern African Universitites Research Programme, 1994, *The Cost of Peace: Views of Political Parties on the Transition to Multiparty Democracy*. Dar es Salaam: Tanzania Publishing House.

Ekeh, Peter P. 1992, "The Constitution of Civil Society in African History and Politics", in Caron, B.A. Gboyega and E. E. Osaghae, "Proceedings of the Symposium on "Democratic Transition in Africa", *CREDU Documents in Social Sciences and the Humanities Series*, No. 1. Nairobi/Ibadan: CREDU.

Fatton, Robert Jr., 1989, "The State of African Studies and Studies of African State: The Theoretical Softness of the 'Soft State'", *Journal of Asian and African Studies*, Vol. 24, No. 3/4.

Fatton, Robert Jr., 1990, "Liberal Democracy in Africa", *Political Science Quarterly*, Vol. 105, No. 3.

Fatton, Robert Jr., 1991, "Democracy and Civil Society in Africa", *Mediterranean Quarterly*, Vol. 2, No. 4, Fall.

Fatton, Robert Jr., 1992, *Predatory Rule: State and Civil Society in Africa*. London: Lynne Rienner.

"Focus on Democracy in Africa", 1992, *Development and Cooperation*, No. 5.

Fowler, Alan, 1991, "The Role of NGOs in Changing State-Society Relations: Perspectives from Eastern and Southern Africa", *Development Policy Review*, Vol. 9, No. 1.

Fowler, Alan, 1993, "Non-Governmental Organizations as Agents of Democratization: An African Perspective", *Journal of International Development*, Vol. 5, No.3.

Garber, Larry, 1993, "The OAU and Elections", *Journal of Democracy*, Vol. 4, No. 3.

Garcin, Thierry, 1992, "Les européens et la démocratisation africaine", *Afrique 2000: Revue Africaine de Politique Internationale*, No. 10.

Geisler, Gisela, 1993, "Fair? What has fair got to do with it? Vagaries of Election Observations and Democratic Standards", *The Journal of Modern African Studies*, Vol. 31, No. 4.

Gibbon, Peter and Yusuf Bangura (eds.), 1992, *Authoritarianism, Democracy and Adjustment: The Politics of Economic Reform in Africa*, Uppsala: Nordiska Africainstitutet.

Gibbon, Peter, 1993, "'Civil Society' and Political Change with Special Reference to 'Developmentalist' States", in *Experiences of Political Liberalization in Sub-Saharan Africa*, (workshop). Copenhagen: Centre for Development Research/Nordiska Afrikainstitutet.

Glickman, Harvey, 1988, "Frontiers of Liberal and Non-Liberal Democracy in Tropical Africa", *Journal of Asian and African Studies*, Vol. 23, No. 3-4.

Glickman, Harvey, 1993, "Towards a New African Political Order: African Perspectives on Democratization Processes, Regional Conflict Management", *Issue: A Journal of Opinion* (special issue).

Guie, Honore Koffi, 1993, "Organizing Africa's Democrats", *Journal of Democracy*, Vol. 4, No. 2.

Hamrell, Sven and Olle Nordberg (eds.), 1990, *State and the Crisis in Africa: In Search of a Second Liberation*, report of the Mweya Conference in Uganda, May 12-17. Uppsala: Dag Hammarskjöld Foundation.

Harbeson, John W., Donald Rothchild and Naomi Chazan (eds.), 1994, *Civil Society and the State in Africa*. Boulder and London: Lynne Rienner.

Harsch, Ernest, 1993, "Accumulators and Democrats: Challenging State Corruption in Africa", *The Journal of Modern African Studies*, Vol. 31, No. 1.

Haynes, Jeff, 1991, "The State, Governance, and Democracy in Sub-Saharan Africa", The Journal of Modern African Studies, Vol. 31, No. 3.

Hayward, Fred M. (ed.), 1987, *Elections in Independent Africa*. London: Westview Press.

Healey, John and Mark Robinson, 1992, *Democracy, Governance and Economic Policy: Sub-Saharan Africa in Comparative Perspective*. London: Overseas Development Institute.

Herbst, Jeffrey, 1990a, "The Fall of Afro-Marxism: (Third World Communism in Crisis)", *Journal of Democracy*, Vol. 1, No. 3.

Herbst, Jeffrey, 1990b, "The Structural Adjustment of Politics in Africa", *World Development*, Vol. 18, No. 7.

Hicks, John F., 1992, "Supporting Democracy in Africa", *TransAfrica Forum*, Vol. 9, No. 2, Summer.

Hoek, F. van, 1993, "Democracy in Sub-Saharan Africa: The Search for a New Institutional Set-Up", *African Development Review*, Vol. 5, No. 1.

Hopkinson, Nicholas, 1992, "Good Government in Africa", *Wilton Park Papers*, No. 54. London: HMSO.

Howard, Rhoda E., 1992, "Communitarianism and Liberalism in the Debates on Human Rights in Africa", *Journal of Contemporary African Studies*, Vol. 11, No. 1.

Hughes, Arnold (ed.), 1992, "Marxism's Retreat from Africa", Special Issue of *The Journal of Communist Studies*, Vol. 8, No. 2.

Hydén, Göran, 1988, "State and Nation under Stress, Recovery in Africa", in *A Challenge for Development Cooperation in the 1990s*. Stockholm: Swedish Ministry of Foreign Affairs.

Hydén, Göran and Michael Bratton (eds.), 1992, *Governance and Politics in Africa*. Boulder and London: Lynne Rienner.

Ihonvbere, Julius O., 1992, "Is Democracy Possible in Africa: The Elites, the People and Civil Society", *Quest*, Vol. 6, No. 2.

Jackson, Robert H. and Carl G. Rosberg, 1982, *Personal Rule in Black Africa: Prince, Autocrat, Prophet, Tyrant*. Berkeley: University of California Press.

Jackson, Robert H. and Carl G. Rosberg, 1985, "Democracy in Tropical Africa: Democracy versus Autocracy in African Politics", *Journal of International Affairs*, Vol. 38, No. 2.

Jeffries, Richard, 1993, "The State, Structural Adjustment and Good Government in Africa", *The Journal of Commonwealth & Comparative Politics*, Vol. 31, No. 1.

Joseph, Richard, 1991, "Africa: The Rebirth of Poltical Freedom", *Journal of Democracy*, Vol. 2, No. 4.

Kalala, Bwabo, 1991, "A l'heure de la démocratie: se départir d'une mentalité d'irresponsabilité", *Zaire-Afrique*, No. 258.

Kalflèche, Jean-Marc, 1991, "Premier handicap de la démocratization: l'indétermination de l'Europe", *Géopolitique Africaine*, Vol. 14, No. 3.

Karikari, Kwame, 1993, "Africa: The Press and Democracy", *Race and Class*, Vol. 34, No. 3.

Keane, J., 1988, *Democracy and Civil Society*. London: Verso.

Kempton, Daniel, R., 1991, "Africa in the Age of 'Perestroika'", *Africa Today*, Vol. 38, No. 3.

Khadiagala, Gilbert M., 1990, "Reflections on Development Theory and Political Practice in Africa", *A Current Bibliography on African Affairs*, Vol. 22, No. 4.

Kibwana, Kivutha, 1990, "Development of Democratic Culture and Civil Society in Africa: An Analysis of Constitutional Initiatives and Models", *Lesotho Law Journal*, Vol. 6, No. 1.

Klein, Martin A., 1992, "Back to Democracy: Presidential Address to the 1991 Meeting of the African Studies Association", *African Studies Review*, Vol. 35, No. 3, December.

Kpundeh, Sahr J. and Stephen P. Riley, 1992, "Political Choice and the New Democratic Politics in Africa", *The Round Table*, No. 323.

Kraus, Jon, "Building Democracy in Africa", 1991, Current History, Vol. 90, No. 553, May.

Kunz, Frank A., 1991, "Liberalization in Africa: Some Preliminary Reflections", *African Affairs*, No. 359.

Lancaster, Carol, 1992, "Democracy in Africa", *Foreign Policy*, No. 85, Winter.

Lancaster Carol, 1993, "Democratisation in Sub-Saharan Africa", *Survival*, Vol. 35, No. 3, Autumn.

Landell-Mills, Pierre, 1992, "Governance, Cultural Change, and Empowerment", *The Journal of Modern African Studies*, Vol. 30, No. 4.

Le Bouder, Jean-Philippe, 1991, "Ajustement structurel, saine gestion de la chose publique et démocratie", *African Development Review*, Vol. 3, No. 2.

Legum, Colin, 1990, "The Coming of Africa's Second Independence", *The Washington Quarterly*, Winter.

Lemarchand, René, 1992, "African Transitions to Democracy: An Interim (and Mostly Pessimistic) Assessment", *Africa Insight*, Vol. 22, No. 3.

Lemarchand, René, 1992, "Uncivil States and Civil Societies: How Illusion Became Reality", *Journal of Modern African Studies*, Vol. 30, No. 2.

Lemarchand, René, 1992, "Africa's Troubled Transitions", *Journal of Democracy*, Vol. 3, No. 4, October.

Leys, Roger, 1984, *Concepts of Democracy and the Democratic Struggle in Africa*. Copenhagen: Institut for Samfundsfag og Forvaltning.

Londregan, John, Henry Biene and Nicolas van de Walle, 1995, "Ethnicity and Leadership Succession in Africa", *International Studies Quarterly*, No. 39.

Lopes, Carlos and Lars Rudebeck, 1988, *The Socialist Ideal in Africa: A Debate*. Research, Report No. 81. Uppsala: Nordiska Afrikainstitutet.

Luckham, Robin, 1994, "The Military, Militarization and Democratization in Africa: A Survey of Literature and Ideas", *African Studies Review*, Vol. 37, No. 2, September.

Magang, David, 1992, "A New Beginning: The Process of Democratization in Africa", *The Parliamentarian*, No. 4, October.

Maganya, E., 1988, "Democratic or Socialist Transformation of the Rural Areas: A Comparative Review of the Experience of Tanzania, Mozambique and Zimbabwe", *The African Review*, Vol. 15, No. 1.

Mamdani, Mahmood, 1986, "Peasants and Democracy in Africa", *New Left Review*, 156.

Mamdani, Mahmood, 1990, "State and Civil Society in Contemporary Africa: Reconceptualizing the Birth of State Nationalism and the Defeat of Popular Movements", *Africa Development*, Vol. 15, No. 3/4.

Mamdani, Mahmood, 1990, "The Social Basis of Constitutionalism in Africa", *The Journal of Modern African Studies*, Vol. 28, No. 3.

Mamdani, Mahmood, 1992, "Africa: Democratic Theory and Democratic Struggles", *Dissent*, Summer.

Mamdani, Mahmood, Thandika Mkandawire and E. Wamba-dia-Wamba, 1988, "Social Movements, Social Transformation and the Struggle for Democracy in Africa", *CODESRIA Working Paper*, No. 1.

Mamdani, Mahmood and Ernest Wamba-dia-Wamba (eds.), 1994, *African Studies in Social Movements and Democracy*. Dakar: CODESRIA.

Mandaza, Ibbo and Lloyd Sachikonye (eds.), 1991, *The One Party State and Democracy*. Harare: Southern Africa Political Economy Series Trust.

Martin, Denis-Constant, 1991, "Le multipartisme, pour quoi faire?: les limites du débat politique: Kenya, Ouganda, Tanzanie, Zimbabwe", *Politique Africaine*, No. 43.

Mavila, J.C., 1992, "L'état africain: quelles perspectives de changement des institutions politiques?", *Annual Conference/African Society of International and Comparative Law*, Vol. 4.

M'ba, Charles, 1992, "Quelles hommes pour conduire la transition démocratique?", *Afrique 2000: Revue Africaine de Politique Internationale*, No. 10.

Mbaku, John Mukum, 1992, "Political Democracy and the Prospects of Development in Post-Cold War Africa", *The Journal of Social, Political and Economic Studies*, Vol. 17, Nos. 3-4, Fall/Winter.

Mbaku, John Mukum, 1993, "Political Democracy, Military Expenditures and Economic Growth in Africa", *Scandinavian Journal of Development Alternatives*, Vol. 12, No. 1.

Mbembe, Achille, 1992, "Traditions de l'autoritarisme et problèmes de gouvernement en Afrique sub-saharienne", *Africa Development*, Vol. 17, No.1.

Mbembe, Achille, 1993, "Diagnostic sur les dérapages de la transition démocratique en Afrique: un entretien avec A. Mbembe (par Michel Lobe-Ewane)", *Africa: Journal of the International African Institute*, Vol. 62, No. 1.

Mbonjo Moukoko, Pierre, 1993, "Pluralisme socio-politique et démocratie en Afrique: l'approche consociationelle ou du 'power-sharing'", *Afrique 2000:Revue Africaine de Politique Internationale*, No. 15.

McFerson, Hazel M. 1992, "Democracy and Development in Africa", *Journal of Peace Research*, Vol. 29, No. 3.

Médard, Jean-Francois, 1991, "Autoritarismes et démocraties en Afrique noire", *Politique Africaine*, No. 43.

Médard, Jean-Francois (ed.), 1991, *États d'Afrique noire: formation, mécanismes et crise*. Paris: Karthala.

Memel-Fôte, Harris, 1991, "Des ancêtres fondateurs aux pères de la nation: introduction à une anthropologie de la démocratie", *Cahiers d'Études Africaines*, Vol. 31, No. 123.

Meyns, Peter and Dani Wadada Nabudere, 1989, *Democracy and the One-Party State in Africa*. Hamburg: Institute for African Studies.

Michalon, Thierry, 1991, "Autoritarisme et hyper-centralisation: l'état Africain contre les libertés", *Annual Conference/ African Society of International and Comparative Law*, Vol. 3.

Michalon, Thierry, 1992, "L'état africain à la recherche d'une nouvelle légitimité", *Annual Conference/African Society of Internaional and Comparative Law*, Vol. 4.

Mkandawire, Thandika, 1988, "Comments on Democracy and Political Instability", *Africa Development*, Vol. 13, No. 3.

Mkandawire, Thandika, 1992, "Adjustment, Political Conditionality and Democratisation in Africa", *Conference on Democracy and Human Rights in Africa: The Internal and External Context*. Harare: SAPES/CODESRIA.

Monga, C'elestin, 1991, "L'émergence de nouveaux modes de production démocratique en Afrique Noire", *Afrique 2000:Revue Africaine de Politique Internationale*, No. 7.

Monga, Célestin, 1995, "Civil Society and Democratisation in Francophone Africa", *The Journal of Modern African Studies*, Vol. 33, No. 3.

Monkotan, J.B. Kuassi, 1990, "Des modes originaux d'expression démocratique en Afrique", *Afrique 2000:Revue Africaine de Politique Internationale*, No. 3.

Mouelle Kombi II, Narcisse, 1991, "La conférence nationale africaine: l'emergence d'un mythe politique", *Afrique 2000:Revue Africaine de Politique Internationale*, No. 7.

Mukandala, Rwekaza Sympho, 1992, "To Be or Not to Be: The Paradoxes of African Bureaucracies in the 1990s", *International Review of Administrative Sciences*, Vol. 58, No. 4.

Munishi, G.K., 1988, "The Institution Building View of the African Development Dilemma", *The African Review*, Vol. 15, No. 2.

Munslow, Barry, 1993, "Democratisation in Africa", *Parliamentary Affairs*, Vol. 46, No. 4, October.

Mustapha, A.R. and S. Othman, 1987, "The Idea of Democracy", *West Africa*, 28 September.

Nannan, Sukhwant Singh, 1992, "Africa: The Move towards Democracy", *Strategic Analysis*, Vol. 14, No. 10.

Narang, Harish (ed.), "Mightier than the Machete", *Africa Quarterly*, special issue, Vol 34. No. 3.

Ndue, Paul Ntungwe, 1994, "Africa's Turn towards Pluralism", *Journal of Democracy*, Vol. 5, No. 1, January.

New Internationalist, 1990, No. 208, "Burden of hope: Africa in the 1990s".

Newbury, Catharine, 1994, "Paradoxes of Democratization in Africa", *African Studies Review*, Vol. 37, No. 1, April.

Ninalowo, Bayo, 1990, "On the Strucutres and Praxis of Domination, Democratic Culture and Social Change: With Inferences from Africa", *Scandinavian Journal of Development Studies*, Vol. 9, No. 4, December.

Nolutshungu, Sam C., 1992, "Africa in a World of Democracies: Inter-pretation and Retrieval", *Journal of Commonwealth and Comparative Politics*, Vol. 30, No. 3.

Nyang'oro, Julius E. and Timothy M. Shaw (eds.), 1992, *Beyond Structural Adjustment in Africa: Political Economy of Sustainable and Democratic Development*. New York: Praeger.

Nyang'oro, Julius E., 1994, "Reform Politics and the Democratization Process in Africa", *African Studies Review*, Vol. 37, No. 1, April.

Nyong'o, Peter Anyang', 1987, *Popular Struggles for Democracy in Africa*. London: Zed Books Ltd.

Nyong'o Peter Anyang', 1988, "Political Instability and the Prospects for Democracy in Africa", *Africa Development*, Vol. XIII, No. 1.

Nyong'o Peter Anyang', 1988, "Democracy and Political Instability: A Rejoinder to the Comments by Thandika Mkandawire", *Africa Development*, Vol. XIII, No. 3.

Nyong'o, Peter Anyang', 1988, "Political Instability and the Prospects for Democracy in Africa", *Africa Development*, Vol. 13, No. 1.

Nyong'o, Peter Anyang', 1988, "A Rejoinder to the Comments on Demo-cracy and Political Instability", *Africa Development*, Vol. 13, No. 3.

Nyong'o Peter Anyang' (ed.), 1988, *Afrique: la longue marche vers la démocratie: Etat autoritaire et résistances populaires*. Paris: Publisud.

Nyong'o Peter Anyang', 1992, "Africa: The Failure of One-Party Rule", *Journal of Democracy*, Vol. 3, No. 1, January.

Nyong'o, Peter Anyang', 1992, "Discourses on Democracy in Africa", *Con-ference on Democracy and Human Rights in Africa: The Internal and External Context*. Harare: SAPES/CODESRIA.

Nyong'o, Peter Anyang' (ed.), 1992, *Thirty Years of Independence in Africa: The Lost Decades?* Nairobi: African Association of Political Science.

Nzongola-Ntalaja, Georges (ed.), 1987, *Africa's Crisis*. London: IFFA.

Nzouankeu, Jacques Mariel, 1991, "The African Attitude to Democracy", *International Social Science Journal*, No. 128, May.

Nzouankeu, Jacques Mariel, 1994, "Decentralization and Democracy in Africa", *International Review of Administrative Sciences*, Vol. 60.

Ojwang, J.B., 1990, "Constitutionalism—in Classical Terms and in African Nationhood", *Lesotho Law Journal*, Vol. 6, No. 1.

Okamba, M. Emmanuel, 1993, "Une analyse systématique des conférences nationales souveraines africaines: de l'état de fait à l'état de droit", *Afrique 2000:Revue Africaine de Politique Internationale*. No. 15.

O'Kane, Rosemary H.T., 1993, "Coups d'Etat in Africa: A Political Economy Approach", *Journal of Peace Research*, Vol. 30, No. 3.

Olukoshi, Adebayo O. , 1992, *The Politics of Structural Adjustment in Africa* London: James Currey.

Olukoshi, Adebayo O. and Liisa Laakso (eds.), 1996, *Challenges to the Nation-State in Africa*. Uppsala: Nordiska Afrikainstitutet in cooperation with the Institute of Development Studies, University of Helsinki.

Olukoshi, Adebayo O., 1996, "The Elusive Prince of Denmark: Structural Adjustment and the Crisis of Governance in Africa". Mimeo. Uppsala.

Othman, Haroub (ed.), 1989, *Alternative Development Strategies for Africa: Report on IFAA/IDS Conference*. London: Institute of Development Studies.

Ottaway, Marina, 1993, "Should Elections Be the Criterion of Democratization in Africa", *CSIS Africa Notes*. Washington: Center for Strategic and International Studies.

Owusu, Maxwell, 1992, "Democracy and Africa: A View from the Village", *The Journal of Modern African Studies*, Vol. 30, No. 3.

Oyono, Dieudonné, 1992, "Du parti unique au multipartisme: environnement international et processus de democratisation en Afrique", *Études Internationales*, Vol. 4, No. 45.

Oyugi, Walter O., E.S. Atieno Odhiambo, Michael Chege and Afrifa K. Gitonga (eds.), 1988, *Democratic Theory and Practice in Africa*. London: James Currey.

"Prospects for Democracy in Africa: Approaches from below and from above", *Africa Today*, Vol. 37, No. 3.

Ramose, Mogobe B., 1992, "African Democratic Traditions: Oneness, Consensus and Openness—a Reply to Wamba-dia-Wamba", *Quest*, Vol. 6, No. 2.

Reyntjens, Filip, 1991, "The Winds of Change: Political and Constitutional Evolution in Francophone Africa, 1990-1991, Journal of African Law, Vol. 35, No. 1–2.

Rijnierse, Elly, 1993, "Democratisation in Sub-Saharan Africa? Literature Overview", *Third World Quarterly*, Vol. 14, No. 3.

Riley, Stephen P., 1991, *The Democratic Transition in Africa: An End to the One-Party State?* London: Research Institute for the Study of Conflict and Terrorism.

Riley, Stephen P., 1992, "Political Adjustment or Domestic Pressure: Democratic Politics and Political Choice in Africa", *Third World Quearterly*, Vol. 13, No. 3.

Rimmer, Douglas (ed.), 1993, *Action in Africa*. London: James Currey.

Romdane, Mahmoud Ben, 1992, "Mouvements sociaux et processus democratique en Afrique, *Conference on Democracy and Human Rights in Africa: The Internal and External Context*. Harare: SAPES/ CODESRIA.

Ronen, Dov (ed.), 1986, *Democracy and Pluralism in Africa*. Boulder: Lynne Rienner Publishers.

Rotchild, D. and N. Chazan (eds.), 1988, *The Precarious Balance: State and Society in Africa*. Boulder: Westview.

Rudebeck, Lars (ed.), 1992, *When Democracy Makes Sense: Studies in the Democratic Potential of Third World Popular Movements*. Uppsala: Working Group for the Study of Development Strategies.

Sandbrook, Richard, 1988, "Liberal Democracy in Africa: A Socialist-Revisionist Perspective", *Canadian Journal of African Studies*, Vol. 22, No. 2.

Sandbrook, Richard and Mohamed Halfani (eds.), 1993, *Empowering People: Building Community, Civil Associations and Legality in Africa*. Toronto: Centre for Urban and Community Studies, University of Toronto.

Schmitz, Gerald J. and Eboe Hutchful, 1992, *Democratization and Popular Participation in Africa*. Ottawa: The North-South Institute.

Schraeder, Peter J., 1994, "Elites as Facilitators or Impediments to Political Development? Some Lessons from the "Third Wave" of Democratization in Africa", *The Journal of Developing Areas*, Vol. 29, No. 1, October.

Shivji, Issa G., 1988, *Fight My Beloved Continent: New Democracy in Africa.* Harare: SAPES Trust.

Shivji, Issa G., 1989, "The Pitfalls of the Debate on Democracy", *CODESRIA Bulletin*, Nos. 2–3.

Shivji, Issa G., 1990, "The Pitfalls of the Debate on Democracy", *Ifda Dossier*, No. 79.

Shivji, Issa G. (ed.), "State and Constitutionalism: An African Debate on Democracy", *Human Rights and Constitutionalism Series*, No. 1. Harare: Southern African Political Economy Series Trust.

Sklar, Richard L., 1983, "Democracy in Africa", *The African Studies Review*, Vol. 26, 3/4.

Sommerville, Keith, 1991, "Africa Moves towards Party Pluralism", *The World Today*, Vol. 47, No. 8–9, August/September.

Stark, Frank M., 1986, "Theories of Contemporary State Formation in Africa: A Reassessment (review article)", *The Journal of Modern African Studies*, Vol. 24, No. 2.

"Surviving Democracy?, 1992, *Review of African Political Economy* (special issue).

Tadesse, Zenebeworke, 1992, "African Debates on Social Movements and the Democratic Process", *Development*, No. 3.

Tadesse, Zenebeworke, 1992, "Conference on Democratization Processes in Africa: Problems and Prospects/Report", *CODESRIA Bulletin*, No. 1/2.

Tandon, Yash (ed.), 1982, *Debate on Class, State and Imperialism.* Dar es Salaam: Tanzania Publishing House.

Tandon, Yash, 1991, "Political Economy of Struggles for Democracy and Human Rights in Africa", *Economic and Political Weekly* (Bombay), June 22.

Tedga, Paul John Marc, 1991, *Ouverture démocratique en Afrique noire?* Paris: L'Harmattan.

Tiangaye, Nicolas, 1992, "Crise de légitimité du pouvoir de l'état et conférences nationales en Afrique", *African Journal of International and Comparative Law*, Vol. 4, Pt. 3.

Tordoff, William, 1993, *Government and Politics in Africa*, London, Macmillan.

Turok, Ben (ed.), 1991, "Debt and Democracy", *Alternative Strategies for Africa*. Vol. 3. London: Institute for African Alternatives.

Vanhanen, Tatu (ed.), 1992, *Strategies of Democratization*. Washington: Crane Russak.

van Hoek, F. and J. Bossuyt, 1993, "Democracy in Sub-Saharan Africa: The Search for a New Institutional Set-Up", *African Development Review*, Vol. 5, No. 1, June.

Vivekananda, Franklin, 1990, "Militarism and the Crisis of Democracy in Africa 1980-85", *Scandinavian Journal of Development Alternatives*, Vol. 9, No. 4.

Volman, Daniel, 1993, "Africa and the New World Order", *The Journal of Modern African Studies*, Vol. 31, No. 1, March.

Wamala, A. S., 1992, "The Role of Workers in the Struggle towards Multi-Party Democracy: Africa's Colonial and Post-Colonial Experience", Eastern Africa Social Science Research Review, Vol. 8, No. 1, January.

Wamba-dia-Wamba, Ernest, 1992, "Beyond Elite Politics of Democracy in Africa", *Quest*, Vol. 6, No. 1.

Welch, Claude E. Jr., 1991, "The Organisation of African Unity and the Promotion of Human Rights", *The Journal of Modern African Studies*, Vol. 29, No. 4.

Widner, Jennifer A. (ed.), 1994, *Economic Change and Political Liberalization in Sub-Saharan Africa*. Baltimore and London: Johns Hopkins University Press.

Wipper, Audrey, 1985, "Riot and Rebellion among African Women: Three Examples of Women's Political Clout", *Women in International Development. Working Papers*, Michigan State University.

Wiseman, John A., 1990, *Democracy in Black Africa: Survival and Revival*. New York: Paragon House.

Wiseman, John A., 1992, "Early Post-Redemocratisation Elections in Africa", *Electoral Studies*, Vol. 11, No. 4.

Wiseman, John A., 1993, "Democracy and the New Political Pluralism in Africa: Causes, Consequences and Significance", *Third World Quarterly*, Vol. 14, No. 3.

Wiseman, John A., 1996, *The New Struggle for Democracy in Africa*. Hants, England: Avebury.

Wodie, Francis, 1992, "Problematique de la transition démocratique en Afrique", *Conference on Democracy and Human Rights in Africa: The Internal and External Context*. Harare: SAPES/CODESRIA.

Woodward, Peter, 1994, "Democracy and Economy in Africa: The Optimists and the Pessimists", *Democratization*, Vol. 1, No. 1, Spring.

Wunch, James S. and Dele Olowu (eds.), 1990, *Failure of the Centralized State: Institutions and Self-Governance in Africa*. Boulder: Westview Press.

Young, Tom, 1993, "Elections and Electoral Politics in Africa", *Africa*, Vol. 63, No.3.

Young, Tom (ed.), 1993, "Understanding Elections in Africa", *Africa*, Journal of the International African Institute, Vol. 63, No. 3.

Index

A

Adelzadeh 227
Adji 147, 148
Affirmative action 196, 198, 210, 224
  226
Africa Demos 11, 17
Agbu 245, 248
Ake 11, 15, 91, 115
Algeria 10
  *political parties and civil society
  organisations*
  FIS (Front Islamique du Salut) 10
Astow 231
Atkinson 227
Azarya 22, 39

B

Bangura 14, 15, 17, 18, 20, 21, 23, 29
Barker 244
Barrell 205
Baskin 200, 218, 221, 222
Bates 17, 48
Bathily 121, 123, 127, 128
Bayart 39
Beckman 11, 17, 21, 23, 172
Benin Republic 25, 27, 31, 148, 162
  political leaders
  Kerekou 27, 162
Berlin Wall 8, 9
Berman 42, 48
Bianchini 121
Bill of Rights 35, 226
bolshevik revolution 13
Botha T 212
Bratton 9, 22, 39
Bundy 229

C

Cameroon 10, 31
capitalism
  democracy 13–18, 176
  political liberties 15
Carter 229

Cornia 29
Côte d'Ivoire 10, 32
Central Europe 8
Chad 31
Chaskalsoni 229
Chazan 22, 39, 175, 181
Chege 57
choiceless democracy 12
citizen 8, 15, 19, 20, 35, 89, 149, 172,
  173, 175, 186, 191, 196, 197, 202,
  232, 242, 249
civic organisations, *see* specific
  country; civil society organisations
civil rights 8, 15, 19–20, 34, 91, 242,
  244, 249, 256
civil society 12–13, 22, 25–26, 51, 53,
  55, 114–142, 195–237
  churches 42, 55, 201, 206
    civil society/civic organisations,
    see specific country; civil society
    organisations
  democratic transition 5–10, 13,
    22–29, 32–35, 39–40, 42–48, 55–
    58, 78, 89, 92, 95, 97, 144–168,
    172–193, 242–263
  extra–legal activities 28, 51
    mobilisation of 5–6, 11–12, 19,
    24–25, 28–36, 40–41, 111, 117,
    120, 126, 127, 132, 134–142,
    175, 180, 181–193, 197, 198,
    199–237, 243, 255
  ethnicity 11, 12, 28, 30, 32, 33,
    40–41, 106, 110, 120, 136, 138,
    150–153, 255
  religion 11, 28, 33, 40, 42, 138,
    139, 140, 256, 259
  professional unions/movements
    32–33, 55, 175, 177, 187, 249
  SAPs *see* Structural Adjustment
    Programmes
  trade unions 25, 33, 49, 115, 117,
    122, 123, 125, 127, 136, 146, 148,
    154, 155, 168, 174, 177, 185, 186,
    197, 198, 199, 201, 203, 208, 211,
    216–223, 226, 228, 232, 234, 236,
    237, 246, 249

women's groups/movements 136, 185, 191, 197, 211, 234
youth and student unions/movements 33, 115, 117, 123, 125, 132–133, 136, 140, 145, 147, 148, 154, 155, 158, 185, 197, 200, 201, 202, 203, 206, 211, 234–246, 249
political parties *see* specific country; political parties
civil society organisations *see* specific country; civil society organisations
Cohen 19
Cold War 9, 13–14, 91
  politics in Africa 9, 56, 94, 116, 228
Collinge 212
Collins 219, 220, 222
colonial legacy 114, 172
Congo 162,
  political leaders
  Sassou Nguesso 162
constitutional conferences 251–254, 260, *see also* national conferences
constitutional reform *see* democratic consolidation; constitutional reforms
communism 9
Copans 138
Coulon 138, 139
Creevey–Berham 138
Cruise O'Brien 138, 139

D

Dabengwa 95
Dahl 14, 244
Ddungu 186
debt burden 16
Decoudras 145
democratic consolidation 10–15, 17–18, 34, 41, 48, 91–142, 144, 145, 177, 195–237
  civil society *see* civil society
  constitutional reforms 10–11, 24–25, 30, 31, 35, 57, 89, 97, 98, 109, 110, 117, 124, 125, 132, 141, 146, 147, 150, 156–157
  economic context *see* economic crisis
  international context *see* international system
  political parties *see* opposition parties

SAPs 11, 12, 13, 26, 33
  the military, 118
democratic transition 5–12, 17–19, 24–36, 39–48, 55–89, 144–170, 171–193, 242–263
  international context *see* international system; democratisation
  international pressure 9, 11–12, 57, 92, 176, 227, 228, 261, 262
  military interventions 10, 33, 145, 152, 164–167, 242–262
  popular pressure *see* civil society; democratic transition
  resistance to 10, 25, 43, 96, 97, 181, 184
  SAPs *see* economic policy; neo–liberalism and political change/democratic transition
development oriented state 13, 33–34
Diamond 14, 22, 183
Diaw 116
Diop 122, 123, 133, 136, 137, 138, 139
Diouf 131, 133, 136, 137, 138
Drake 175
Duncan 14

E

Eastern Europe 8, 93, 215
economic development
  democracy and 13, 16–19, 114
economic crisis 16, 19–28
  explanations of 16, 20, 40
  popular protest 8, 20–21, 24, 25, 26
  democratisation 6, 11, 13, 16–28, 33, 34, 39–40, 42, 43, 89, 121, 132, 138, 139, 140, 155, 160, 161, 200, 261, 262, 263,
  SAPs *see* Structural Adjustment Programmes
economic policy
  liberalism and democracy 8, 19
  neo–liberalism 20–23
  political change/democratic transition 9, 11–19, 21–29, 33–34, 39, 89, 101, 102, 129, 131, 139, 140
economic reform 11–13, 26, 27
  conditionality 11, 23, 25, 26, 200
  popular protest 13, 23, 25, 129–130 134, 147
  SAPs *see* Structural Adjustment Programmes

elections 8–10, 19, 24–25, 31–33, 91, 172
  boycott 30, 132, 246
  electoral system 96,99,130,134,157
    Westminster 31, 227
  Kenya *see* Kenya; elections
  monitoring 8, 30, 153, 246
  Niger *see* Niger; elections
  Nigeria *see* Nigeria; elections
  opposition cohesion *see* opposition parties; cohesion
  outcomes of 9–10, 25, 31, 83, 95, 98, 100, 103, 104, 125, 126, 130, 136, 147, 151–155, 158, 159, 167–168, 185
  rigging 29–30, 33, 49, 104, 168
  South Africa *see* South Africa; elections
  Uganda *see* Uganda; elections
  Zimbabwe *see* Zimbabwe; elections
Ethnicity
  politics 11, 12, 16, 40–89, 95, 106, 150–153, 154, 176, 177, 178, 179, 181, 183, 184, 196, 227, 246, 250, 252, 253,
Europe 17
European Union 260

F
Fako 215
Fall 123, 125, 126, 132
Fascism 14, 15, 18
Fatton 123, 138
Fine 212
Francophone Africa 8, 162
Friedman 212, 227
Fuglestad 167
Fukuyama 14

G
Gabon 31
Gambia 10
  political leaders
    Jawara 10
Gathiaka 53
Gender issues 102, 225
Germany 8
Gertzel 43, 45, 48, 50
Ghai 12, 24

Ghana 10, 31
  political leaders
    Nkrumah 196
Gibbon 8, 9, 12, 16, 21, 23, 197, 232
Goulbourne 19
Greece 14
Group of Seven (G–7) 12
Guinea 31
Guinea Bissau 10
Gutto 40

H
Haggard 26
Haysom 206
Havnevik 8
Hermet 91
Hesseling 116, 124
Hughes 229
human rights 25, 32, 34, 97, 172, 191, 245, 246, 249, 256, 260, 262
Huntington 172
Hydén 16, 39

I
Ibrahim 25, 167
International Monetary Fund (IMF) 11, 12, 20, 21, 26, 27, 32, 101, 147, 150
international system 121, 129, 132
  changes in 8–9
  democratisation 8–10, 12, 35, 93
Islam 10, 121, 123, 137–141

J
Jackson 39
Jacobs 211
Jochelson 229

K
Kanogo 42
Kanyinga 25, 48, 53, 55, 61, 62
Kanté 133
Kasfir 178, 185, 186
Keane 14, 15
Keet 212
Kenya 6, 10, 24, 25, 39–90, 175, 224
  opposition politics 25, 29, 31, 31, 32, 33, 35, 41–50, 56–89, 176

elections 45, 49, 54, 58, 63, 68, 69,
70, 75, 76, 79, 80, 83, 84, 86, 88, 89
*political parties and civil society
organisations*
  CAPU, Coast African People's
    Union 46
  CMS, Church Missionary Society 42
  COTU, Central Organization of
    Trade Unions 53
  Dinya Kaggia 42
  Dinya Msambwa 42
  DP, Democratic Party 61, 62, 65,
    67–71, 83, 84, 85, 86
  EAA, East African Association 42
  FORD, Forum for Restoration of
    Democracy 57, 58, 59, 60, 67
  FORD–Asili, 57, 60, 61, 62, 75–79
  FORD–Kenya, 57, 60, 61, 62, 69,
    70, 71–75, 76, 86,
  GEMA, Gikuyo Embu Meru
    Association 52, 53, 67, 68, 69, 83
  IPK, Islamic Party of Kenya 57
  KADU, Kenya African Democratic
    Union 47, 48, 49, 50, 58, 63, 64, 66,
    86, 88
  KANU, Kenya African National
    Union 46–54, 57–70, 72, 74, 76,
    78, 79, 81–88
  KPA, Kalenjin Political Alliance
    46
  KAPP, Kenya African People's
    Party 46
  KAU, Kenya African Union 42,
    44, 47
  KCA, Kikuyu Central Association
    42
  Kavirondo Tax Payers Welfare
    Association 43
  KIM, Kenya Independence
    Movement 46
  KNC, Kenya National Congress
    65
  KNP, Kenya National Party 46
  KPU, Kenyan People's Union 49,
    50, 51
  KSC, Kenya Social Congress 57
  Luo Thrift and Trading
    Corporation 44
  Mau Mau movement 43, 44, 46,
    47, 48, 51
  MUF, Maasai United Front 46

  NKCA, North Kavirondo Central
    Association 44
  Nomia Church 42
  SAFINA 72
  SNA Somali National Association 47
  Taita Hills Associations 44
  Ukamba Members Association 44
political leaders
  Kaggia 48, 51
  Kenyatta 47–54, 63, 67, 77, 79, 85,
    87, 224
  Kibaki 63, 67, 68, 85
  Matiba 59, 60, 62, 65, 75, 76, 77,
    78
  Mboya 48, 49, 50
  Moi 45, 46, 50–57, 61–64, 66– 68,
    73, 76, 77, 80–82, 85, 171, 175,
    176
  Muliro 45, 46
  Ngala 46
  Oginga Odinga 44, 48, 49, 50, 51,
    58–61, 69, 71–73, 75
Keynesianism 12, 21
Kiggundu 178
Kriger 197, 233

L

Laakso 11, 19, 28, 196
Lambert 217
Lanegran 212
Latin America 17
Lavergne 137, 139
Legum 8
Lensink 16
Lesotho 28
Levin 213
Liabes 18
Liberia 28
Lodge 198–206, 212, 229–231
Lonsdale 42, 48
Lusophone Africa 24, 31
Ly 117, 121

M

Machiavelli 23, 24
Madagascar 31
de Madariaga 244
Mahamadou 165
Maidoka 147

Mali 28, 165
Maloba 42
Mamdani 33, 41, 42, 172, 181, 196, 197, 200, 220, 224, 231, 232
market 11–12, 14, 21–24, 26, 40
Markoff 14, 17
Markowitz 138
Marx A. W. 198–200, 202, 203, 210, 229, 230
Marxism 19, 114–116, 120, 121, 124, 125, 128, 132, 135, 152, 229
Matabeleland 92, 96, 106
Mathiane 203
Mayekiso 212
Mduli 212
Mill 171
military rule 5, 8, 35
Mkandawire 12, 16, 18, 21, 23, 26, 33
Molamu 215
Morobe 206, 208, 236, 237
Moyo 99
Mozambique 10
multi–party democracy 6, 8–11, 19, 25, 29, 30, 32, 33, 35, 40, 41, 50, 54–60, 62, 77, 86, 88, 89, 91, 92, 113, 114, 118, 128, 139, 145, 147, 148, 150, 154, 156, 161, 171–176, 181–183, 185, 187, 191, 196, 207, 227, 228, 237
    African alternative to 10, 180, 193
Murray 198, 199, 229, 230
Mustapha 20
Muslims see Islam or religion

N

Naidoo 229
National conferences 8, 24, 31, 113, 144, 145, 148–151, 155, 160, 166, 167, see also constitutional conferences
Nelson 22
Neocosmos 25
Neo–patrimonialism 15, 16, 17, 18, 22, 39, 41
Ngcobo 212
Ngunyi 53
Niger 28, 31, 144–170
    opposition politics 6, 35, 144–168
    elections 145, 147, 149, 152, 153, 155, 158–167

political leaders
    Abdoulaye 159
    Amadou 150, 160, 165
    Cisse 160
    Diori 145, 167
    Djermakoye 150, 152, 153, 155
    Issoufou 152, 155, 156, 163, 165
    Jackson 152
    Kountché 145, 147, 150, 151, 167
    Mainasara 164–168
    Ousmane 152–155, 157–159, 163, 165
    Saibou 149, 156
    Salifou 149, 156
    Tandja 150, 151, 154–156, 162
political parties and civil society organisations
    AFC, Alliance Forces for Change 153–163
    AMACA, Association Mutelle pour la Culture et les Artes 152
    ANDP, Alliance Nigerienne pour la Democratie et le Progrès 152–155, 157, 159
    CAMAD, Club des Amis de M.A. Djermakoye 153
    CDS, Convention Democratique et Sociale 151, 152, 154, 155, 157, 159, 168
    CND, Conseil National de Développement 146
    COCD, Comité de Coordination des Luttes Democratiques 154
    Energie de l'Ouest 152
    Islamic Association of Niger 145
    MNSD, Mouvement National pour la Société de Développement 145, 147–149, 151–156, 158–162, 164
    PNSD, Parti Nigerien pour la Democratie et le Socialisme 152, 153, 154, 155, 157, 159, 161
    PPN/RDA, Parti Progressiste Nigérien/Rassemblement Démocratique Africain 153, 154, 159
    PUND, Parti pour l'Unité Nationale et le Développement 153–155, 159
    UDP, Union pour la démocratie et le progrès 153, 154

UDPS, Union pour la démocratie
et le progrès social 153–155, 159
UPDP, Union des patriotes
démocrates et progressistes 154,
156, 159
USTN, Union des Syndicats des
Travailleurs du Niger 148, 168
Nigeria 6, 10, 20, 242–263
opposition politics 35, 242–262
elections 242, 243, 246–251, 255,
258, 259, 262, 263
political leaders
Abacha 243, 246–256, 258, 259,
261, 262
Abiola 10, 246, 248–253, 255, 259,
261, 262
Babangida 10, 151, 242–248, 250
252, 254, 262
Balewa 253
Buhari 244, 253
Enahoro 258
Gowon 253
Idiagbon 244
Ironsi 253
Kingibe 249
Muhammed 253, 254
Obasanjo 252–254, 258, 261
Okparaji 256
Ransome–Kuti 261
Saro–Wiwa 256
Shagari 254
Shonekan 247, 248, 250, 253, 254
Soyinka 256, 261
Yar'adua 252, 258, 261
*political parties and civil society
organisations*
ANC, All Nigeria Congress 256, 259
CAN, Christian Association of
Nigeria 259
CBCN, Catholic Bishops'
Conference of Nigeria 259
CD, Campaign for Democracy
246, 247, 256
CDHR, Committee for the
Defence of Human Rights 256
CLO, Civil Liberties Organization
247, 250
Council of Ulema 259
CRP Constitutional Rights Project
247, 256

EMU, Eastern Mandate Union
256, 258, 260
Imeru Unity Group 256
Middle Belt Forum 256
MNR, Movement for National
Reformation 258
MOSOP, Movement for the Sur-
vival of the Ogoni People 244, 255
NADECO, National Democratic
Coalition 254, 256–260, 262
NALICON, National Liberation
Council 256m 259, 261
NAM, National Awoist Move-
ment 259
NANS, National Association of
Nigerian Students 247
NBA, Nigerian Bar Association
247
NDAC, National Democratic
Awareness Committee 256
New Dimension 259
NLC, Nigerian Labour Congress 247
NPDA, National Patriotic Demo-
cratic Association of the 4th
Force 259
NRC, National Republican
Convention 245, 247, 248, 249
NUC, National Unity Club 256, 259
NUCN, National Unity Council of
Nigeria 258, 259
PCF, Peoples Consultative Forum
256, 259
PDM, Peoples Democratic
Movement 256, 258, 259
PPA, Patriotic Peoples Association
259
SDP, Social Democratic Party 245–249
SDU, Social Democratic Union
256, 259
Nkiwane 29, 101
Non Governmental Organisations
(NGOs) 24, 106, 175
Nyiam 260
Nyong'o 18, 40, 53, 173
Nzo 195
Nzongola–Ntalaja 196
Nzimande 212

O

O'Donnell 18
Olagunju 245

Olukoshi 9, 11, 16, 18, 19, 20, 21, 23, 24, 27, 196, 245, 248

Onimode 24

opposition parties 5–6, 10–12, 18–19, 23–35, 41, 55–89, 173–177

   cohesion 25, 32–34, 41, 57, 58, 63, 64, 69, 70, 78, 108, 110, 111, 115, 118, 121, 128, 130, 132, 135, 137, 141, 161, 192, 244, 250

   financing 31–33, 132, 152, 177, 182, 192

   political base 32, 35, 78, 101, 102, 103, 105, 106, 111, 119, 121, 124, 126, 132, 145, 151, 177, 178, 181, 184, 185, 186, 188, 190, 197, 109, 256

   mobilisation of see civil society;

   organisation of/leadership 6, 12, 30, 55–89, 101, 102, 105, 107, 109, 111, 118, 130, 131, 135, 156, 177, 179, 181, 183, 184, 191, 230, 233, 234, 235, 237, 258

   political agenda 47, 48, 49, 100, 102, 105, 109, 111, 120, 127, 128, 129, 135, 197, 209, 222, 223–237, 243, 256

   popular participation see civil society; mobilisation of

Orkin 221, 222

Ottaway 16, 17, 18, 19, 21, 22

P

Padayashee 227

Paye 133

Pieterse 212, 233

Pityana 221, 222

political parties 19, 25

   see also opposition parties

political theory

   democracy 13–19, 33–35, 91–92, 244

popular politics school 39–40

R

religion

  identity 31

  politics 11, 28, 31, 32, 33, 40, 121, 123,137–141, 246, 250

rent-seeking 15–18

Robinson 146, 149

Rosberg 39

Rousseau 149

Rudebeck 18

Rwanda 28

S

Sachikonye 97

Sandbrook 22, 39

Sapine 229

de Sardani 165

Sartori 96

Schatzberg 183

Seekings 204, 229

Senegal 113–143

   opposition politics 6, 32, 35, 113–142

   elections 114, 117, 123, 125, 126, 129–132, 135, 136, 138, 140, 141, 142

   political leaders

     Bathily 129, 132, 141

     Cissoko 115, 116

     Dia 117, 119, 128, 129

     Diop Cheikh Anta 117, 118, 119, 126, 127

     Diop Majmouth 115, 116

     Diop Momar Coumba 114, 119, 121, 123

     Diouf Abdou 126, 128–138, 142

     Guèye 118

     Ly 118, 119, 120, 128

     Ndoye 128

     Niang 115, 135

     Savané 135, 141

     Senghor 114, 115, 117, 118, 122, 124, 125, 127, 130, 131, 133, 138,

     Sy 117

     Thiam 128, 131, 137

     Wade 126, 130, 131, 132, 134, 135, 136, 137, 141, 142

   political parties and civil society organisations

     ADS, Senegalese Democratic Alliance 129, 130, 132

     AJ/PADS, And–Jëf/Parti Africain pour la démocratie et le Socialisme 135, 141

     Association of Senegalese Democrats 128

     BMS, Coalition of Senegalese Masses 117, 118, 119

COSU, Coordinating Association for the United Senegalese Opposition 128
FNS, Senegalese National Front 117, 118, 119
LCT, League of Communist Workers 129
LD/MIT, Democratic League/ Workers' Party 125, 132, 141, 142
MDP, Popular Democratic Movement 129
MFDC, Movement of Democratic Forces of Casamance 132
PAI, African Independence Party 115, 116, 117, 119, 120, 123, 124, 125, 127, 128, 129
PDS, Senegalese Democratic Party 124–127, 129–132, 135–137, 141, 142
PIT, Parti de l'indépendence et du travail 135, 137, 141
PLP, Parti pour la libération du peuple 127, 135
PPS, Senegalese People's Party 117, 119, 120, 124, 129
PRA, Parti Rassemblement Africain 115–122
PS, Parti socialiste 114, 125, 127, 129–140, 142
RND Rassemblement National Démocratique 126, 127, 129
UPS, Union Progressiste Sénégalaise 114–120, 122, 124, 126
UTLS, Union of Free Workers of Senegal 129
Seychelles 10
Shaw 221
Shivji 11, 40
Sidell 21
Sierra Leone 10
  political leaders
    Momoh 10
  political parties
    APC All People's Congress 10
Sikhosana 212
Simone 212, 233
single party rule 5, 8, 9, 55, 62, 63, 86, 97, 114, 123, 147, 154, 182
Sisulu 204

Sitas 229
Sithole 95, 96
Sklar 175
Slovo 215, 233
social contract 18, 20, 21, 34, 36
Socialism 12, 155, 179, 235, 236
  democracy 13–15
  political liberties 15
Solomon 213
Somalia 28
Souley 25, 147, 150, 161, 164, 65, 166
South Africa 10, 195–241
  opposition politics 6, 24, 25, 35, 199–237
  elections 198, 201, 202, 210
  political leaders
    Botha 202, 209
    Cronin 214, 215, 229
    Lekota 209
    Mandela, Nelson 10, 214, 234
    Mandela, Winnie 208
    Naidoo 219
    Sebina 203
    Shilowa 224
  political parties 201, 210
    ANC, African National Congress 199, 205, 206, 208–212, 214–216, 220, 221, 223–225, 227–230, 233–235
    COSATU, Congress of South African Trade Unions 206, 208, 217, 219–224, 230, 233
    FEDSAW, Federation of South African Women 225
    FOSATU, Federation of South African Trade Unions 217, 218, 219
    Inkatha Freedom Party 215, 227
    MAWU, Metal and Allied Workers Unions 218, 219
    NP, National Party 199, 220, 227, 228
    PAC, Pan Africa Congress 216
    PEBCO, Port Elizabeth Black Civic Organisation 201
    PFP, Popular Federal Party 209
    SACP, South African Communist Party 214, 220, 233, 235

SACTU, South African Congress of Trade Unions 216
SANCO, South African National Civic Organisation 210, 211
UDF, United Democratic Party 198, 201–212, 214, 218, 226, 229, 230, 231, 233
Southern Africa 28
Soviet Union 19, 56
Sparks 199, 234
Structural Adjustment Programmes 8, 11–13, 20–33, 129–131, 139, 155, 196
  democratic consolidation *see* democratic consolidation
  democratic transition *see* economic policy; neo–liberalism and political change/economic transition
  socio–economic consequenses of 11, 12, 20–21, 23–29, 33, 131, 134, 139, 155, 200
Swilling 202, 212, 218, 219

T

Tanzania 31, 232
  political parties and civil society organisations
    TANU Tanganyika African National Union 233
Tarp 16
Third World 12
Throup 42, 51, 53
Tordoff 174

U

Uganda 171–194
  opposition politics 6, 30, 35, 179–193
  elections 183, 185, 186, 189, 190–192
  political leaders
    Bataringaya 188
    Museveni 35, 172, 180, 182–185, 190
    Obote 182
  political parties
    DP, Democratic Party 179–181, 183, 185, 188, 189
    KY, Kabaka Yekka 188
    NCD, National Caucus for Democracy 190

NRM, National Resistance Movement 35, 172, 179–189, 191, 192
UPC, Uganda People's Party 179–183, 185, 187, 188
UNDP, United Nation Development Programme 16
UNRISD, United Nation's Research Institute for Social Development 11, 29

V

Villalon 140
de Villiers 205

W

van de Walle 39
Wamba-dia-Wamba 196, 235, 236
Warsaw pact 8
Wasserman 46
Webb 26
Webster 198, 217, 218, 220
Welfarism 13, 20–21, 34
White 205
Widner 16, 17, 18, 19, 22
Wiseman 19, 24
Wohlgemuth 9
World Bank 11, 12, 20, 23–27, 32, 92, 101, 150, 227

Y

Young 11, 133, 175

Z

Zaire 29, 30, 175
  political leaders
    Mobotu 175
Zambia 25, 27, 31, 33, 162
  political leaders
    Chiluba 27
    Kaunda 25, 162
  political parties and civil society organisations
    MMD, Movement for Multi–party Democracy 27, 32, 108
    UNIP, United National Independence Party 25, 27
Zimbabwe 91–112, 233
  opposition politics 6, 29, 35, 91–112
  elections 95–99, 102–105, 107, 110, 111

political leaders
  Chakaodza 101
  Chikerema 95
  Dongo 104, 109–111
  Dumbutshena 102
  Magoche 101
  Mudehwe 105
  Mugabe 92, 95, 98–100, 104, 105, 110–112
  Muzorewa 95, 98–100, 108
  Nkomo 92, 94
  Sithole 95, 99, 100, 108
  Smith 98, 108
  Tekere 97, 98, 101, 108
political parties and civil society organisations
  ANC, Southern Rhodesia African National Congress 94
  CAZ, Conservative Alliance of Zimbabwe 108
  DP, Democratic Party 110
  Forum Party of Zimbabwe 102, 103, 106, 110
  FPD/MPD, Front/Movement for Democracy 101–102, 110
  Movement for Independent Candidates 109
  NDP, National Democratic Party 94
  PF, Patriotic Front 95
  PF–ZAPU, Zimbabwe African People's Union 92, 94–97, 106, 107
  RF, Rhodesian Front 96
  UANC, United African National Council 95, 98, 100, 108, 110
  United Methodist Church 99
  UP, United Parties 99–100
  ZANU, (Ndonga) 100, 108, 110
  ZANU, (Sithole) 96, 98
  ZANU–PF, Zimbabwe African National Union 92, 94–98, 100–111
  ZUM, Zimbabwe Unity Movement 92, 98, 99, 101, 102, 106–108, 110
Zuccarelli 119, 120